WHEN SALEM CAME TO THE BORO

Stuart Bell was born in a north-west Durham pit village fifty years ago. He left school at sixteen to work in the colliery office. At seventeen he became a newspaper reporter and at eighteen moved to London, where he spent four years doing a series of clerical jobs in the City. He turned his hand to law and qualified for the English Bar. He practised private international law in Paris before entering politics. In 1983 he was elected the Labour Member of Parliament for Middlesbrough. He became Parliamentary Private Secretary to the Deputy Leader Mr Roy Hattersley, and Northern Ireland spokesperson in 1984. He quit his front-bench post in order to deal with the Cleveland child abuse crisis.

Stuart Bell MP

WHEN SALEM CAME TO THE BORO

The true story of the Cleveland child abuse crisis

A PAN ORIGINAL
Pan Books *in association with Sidgwick & Jackson*

First published 1988 by Pan Books Ltd,
Cavaye Place, London SW10 9PG
in association with Sidgwick & Jackson, Ltd
9 8 7 6 5 4 3 2 1

ISBN 0 330 30503 4

Photoset by Parker Typesetting Service, Leicester
Printed and bound in Great Britain by
Richard Clay Ltd, Bungay, Suffolk

To Margaret and Malcolm

This is the story of events in Cleveland during 1987.

It is right that this story should be told, so that we may all know and better understand the country in which we live, and why it is that such events can happen. The names of the children, their parents and their doctors, among others, have been altered to protect the anonymity of the children, so that they may grow up and live normal lives and forget the traumas that beset them. The vocations and professions of their parents and the location of their homes have also been changed for the same reasons. These disguises are thick rather than thin but do not detract from the truth of the story.

The names of the other major participants remain, of course, for they too have a tale to tell, they too have voices that should be heard, they too have a case to put. The sincerity and the motives of these participants is not in question.

Contents

PROLOGUE

The body that turned slowly and sadly in the wind was that of Bridget Bishop, the first of the Salem witches to be hanged.

Bridget Bishop had been unfortunate from many points of view. She had had a poppet in her home, a sure sign she was a witch; she had been a flashy dresser and particularly liked a red paragon bodice that offended Puritan tastes; she had kept two ale houses, known as ordinaries, had allowed young people to loiter there, to play shovel-board, and by their rowdiness to keep neighbours from their sleep. Worse, as a witch her spectral shape had hovered over the beds of many a decent Puritan, so that even the jury, let alone the judges, had no difficulty pronouncing upon her witchcraft. The difficulty, however, lay in the law. For witchcraft was not a capital offence in Massachusetts. Therefore, on 8 June 1692, the general court legalized the sentence by reviving an old colonial law, and two days later the high sheriff personally took Bridget Bishop to the top of Gallows Hill, where she was hanged from the branches of an oak tree.

To this day, there are those who still believe in the Salem witches. One American historian, Chadwick Hansen, concluded that not only had they existed but they had caused great harm to the community. Hansen argued that 'the indiscriminate accusations that had resulted in the execution of innocent people' had been the consequences of 'a general public fear and panic in response to a psycho-social situation, not to the exhortations of clerical bigots'. Those who denied they were witches were sincere in their denials; but those who tried and hanged them believed equally sincerely that they were doing God's work.

Sincerity, it appears, has as many crimes to its name as liberty itself.

In all, nineteen Salem citizens were hanged between May and October 1692. Five went in a single day – 19 August. They were trundled out in a cart and jostled through the streets before spectators who were more sympathetic than angry, more convinced of their innocence than were their judges. Indeed, some surged forward to prevent the hangings, but they were swiftly rebuked for attempting to do the Devil's work. Another eight were hanged on 22 September. They had the grim satisfaction of a final look beyond the waters of Massachusetts Bay and the knowledge that thev died as they had lived. Had they confessed, their executions would have been remitted. But as they had not lived a lie, nor could they die for one.

Others would escape the high sheriff's rope by fleeing while the authorities looked the other way. One Hezeikiah Usher, a prominent Boston merchant who happened to be in the vicinity, was ordered to prison but quietly – and quickly – left the village and the province. Another, Giles Corey, whose wife had already been hanged, stood mute and therefore disrespectful of the court. By refusing to confess, he ensured that his estate would pass to his heirs. He was pressed to death and thus became the twentieth victim of the Salem witchhunt. He was one of those fractious fellows who had given Salem village a bad name, one of those who liked to declaim against men in public life and tended to 'the disturbance of the common peace'.

The origin of Salem witchcraft was not cantankerousness, but the arrival of the Reverend Samuel Parris who had come to the parish in 1688. He had been educated at Harvard, which in those days was a theological school, but had tried his hand at the West Indian trade runs, and had returned with two slaves, Tituba and John, 'half native, half negro', who had accompanied him to Salem. He came with his wife, his daughter Elizabeth, aged nine in 1692, and his niece, Abigail Williams, aged twelve. Tituba would tell voodoo stories to Elizabeth and Abigail and a neighbour's daughter, Ann Putnam, and such was the fascination of Abigail at least that some of the older village girls were also brought along to listen.

Soon a kind of mass hysteria broke out. First the girls became prey to absent-mindedness. They they fell to writhing, braying and convoluting in parlours. As word passed among the affrighted villagers, so too did the hysteria, as other girls joined in. But it was Abigail Williams who excelled herself. She threw grievous fits. She tried to fly, 'hurrying with violence to and fro', she leapt into the fire, she threw firebrands around the house, she sought to climb up the smoking chimney. She saw spectral yellow birds at the church service, either sitting on the rafter or perched upon the preacher's hat.

Their hallucinations left the girls none the worse for wear, or as one contemporary put it, they remained 'hale and hearty, robust and lusty'. Unfortunately there was no doctor in the village who could diagnose psycho-neurosis, although some of the menfolk, in a rare fit of common sense, did suggest a good thrashing for the girls to bring them to their senses. Instead, the village physician pronounced the girls bewitched. The superstitious suggested that the witches should be flushed out by the baking of good old-fashioned witch bread, which consisted of rye meal mixed with children's water and baked in ashes. But this was soon dismissed as medieval by examining church ministers brought in from Salem town.

They began to put to the girls leading questions, including the names of suspects who were particularly unpopular with the local inhabitants. There was Tituba, of course, the slave woman who had led the girls astray. She was arrested, together with Sarah Good, the village tramp, and Sarah Osborne, who had taken another man into her home after her husband's death. The fact that she later married him did not redeem her in the eyes of the village. The warrants were issued on 29 February 1692 – this being a leap year – and the prisoners were shackled and taken to Salem prison. They were the first of many the girls would name: so many, in fact, that by May the prison would be crowded as the accused awaited a court session.

The evidence against the so-called witches was spectacular, and, in the first instance, consisted of the touch test. This involved stripping the accused and searching for devil marks, examining the bodies minutely by running pins through any abnormality that was found. In the case of Bridget Bishop, they discovered 'a witch's tet' between 'ye pudendum and anus' and it did not matter that, after her trial, a second investigation revealed that the 'tet' had withered to dry skin. In the second instance, there were the hallucinations, dreams, visions, ravings if you like, of the girls themselves, who by now claimed they had been 'visited' or 'attacked' by the witches' 'shapes' or other apparitions. This became known as spectral evidence and would be the most telling of all.

Spectral evidence was best described by the Reverend Deodat Lawson, writing not for posterity but with the immediacy of the times. He had formerly been the Salem priest, and had been rapidly called back when the 'witch fever' broke out. There were three reasons why he was recalled: the fact that the witch fever had broken out in the home of his successor; the fact that he was the former priest; and the fact that, according to the girls, his own wife and daughter who had died at Salem had been driven to their graves by 'the infernal powers'. He arrived back on 19 March 1692. Salem village was no more than a cluster of farms around a meeting house and an ordinary. Lawson stayed at the ordinary and was met by Mary Walcott, daughter of the commander of the village militia. She was one of the afflicted children and was now aged seventeen.

In the ill-lit tavern there suddenly came a scream from Mary. A hoisting of a candle revealed that her wrists had been bitten: the marks of teeth, both upper and lower set, were visible on each wrist. But whose spectral shape had done the biting? This was admissible evidence in the general court on the grounds that the Devil could not assume the shape of an innocent person and must therefore express himself through his appointed witch. The burden of proof was thus reversed for those unfortunate enough to be named by the demented girls. For how can a man or woman – a wizard or witch – prove that his 'shape' has not entered another? This soon gave rise to sexual connotations and one young woman, Susanna Martin, found herself accused of using her 'supernatural witch shape' to molest men in their bed chambers. One Joseph Ring claimed that by such devious means Susanna had enslaved him, for at night he heard a 'scrabbling at the window' and there was Susanna's spectral form, hopping down from the sill and getting into bed.

Emboldened by their success, since few doubted their word in a world of strange goings-on that could only be attributed to witchcraft, names began tumbling from the lips of the girls. More members of the Salem community were arrested. Farmers ceased their chores and their wives stopped picking berries in order to crowd into the large meeting house to hear the evidence and, more particularly, to see how the girls could twist and turn on the floor when spectral shapes entered them. Their wailings were also a wonder that afflicted the ears. Who could doubt that they were sorely demented and that the witches should be punished? Thus it was that an upstanding countrywoman, Martha Corey, was sent to jail, followed by respected church members such as Rebecca Nurse, John Alden and a former minister of Salem parish, George Burroughs.

One of the young girls, Mary Warren, brighter than the rest, began to recoil from the consequences of her acts. If it was a joke, it had gone too far. But such was the strength of the current flowing against witches and witchcraft that there were dangers even in recantation. The magistrates felt that the Devil had entered into her too, and she was arrested. Her only hope of salvation was to confess that the Devil had indeed paid her a visit, and that he had been sent by her employer, who was also arrested. Even when the girls started to ease away from their accusations, the magistrates would not gainsay them and encouraged more confessions and more names until, in the end, the wife of the Massachusetts governor was implicated.

She, of course, was not arrested. Nor was another whom the children had named. This was Mrs Margaret Thatcher, who had the good fortune to die in her bed two years later rather than on Gallows Hill. She had no doubt escaped the issuance of a warrant because of her wealth and station: she had married the richest man in Boston. In fact, it was her fate, or lack of it, that occasioned 'much discourse and many hot words', for there were those who said that justice should be distributed equally and without respect to persons. Others felt it was a mercy the afflicted children had named the governor's wife, for this moved the governor to treat the witchhunt more seriously and take steps to bring it to an end.

After Bridget Bishop was hanged, the witchhunt spread to another Massachusetts village, Andover, where several people were ill. Lacking any clear diagnosis of what was wrong with them, the good people sent for the children of Salem, so that they might come and name those melancholic witches who were bringing so much illness into the community. Thus Ann Putnam came eager to justify her powers. She, with an afflicted friend, visited the homes of the sick, and sure enough saw the spectral vision of a witch at the top of each bed. But whose was the spectral shape? The girls duly fell around the hearth or sick bed, their screeches bringing the half-dead from their slumbers; but when it came to naming names they had a difficulty. They had never strayed beyond Salem in their lives. They knew no one in Andover.

The elders resolved this difficulty by arranging an identity parade. Of course, a witch being a witch, it was felt that not more than two or three would be trawled in Andover, but the young girls identified no fewer than forty before their day was done, so that the magistrate who had to sign the warrants of arrest gave up. Andover would soon lament its folly and become 'an object of great pity and commiseration'. In Salem too the foreboding mounted. It was one thing to arrest vagabonds and errants as witches. It was another to accuse respected pillars of the church.

One eminent opponent of the Puritan theocracy, Thomas Brattle, wrote: 'There are several worthy gentlemen in Salem who account this practice as an abomination, have trembled to see the methods of this nature which others have used and have declared themselves to think the practice to be very evil and corrupt; but all avails little with the abettours of the said practice.' The worshipful magistrates were also astonished when those whom they arrested for witchcraft wished to turn to prayer. After all, it was something they had done all their lives. But still that had not saved them from the afflicted children who accused their spectral spirits of 'biting, pinching and strangling'.

Puritans themselves began to urge 'exquisite caution', and others began to put it abroad that if the Devil wished to destroy a community he had gone the right way about it by sending his spirit into the young girls and forcing them to name respectable citizens. The president of Harvard entered the controversy and timorously suggested that it would be 'better that ten suspected witches should escape than one innocent person should be condemned'. Massachusetts itself was now beginning to take a calmer and firmer view of events in Salem, and on 23 November and 16 December 1692 special sessions of the superior court were appointed to complete the Salem trials. The judges remained the same but there was now one bold innovation: spectral evidence would be eliminated.

This had startling consequences. Until then the young girls had participated in the legal proceedings, but since they were no longer there, writhing on the floor staring with eyes out of their sockets, forty-nine acquittal verdicts were returned, with only three convictions based upon the confessions of the accused. Even these were unfortunate, for until now a confession was a sure way of having the death sentence remitted. That and proclaiming one was pregnant. But, nevertheless, there would be no more hangings, and by May 1693 the Massachusetts governor discharged all those witches still in jail and issued a proclamation of general pardon.

Almost three hundred years later, in the county of Cleveland, England, there was visited upon the town of Middlesbrough a phenomenon not dissimilar to the hysteria that had afflicted Salem.

The town owed its existence to the extension in the nineteenth century of the Darlington-to-Stockton railway. More staithes were needed on the Tees, more port facilities to export the coal of south-west Durham, and on 2 August 1829 one Joseph Pease took a boat from London and sailed up the river to the site that became the town of Middlesbrough. As he wrote in his diary: 'Its adaptation far exceeded my anticipations. I was fancying the coming of a day when the bare fields we were then traversing would be covered with a busy multitude and numerous vessels crowding to these banks denoting a busy seaport. Time, however, must roll many successive tides ere the change is effected.'

In addition to the exportation of coal, there were outcrops of ironstone on local slopes that would make the good coking coal of south-west Durham particularly advantageous to the production of steel. The port was deepened, the iron trade flourished, immigrant Irish labour built up the mills. If Middlesbrough became famous for anything at all it was for the steel that built the Sydney Harbour Bridge. Soot and grime blackened its horizon and seared lungs, for Middlesbrough is a child of the Industrial Revolution, with chemicals and shipbuilding to complement the steel and export traffic. Foundries glowed in the night and the burning of excess gases from the chemical plants traced the sky with an angry orange and gold.

Football was the focal point for much of the town when the week's work was over. The town's postwar soccer stars were Wilf Mannion and George Hardwick – Hardwick for several seasons actually leading the England team on to the field as captain. It would take some thirty years for the club to offer its erstwhile stars a benefit match, and this it did on 17 May 1983, bringing the redoubtable Kevin Keegan down from Newcastle United to add lustre to the England team which played against the Boro. The club never did win either Cup or League and in the summer of 1985 it went into liquidation, the first Football League club to do so. However, a new club rose from the ashes of the old, and within a season Middlesbrough had played themselves from the third to the second division in a new burst of self-confidence.

This confidence was badly needed in a town that ten years earlier has seen itself as a growth point in Europe with an industrial basin that would challenge any within the Common Market. The steel mills were to be doubled and an extra blast furnace had been ordered; the chemical plants bestraddled the river at Wilton and Billingham; the dockyards turned out vessels at Haverton Hill and Smith's Dock; and seventy or so foundries lit up the night sky all along the river bank. Middlesbrough had something else. It had the work ethic. This human resource would soon be augmented by a natural resource with the building of the Kielder Dam in the hills of Northumbria, with underground pipes burrowing beyond the Tyne and Wear dales to provide water for growing industry.

The chant at the football ground might be 'Up the Boro', for that was what the locals called the town, but this chant turned to despair when, as the nation veered into the eighties, it also dipped into the world recession: the plans for a second blast furnace at British Steel were scrapped, the work force reduced from 25000 able bodies to 7000; Imperial Chemical Industries diverted into world markets and reduced its work force by 3000; the dockyards at Haverton Hill and Smith's Dock closed; the foundries were reduced to a handful. The job losses amounted to 46000 – enough to fill the football stadium at Ayresome Park three times over.

The water from the Kielder Dam was never used, except for one occasion, when it flushed out the river Tees.

With unemployment at twenty-eight per cent, some spirit went out of the town. Council-housing stock deteriorated because of government cutbacks; the river frontage fell into dereliction; there was more vandalism and violence; and for the families at the bottom end of the scale, more dependence on Cleveland Social Services. This turned out to be one of the few growth industries and by the summer of 1987 its work force stood at 4600, almost equal to that of British Steel, but climbing to meet the needs of an area that was rapidly becoming impoverished.

Middlesbrough seemed to turn the corner as it moved towards the nineties. The government granted money for a Teesside Urban Development Corporation, whose ideals would be talent and initiative; its people understood that the days of the Industrial Revolution were over, but there were module yards on the river and Nissan loading and unloading car parts from Japan for its new factory up the coast at Sunderland, with some of the finished products destined for the Common Market. The sagging spirits of the early eighties began to revive.

But in the spring and early summer of 1987 a phenomenon hit the town the likes of which had not been seen in the western world since Salem.

Over a six-week period a staggering total of 197 children were taken into care on allegations of sexual abuse. The figure would later move up and down, frontwards and sideways. It was 197 according to Mr Mike Bishop, director of social services, when he wrote to foster parents on 25 June; it was 197 according to Dr Marietta Higgs when she issued her one and only press statement on the same day, though the figure she had in mind covered child abuse over the whole year. Another participant in what would become a rapidly moving drama, Ian Donaldson, district general manager of the South Tees Health Authority, also confirmed the 197 figure. But when public outcry was at its height Cleveland county shaved the numbers downwards to 113 and accused the press of 'inventing' the figure of 197.

Public bewilderment did not end there. For at the judicial enquiry that opened in Middlesbrough on 4 August, Mr Alan Glyn Cooke, clerk to the Teesside justices, announced that his magistrates had signed 270 place of safety orders, taking children from their parents and into care. Later again, Dr Higgs and her fellow consultant paediatrician, Dr Geoffrey Wyatt, stated they had made 121 diagnoses of alleged child sexual abuse. Mrs Justice Butler-Sloss, who had been appointed by the government to head the judicial enquiry, sought for several weeks the true number of children taken into care before announcing that the doctors had made forty-five diagnoses in May and forty-seven in June.

But did the figures really matter? What did matter was that children who had never been abused had been taken away from their parents, siblings had followed suit, and families had been broken up. One father suffered a heart attack, a mother decided upon an abortion rather than have another child taken from her, there was one arson attack on a home, windows were smashed, one family had to be evacuated, fathers and grandfathers and neighbours were falsely accused. The children's casualty ward at Middlesbrough General Hospital filled up with well children and their mothers slept on campbeds or cots by their beds. The tension thus generated eventually created a near riot and hands were laid on a consultant paediatrician, who called the police. Nurses were horrified at midnight checks on their wards for sexual abuse and complained to the South Tees Health Authority. In the end, the parents, out of fear and frustration, took to the streets. They also went to their Member of Parliament.

Conflicts arose among professionals. There were greater conflicts between three powerful bureaucracies: Cleveland Constabulary, Cleveland Social Services and the Northern Regional Health Authority. The careers of the participants, together with their reputations, would be confirmed or destroyed. There was a national outcry, a national debate, statements on the floor of the House of Commons, and a judicial enquiry that sat from 4 August to 17 December 1987, with final submissions beginning on 27 January 1988: the longest judicial enquiry in British history.

A mass hysteria had enveloped Middlesbrough as children were taken from their homes by social workers. They were brought to the hospital to be examined by two consultant paediatricians. If sex abuse was alleged, the social worker filled out a photostatted place of safety order and hurried off to a justice of the peace, who would sign it in his home. A legal process had begun that would separate children from parents for many a long month or year. Mothers and fathers, grandmothers and grandfathers, friends and relatives, were left to fret as to the children's whereabouts and wellbeing. Their classmates at school wondered where their friends had gone. Neighbours wondered what parents had done to their children. And so doubts and uncertainty built up till families who wished to take their children to hospital for the treatment of routine ailments began to hesitate.

These events were not dissimilar to Salem because, just as in the Middle Ages and beyond there were those who believed in witchcraft, so there were those in Cleveland who believed that child sex abuse existed on a hitherto unknown scale. Both had their own elements of truth. Pockets of witchcraft exist to this day. Sorcery and satanism arose from the belief that if good and evil existed, then God and the Devil must equally exist. The war between the two was 'more actual, more cruel, more momentous, than any fray of flesh and blood.'[1]

This view itself was a product of thirteenth-century theology and received a mighty boost when the Holy Inquisition equated witchcraft with heresy, threw in diabolic sects and the witch sabbath, and by thumbscrews, pressings and other divers tortures extracted confessions and accusations that proved witches abounded. Thousands were burned at the stake. Hundreds would go in a single day. The contagion, for such it was, spread from the Continent to England and Scotland, and even during the Civil War witches were put to death by the score in 1645–7. The Puritans took their superstitions with them to New England and the tide lapped as far as Salem before receding. The phenomenon gradually died out in the next century and the last trial for witchcraft took place in 1717. Parliament abolished witch trials in 1736.

There are those in modern society who have an equal and sincere belief in the prevalence of child abuse. The break up of family life, with more one-parent families, more latchkey children, more divorces, more boyfriends and strangers coming to the home, makes more likely the abuse of children unrelated by blood. And even among blood relatives the abuse has gone on. But although child sex abuse exists, there is no evidence to support the hysterical figures

[1]George L. Burr, *Narratives of the Witchcraft Cases 1648–1706*. (Barnes & Noble, New York, 1914)

given by one councillor that 14000 girls and 7000 boys were being abused in Cleveland county; or the view of child abuse consultant, Mrs Sue Richardson, that one in three children was being abused. Or even the view of 'one in ten' that would enter folklore through regular peddling on television and in the newspapers. The consequence of this misinformation was as dire as the decision of the physician in Salem who, at a loss to explain mass hysteria, fell back upon witchcraft as the only diagnosis. So when consultant paediatricians developed a new technique which they believed to reveal anal abuse, there were enough hands ready, willing and able to be set upon innocent children.

What was equally astonishing was that anal abuse of children was readily believed to be as common as battering, as common as incest, fondling, mutual masturbation, digital penetration or oral-genital contact. Any reflective person could only construe anal abuse as sadistic abuse. But more that that: anal abuse could be linked to a child's failure to thrive. Thus children admitted for routine examinations in outpatients' clinics were diagnosed for alleged sexual abuse even when they had attended with complaints as routine as croup or asthma. Children taken into casualty also found themselves diagnosed. One child on an intravenous drip feed suffered the indignity of an anal examination. The 'failure-to-thrive' theory was attractive if tenuous, but the lack of additional evidence in no way lessened the conviction of those paediatricians who made the diagnoses.

They were able to take comfort, however, from the literature of other experts in the field who charted the public's likely response to such new discoveries. First, the public would deny that child sex abuse existed to any significant extent; then the community would wilt before the facts and begin to pay attention; the community would become more attentive still when it understood the link between abuse and failure to thrive; and of course the community would leap to its collective feet when it perceived the full extent of sexual abuse. The sixth stage in public perception would be when the community accepted that each child needed to be truly wanted and provided with loving care.

We can all agree to protect children. We can all accept they need loving care and attention. To state otherwise would be, as the Italians say, an *infamia*. What the theorists did not ask, however, was 'Who will provide the love and the care that each child badly needs?' Would it be the state, through paediatricians and social workers? Or would it be the family unit? Who would have power over children? Would it be the families into which they had been born? Or would an artificial security be provided by others who knew better than parents what was in the best interests of their children? This would become the battleground in Cleveland. The terrain was ideal. For the child care professionals believed that pools of deprivation were sufficiently murky to breed child sexual abuse: 'In families where the father is out of work and experiencing financial problems, or is ill and injured, he will be more often at home and is more likely to be depressed or drinking excessively than his counterparts in full employment. These factors may lead him to molest his children.'[2]

The tragedy of Cleveland was that it actually set back the cause of rooting out child sex abuse, prosecuting its perpetrators and protecting innocent families. The opposite face of a caring society showed itself – there was a fundamental attack on family life. There was a moral crusade to save children, to pluck them out of one environment and place them in another in their own best interests; but neither the interests of the child, the family nor the crusaders themselves would be served. All in the end would be victims. As the accuser of Bridget Bishop would say in later life: 'We walked in clouds and would not see our way. We must have moral cause to be humbled for error.'

Another writer, Marion L. Starkey, in the preface to her book, *The Devil in Massachusetts* (Robert Hale, London, 1952), wrote: 'One would believe that the leaders of the modern world can in the end deal with delusion as sanely and courageously as the men of old Massachusetts dealt with theirs.' It was not national leaders, but a coalition of men of the cloth, Members of Parliament, the legal profession, the media and the police that got to grips with its modern equivalent some three hundred years on, seeking to understand what was happening to their children and their family life.

The innocent, divided families knew little of the wider issues, the clashing of powerful bureaucracies, the deep conviction of the participants, the attitudes of mind that classified anal abuse as sexual, rather than sadistic, abuse, and linked its discovery to 'improved diagnostic technique'; and used place of safety orders as instruments of the state to take children away from their parents. All that the families perceived was a conspiracy against them, a conspiracy that whether sullen or hostile, overt or covert, had the same result. It

[2]*Child Sexual Abuse Within the Family*, The Ciba Foundation

deprived them of their children. Who was behind the conspiracy they neither knew nor cared. But not only were children taken away, fathers would be accused of a heinous crime, perhaps the most heinous of them all: molesting their own children.

They stood falsely branded, falsely accused. And beyond their indignation was the sorrow of returning to empty homes, full of dolls and toys and books and puzzles and children's videos. But there would be no chatter, no laughter, no tantrums, no sleepless crying nights, no asking for drinks of water in the small hours, no one to see off to school in the morning, no messages to give to teacher. There were no tears. Except the tears of wives and mothers who, like Rachel, wept for their children because they were not.

This then is the true story of these events, in May and June 1987, when Salem came to the Boro.

Book One

SUFFER THE LITTLE CHILDREN

1

Bill and Norma Yardley were young and upwardly mobile.

They were not part of the Middlesbrough subculture that was impoverished and underprivileged. Both in their early thirties, both good looking, both on the small side, they had settled in the town some three years earlier when Bill was appointed to a new job. He was a professional man in a position of trust. The Yardleys did not live on one of the council estates that clustered in the centre and east of the town; their house was a private, three-bedroomed semidetached with bay windows, a rose garden and crazy paving leading down the garden and out to the road. Their lives centred around their three children: Elaine aged seven, Susan aged two and Anne, who in the summer of 1987 was not yet one year old. But the Yardleys were sociable enough to get on well with their new neighbours, one of whom had two children of her own, aged twenty and eighteen, and who enjoyed having smaller children around.

This neighbour had become particularly friendly with Norma Yardley when Susan was born, and through Norma she had got to know the eldest child, Elaine. 'They came to see me often,' she recalled. 'I called to their house also to see them. The friendship has continued and I still see Norma and the children often as well as Mr Yardley.' The neighbour found both Elaine and Susan very active children: extrovert, contented, normal. 'Both are self-confident and are quite happy in the presence of adults. I have seen the children at other places when we have been out socially and they behave totally normally. They are well-behaved children who do as they are told by their parents and also by other adults. Elaine has a mind of her own and can be quite strong-willed.'

At seven years old, Elaine Yardley was enjoying life. She had a settled environment, loving parents, caring neighbours, regular holidays, play-friends at school, a younger sister and a third child just brought in by the stork. Like many an elder child, she was full of herself and liked to chatter away about everyday family life. She was sunny and bright and even when her mother and father had an argument – there were flecks of red to Norma Yardley's hair – she felt sufficiently comfortable with her family's neighbour to mention this too. Norma Yardley knew Elaine treated her friend as an aunt. The neighbour said: 'It would be very difficult to stop her telling me if anything was wrong, particularly if she had been assaulted or ill-treated in any way.'

Elaine was also popular at her local school. The deputy head teacher wrote that she was 'a happy, lively and friendly girl, gently confident and secure, with a close, loving family. She is well behaved and sensitive to other children's needs. She talks easily and is making normal progress at school.' Of the parents, the deputy head wrote: 'Mr and Mrs Yardley have established a very friendly relationship with school and have regularly taken an interest in the various functions and have been very supportive of the school and their children. The birth of Elaine's two younger sisters was greeted with delight and Elaine is very anxious of her role as Big Sister which she fulfils admirably and she shows obvious delight in being with the family.'

The deputy head had been in teaching for thirty years. She considered she had a deep understanding of children and was alert to those with 'unvoiced emotions'. But she wrote: 'In the case of Elaine I have never had any sign that would suggest any sort of problem either at home or elsewhere.' Elaine had good health to go with her sunny disposition. She had been prone to tonsillitis, but this never kept her from school, and while she had the normal healthy appetite of a seven year old, she drank little liquid. She had never been to the family doctor for any serious complaints of constipation, but nevertheless she had a slight problem in that she did not go to the toilet regularly. In the words of her mother, such was her enjoyment at playing with friends at school that she would 'hold on for as long as possible'.

This problem did not matter greatly in the normal world but later it would have some significance. For when she 'paid a visit' she complained that it 'hurt a bit' and one week she was sent home from school because she was suffering from stomach pains so severe that they bent her double. In fact, she had to be carried home by her mother. She slept for a few hours and then paid a visit, again complaining that it 'hurt a bit'. Both mother and father looked upon this as nothing more than a childhood ailment, an unremarkable episode in the life of a girl growing up.

The Yardleys' second child, Susan, was also healthy and well nourished. Only once had the doctor been called. This had been for a virus infection. The health visitor had regularly called by to see Anne, the newborn in the household, but there was nothing in the health of Susan that gave the health visitor cause for alarm. She suffered from a dry skin which was so persistent that her mother took her to the local skin clinic at a hospital in the centre of Middlesbrough. The complaint appeared to grow worse as Susan cut her teeth. Later Dr Higgs would say that Susan was 'inarticulate', a remark which when it came to the ears of Norma Yardley cut her to the quick.

Anne had been born in the autumn of 1986. The Yardleys had had the same family doctor since their arrival on Teesside; she had seen Norma Yardley through her second and third pregnancies and had always been impressed by the care shown to the children by the parents. As she later wrote: 'The children have always struck me as being happy, contented and natural in their relationships with their parents, and I have never been concerned about the children's care.' Nor was the doctor concerned at the children's slight build: 'I have seen the children quite regularly and I was not concerned that the children were slight in stature as both parents are slightly built.'

But if the first two Yardley children enjoyed good health this bounty was not to be bestowed on the newborn Anne. Hers was a breech birth. The baby's feeding patterns were irregular, she slept continually and had to be woken for her feeds. She did not take her mother's milk and had to be weaned on good, old-fashioned Cow and Gate Premium. When she was six weeks old, she was taken for a check-up. She had a slight cold, which the doctor put down to the time of year. Norma Yardley mentioned this to the health visitor; also that Anne was 'sleeping through', and the fact that she did not appear to be gaining weight.

During the first week of January 1987 Anne developed a cough and a cold. The regular doctor was away and a substitute doctor from the same surgery was called. He arrived on Saturday morning, 10 January, and gave the baby some antibiotics, saying that if the parents were still worried they should not hesitate to give him a call. The following day Anne would take neither food nor drink and the parents began to worry that she might be dehydrating. On Monday 12 January the substitute doctor was called again and he was so concerned that he decided to admit Anne immediately to Middlesbrough General Hospital.

Two-and-a-half-month-old Anne Yardley became, therefore, one of the first patients to be seen by Dr Marietta Higgs in her new consultancy on Teesside.

Norma Yardley found Dr Higgs a slim, sprightly woman, alert and conscientious. She too was in her thirties and there was little age gap between the worried mother and the caring doctor.

Anne remained poorly for a further two weeks. The original diagnosis was that of an acute chest infection which led to feeding and weight problems. She was placed in an oxygen tent and tube-fed. Eventually the child's infection eased, and as she still would not take any quantity of milk from a bottle Norma was taught how to tube-feed her, so that Anne could return home and be cared for there.

Anne spent sixteen days in Middlesbrough General Hospital. Norma spent the morning on ward ten with Anne, taking Susan to the hospital with her, and returning home at about two o'clock in the afternoon. Bill would go straight from work and spend several hours at the hospital, being relieved by his wife at around nine o'clock. Norma would pick up Elaine from school at four and later see that she and Susan were in bed, the babysitter safely ensconced, before nipping back to the General.

Anne was discharged on 28 January 1987 but returned to the hospital three days later for a check on how the tube-feeding was going. Norma was advised gradually to reduce the tube-feeding and start weaning Anne on to more solid foods, such as rice from a spoon. The baby returned to the hospital again on 13 February, where she was again examined by Dr Higgs. She was concerned about the general 'floppiness' of the baby and her poor weight gain, though Anne was still making progress. The Yardleys found themselves helpless before the child's many ailments, though they were content that the staff at Middlesbrough General Hospital, from nurses to junior doctors, were doing the best they could for their baby. They were equally reassured by the thoroughness of Dr Higgs.

On Friday 6 March Anne had another appointment with the consultant doctor. She had another full examination and Dr Higgs sent her over from outpatients' for an X-ray because she was not satisfied with the child's hips. It was part of paediatric routine to check if a baby less than a year old had fully abducted hips. Anne was again taken to hospital on 3 April because her weight was down, she suffered from diarrhoea, and again there was general concern for her health. She was kept under observation and the weight loss was put down to another virus infection. Throughout this period of observation Anne was fully examined daily by Dr Higgs, and on 10 April the child was again discharged back to the family home.

The fine spring weather did nothing to alleviate the child's ill-health and Anne Yardley again returned to Middlesbrough General Hospital on 1 May. There was yet another thorough examination: a blood sample was taken and concern expressed that she might be suffering from a urinary infection. The question of the urinary infection subsequently faded and there was never any further mention made of this by Dr Higgs to the parents when Anne Yardley next visited the hospital. Dr Higgs noted that the child seemed to take a long time to recover from her earlier stay in the hospital and was still feeding poorly.

Dr Higgs did say that the child needed building up and she wished to pass her on to a dietitian. This too, like the urinary infection, was not to be mentioned again to the parents. By now Bill Yardley was accompanying his wife on every visit to the hospital and the anxiety was reflected in his face. However, the baby's health began to improve and by the time of the next appointment – on Friday 12 June – she had put on two pounds in weight. The nurse who weighed the baby was particularly pleased, for she had been nursing Anne all these months during her various stays on the ward.

It seemed that after all this time baby Anne had turned the corner.

But at the outpatients' clinic Dr Higgs expressed some concern for Anne's chest, and she was sent for an X-ray. The X-ray revealed a mild infection on her right side and therefore she was again admitted to Middlesbrough General Hospital where she was kept under observation. This did not unduly worry the Yardleys because it seemed remote from the child's earlier ailments and hospital would be the best place for her. Their satisfaction had come from the weight increase as the baby had moved on to solids: Ready Brek, rice, yoghurt and fruit. As Bill Yardley recalled: 'She had four meals a day. Because she had never taken to milk from a bottle, she had been drinking only from a spoon for the last three months. Thus there might have been an imbalance of liquid intake.' This might have explained why the child had difficulties on the toilet and strained considerably when on her potty.

The general satisfaction about her improvement in health would, however, be short lived.

2

While checking the child's hips on 12 June Dr Higgs had noticed bruising to her anus. Or to use her words: 'The bottom did not look right.' She got on to her knees to separate the child's legs and thus have a closer look at the anus. She felt this confirmed the bruising; a subsequent examination showed a bruised anal orifice. Having been 'warned' by what she saw, she realized she would have to sit and talk at length to Norma Yardley. The truth was – which explained the repeated examinations – that Dr Higgs had never been quite satisfied with the progress Anne had been making. She admitted to having been 'worried' when she had first seen the baby on 12 January; she wanted to know the reasons for what she considered to be general 'floppiness' and poor weight; and then there was the question of whether the child had dislocated hips.

All these were genuine paediatric concerns. At nine o'clock that evening, with her mother not present at the hospital and not aware of what was going on, Anne was examined again in the presence of two nurses. Photographs were then taken of the baby lying on her tummy, with Dr Higgs gently parting the bottom. She again felt it was bruised and discoloured. With the child in the same position, another picture was taken of the anal sphincter, which in fact opened so that she could see inside the orifice. It was, in her words, 'gaping'. She also ascertained fissures at eleven o'clock, two and six o'clock. Later, however, these would be difficult to discern when the slides came to be analysed.

Normally, according to Dr Higgs, when the buttocks are parted, the sphincter contracts and stays shut; on this occasion Dr Higgs noted it had opened five centimetres. She did not in this instance record the time it remained open. But normally it would be twenty to thirty seconds. Of course, patient cooperation would be essential in such an examination, but this would not be forthcoming from a small baby. But Dr Higgs knew of no other cause for anal dilatation than external penetration, apart from the normal physiological one of allowing for bowel movements. She discounted constipation, and Crohn's disease did not apply, since the child was not suffering from this.

What then had penetrated?

Dr Higgs would later decline to speculate.

'That would be very difficult to answer.'

'Could it be a thermometer up the bottom?'

'Thermometers don't cause this. If a child has stomach pains and fingers were used to investigate, they would not cause this either.'

The following day, when Norma Yardley visited the hospital, Dr Higgs mentioned Anne's sore bottom. Were there hereditary problems? Not that Norma Yardley knew of, but she shared in the doctor's concern: it had been that way for two weeks. Dr Higgs suggested that Norma Yardley return home and bring to the hospital the two other children, Elaine and Susan. Such was the satisfaction of Norma Yardley with Dr Higgs' examinations of her youngest child that she immediately complied: whatever was wrong with Anne she hoped would not equally be wrong with Elaine and Susan.

Bill Yardley shared his wife's anxiety and he too returned to the hospital this Saturday afternoon, 13 June. The parents and children arrived at quarter to three. They waited for two and a half to three hours before Dr Higgs arrived. She was as usual very busy, always alert but always on the move: this was indeed a busy time for her. In fact, so busy that the staff at the hospital were not aware that Dr Higgs had asked to see the other two Yardley children. The older girls could not understand what they were doing there, and as the time passed the children became bored and angry. The concern of the parents mounted.

When Dr Higgs did arrive she brought Dr Geoffrey Wyatt, a fellow consultant paediatrician at Middlesbrough General Hospital. According to both Bill and Norma Yardley, they made no apology for their late arrival, and since they were upstairs on ward ten the doctors simply gestured and asked for the mother and father, with Elaine and Susan, to follow them. The two doctors weighed and measured the children. They then took the children back to an examination room on ward ten. Susan was examined first. The doctors looked in her ears and then at her chest. In the words of Bill Yardley: 'She was then turned over, placed on hands and knees with her bottom in the air. Dr Higgs took one look and made the comment: "Tut, that's not right!" '

Dr Higgs also registered concern at Susan's poor speech. She felt a child of that age should be doing better. So far as she was concerned, however, there was no doubt about it: Susan had signs consistent with anal sexual abuse. She acknowledged later that the so-called signs might have had something to do with poor hygiene, but she really did not have any explanation for reflex anal dilatation other than that sexual abuse had taken place: there was no explanation in medical literature other than that of trauma caused to the anus. She had considered medical articles in the *Lancet* by two paediatricians working out of Leeds; she had seen literature from other countries and had even discussed this with colleagues in the United States; but she had not heard of another explanation.

Elaine was then examined: ears and then chest. Again, in the words of Bill Yardley: 'They then took off her pants in order to examine the lower region. Upon doing so they noticed that Elaine had delayed in going to the toilet and had slightly messed her pants. This caused great embarrassment to Elaine. Dr Higgs examined Elaine's back passage then looked in her vagina. Dr Higgs asked if "she was sore in that area", to which Elaine answered "Yes". Dr Wyatt did not speak at all. Anne was not examined throughout this period.' Unbeknown to Bill Yardley his baby child had not only been examined, but had also been photographed the night before.

According to the recollection of Dr Higgs, she found Elaine to be normal, except she looked thin for her height. When she first applied pressure to the buttocks, the anus appeared lax and later opened. The anal verge and skin folds were thickened. She also looked at Elaine's vulva but did not get a look at the hymen because the orifice was quite small. There was no doubt in the mind of Dr Higgs that the signs in relation to the anus were consistent with sexual abuse.

The examination of the two older children now completed, a nurse was called to take both Elaine and Susan back to Anne's cubicle on the ward. Dr Higgs wanted to talk to the parents. The parents were anxious to hear what she had to say. For while they had been worried about the health of Anne, they now had to worry about the health of Elaine and Susan. Whatever thoughts went through their minds, whatever childhood afflictions might have crossed their consciousnesses, nothing in their life experiences would prepare them for the news that was about to be imparted to them. Bill Yardley tried to remain as noncommittal as possible when he recalled: 'Dr Higgs said there was reason to believe and evidence in all three girls that they have been abused – sexually interfered with.'

Dr Wyatt who was present made no comment.

It says much for the strength and closeness of the marriage between Bill and Norma Yardley that they did not stumble into mutual accusation and recrimination. For here was a consultant paediatrician, duly appointed by the National Health Service, skilled in her work with babies and children, making the most serious of accusations, that their three children had been buggered. It seemed incredible to both parents – so incredible that neither for one moment thought of accusing the other. 'My wife and I immediately thought that Dr Higgs was totally and utterly wrong in her diagnosis and assumption,' Bill Yardley recalled. 'We put forward reasons as to why we thought she was wrong and even details of the family's medical history. Dr Higgs was very evasive when pressed on the extent of the evidence. Her attitude was one of: "I've told you it's happened or happening. Don't you believe me?" '

For her part, Dr Higgs would recall that she found the eldest child, Elaine, 'quiet and reserved'. She was guarded when answering questions. Dr Higgs explained that she was worried about Elaine's bottom and could she explain what caused it? From the child's point of view, she was seven years old, she was not ill, she had been brought to a hospital on a Saturday afternoon, and she had been examined in the most intimate of places. Nevertheless, she was able to describe 'stretching feelings of her anus', which was 'painful red' and which she had herself examined using two mirrors. She couldn't really remember very much, and found it difficult to talk about the reasons why her bottom was 'painful red', and 'didn't want the nurses to know'.

Of Anne, Dr Higgs would write: 'Anne is failing to thrive and has developmental delay for which no obvious cause has yet been found.' So far as Elaine was concerned, she was 'grossly underweight for her age and height', whereas Susan's speech is 'poor for her age'. Dr Higgs concluded in writing that all three children had physical signs 'consistent with sexual abuse' and went on: 'I think it is unsafe for these children to be released from care until a full assessment, including continuing disclosure work with Elaine in particular, has been undertaken.' Dr Higgs made an observation more fitting perhaps to a social worker: 'Disclosure work in this situation requires a period of separation from the parents.'

3

Bill and Norma Yardley, that Saturday afternoon, in a daze at the hospital, did not quite know what to do next. Drs Higgs and Wyatt took Elaine with them in order to carry out their own 'disclosure' work. 'We assumed that their talk would be brief,' Bill Yardley recalled, and that 'they would bring her back to the examination room. This they did not do. Instead, they took Elaine away from Susan to a room well away from the examination room, away from the ward, and without the presence of either myself or my wife.'

While Bill and Norma were left alone, a nurse came in and asked for particulars on Susan. When the parents asked why she required particulars she replied: 'Didn't you know we are keeping Susan in?' Such was the reaction of the Yardleys that the nurse too became upset. '*You too, I'm afraid*,' she said through her tears. The Yardleys went to see Susan and Anne and found that Anne had been moved from one cubicle to another and that another cot had been added for Susan. No one other than the nurse had informed the couple that all three of their children were now to be detained.

Elaine returned to the cubicle. 'We asked her what she had talked about,' Bill Yardley recalled. 'But she appeared embarrassed and slightly vague. However, she remembered being asked where she slept and with whom. She was given a pencil and paper and asked to draw a picture of where we all slept' (grandparents had stayed the previous few days and thus sleeping arrangements had been altered). The Yardleys would later see this as explaining why Drs Higgs and Wyatt were 'grasping the wrong end of the stick'.

As Dr Higgs recalled it, she had asked about the sleeping arrangements in the house. Elaine said she slept in bed with one or other of her parents; and sometimes both. But 'she was not happy to talk as to why her bottom was "painful red"'. Drs Higgs and Wyatt then sent for the couple. 'Dr Higgs again made the allegation of sexual abuse but by whom she would not say. She supported her view this time with the words: "From what we've asked Elaine and what she's said, we know something is happening in the home. And it has to stop for the sake of the children".' The two paediatricians were now embarking upon disclosure work with the Yardley children as well as examining them for sexual abuse, but these fine points were lost on Bill and Norma Yardley.

This young couple with everything to look forward to in life were distraught almost to tears. They strongly rejected the allegations. They demanded to know what had been said or discussed with Elaine. Dr Higgs refused to say. 'Her view was that she was not prepared to enter into a discussion: "All I know is that it is happening in the home – by whom and with what I'm unable to say".' This did not amount to an accusation against Bill Yardley, but the implication was plain. So far as he registered anything at all, it was the implication that he had consistently buggered his eight-month-old daughter, he had been doing it from birth, and it was for this reason the baby was consistently unwell. The fact that both parents were slight of build and that this might be the hereditary cause of their own children's smallness did not seem to him to have been taken into account.

'By now our manner was that of complete shock,' Bill Yardley recalled. 'We made very strong denials on behalf of the children. We again put forward "evidence", alternative theories and the like. They were all met with a complete and utter refusal even to consider them. Drs Higgs and Wyatt then left the room saying "sorry". Later Dr Wyatt returned with a social worker. The social worker was on the side of the doctors. Her view was that if the doctors had diagnosed sexual abuse then it must be so.'

Bill Yardley began to fight back. Could Dr Wyatt give reasons? Could he answer questions? On what time scale, for example, had the abuse allegedly taken place? What had been the extent of the injuries? Dr Wyatt replied that 'it had happened in the last few days'. He did not elaborate on which child he meant or whether he meant all three. Dr Wyatt and the social worker also then left the room, but when the social worker returned she was carrying three pieces of paper which she handed to Bill Yardley.

They were place of safety orders.

These would become familiar documents to many a Cleveland family in the weeks and months to come. Their origins lay in two Acts of Parliament designed to protect children: the Children's and Young Persons' Acts 1933 and 1969. They provide for emergency situations where children may be so at risk that they should immediately be removed from their environment for their own safety. Powers under a place of safety order are formidable because once signed by a justice of the peace they permit a child or young person to be removed from the parental home to 'a place of safety'. This can be for as long as twenty-eight days.

The pattern quickly established in Cleveland was that a social worker would take such a place of safety order to a justice of the peace – for the most part in his own home – who would take out his Bible and make the social worker swear an oath that what he was about to say was 'the truth, the whole truth and nothing but the truth'. There would be no other person present, however, no submissions made from parents, and once the place of safety order was signed by the justice of the peace there would be no rights of appeal either for the children or young persons or their parents. There was not even statutory provision for the keeping of proper records.

In the case of the place of safety orders on the Yardley children, they had indeed been made out by the social worker – they contained the names of the three children, and they said that the children were to be taken away from their parents for a period of twenty-eight days. They had been signed by a justice of the peace. And such was the haste of social services that they had been written out by hand. The social worker who had presented the place of safety order to the justice of the peace had testified to the 'moral and physical danger' in which the children found themselves and, of course, with the children's interests paramount, the justice had signed.

The Yardleys had been told not more than an hour ago that all three of their children had been allegedly sexually abused; they had been told not more than half an hour ago that it was proposed that Susan and Elaine should join Anne at the hospital for what they believed to be observation; and now they were being told that all three children would not be coming home at all. At lunchtime Bill Yardley had not even known that Dr Higgs had asked for his two other daughters to go to the hospital. And if there was anything worse, the clear implication was that he had committed acts of gross indecency against all three of his children.

All they could do, with evening approaching, was to return to the cubicle and settle Susan and Anne for bed. They went through the motions as if they were at home. Susan was by this time upset and crying: with the instinct of a young child she knew she was being placed in an alien environment. She did not want to be in hospital. She was not sick and she wanted to go home. Elaine was downstairs on ward nine. Because the child was older and also unlikely to sleep in a strange hospital bed, with the excitement and all, the Yardleys stayed till darkness set in and did not leave the hospital till around half past ten or eleven o'clock.

They returned the following day before Sunday lunch: 'Elaine was in bed feeling very poorly. She had developed tonsillitis and had been sick on numerous occasions,' Bill Yardley recalled. 'She had had no contact with Dr Higgs but mentioned that after my wife and I had gone home and Elaine had gone to bed she was woken up and taken to have her bottom photographed. I asked if this was done by an X-ray machine and Elaine said: "No. They used an ordinary camera".'

The meeting this Sunday was not pleasant. This was no longer the kindly, if slightly harassed, doctor the Yardleys had known since January. They had always found Dr Higgs difficult to communicate with, but they had put this down to her heavy schedule and desire not to be engaged in small talk. Now the Yardleys forthrightly challenged her clinical judgement. They took on her diagnosis. How could she be sure she was right? She for her part refused to accept any alternative explanations and, of course, no one could challenge the clinical judgement of a paediatrician. The Yardleys again expressed their disbelief at what had been said, but all they could get from Dr Higgs was: 'Well, there are signs of interference in all three girls.'

It was not only the Yardleys who were anxious. The nursing staff had been looking after Anne almost since birth. They had grown attached to the baby. One nurse had twenty years' experience in bowel complaints and spoke to the parents expressing her disbelief. She admitted that she had had a quiet look at both Susan and Anne. She said that Anne's bottom was 'a little sore' but that was probably due to her diet. And as for Susan, there was 'nothing wrong at all, just a normal bottom'.

By now the Yardleys had been roused to anger at the loss of their children. Who had asked for a place of safety order? Who had made the decision to take their children into care? Dr Higgs, when later asked the question, was quick to point out that a doctor could not ask for a place of safety order. This was a matter for the child protection agency. Or rather, Cleveland Social Services. Normally Dr Higgs would ring the duty social worker, tell the social worker what the signs were, and this would be followed by a discussion. In the case of the Yardley children, Dr Higgs had been 'very concerned' at those signs in relation to Elaine and had therefore considered a place of safety order appropriate. Dr Higgs' view, later to be expressed in court, said little for the independence of the social worker.

What she had been anxious to do with Elaine was remove her from her parents, so that the child could 'disclose' to social workers. But a High Court judge would later point out that Dr Higgs had led him to believe that 'she would never be satisfied until the children had made some admissions as to sexual abuse. Thus if the children were to be kept in care, as she advocated, until at any rate some admissions were forthcoming, I can see endless stalemates should the children stick to their guns.' And even if the child did make some kind of confession, what then? 'One wonders what evidential effect such admissions would have. In all probability, I should have thought, nil.'

Dr Higgs was always careful not to indicate who she thought the alleged perpetrator might be. This was why she wanted the maximum time to obtain a disclosure. 'I could not say who the perpetrator could be,' she recalled. 'Elaine needed to talk.' It was significant by this stage that abuse of Anne was no longer talked about; nor did Susan come into the reckoning. But then the first child was no more than a few months old; the second was 'inarticulate'. Only the 'bright and sunny' Elaine seemed willing to babble away, but never to the point of admitting she had been sexually abused. She would later, however, be the focus of a great deal of attention.

As for Anne, did Dr Higgs know of a lower limit on child sex abuse? She didn't, she confessed. 'I've certainly heard of it in very small babies of two to three weeks old.' She could not, however, recall whether she had read this in a paper or someone had spoken of it. She thought that disclosure work was part of the process of getting to the heart of child abuse. 'In the generality of cases, disclosure work has been of use in proving suspicions aroused in the first place.'

Meanwhile, at the hospital, a student nurse told the Yardleys that while she was downstairs on ward nine Elaine had come up to her, sat on her knee quite naturally, put her arms around her and said: 'They think that someone has been touching mine and Susan's bottom. But they haven't. They haven't.' Elaine repeated this at a later time. The student nurse had then reported this to other staff nurses. Indeed, the student had been so upset that she cried at home and had nightmares about it. It was an inauspicious start to her nursing career.

The Yardleys were back at the hospital on Monday. Bill had forgotten all thought of going to work that day. He rang in to say there was a bit of family difficulty and could he be excused? The Yardleys also called their own doctor, who by now had returned after an absence of three months. She said she could not believe what had happened and she would come to the hospital as soon as possible. Two social workers arrived at one-thirty. The social worker assigned to Elaine not only remained in communication with Dr Higgs, asking her to speak to the child again, but she later made a name for herself as the Yardley children became the centre of yet another drama.

This social worker noted: 'Cleveland social services department have had no previous involvement with this family and at this stage very little is known about their background. However, they project themselves as a happy and united family.' Despite this honest report made from direct observation, the social workers had even more shocks in store for the Yardleys. For no one had told them that their children were to be fostered out. They thought they had lost their children to the social services and the General Hospital. They now discovered their children were to be given alternative homes with substitute parents.

The Yardleys were even required to assist in the process. 'The social workers asked if I would escort and carry Elaine and Susan to their car in order to ease the children's distress,' Bill Yardley recalled. 'They also mentioned that they would come back for Anne later in the afternoon. The social worker, incidentally, had mentioned to Elaine that she was being taken to somewhere *safe* because Dr Higgs had told her she had a sore bottom.' The Yardleys were deeply irritated at this. Especially when they saw their children 'crying uncontrollably' as they were driven away.

Bill then went back into the hospital to see his wife and daughter Anne. They decided it would be too heartbreaking to be around when the social workers returned for Anne. But as they left the hospital grounds their own general practitioner arrived. 'We asked her to examine Anne before the social workers took her,' Bill recalled. This she did. She remarked: 'Well, I've certainly seen worse bottoms than this.' At this point, Dr Higgs hurried into the examination room and asked if she could have a word with her outside. Dr Higgs complained that the general practitioner should not be examining Anne Yardley who was now a hospital patient. She could not examine her without her consent. In this Dr Higgs was strictly correct. The doctor had therefore to apologize before returning to the ward.

Later the doctor wrote: 'I have no doubt at all that the Yardleys are good and caring parents who have done everything necessary to safeguard the health and wellbeing of their children.' After her discussion with Dr Higgs, the doctor returned to the Yardleys. They spoke about the possible reasons for Anne's condition. The doctor said 'it was probable that it could be caused by constipation'. A nurse was present when this conversation took place, but by this time the social workers had returned and Anne too was taken away. The Yardleys had not even been spared seeing the back of their smallest child as she too was placed in a car and driven off to obscurity.

The Yardleys returned to their empty home. One room had been painted specially for Elaine. Anne's cot stood unmade. Susan had left her dolls and toys lying around and now her mother cleared them up and stacked them in a corner. How would they settle without their children? What would they say to those caring neighbours who had befriended them? How could they explain their children had suddenly been taken from them? And what reasons would they give for their disappearance? Could they be honest and say they had been taken away because Bill Yardley had allegedly interfered with all three of them? Or would there be a hysterical reaction from their friends? And what about Bill's job and career prospects? Suspension and dismissal from his position of trust stared him in the face.

In fact, all these considerations were swept aside. The Yardleys were innocent. They had nothing to hide. They decided to call their family solicitor and battle it out. They would take on the regional health authority, Cleveland Social Services, social workers, doctors, the lot. The battle began now. And it began in a traditional way – in prayer. The Yardleys were not church-goers but their neighbour was. They asked him to contact a local vicar who might join them in prayer. The name of this vicar was the Reverend Michael Wright. It was Michael Wright's first involvement in Cleveland child abuse. It would not be his last.

The Yardleys would not rest till their children were returned. It would be a long hard road, but sitting in an empty and still house in a state of shock was not the answer. The Yardleys might be diminutive but they could take comfort from the words of the Irish boxer Barry McGuigan. It was not the size of the dog that counted. It was the size of the fight in the dog.

Throughout these past few days, one phrase had been running time and again through the head of Norma Yardley. It had wakened her in the night. It had caught up with her during the day. She could not forget the tears of the nurse who had been looking after Anne. She could not forget how upset she had been when she learned that the Yardley children were to remain in hospital. What were the words she had used? And remembering the words why had she used them? '*You too, I'm afraid*', she had said. What had that meant? Did it mean that there were more children and more families in the same deadly predicament?

Norma Yardley did not know but she would soon find out.

4

Marietta Higgs was born in occupied Germany on 28 October 1948.

Her mother Johanna had been living in Poland with her German family, where her grandparents had an estate, but they had fled to Germany before the path of the Russian advance. Marietta's father was a Yugoslav. Obrad Kljajic had been too young to be in the Yugoslav Royal Army and had joined a civilian watchman service. He too found himself in Germany in the years after the war and met his future wife at a local cinema. Their love was born out of the chaos and deprivation of a world war. But did Johanna love Obrad? She was not sure. He continued his pursuit, her mother raised no objection, and so they married and settled near Munich.

Their future looked grim. In Germany the rubble lay all around. There were food shortages. The country was split between the Allies and there was the Berlin blockade. Emigration to Australia seemed a way out, not only for the Kljajics, but for thousands of others who wished to avail themselves of a free passage. The vessels were cramped, but for those who had suffered so much in wartime the promise of a new life in a new country was overwhelming.

The Kljajics arrived at the small whaling port of Albany in South West Australia.

Obrad Kljajic, now aged sixty-four, recalls how happy he was when the emigration papers came through. Like other emigrants, the Kljajics knew their life in Australia would be hard; they knew they would have to learn not only language but tradition and culture. Many of this generation would rise to become successful businessmen in their own right; others would fail. All knew that if they themselves did not make it, they might at least create opportunities for their children.

Johanna Kljajic had carried in her arms to Australia the nine-month-old baby Marietta. A few months later her sister Sonya was born. Obrad Kljajic did his two years' compulsory service for the government. As Obrad recalled: 'We went to a place called Lake Biddy to do farming work at first and then I got a job with the roads. That was when we busted up, Johanna and me.' On the farm Obrad teamed up with fellow countryman, Marko, four years older than he, who became his life-long friend. Marko had a young German wife and struggled like the rest of them to come to terms with his new life.

Marko and Obrad whiled away their spare time talking of Europe and the old country, and when Marko was transferred back to Albany Obrad wangled a way to follow him. 'They sent us out into the bush from Albany,' Marko recalled. 'It was to do survey work for a week. It lasted twenty-seven years. In that time I lost my own wife to another man and I saw Aubrey [his name for Obrad] go to pieces pining – yes, that's the word, pining – for his children.' The fragile love of Johanna and Obrad had hardly survived the crossing to Australia and their marriage had begun to fall apart even in the small whaling town.

As Johanna recalled in December 1987, at her home in East Fremantle, south of Perth: 'I think it was on the ship coming over to Australia, with Marietta in my arms and a second baby on the way, that I began to realize I didn't love him.' The parting was blunt. She threw Obrad out. She recalled: 'He became very bad tempered. He loved our children, but he was against me. Then he wanted to come back but it was too late.'

Johanna and her children settled in Albany and soon she was joined by her mother and her brother Helmut. Obrad stayed in touch with his children, calling at the family home on a Sunday when he had access and taking them for rides. At the home Obrad was always on his best behaviour and when he took his children back at the end of access time he could 'never bear to part with them'. Marko recalls that his friend 'got into a big depression after that'. Soon Obrad became 'depressed and bitter' and stopped visiting the Kljajic home altogether.

Obrad and his daughters became so estranged that when Sonya was shown a photograph of her father, she said: 'I'm flabbergasted to learn he is still alive. I thought he had died of stomach cancer. This is my biological father. I'd forgotten all about him. I have photographs in my home and this is him. Marietta has his nose.' Sonya Gottfried, as she now is, had returned to Europe some twenty years ago and now lives in an affluent suburb of Cologne. She shook with emotion when shown the photograph of a father she thought had died years ago.

Sonya, married with a small child, is a teacher and speaks fluent English and German. She recalls little of her father or the events of her childhood. But she does remember that after her parents' divorce Obrad had been granted access to her and Marietta, who was eighteen months older. 'He would take us to Woolworths to buy cheap toys and patent leather shoes. My mother disapproved of what he bought us. On the Monday she would return them to the store and ask for a refund.' Both Kljajic children would 'shut their father' out of their minds, as Sonya would say. 'He means nothing to me. Neither I nor Marietta had a close relationship with our natural father.'

Sonya felt that Obrad had been put in a position where he could not 'cope'. She felt 'probably it wasn't his fault. He had to emigrate from Germany but he did not have the character to take the pressure.' Did the fact that there had been no father in the home have any impact on their upbringing? 'We were not affected by his behaviour,' Sonya recalls 'because we had two strong women behind us when he left – our mother and our grandmother.'

She added: 'Everybody's psyche is a product of their childhood. But nothing that Marietta has done has had anything to do with him or is because of him. There are no skeletons in her cupboard, whereas there may be in other people's.' For her Marietta was 'unimpeachable'. 'She has the courage of her convictions and she can stand up and say what she knows is right and what she feels because she is on solid ground. It is ridiculous to say that Marietta's behaviour now is based on her childhood experience.'

Marko blames the Kljajic split on the arrival of Johanna's mother: 'Aubrey was devoted to the kids – Marietta's baby sister had come along by then – but he believed the old lady was coming between him and them.'

Though the Kljajic sisters had no father, they did have uncle Helmut Templing. A neighbour recalls the closeness that developed between Helmut and the girls. This attachment came to a tragic end on 9 July 1960 when Helmut was killed in a motorbike accident at the age of only nineteen.

The sisters badly felt the loss of their young uncle. Both were 'devastated', but it was Marietta who was most 'affected'. Mrs Sue Wheatcroz was a former close friend of Marietta when at school. She now lives next door to Obrad Kljajic. Thinking on those bygone days, Sue Wheatcroz recalls that Marietta was 'a lovely girl. Very quiet. Very studious. She always had her head in a book.' Both Marietta and Sonya went to the John Curtin School in Fremantle, named after a former prime minister, and over the next four years both proved to be first-class students. Marietta developed an interest in the sciences and learned at the age of seventeen that she had been accepted at the University of Western Australia.

Before taking up her place she had a journey to make. Her mother had remarried. Her new husband was a Glaswegian, Duncan Halliday. With Obrad out of the house, Johanna had had to bring up her children as best she could, aided by her own mother. She had done laundry for the local maternity hospital. She had worked as a barmaid. However hard the life there was a dramatic change when a wool ship came into port with the Scottish mariner Duncan Halliday on board.

The courtship was different from the one with Obrad and had happier consequences. Duncan Halliday met the children and got on with them. He proposed and was accepted and the Halliday family, as it became, settled in Fremantle. Duncan's brother-in-law was a prominent Dundee gynaecologist. Marietta's grandmother, Johanna Templing, had by now returned to Germany. Marietta went to see her grandmother and also visited her stepfather's brother-in-law. This might not be a grand European tour, but it took Marietta to Scotland where she watched her step-uncle at work in his hospital.

Perhaps it was this experience which led Marietta to settle upon a career.

Her mother said: 'We think it was during that visit to Scotland that her future with children was subconsciously decided – although she never said so herself.' When she returned to Western Australia, she enrolled at the university. This was 1967. She was in her nineteenth year. She studied biology, chemistry, maths and physics, but the results were not in accord with the studious ambition. Marietta failed her exams. According to her mother, this was because she had fallen in love. She had met her future husband, university lecturer David Higgs, son of a Sydney antique-book dealer. David asked Marietta to marry him and she went home to give her mother and stepfather the good news.

They expressed their concern. Marietta was the same age as Johanna when she had married in Germany. 'I didn't want Marietta to go through the same mistake I had made,' Johanna recalls. 'And David, I thought, was too old for her. He was twenty-eight.' Marietta, with a determination that would prove characteristic, had made up her own mind, so that the only remaining questions were whether she would try for her degree again, and where she and David would settle. They decided to move to Adelaide. Housing might be cheaper there and, besides, the university said that they would accept her.

David Higgs' father travelled a thousand miles from Sydney to help find the newly-weds a home of their own, which they did in

Jenkins Avenue, in a peaceful suburb known as Myrtle Bank.

In 1968, the year of student restlessness throughout the world, Marietta Higgs was busy starting a family. It was a further three years before she was able to take up her university place. By then she had two children of her own, Nicholas and Robin.

Those who recall her days at the university remember her 'shyness and self-effacement'. Often she would leave her children in the university nursery and when she returned to pick them up she would do so in the company of a friend, Antonia Turnbull, now a prominent paediatrician in Adelaide. Dr Turnbull recalls that she probably knew Marietta better than anyone: 'Yet in many respects I did not know her at all. I was never aware of her family. But she did speak about the difficulties she and David had trying to raise children while building their own careers.' By 1975, however, after she had gained her Bachelor of Medicine and Bachelor of Surgery, the *Medical Gazette* was listing her as a medical practitioner.

She qualified with what an Adelaide university official described as 'a reasonable degree' and carried out her pre-registration year in medicine and surgery as a house officer at the Royal Adelaide Hospital. She did a further year's training at the Adelaide Children's Hospital. Her mentor was Professor George Maxwell, head of the paediatrics department of Adelaide University, associated with the hospital, and chairman of the research committee of the Children's Medical Research Foundation of South Australia.

The credentials of Professor Maxwell were impressive. He had graduated in Edinburgh, where he had also done his training; he had gone to the United States where he had been a member of the academic staff of the University of Wisconsin. In 1959 he had moved to Australia and taken up the chair as professor of paediatrics. It was Professor Maxwell who documented the first cases of child abuse reported in Australia in the early 1960s, setting up a well-organized scheme for the recognition and treatment of abused children.

Professor Maxwell remembers Marietta well because 'she stood out as a dedicated and conscientious trainee in the field of paediatrics'. He recalls her as 'a sensible, mature graduate who always accepted the right degree of responsibility'. She was cooperative and would put evidence together and interpret it with 'caution'. She would call for the appropriate confirmation and tests and all in all displayed a degree of clinical judgement which was 'quite impressive for someone who was newly graduated'.

And like all trainees she was exposed to the problems of child abuse.

Professor Maxwell says: 'Marietta's training in sexual abuse would have begun in England where techniques have been streamlined in recent years.' Professor Maxwell pointed out that cases of sexual abuse would be much more difficult to diagnose than physical cases: 'Very often the diagnosis finishes up on the basis of the perpetrator admitting it because there is sufficient evidence to persuade him to admit it.' Professor Maxwell was 'less able to be certain about sexual abuse and therefore we did not push this too much with the undergraduates and junior doctors'. There might have been the odd case of sexual abuse for Marietta to deal with but generally she would have dealt with physical abuse.

In 1976 Marietta and David Higgs came to Europe in circumstances not entirely different from those in which Marietta's own parents had emigrated. Her mother had left Germany with one baby in her arms and another on the way; Marietta, who had married at the same age, left Australia with two children and a third expected. Her family would not interfere with her medical career; her husband David took it upon himself to bring the children up.

Marietta worked first as a locum in Nottingham and then became senior house officer in Chatham, Kent, before moving to Newcastle upon Tyne in 1979. There she joined a research team looking into cot deaths. The following year she joined a two-year rotation scheme for registrars with the local health authority. The first year she specialized in general paediatrics, the second year she did six months of neonatal intensive care and six months in paediatric cardiology. She also completed her family and by the time she came to live in Middlesbrough she had five children – Nicholas aged sixteen, Robin fifteen, Zoe ten, Thomas seven, and Kate five.

It was in 1980 when she was a registrar in Newcastle that Marietta Higgs developed her special interest in child abuse.

5

It is true to say, however, that while her career was *child-oriented* it was not *abuse-oriented*, a point many overlooked in 1987. She later recalled, echoing the words of Professor Maxwell, that while in Australia she had certainly come across children who had been physically abused; but 'it tended to be dealt with really as a social problem, that social agencies dealt with rather than doctors'. As a junior doctor she had dealt with neither emotional nor sexual abuse. Her career was positively steered in this direction when she came to work with Dr Christine Cooper in Newcastle. This paediatrician, known to her friends as Tina, took the view that doctors should play a more active role in child abuse generally; she thought paediatricians should be involved in the recognition of child abuse, and once it was recognized, 'be instrumental in trying to assess the families in which these problems occurred'.

What did this mean?

As Dr Higgs explained it: 'An assessment of the child would be carried out, usually by a paediatrician, possibly a psychiatrist or psychologist. Further family assessments would be carried out by other agencies. But certainly the paediatrician should play an active role in assessment and making recommendations for future rehabilitation.' Dr Higgs saw at first hand the children with whom Dr Cooper had to deal: 'Children that had been bruised, that may have come from families, that had perhaps young parents, severely stressed, difficult problems, and children who were being emotionally abused. Failing to thrive, where there was evidence of neglect of these children.'

Dr Cooper looked into these families and tried to get an idea of the backgrounds in which parents were not able adequately to care for their children. It was the view of Dr Cooper that one should, in the words of Dr Higgs, 'continue to keep the optimum development of the child to the forefront'. Dr Higgs explained her own view of poorly children in relation to their family: 'It can be very difficult for families to accept that possibly their care of the child is not optimum for the child, and one needs to have some control and authority over the situation to help the parents adjust and change in order to appropriately parent their child or children.'

She added: 'I think one thing that we all need to remember is that childhood is short. There are time limits on the sorts of developments that children need to undergo, physical, emotional, psychological, and so on. So one does need to try and improve the parenting within the time limits that the child has, and that sometimes needs an authoritative approach. Ideally, it would be nice to be able to persuade the parents round to your view, but often that takes a very long time and may never happen.'

Dr Higgs had learned from Dr Christine Cooper that, in general terms, 'paediatricians should always be honest with parents'. Dr Higgs admitted that there might be difficulties in this. She might have to face the anger and hostility of the parents, but it was for the paediatrician to 'work one's way through that part of the process in order to then go on and move forward to work with the parents and their children'.

Following her stint on the two-year rotation scheme, Dr Higgs crossed the river Tyne to work in Gateshead at the Queen Elizabeth Hospital. As a part-time registrar she worked eight sessions a week, which meant four days a week; she was on call one night in three. The job was considered 'part-time' but it was generally a very heavy schedule for Dr Higgs: 'Gateshead is a busy district general hospital which involved general paediatrics,' she recalled. 'They also have a special care baby unit and I remained involved in that aspect also, although they did not "ventilate" babies at Gateshead.'

Dr Simon Court, consultant paediatrician at the Queen Elizabeth Hospital, wrote of Dr Higgs: 'She is incredibly hard-working and careful. The interests of the child are paramount in her thinking and the principles under which she works would stand the closest scrutiny.' Dr Court added a final comment to sum up Dr Higgs: 'She is a very well-trained paediatrician.' She continued her studies and obtained her membership of the Royal College of Physicians in 1983. She kept up her clinical work, passing back over the river to attend regular sessions with the Nuffield Child Psychiatry Unit in Newcastle. Over the next two years she immersed herself in her work with children: 'The sort of children that I was dealing with were perhaps children with behavioural problems, soiling, constipation, and also there were a number of children who had been sexually abused.'

Here Dr Higgs learnt how to communicate with children in a much more detailed way: 'The sort of help that I was offering children was individual therapy, and also therapy sessions. I learnt to spend more time trying to understand children and trying to learn to speak with them, communicate with them.' Dr Higgs saw at first hand during this period of her career the really damaging effects of child sex abuse: 'I remember one little girl in particular, who was nine years old and who had been sexually abused by a stepfather. Her mother had married, I think, four times. She had also been abused by her older brother, who was I think sixteen or seventeen at the time.'

Dr Higgs had seen the child for over a year, initially weekly and then fortnightly. 'The thing that she taught me was how damaging it could be in terms of being able to trust and to form relationships,' Dr Higgs recalled. 'I do not think I ever, even in that length of time, managed to begin to form a relationship with this child. She just would not allow anyone near her in that way.'

Towards the end of that year Dr Higgs was working in an attic room in a Victorian terraced house. The girl 'would sit on the rafter over the window and would spend the entire session asking who would care, what would happen if she threw herself from the window. What would I do? Would I care? And that was after a year. She was beginning to test out whether she was worth caring for. It was a very sobering experience for me to have met that child.'

In 1983 Dr Higgs attended a two-day conference on child sexual abuse that had been organized at Northumbria police headquarters. The lesson she learnt from this conference was that 'it was going to be very important for professionals dealing with this problem to come to terms with it themselves and also to be able to share experiences with colleagues and that, in working on this problem, it was also very important to have support to be able to do that.' Dr Higgs gained the impression that child sex abuse was really 'a very common problem' and had gone largely undetected in the past, but 'as professionals were gaining increasing knowledge and awareness of it, the incidence seemed to be increasing. Or the incidence of detection seemed to be increasing.'

Dr Higgs returned to Newcastle in September 1985 to the Princess Mary Maternity Hospital to gain further experience in her chosen subject of neonatal intensive care. Her job description was that of 'first assistant to the senior registrar in child health'. From the Princess Mary she also covered the Fleming Hospital next door. In the Fleming was the residential assessment unit of Dr Hans Steiner. This family assessment unit greatly impressed Dr Higgs. As she explained it, its function is 'to assess parenting of children where there has been a recognized difficulty, whether it is in terms of emotional abuse or physical abuse. And also, where you have young single mothers where their parenting skills have not yet been tried, to enable you to assess that and to try and help improve it. I think the most important feature of the unit is that it is residential, and is able to admit whole families so that you do not separate children from their parents while assessments are going on and yet the children are safe.'

Families would stay in the unit for a month to six weeks, depending very much on the family, the problem, how the assessment was going, and what sort of work needed to be done: 'The aim is to help the parents to learn of the problems with bringing up children and how to deal with them.' Dr Higgs had in mind to set up a similar unit for Teesside when she first heard of a vacant consultancy post at Middlesbrough early in 1986. She learned of it through the medical grapevine. One consultant paediatrician at the Middlesbrough General Hospital had passed on the job prospect to Dr Higgs' superior in Newcastle. This was Dr Edmund Hey.

As Dr Higgs recalled it: 'He felt, knowing me and knowing my interest, that it was really quite an ideal job for me because it would allow the combination of not only being able to continue in general paediatrics but also continue with my interests in neonatal intensive care.' This was, after all, 'a major part of the job'. Dr Higgs, however, saw an additional opportunity in taking up the Middlesbrough post if it were offered: 'Someone was needed in Middlesbrough who had an interest in child abuse and parenting problems.' Dr Higgs would find enough of both these problems and in doing so would put the iron town on the map in a way it would rather have done without; put the county of Cleveland on the map in such a way that there were those who thought, in the end, it should change its name; and put herself into the medical history books in a way, probably, she herself would have liked least.

All these future events were inconceivable, however, when Dr Higgs came down the A19 from Newcastle to see for herself the town of Middlesbrough.

6

She was shown around the wards at Middlesbrough General and Maternity hospitals by Drs Wyatt and Morrell. She also met the senior paediatrician, Dr Hilary Grant. Born in 1927, Dr Grant had been appointed consultant paediatrician in 1966. She worked out of the South Tees Health Authority but did some work in the neighbouring North Tees. Peter Morrell was next in seniority. He had been in paediatrics since 1974. His speciality was neonatology and the needs of handicapped children. And then there was Geoffrey Wyatt, aged thirty-seven, appointed a consultant in paediatrics and neonatology in 1983. He did most of his work out of Middlesbrough General Hospital but also occasionally crossed the river to the North Tees Hospital.

Dr Higgs had already known Dr Morrell from the days when he was senior registrar at the Princess Mary, but this was her first encounter with Dr Geoffrey Wyatt. The two found themselves instantly compatible. Perhaps it was their age. Perhaps it was their outlook. Perhaps it was their desire to see an expanded paediatric service covering more ground in the deprived and underprivileged areas of Middlesbrough. However, such was the chemistry that although Dr Higgs was junior to Dr Wyatt, the consultant paediatrician referred for her appraisal a case involving twin boys: 'The boys were very seriously failing to thrive,' Dr Higgs recalled. 'They had moved up from somewhere south but had been in Middlesbrough, I think, for about seven or eight months, and it had been recognized from their arrival that there was going to be a need for social work input for the family.'

There was no question of sexual abuse with the twins, but Dr Higgs had felt that while the parents had been 'very well supported, had received help and advice on the care of their children', it did not seem to her that this was making very much difference to the boys. Her recommendation was that the children should be removed from their mother and father and from the family home, a draconian solution that would become well known to Middlesbrough families. It was her view that, 'having had that amount of very intensive social work input, that a period of a trial of fostering should be tried to see if that would improve the boys' growth'. The paediatrician had made a recommendation for social services and case conference workers alike, but much to the satisfaction of Dr Higgs, the children were indeed fostered and made, in her words, 'a very dramatic weight gain in care'. According to Dr Wyatt, this amounted to twenty per cent in three months. He attributed their condition to 'previous emotional deprivation'.

The link between child sex abuse and failure to thrive would be an important element in Dr Higgs' views in the months to come. In her mind, failure to thrive is 'inadequate growth of children when there is no obvious medical cause to account for it'. As Dr Higgs explained, 'children grow at a defined rate through childhood. They come in all shapes and sizes. There are small children and large children, but the rate of growth should be fairly uniform with all children. If the rate of growth is inadequate, then there is what is considered to be failing to thrive, that they are not reaching their own potential for growth.'

The appearance of such a child was that he would be 'very small, very underweight. Often they look much younger than their years. These two boys, for instance, were almost three years old, and they really looked like eighteen-month-old children. They still have very large pot bellies; the proportion of their legs was in keeping more with infantile proportions rather than that of a three-year-old child. So very small, very underweight children who looked very immature for their age.' Dr Higgs noted that, in the case of the twins, there had been a dramatic improvement in their health: 'Instead of growing along the normal rate there was a much accelerated weight gain.' It was clear that the children had been put into 'a nurturing environment where they were clearly adequately fed and parented. It highlighted the deficiency of the parenting that they had had prior to that.'

These were ominous tidings for Middlesbrough parents who had sick children, but they reflected the views of those who felt that the child's interests were pre-eminent, and that if there were to be solutions for children with ill-health they might equally well be found out of the family as within it. So long as the child came first, so long as he thrived, it hardly seemed to matter what environment he was in. The solution for the twins which had escaped Dr Wyatt was easily found by Dr Higgs when the children were taken into care and subsequently did better in the foster home.

The consultancy post in Middlesbrough was duly advertised in June 1986. Satisfied with the opportunities that awaited her in the paediatric field, Dr Higgs applied for the job and attended an interview on 14 July. There were two other applicants, one of whom had been a colleague of Dr Wyatt when he had worked in the south of England. At the interview, as Dr Higgs recalls it, she discussed all her interests: 'That of wishing to continue to work as a general paediatrician with a special interest in neonatology. And also in child abuse and parenting problems.'

There were many within the Teesside health community who did not look upon Dr Higgs' appointment as 'a good one'. There was the question of experience. Dr Higgs had been a senior registrar for all of eleven months. Was it unusual for a registrar to be promoted to consultant so quickly? 'It would depend on the training before that,' Dr Higgs explained. 'I had been part-time registrar for a little while before I took up the full-time post and had had a number of years as a registrar.' Generally, however, as Dr Higgs would accept, it would be usual to spend five years or the equivalent in a senior registrar's post before such an appointment is made. Dr Higgs did not become accredited to the Joint Committee of Higher Medical Training until after she had been made a consultant. But it was the enthusiasm of Dr Wyatt that was decisive. He remembered the referral of the twins and 'because of this and other contact which I and my colleagues had with Newcastle in the normal course of our work, I knew of Dr Higgs and of her interest in disadvantaged and abused children'. At this time, however, even Dr Wyatt did not know of her interest in child sexual abuse.

Prior to being interviewed, Dr Higgs attended yet another conference on child sex abuse held in Leeds. She went with her mentor, the by now ailing Dr Christine Cooper.

Dr Cooper had been a founder member of BASPCAN, the British Association for the Study and Prevention of Child Abuse and Neglect, in the north east and she had invited Dr Higgs to join it. Dr Cooper had set up the north east branch during 1984–5 and in the previous years she had involved herself in the Ciba Foundation, an international scientific and educational charity, which had turned out a useful manual on child sex abuse within the family. Clearly, the interests of Dr Cooper extended beyond that of an enlightened advancement of paediatric services in child care: the issue of child sexual abuse was important to her and she funnelled her energies and her devotion to the cause through BASPCAN.

Dr Cooper had recently retired, having been ill for some time, but she had sought not to let this interfere with her work, nor, as Dr Higgs recalled, 'her approach to life and its problems'. The dedication of Dr Cooper was such that despite her illness, despite her retirement, she was still seeing patients – 'not many, but seeing them'. She also continued her work with BASPCAN.

The association itself had been set up in 1979. Its origins could be traced back to a Tunbridge Wells study group in the early seventies, when a number of prominent people came together to work out ways of 'professionalizing' the study of child abuse. A study group had been set up in 1973, and in 1976 the International Society of Child Abuse was formed. 'Really,' the BASPCAN chairman, Mr Norman Dunning, would say, 'the association grew out of a number of more informal contacts between professionals that were taking place early in the seventies'. It had its own child abuse review and in 1981 published a book on child abuse which sold 18000 copies.

As Cleveland county turned the corner into 1987, BASPCAN had some thousand members drawn from a range of disciplines, all of them involved with child abuse: social workers, doctors, lawyers, nurses, teachers, representatives from self-help groups and lay people. BASPCAN organized, with the Ciba Foundation, contributions and publication of *Child Sexual Abuse Within the Family*. It organized seminars and conferences. These were done locally through branches and nationally through the association. In the words of its chairman: 'We are essentially a body which aims to promote understanding and training. We do not regard ourselves as any sort of pressure group. In fact, we do not have single views. We are more of a debating society, a place where people come to exchange ideas and to learn from one another.' The people who came together, however, were all of like mind and held similar, if not identical, views.

These views could be summarized in a series of basic principles that bound BASPCAN members together. The first of these was the needs of a child. This was in fact the central principle that guided all the professional groups who found themselves immersed in BASPCAN: 'The child's needs must come first. We think it is the most important starting point because of the powerlessness of children and their particular vulnerability in cases of child abuse.' Dr Dunning stated: 'Clearly, the thing which is most effective for children in any situation where they lose, temporarily or otherwise, the guidance and protection of parents is that they are placed in an extremely vulnerable position and do not know whom to trust.'

In these circumstances, it would be up to the professionals to accept their responsibilities and try to promote the interests of the child. There were, of course, clear dangers in this philosophy: if parents were unable to look after children, who was to say that social workers and doctors would do any better? Was it being implied that family life could no longer be trusted as a unit and that professionals skilled in child care should replace parents? Where was the thin line between the child who had been abused and needed protection and the child who had *not* been abused, who needed protection both for itself and for the family? And who was to be the arbiter between what might turn out to be competing interests of family and professionals?

But on the basic principle everyone could be agreed: *the needs of the child must come first.* On this would be built the remaining principles of BASPCAN: inter-professional work; reporting of public attitudes towards child abuse and child care practice; guidance from government in the field of handling child sex abuse; and skills, training and resources for those field workers having to deal with the problems of child abuse. These laudable principles were the foundations of a philosophy that would unite many of the participants in the Cleveland drama. Dr Higgs was a member of the north east branch of BASPCAN and served on its committee; Dr Jane Wynne was a member in Leeds; and the Cleveland child abuse consultant, Mrs Sue Richardson, was also a member. Dr Christopher Hobbs, another Leeds paediatrician who would gain notoriety out of events in Cleveland, was on the executive committee.

Mrs Margery Bray – known as Madge to her friends – was also a member. She had worked for thirteen years in the child care field. She had been involved in both fostering and adoption and had held a management post with Shropshire County Council. She would be called upon by Mrs Richardson to effect disclosure work on children suspected of alleged abuse in Cleveland. Mrs Marjorie Dunne, employed by the South Tees Health Authority as a senior nurse and designated officer for child abuse in the Langbaurgh district of Cleveland, was also a member.

Dr Higgs herself, recognizing the number of professionals in Cleveland whose work brought them face to face with alleged child sexual abuse, sent out a letter proposing that they get together. She in effect formed her own group, named the Cleveland Sex Abuse Group, which had its first meeting on 2 April. There was in the beginning a formal organization, with proper minutes being kept, but this fell away somewhat at later meetings. Dr Higgs would be reluctant to take the credit for forming the group: 'I certainly sent out the letters, but it came about because I had been discussing this problem with a number of other people and it seemed that there were individuals within Cleveland who were working with children, that their expertise and ideas had not been drawn together in any way, and it seemed that it was a good thing to try to do this.'

Other meetings were held on 30 April, 11 June and 23 June. Dr Higgs would not attend the last meeting but she was so concerned that nursing staff at the hospital should come along that she publicized the second June meeting in the sisters' offices of wards nine and ten at Middlesbrough General Hospital.

BASPCAN organized the Leeds seminar which Dr Higgs attended with Dr Cooper in June 1986. The principal speaker at the seminar was Dr Jane Wynne, consultant paediatrician at St James's University Hospital and the General Infirmary, Leeds, who together with her colleague Dr Hobbs had pioneered the technique of reflex anal dilatation. The best description of this technique would ultimately be found in a High Court judgement rendered by Her Honour Judge Cohen QC: '*A normal reaction when the buttocks are parted gently is for the anus to remain tightly closed, because the sphincter muscle is in a natural state of tension and cannot be voluntarily opened, only closed.*'

Judge Cohen went on: '*It is only opened by the expulsion of faeces from the rectum downwards and not normally opened in the reverse unless pressurized to do so by some form of external penetration. But if there has been repeated anal penetration, the muscle can train itself to react to minimize, presumably, any pain and discomfort caused by that penetration. In other words, the sphincter muscle will teach itself to relax and it will then open the anal orifice by reflex action in anticipation.*' It was the view of those paediatricians who supported reflex anal dilatation as a diagnostic technique that, in the case of an abused child, a doctor could actually see this happening. Hence the conclusion that if the anal orifice opened by reflex action there must have been a prior penetration to cause it. There was, in addition, a negative aspect to this. For if the opening of the anal canal constituted child sexual abuse – and there was no known explanation as to why the canal had opened – then child sexual abuse could be diagnosed *ipso facto*.

It was this technique that was at the heart of Dr Wynne's presentation at Leeds. According to Judge Cohen, the technique was actually introduced at this seminar. Dr Marietta Higgs was therefore in on the ground floor. The broader views of Drs Wynne and Hobbs were set out concisely in an article in the *Lancet* published 4 October 1986. In an article entitled 'Buggery in Childhood – A Common

Syndrome of Child Abuse', the two paediatricians claimed that, in the case of sexually abused children, 'under-reporting' was usual. They cited their own experiences in Leeds where, over a three-year period, the number of cases brought to their attention had risen from ten in 1983 to 106 in 1985; there were 104 in the first six months of 1986.

Drs Wynne and Hobbs linked their findings to a MORI poll in September 1984 which, on the basis of retrospective recall, allegedly showed that one in ten had been sexually abused as children. The article did not give the MORI poll's definition of sexual abuse: '*A child (anyone under sixteen years of age) is sexually abused when another person, who is sexually mature, involves the child in any activity which the other person expects to lead to their own sexual arousal. This might involve intercourse, touching, exposure of the sexual organs, showing pornographic material or talking about things in an erotic way.*'

There was no question of this poll showing by way of psephological evidence that one in ten children had been interfered with as children. In fact, the poll showed that seven in a thousand had actually been interfered with, a high enough incidence of child sex abuse, but far removed from the figure of one in ten which was to enter into mythology and which was subsequently to be denied by the poll's founder, Mr Bob Worcester, in an article published in *The Times* on 2 December 1987.

Drs Wynne and Hobbs described in their article how they had seen in Leeds as many cases of sexual abuse as physical abuse: 'Ano-rectal abuse of young children is more common than the battered child syndrome in this age group,' they wrote. 'Although recognized cases of all types of abuse, including fondling and touching, masturbation, child prostitution and pornography, and intercourse (oral, anal and vaginal) have risen, we have become aware of more cases of anal abuse than any other forms of sexual abuse in very young children of both sexes.'

These were sweeping statements: more parents buggered their children than beat them. And it was not simply that more abuse was being *detected* now: there was actually a *rise* in sexual abuse in relation to past times, the article claimed. There was an increase in fondling, touching, masturbation, child prostitution, pornography and intercourse of every sexual type, but there were more cases of anal abuse than of any of the other forms.

In an article entitled 'Management of Sexual Abuse', published in *Archives of Disease in Childhood*, 1987, Drs Wynne and Hobbs declared that the United Kingdom was 'witnessing the beginning of an explosive epidemic of reported cases of the sexual abuse of children. A similar epidemic started ten years ago in the United States.' In the view of the paediatricians, this had arisen 'because of greater public and professional awareness and willingness to intervene in a problem that has been well known for generations.'

The one-in-ten figure would still not lie down: 'Recent research on both sides of the Atlantic has shown that as many as one in ten to one in three children – boys and girls – are sexually abused in some way during childhood or adolescence.' There was no definition as to what the surveys indicated to be child sexual abuse; but on the broad-brush canvas of child abuse that was painted at Leeds, in June 1986, the diagnostic technique married to such a massive increase in alleged child abuse would leave a startling impact on the mind of at least one of the participants: Dr Marietta Higgs.

Slides were shown of sexually abused children. Similar slides were shown to interested Members of Parliament in the House of Commons on 28 October 1987. They clearly showed child anal abuse in all its abhorrent forms. But did they show a clear link between child abuse and its detection by the means of reflex anal dilatation? Since the professionals who attended this seminar were all of one mind, perhaps the question was never asked. But if Dr Higgs had been impressed by the diagnosis she was equally impressed by its pioneer: 'This was the first occasion on which I heard Dr Jane Wynne speak and show slides of physical findings which she had seen,' Dr Higgs recalled. 'I realized for the first time the numbers of children that could be involved in this problem and the importance of the medical examination.'

She recalled the earlier conference she had attended in 1983, where the medical examination of a child had not been seen to play an important role. 'I think what was impressive about the Leeds conference is that there were doctors who had been working in the field, who had had a number of years' experience. They had children with physical findings and were actually then able to relate these to histories from the child of abuse and also admission by the perpetrators.' Other facets of the seminar also impressed Dr Higgs: 'The numbers of children who had this problem were increasingly being diagnosed in Leeds, and the figures were rising quite quickly over the previous two to three years.'

Prior to her visit to Leeds, Dr Higgs had not spent a lot of time on children's bottoms. She had, of course, come across urinary tract infections or rectal bleeding, constipation and the like, but after her attendance at Leeds her practice changed and she 'tried to consciously familiarize' herself with normal appearances and, when appropriate, would in fact 'clinically examine children' in that area. Dr Higgs agreed that while such examinations were part and parcel of general paediatric practice, nevertheless she thought 'conscious examination of the genitalia and anus is something that has probably been done more, recently, than it has been done before.'

Dr Higgs was told at Leeds that of children who had been physically abused some twenty-five per cent had been sexually abused. She was impressed that the seminar was addressed by representatives from the police, social workers and other professionals working in Leeds. She said later: 'It was at this meeting that I first heard described the technique of anal examination which Dr Wynne used, and I particularly recall that both the slides shown and the statistics put forward by Dr Wynne made a deep impact on me.' They equally made a deep impact on Dr Cooper, and the senior and junior doctor discussed both the slides and the statistics as they related to 'the potential difficulties and importance of dealing with sexual abuse'.

Dr Higgs recalled 'that what they were describing was new'. But she did not get the impression, either from the meeting or the questions asked, or indeed from the discussions which she had later with Dr Cooper, that the diagnosis of reflex anal dilatation was 'a highly controversial subject'. She accepted that new findings were being presented. 'Also it was a new approach to the problem in which paediatricians had become involved. That was the way that I remember that meeting. But the issue of controversy did not loom at all.'

It was in this frame of mind that Dr Higgs and Dr Cooper returned from Leeds to Newcastle. Unfortunately Dr Cooper died shortly thereafter, thus depriving the junior doctor of what might have been a steadying influence; Dr Higgs duly saw her appointment as consultant paediatrician at Middlesbrough General Hospital confirmed by the regional health authority; and the way was clear for her to join the medical elite of consultants. She did not take up her post immediately, for she wished to finish her research in Newcastle. It was for this reason that the health authority agreed to what amounted to a late kick-off, that is, 1 January 1987.

Meanwhile, Dr Higgs had an early opportunity of finding out at first hand what reflex anal dilatation was all about.

7

Whereas Bill and Norma Yardley were 'upwardly mobile', it was plain that Joseph and Mary Dixon were not in the same category. Both were twenty-four years old. Both were unemployed. Indeed, neither of them had worked in their lives. They managed by skimping on unemployment and supplementary benefit to bring up a family. They lived in a Middlesbrough suburb, in a council house on one of the estates built in the early fifties; they had married young and in July 1986 had two children, Vera aged four and Angela aged eighteen months. Vera had been born at full term by emergency caesarean, but the child was none the worse for that and would later be described as 'an easy, happy baby who had given her parents no cause for concern until Angela was born'.

Angela was also delivered by caesarean but was not so lucky as her elder sister. Mary Dixon was ill for several weeks following the birth with infections which needed hospital treatment, and Angela had problems with vomiting and poor weight. In other words, she failed to thrive. As Dr Higgs would later write: 'Her symptoms have been extensively investigated both at Middlesbrough General Hospital and at the Fleming Memorial Hospital on a previous admission and no medical cause has been found.' Because of the recurring bouts of vomiting, Angela had from the age of three months been under the care of Dr Geoffrey Wyatt, who felt that the child's problems might stem from a narrowing of the gullet.

Dr Wyatt recommended an operation but the parents hesitated. Could they have a second opinion? The child was therefore sent up to the Fleming Hospital in Newcastle, where a consultant surgeon concurred with the opinion of Dr Wyatt. Further tests were carried out on Angela, who was admitted to the Fleming for two days, after which the consultant surgeon changed his mind. No operation was carried out and Angela was readmitted to Middlesbrough General Hospital while doctors and nurses pondered what to do with her and looked for solutions to her problems.

In these first fragile months of her life, Angela Dixon was constantly in and out of hospital. Sometimes she would be there for days, sometimes for weeks, and sometimes even for months: she suffered a series of infections, particularly to the eyes and chest. The referrals to the hospital were at the request of the family doctor, or Dr Wyatt himself when the child visited his outpatients' clinic at

Middlesbrough General. At six months old, Angela had further tests on her gullet, this time at North Tees Hospital, and consequently she was put on a gluten-free diet. So, in the first eighteen months of her life, the child had seen the inside of three hospitals: the Middlesbrough General, the North Tees and the Fleming Hospital in Newcastle.

However, it was the health of the well child, Vera, that was drawn to the attention of the authorities. On 9 July 1986, when a health visitor came to the house to enquire after Angela, she noticed a bruise on Vera's bottom. The four year old also had a dimpled bruise at the top of her left shoulder blade, one on her left temple, and three little bruises on her left wrist. There were two other bruises on her right wrist, and bruises to her shins. All these were shown to the health visitor by Mary Dixon. The health visitor suggested a visit to the family doctor and when the Dixons arrived they were surprised to see the health visitor in the doctor's surgery, apparently explaining to the doctor how the bruises had come about: 'She was smacking her own backside and getting hold of his arm in a grasping motion how she thought that the bruises had come about on the child,' Mary Dixon recalled.

The family doctor asked the Dixons if they had been responsible for the bruises.

'No,' they replied.

The Dixons were asked to leave the room and ten minutes later were called back and told to have the child examined by Dr Wyatt at Middlesbrough General. This examination took place on 9 July 1986. In a letter to the area office of Cleveland Social Services, dated 11 July, Dr Wyatt had this to say: 'I talked to Mr and Mrs Dixon and they were unable to explain the bruises which I think were over her left buttock and the backs of both arms. I would go along with them that the small one-centimetre-diameter bruises on the child's legs were clearly accidental, and I did demonstrate to the mother that it was possible to cause the bruising on the back of the arms by holding the child's arms tightly and causing indentation by the fingers, but Mrs Dixon could not remember an incident that might have caused this.'

In fact, Mary Dixon pointed out that the child had started playschool three days earlier, the child bruised easily, and it might be that schoolyard activities had caused the bruising. Dr Wyatt went on: '*I examined the child and thought she was delightful, I could not find any other physical signs and there were certainly no injuries that were clearly non-accidental. I think I would go along with the fact that these are unexplained injuries but knowing Mr and Mrs Dixon, at present I would view these unexplained bruises as accidental.'*

Dr Wyatt ended his letter to Cleveland Social Services by stating that he had sent a copy to the family doctor, 'but I have not asked for any further action to be taken'. This ought to have been the end of the matter for the Dixons, but in fact it was only the beginning of a nightmare that would last for almost two years. The following day a car drove up to their house. There were two social workers in the car. They wanted to know where the children were. Mary Dixon explained that Vera was at playschool and Angela was asleep in bed. The social workers said that Angela should be taken to Middlesbrough General Hospital immediately and Vera would be picked up from playschool.

The children apparently did not like the idea of being taken to hospital, for they cried all the way there and again in the admission room. Dr Wyatt examined both children, with the assistance of a junior doctor. As Joseph Dixon recalled: 'We did not know the purpose of the examinations. Nobody told us anything. It was just a nightmare, but we thought it was just to do with the bruises that he had seen the day before.' The examination of the children continued: eyes and ears, hearts and lungs.

'Then Vera was told to stand up and take her knickers off,' Joseph Dixon recalled. 'When she was standing up, Dr Wyatt parted her legs to look at her vagina and parted the vagina just slightly. And then she went on to the bed in a kneeling down position, her buttocks were parted, and a light was shone upon her bottom.'

'What are you doing with my child?' Joseph Dixon demanded.

He was told the doctors were looking for 'sore parts'.

'The child doesn't understand what you're doing.'

By this time the child was crying. But now it was the turn of Angela. As Joseph Dixon recalled: 'Angela had her nappy taken off and Dr Wyatt just sort of leaned her on the bed, parted her buttocks, had a look at her anal passage and her vagina. It did not take long.'

Dr Wyatt asked Mrs Dixon to fasten the child up again. He told the parents both children were fine. Blood tests were then taken and X-rays. A diagram was made of Vera's bruises and arrangements were made for the Dixons to go to the X-ray department with both children and the two social workers, together with a nurse. There was, however, great difficulty in getting Vera X-rayed at all, so that Joseph Dixon had to assist in holding his daughter steady. The same turned out to be the case with Angela.

When the X-rays were eventually completed, one of the two social workers, who had slipped away during the X-ray session, returned with two pieces of paper. One was given to Joseph Dixon. The other was given to his wife. They were place of safety orders. Neither of the Dixons knew what these documents meant. The social worker declined to explain. 'Talk to Dr Wyatt,' she said. The Dixons waited for two hours. When Dr Wyatt did arrive, Joseph Dixon asked what was going on. Dr Wyatt asked him not to get too excited.

'Too excited at what my children have gone through today?' Joseph Dixon said.

'Don't worry,' Dr Wyatt said. 'The X-rays and the blood tests, I've got them here.' Dr Wyatt did indeed have both in his hands. The Dixons followed him into a room, where he put the X-rays on the viewing machine and described them as 'lovely and clear'.

'There's nothing the matter with the children,' Dr Wyatt said.

But he was concerned by what he described as Mary Dixon's 'back history'.

'Are we talking about my children's safety or my wife's back history?' Joseph Dixon wanted to know.

'The wife's back history. I would like to go into further detail. That's why I would like the children to stay in hospital for a while.'

This was 10 July 1986. On 11 July, Dr Wyatt sent a letter to the Dixons' doctor, saying no further action need be taken. But he decided to continue the letter overleaf and stated that he had made further enquiries following an hour-long interview with the Dixons. He had given them, he explained, a possible interpretation of events which, while not related either to the medical examinations or to the injuries he had already described as accidental, requiring no further action, had indeed everything to do with Mary's 'back history', as he called it.

What was this 'back history'?

The mother and father of Mary Dixon had split up when she was four and a half years old. On the divorce, her father had gained custody of both Mary and her brother. Mary's father, Jonathan Smith, remarried when Mary was twelve and a half years old. She went to live with her father and stepmother in a suburb of Middlesbrough. Her brother, despite the custody order, had actually gone to live with her mother. However, Mary's stepmother, having had two children to Mary's father, had a nervous breakdown and was admitted to the local psychiatric hospital.

Mary went into voluntary care and as her stepmother came in and out of hospital so Mary came in and out of care, until she was seventeen and a half and got her own flat in Middlesbrough. She married Joseph Dixon in September 1982. Her first pregnancy ended in miscarriage at about three months but both Vera and Angela were planned pregnancies. It was the family background, however, which preoccupied Dr Wyatt and to which he referred as the 'back history'. He gave his own interpretation as to how this might be affecting the health of the children, or rather the health of the eighteen-month-old Angela: 'Mrs Dixon went into care herself as a child at the age of four,' he wrote in the continuation of his 11 July letter.

He added: 'She stayed in a variety of children's homes and at the age of twelve was reunited with her father.' She had lived with a sixteen-year-old girl, who had subsequently had a baby. Her father had taken an overdose. She had then met Joseph Dixon. 'It was while Mrs Dixon was living in the accommodation as a teenager that she got to know Mr Dixon because he lived across the road, and that is the explanation as to why there is an odd situation of Mrs Dixon who lived opposite her mother with whom she has no contact verbally at all – and yet living just across the road.'

Dr Wyatt found it strange that a daughter separated from her mother at the age of four, and therefore before the age of memory for most of us, having been brought up by her father, and having been taken into care when the father could no longer cope, should feel little inclination to be in contact with her mother now she had reached the age of seventeen: 'I'm not sure really whether during the conversation we really acknowledged that this was an odd state of affairs and it was difficult to get Mrs Dixon to agree that her parenting skills may have been prejudiced by her upbringing.'

The conversation on 10 July upset Mary Dixon who, having pointed out a bruise on her daughter's bottom which the doctor had attributed to an accident, now felt herself being questioned on her role as a mother. For his part, Dr Wyatt complained that he did not seem to be getting through to Mary Dixon. And having once diagnosed Angela's sickness problems as 'a narrowing of the gullet' he now indicated that there might be other non-medical reasons: 'I said that one possible explanation for Angela's illnesses that resulted in a large number of admissions as an infant was because the mother did not love the child.'

Dr Wyatt perceived that Mrs Dixon was 'mildly offended' at this suggestion. She reminded Dr Wyatt he had given endless accounts as to why the child had been vomiting. He had never before mentioned emotional deprivation.

'I agreed with her,' Dr Wyatt said and suggested that possibly he had led the family 'up the garden path a bit in pursuit of an organic cause for the child's vomiting where in reality there was a psychological problem.' Having confessed gratuitously to Mary Dixon that his advice might have been wrong for the past several months, he then admitted that the treatment he had prescribed seemed to be working. 'The child', as he wrote, 'seemed better.'

By this time, as Dr Wyatt admitted, the Dixons were getting extremely agitated. The doctor had already said that Vera's bruises were accidental, but he was now saying that Angela was ill because her mother did not love her and was a poor parent. That at least was how the Dixons construed his words. No doubt Dr Wyatt was seeking to express himself in the best interests of parents and children alike. They in turn pointed out that Vera could easily have been bruised at playschool, which was new to her, and where she was forever throwing herself around a play area full of balls.

If this was criticism, the doctor took it to heart. He went to the playschool to see for himself the following day. He was surprised, however, to see that the Dixons were also there: 'This wasn't part of the arrangement and I think they are becoming increasingly obsessive and have a view that they are being persecuted,' he wrote. The Dixons might be forgiven a mild hysteria but Dr Wyatt wished to dampen such feelings down. He therefore drove the Dixons home from the nursery. He went round to their house. What he found, however, seemed to belie the statements that he had made to Mrs Dixon, the implication being she did not love her children and that she lacked parenting skills: 'I was impressed by the number of toys,' he wrote to the family doctor. 'Though clearly this household is financially restricted and therefore materially rather deprived, it is by no means a danger to the children and probably very similar to many households in this health district where unemployment is rife.'

Next Dr Wyatt drove the family to the post office.

Joseph Dixon went inside and again Mrs Dixon expressed her annoyance that there had been a series of intrusions into her life, that she had not told anyone in the family, but that she would be glad to provide character references. In his letter of 11 July 1986, Dr Wyatt wrote: 'I don't think that she really understood anything I was talking about the evening before. I'm not sure whether she is of limited intelligence or whether this resistance is an emotional reaction. However, I remain ill at ease with the whole business, as I must say that I have always been, knowing this family.'

Dr Wyatt would then dictate a post post scriptum to this letter which would have significant consequences for the Dixon family. Someone had told him that Vera had been used in a physical 'tug of war' between the Dixons and this had resulted in the bruising. The information had been anonymously given within the hospital. Mary Dixon knew nothing of this anonymous allegation and would not learn of it until court proceedings were pending. Then her only explanation was that a message had been sent to her father and stepmother that Mary's children were in the hospital and that her father could not believe they had been admitted on the basis of bruising only – hence the garbled story of a possible 'tug of war'.

Whatever the source, and whether the allegation made to Dr Wyatt had been malicious or innocent, or whether it had any impact on social services' thinking, the fact is that application was made on 18 July for an interim care order on the Dixon children and this was granted by Teesside magistrates.

The Dixons claimed they knew nothing about these proceedings. In any event, they would not have understood them. They did not know that control had already passed from them as parents to social services. Everything had happened so quickly, within a matter of days, that they had been left completely mystified. Their daughter Angela had been sick from birth. She had required medical attention. Their elder daughter Vera had had bruises which no one could explain other than that they had happened in a playschool but which Dr Wyatt had considered to be accidental. And yet place of safety orders had been converted into interim care and everything that was now to be done with their children had to be done under the auspices of social services.

But if the Dixons thought all this bad enough, worse was in store.

8

There had been a social services case conference on 15 July at which it had been agreed that an interim care order should be sought in respect of both the Dixon children. It was also agreed that enquiries should be made to see whether it would be possible to have the family placed on ward two of the Fleming Hospital in Newcastle for 'assessment'. The Dixons made a reconnoitring trip on 16 July to meet nurses and doctors. They also met Dr Marietta Higgs. The Dixons were to be assessed over a six-week period and the entire family was taken to ward two – the Steiner Unit, so called after its founder and leader Dr Hans Steiner – by social workers on 19 July, which was a Saturday.

Their residence did not get off to an auspicious start: 'On the Sunday,' as Mary Dixon recalled, 'my husband was taken to the Royal Victoria Infirmary with suspected food poisoning and Angela and Vera came down with it and myself and the two little girls were confined to our rooms.' Vera had been vomiting all over the place. A nurse said: 'Hasn't anybody seen about the child?' They called a doctor from the Princess Mary in Newcastle so that she might be checked over.

Joseph Dixon stayed at the Royal Victoria Infirmary for two days and returned to be with his wife on the Steiner Unit. On Wednesday 23 July 1986 they received another visit from Dr Marietta Higgs. It was because Dr Hans Steiner himself was on holiday that Dr Higgs had been called in to meet the family. Dr Higgs, however, had a different explanation. The consultant covering the children should have been Dr Hey, her senior, but because Dr Hey knew of her 'interest' the family was referred to her as 'the person who would probably undertake the work with them'. The background to this 'interest' would not be explained to the Dixons, but it had happened that, on 15 July, while on duty at the Fleming Memorial Hospital, as Dr Higgs always called it, she had received a telephone call from a Teesside social worker to discuss the possible admission of the Dixon family. The social worker wanted an assessment of their parenting. Dr Higgs was told that non-accidental injury to Vera had been diagnosed at Middlesbrough General and that, at the case conference that day, it was reported by several people who knew the family that 'there had been long-standing concerns about the parenting of the children'.

No one had told the Dixons about this case conference, or about the fact that someone had converted their child's injuries from accidental to non-accidental. What came next would equally floor them. 'Dr Higgs talked to us about my back history,' Mary Dixon recalled. 'She asked me about my background and how I got on with my neighbours and then about my neighbours' backgrounds and the environment they lived in.' The Dixons chatted about a man in the street who had had a baby boy to a fifteen-year-old girl, and the police had kept his house under surveillance. The police had used the Dixons' house for their activities: 'We had let them do so. They were looking for other young girls going in.'

Dr Higgs then spoke directly to Joseph Dixon: 'Well,' she said, 'I think it is an appropriate time to tell you my suspicions about Vera, your oldest daughter. I strongly suspect she has been sexually abused.' Mary Dixon recalled: 'At this time we were made numb and my husband asked what she meant by "sexually abused". From her reply we gathered that she was implying that the man in the street we had been talking about had done it. I said to her: "If it's him I'll kill him." She turned to my husband and said: "Oh no, Mr Dixon. I strongly suspect a penis has penetrated through the anus." My husband then said: "Where and how?" She said: "Between leaving Middlesbrough General Hospital and getting into the Fleming."'

This astonished and perplexed the Dixons. They were being told that their four-year-old daughter had been sexually abused. More extraordinarily still, they were being told this abuse had occurred while the child was in the care of Cleveland Social Services, on a trip from Middlesbrough to Newcastle, with two social workers in the car. Joseph Dixon told Dr Higgs that this was impossible. He told her it was even more far-fetched, since he had been the only male in the car. Dr Higgs moved away from the possibility that there had been penile penetration.

'It could be fingers or an instrument,' she suggested.

This upset Mary Dixon even more.

'They won't be just blaming you,' she said, 'they'll be saying that I have shoved something up her.'

Dr Higgs left the room and called the police.

This, then, had been her first diagnosis of alleged child anal abuse following her trip to Leeds and her exposure to the diagnostic techniques of Drs Wynne and Hobbs. Dr Geoffrey Wyatt, who had been the children's doctor, later wrote: 'Historically, the Dixon children were the first of my patients ultimately to be diagnosed as sexually abused who were seen by Dr Higgs. These children had been on the ward at Middlesbrough General Hospital under my care many times.' As for Dr Higgs, she acknowledged there was no reason for her to examine the bottom of either child, but her Leeds experience was fresh in her mind: 'Because one of the findings made by Dr Wynne and given at the Leeds conference was that approximately twenty-five per cent of children who were physically abused were also sexually abused, I felt it was appropriate for me to examine the bottoms and genitalia of the family.'

Dr Higgs described the Dixon children thus: 'There were two little girls in this family and I examined both the children. The oldest girl, as well as having signs of fading bruising that was consistent with non-accidental injury, also was underweight and the most worrying aspect of her examination was that she demonstrated reflex anal dilatation. The younger girl was fine and her anus was quite normal on that examination.' Why was this the first time Dr Higgs had come across this diagnostic phenomenon? As she explained: 'One reason possibly is that in medicine, if you do not know what you are looking for, or at, you may not see it. An important aspect of looking for this sign is that you must look for longer than you normally would in routinely inspecting an anus for abnormalities. You must be patient and take a little longer to see if the anus does dilate in that way.'

Dr Higgs recalled the day she examined the Dixon children: 'The day that I examined the children, the parents and children had come up just to meet the staff, to see what the accommodation was like. They were still in-patients at Middlesbrough General Hospital.' This examination had taken place unbeknown to the parents. The cause of the examination was equally unknown to them and would no doubt have startled the Dixons who thought they were coming to the Steiner Unit so they might 'rehabilitate' as a family. The view of Dr Higgs was different because her emphasis was different: she thought only of the children. She did not mention her diagnosis of reflex anal dilatation on that day because she knew the children were 'safe' in Middlesbrough General Hospital.

On examination, Dr Higgs found Angela to be 'a fractious unhappy child'. She found numerous leg bruises consistent with toddler activities. The examination was otherwise normal. As for Vera, she was 'shy and friendly' and remained passive throughout the examination. There were numerous bruises on her body, again consistent with being an active three year old. However, Dr Higgs felt that the 'fading yellowish-green bruises' overlying the middle of her spine, and also on the backs of both her forearms, were typical of fingertip bruising.

Dr Higgs found a large purple bruise on the lower outer aspect of her right buttock, but the most worrying thing of all was the finding of a lax anus, which 'demonstrated reflex relaxation on gently parting the buttocks'. Vera was re-examined on Tuesday 22 July: 'The appearance of her anus was the same, although the degree of reflex relaxation was less than that seen the previous week.' This was Dr Higgs' first confrontation with reflex anal dilatation. She therefore did the prudent thing and called Dr Jayne Wynne in Leeds for advice. 'Her view on my description,' as Dr Higgs recalled, was that 'there could be no other explanation for it and that sexual abuse had to be considered.' Even then Dr Higgs was not sure. She therefore did something which many considered to be astonishing and which one Queen's Counsel would describe as 'a bizarre practice'. She went to her home in Jesmond, Newcastle, and tried the technique out on her youngest children 'to see whether I could elicit reflex anal dilatation on their bottoms. It did not happen. It was quite a striking finding.'

With the Dixon children admitted to the Steiner Unit and therefore no longer in the custody of Middlesbrough General Hospital, Dr Higgs was anxious to bolster or allay her suspicion with a second opinion. As a further precautionary measure, she alerted Cleveland Social Services and Cleveland Constabulary of what these 'suspicions' were. As to the second opinion, she wanted this prior to approaching the Dixons. But things did not work out that way and, in the course of taking further details of the Dixon family on 23 July, the topic of sexual abuse arose. The Dixons themselves were finally informed about these 'suspicions'.

Dr Higgs' version of the conversation on 23 July was as follows: 'I told the parents of my concerns,' she recalled. 'It seemed an appropriate time to voice my suspicions about the possibility of sexual abuse of Vera. Both parents appeared shocked by the suggestion and then Joseph said something to the effect: "You know what they will do next, they'll start accusing me of doing it."' According to Dr Higgs, Mary replied: 'Not necessarily, they may say it was me.'

The account of Dr Higgs was nothing if not graphic: 'Joseph looked puzzled and said: "How?" Mary replied: "Well, I could have pushed something up it, like two fingers." Then quickly said: "If it's him I'll kill him [meaning the neighbour].""

Dr Higgs told Joseph and Mary Dixon that she had arranged for a second opinion and that Dr Ellis Fraser would be seeing Vera that afternoon. Both parents insisted that they wanted to be present. Dr Higgs later found it 'interesting' that although both parents knew the doctor would be arriving at three o'clock, Mary Dixon ran a bath for herself at ten minutes to three. The bath, as it turned out, had been for her husband, which explained why Mary Dixon was attentive and present when Dr Ellis Fraser arrived.

Dr Ellis Fraser was a medical practitioner of long standing: she had graduated from Edinburgh University in 1941. Since then she had been in practice at the Edinburgh Hospital for Sick Children, she had been in general practice for fifteen years in South Shields, and in all she had spent thirty years in family planning. She was also a member of the Northumbria Police Women Doctors Group, a body set up in 1983 to which Dr Higgs was greatly attached because, as she saw it, they espoused the same views towards child abuse as she did. For the last three years until 1986 Dr Fraser had been examining victims of rape and child victims of physical and sexual abuse.

Dr Higgs was asked why it was she had turned to two doctors of like mind for a second opinion on a child allegedly sexually abused. Why had she gone to Dr Jayne Wynne and Dr Ellis Fraser? Why had she not turned to her immediate superior, Dr Hey? Why had she not waited until Dr Steiner returned from holiday? Dr Higgs recalled that she wanted what she thought would be 'a good opinion: I knew that Dr Fraser had had a lot of experience in looking at sexually abused children. She had been recommended to me in the past as being a good person to look at children who had been sexually abused.' As to the other consultants she might have gone to, 'their experience of sexual abuse was not very great at that stage. I wanted to have an expert opinion on the child whom I had responsibility for.'

It was for these reasons, therefore, that Dr Ellis Fraser found herself hurrying to the Fleming Hospital to examine four-year-old Vera Dixon. 'I managed to persuade Vera to kneel on the examination couch, put her head on the pillow and raise her buttocks. I then gently parted the buttocks and noted that the anal sphincter was of a perfectly normal appearance. It was tightly closed and there were no signs of any trauma at all.' According to this examination, therefore, there had been no sexual abuse. But this would not be the story that was presented to the Dixons.

It was the view of Dr Fraser that any overstretched sphincter, if left alone, would return to normal within three to six days. In the words of Dr Fraser, 'the fact that Vera's anus was perfectly normal when I saw it compared with what it had been like when Dr Higgs had seen it previously had serious implications'. These implications were that, not withstanding the disappearance of the evidence, Vera had, nevertheless, been abused. The response of the Dixons was prompt: they became aggressive and, untutored as they were in the ways of the law, began threatening the doctors with solicitors.

It did not apparently occur to either doctor that if what they were saying was true, then Vera Dixon was being abused in a hospital ward, in which case that hospital ward should be shut down in the interests of the children who might be detained there. In the case of the Steiner Unit, this would have been a tragedy, given the excellent work in the rehabilitation of families that had been carried out by Dr Hans Steiner; but if it turned out to be true that children were being anally abused when in hospital care, then the children's side of the health service would come apart. However, these were not the considerations uppermost in the minds of the doctors. They wanted to be sure, they wanted to be right, and they wanted to protect children.

Dr Higgs would say later, even when dilatation had disappeared, 'with the description of what I had seen and she [Dr Fraser] found on examination, she felt that sexual abuse was the most likely explanation'. On Thursday evening, 24 July, Dr Higgs received a telephone call from a member of the nursing staff at the hospital to say that she was passing on a message from the nursery staff, who had been looking after Vera Dixon during that day: 'They rang me at home that evening to say that the child had complained of her bottom being sore. In the course of the conversation, although the little girl's speech was very poor, the word 'daddy' was mentioned in relation to this sore bottom. So there was concern there.'

When Dr Higgs re-examined the child the following morning the reflex anal dilatation had returned. What then was the explanation for the fact that reflex anal dilatation was there one day but not the next? As Dr Higgs explained it: 'My concern was then, and still is, that the child had probably been abused in hospital. Although that sounds preposterous, the way the ward is laid out is that there are cubicles for the families. Parents have free access to their children.

There is certainly opportunity for privacy. This problem has been described as one of a compulsive behaviour disorder in people who carry out sexual abuse. *I did not have any other explanation for it.* The child was not constipated, which is another slight possibility. There was no other explanation for the disappearance and the return of the sign.'

Mary and Joseph Dixon had been there at this second examination of their child. Some fifteen days ago, they had been sitting in their council house with two children, one of whom had bruises to her body which Dr Geoffrey Wyatt had considered to be accidental. Since then Vera, aged four, had been examined at Middlesbrough General Hospital on 10, 11 and 15 July by Dr Wyatt; she had been examined in Newcastle by Dr Higgs on 16, 22, 23 and 25 July. Now, because Vera had complained to the nursery nurse on the ward the previous day of a sore bottom, while sitting on the toilet, she was being examined again.

On this occasion, as Dr Higgs described it, her anus was again very lax and there was gross reflex relaxation: 'There were no tears or bruises visible.' Later that day, Dr Fraser arrived back at the hospital. She too found a relaxed anal sphincter that indicated some 'overstretching' since she had last seen Vera, and there was no doubt in her mind that this had been caused by 'something having been pushed into the child's anus'. With the findings confirmed, photographs were taken; but this was not the end of the examinations of Vera Dixon. She was examined again by Dr Higgs on 28 July. She found the sphincter normal: 'These findings were indicative of temporary damage to the anal sphincter which could only have occurred by something large being pushed from the outside to the inside of her anus.'

Dr Higgs' assessment of Mary Dixon, the twenty-four-year-old mother of two, was harsh: 'It was noticeable during this admission both to the nursing staff and myself (even though it was cut short and was also stressful) that Mary was quite unable to put her children's needs before her own and that there was very little evidence that she was able to play with them.' Dr Higgs noted that it was Joseph who responded quickly when either of the girls was 'unhappy' and also played with them.

It was no doubt because of these genuine reasons for concern about the Dixon children that Dr Higgs felt there were 'very serious implications' in this behavioural pattern: 'My own observations (although brief) of this family while on the ward, along with the total denial of any problems by the parents in the face of the evidence, lead me to conclude that there is little hope of rehabilitation, and that it is in the best interests of these children that a care order be granted.' As with the twins she had seen earlier, at the request of Dr Wyatt, the solution that was in the best interests of the Dixon children was to separate them from their parents. These words were written on 16 September 1986, prior to what was expected to be a full hearing on the interim care order that had been issued on 18 July. Dr Higgs added a phrase which might be considered unkind in the circumstances: 'I also feel that the parents, particularly Mary, are in urgent need of help in their own right.'

On Monday 28 July, whether in need of help or not, Joseph and Mary Dixon were arrested on suspicion of assault and buggery on their daughter Vera.

9

They were taken to a police station on the outskirts of Newcastle and held in police cells for six hours. When they were questioned, it was on the basis that together or separately they had 'done something to Vera'. Eventually they were bailed to appear at their own local Cleveland police station some six weeks later. From the time of their arrest they were not to see Vera or Angela for seventeen long months, or even to know where they were or how they were doing. From time to time they were allowed to take presents to the social services department in Marton Road, Middlesbrough, but this was on the understanding that the children were not to know who the presents were from. Even Easter and birthday presents would be passed on but the children would not be allowed to know who had sent them.

In these latter days of July the Dixons had to defend themselves against police questioning and protest their innocence against crimes which, to say the least, both of them found odious and offensive. Mary Dixon, a young and sensitive woman, was questioned on the following lines: 'I had been very clean in the hospital, constantly disinfecting the room, and I had been a bit too particular, and when

I was wiping Vera's bottom I had accidentally slipped my finger up her back passage?' Mary Dixon indignantly denied this suggestion and the matter was not taken further. There were no charges against Joseph Dixon.

When the time came for them to surrender to their bail at a Middlesbrough police station they were told that no charges would be brought and they were free to return home. They were not to hear from the police again. They now had to settle down without their children. This was something of a nightmare to both of them and neither could understand how these things had happened. They were not educated. They had never before in their lives taken legal advice. They had not been represented when social services had applied for and been granted an interim care order which had taken their children from them. They knew nothing about such things as the right of access. As a mother, Mary Dixon was particularly upset: 'I was so concerned about everything, the things that had been said about me, and the questions they had been asking me, of my background and so on, that I went off my own bat to a solicitor.'

Perhaps she too felt in need of some of the help suggested by Dr Higgs, for when her solicitor was granted legal aid in order to permit him to take up her case, the first thing he arranged was for her to be examined by a consultant psychiatrist. The psychiatrist could not believe the story he had been told. He also examined Joseph Dixon and came to the conclusion: 'Somebody is pulling the wool over somebody's eyes.' The psychiatrist found no sexual overtones in the background of Mary Dixon, or 'even anything that was relevant that would affect the children'. Armed with a solicitor, the Dixons began court proceedings to recover their children. These proceedings would be lengthy, so lengthy that Dr Higgs was asked for an explanation. She replied: 'Part of the delay with the Dixon girls was delay in court proceedings. I think because of the parents' request to have further information.' The implication was that the Dixons, having lost their children in the first place, were also responsible for the delay in getting them back.

If the Dixons felt they had suffered at the hands of the National Health Service, they were devastated by a letter they received from Cleveland Social Services on 12 November 1986. It warned them that should the court uphold the interim care order taken out on 18 July their children would not be returned to them. In other words, steps were now being taken to have the children permanently removed: 'It is only right that you should know that the plan will be for the children to be provided with a permanent alternative family with the intention that adoption will be the outcome.'

There was something else: 'In the light of all that has happened the department has to consider very carefully the future of any other children that you might have. If any children that you have in the future are to remain in your care, the department would require a period of assessment to be carried out. Discussions would include areas such as your pasts, both as individuals and a couple/family, your present marital relationship, your past relationship with Vera and Angela, including any injuries, and your extended families . . .'

Social services did not mean that any future children would then be entrusted to the Dixons: 'There would be no guarantees from us that you would be entrusted to look after any child you may have.' And even so there was a catch: 'It may take some time to come to a decision to do this and *it certainly will not be possible while you are opposing the care proceedings*.' In short, if they abandoned their rights to their children they might possibly, although not certainly, be able to keep any unborn children. The Dixons decided to press on with their fight to retain their children no matter what threats emanated from social services.

But what to do when Mary Dixon became pregnant?

All three pregnancies of Joseph and Mary Dixon were planned because they loved children and wanted a big family. The first had miscarried, the second two had entered the world by caesarean birth; but no one had suggested to Mary Dixon that she should not have another for medical reasons, and therefore when she became pregnant, as she did in the early part of 1987, they had to decide what they should do. Should they place themselves in a position of further assessment in the Steiner Unit where they had been unjustly accused of interfering with Vera? Should they allow themselves to be further counselled for three months? And even then accept that when the three months were up there was no guarantee that they would be able to keep their child? Mary Dixon dreaded any more discussions about her so-called 'back history'. She now felt that not only was she being persecuted as a mother in her own right, but that she was being persecuted because she came from a broken home, because she had been in and out of care, because she had not talked to her mother who lived across the road but whom she hardly knew, and if three months' counselling meant going through all of this again it might be better opting out.

Even then Mary Dixon was reluctant to take a decision that would terminate her pregnancy. She and Joseph Dixon therefore went to the local social services office and spoke to a social worker whom they knew. 'My husband said to her at the appropriate time – he didn't just lunge straight into it – he asked her: "What would happen if my wife fell pregnant?" The social worker referred to the letter that had been sent but Joseph Dixon again repeated the question: "What would happen if my wife fell pregnant?"'

As Mary Dixon recalled: 'To put it bluntly, she told me in that room that the child would be taken off me from birth, so when I found out I was pregnant what option did I have? I saw my own doctor and had an abortion. I hate that word. I feel degraded to think that I have been in hospital and got something like a termination of pregnancy done because I think that a child has got a life to live just as much as the other two children.'

The abortion was performed on 18 May 1987.

The Dixons continued to worry and fret about their children but in fact they were in good hands: such good hands that the foster parents wanted to adopt them when all of the court proceedings were terminated. The foster parents were Mr Matthew and Mrs Ruth Allan, who lived across the Tees in another part of Cleveland.

The Allans had three children of their own: Selina aged ten, Rebecca aged eight and Eleanor aged two. They were called by Cleveland Social Services on 25 July 1986 (the day of Vera's final medical examination) and asked to foster Vera and Angela Dixon. In fact, there is evidence that a case conference was held at the Steiner Unit even before Vera Dixon had been examined a second time; that the conference had been attended by representatives of both the police and social services; and that the decision had already been made to foster out the Dixon children even before the second diagnosis had been made.

As Matthew Allan recalled: 'The children had been examined by Dr Higgs and a police surgeon. They came to us that very day [25 July]. During that period of time they were withdrawn, but they were seen by a social worker on average once every three weeks. Sometimes it was more often than that.' The Allans were told that when the children had entered the Steiner Unit there had been eighteen bruises on their bodies, a fact not borne out by any of the doctors who examined the children – and there had been eight examinations over an eighteen-day period.

The commotion had seriously affected the health of both children, however, and the Allans found both Vera and Angela Dixon seriously underweight. In the new household and in a settled environment, with foster parents who loved children and took a professional approach to their work, the children began to thrive and put on weight. 'We have weight charts to prove that their general condition improved,' Matthew Allan stated. 'The eldest child's speech improved. We took her to therapy. Both children improved dramatically. During this time they were sent for a total of five medicals and seen by a local doctor. The last visit was on 20 April 1987.'

With the court proceedings still pending, Dr Jane Wynne had written a letter to the Dixons' solicitor dated 21 October 1986. At this time she had seen neither child but she did recall the telephone conversation with Dr Marietta Higgs: 'Dr Higgs telephoned me in July about a case which was worrying her. This may be the one. I advised her to get a second opinion and to photograph the signs.' Dr Wynne based her report on the statements of those who had advised her; the health visitor, who wrote to say the child had had twenty-two bruises (the bruises were clearly inflationary), that Angela Dixon had been in and out of hospital 'for no apparent reason' (no mention of the 'narrow gullet' which had once so preoccupied Dr Geoffrey Wyatt); and she found it 'extremely worrying' that Mary Dixon had said: 'Well, I could have pushed something up it, like two fingers' (the fact that Mary Dixon had not been charged with any criminal offence was not mentioned).

Of this comment, Dr Wynne had this to say: 'This is an unusual response unless there is substance to it. Women may be perpetrators and Mrs Dixon has had a difficult past.' Dr Wynne did not indicate that the child had been sexually abused. She merely noted that Vera appeared to be 'passive, underweight', and there were 'bruises, soiling', which she described as 'signs consistent with anal penetration'; and that Angela had had 'early difficulties, mainly feeding, thriving, with worries about bonding and is now thriving'.

A social worker had been called in to undertake a 'play assessment' of Vera with a specific intention of attempting to ascertain what her experience had been with regard to 'sexual abuse'. The social worker was Mrs Madge Bray. Her responsibilities with the council included 'placing and reviewing' the progress of children in residential care.

As Mrs Bray wrote: 'I left local authority social work in July of 1984 to concentrate on teaching communication skills for working with children who have suffered emotional damage.' In fact, Mrs Bray did something else. She set up an agency with another social worker, Mrs Mary Walsh, and offered advice to social services where children were already in care.

The agency set up by Mrs Bray with Mrs Walsh was the 'Sexual Abuse

Child Consultant Service' (Saccs). This agency earned £150 a day from conducting 'disclosure' interviews, where children played with toys, in the belief that they might then describe their alleged child abuse experiences. It was on this basis that Mrs Sue Richardson recommended that Mrs Bray be retained by Cleveland County Council.

Indeed, such was the 'demand' for Mrs Bray's services in Cleveland during the month of May that Mrs Richardson recommended that she lead an advanced level workshop offering 'consultancy and further training' in disclosure and case management. As Mrs Richardson wrote on 27 May, 'Madge is keen to help others develop their expertise based on her knowledge of current issues in Cleveland'. Mrs Richardson recommended that, since Mrs Bray was 'heavily booked', it would be advisable to confirm the appointment 'as soon as possible'.

A play session was conducted with Vera Dixon on 11 April 1987 in the Allan foster home. Mrs Bray did keep notes of this interview. In the words of Mrs Bray: 'The child is allowed to play freely with whatever play material is available and my normal practice is simply to feed back what the child is expressing. In my experience children who have been abused are struggling very often to make sense of these experiences and use the play materials to effect that process "playing out" traumatic experiences.' In the case of four-year-old Vera Dixon, she began by going through some items in the toy box which had been placed at her disposal.

She picked up a spider and played with it. She put it in her mouth. She then took it out and said: 'Can't.'

Vera, pointing to the snake: 'What that? Nake. Can't walk.'

Mrs Bray: 'Can't walk.'

Vera: 'Bite you,' gesturing towards Madge with the snake. Then she picked up the frogs and said: 'That bite you too.'

Mrs Bray then took some other toys out of the toy box.

In her report on the interview of 11 April, Mrs Bray said of both Dixon children: '*It would appear that whatever they have experienced in their early life has had major implications for both their physical and emotional development and it would appear that when they came to the foster parents' home they were showing many signs of children who have suffered abuse.*'

What seemed to be the key to the alleged abuse suffered in their own home was the manner in which they had responded in the foster home. In the words of Mrs Bray's report: 'Both Vera and Angela have made significant progress over the last few months since they came into foster care.' Dr Wynne noted that Angela in particular was now 'thriving'. Again Mrs Bray wrote: 'Since their arrival at the foster home the children have not had any significant illnesses and have never required hospitalization. They are now progressing along much more normal lines, although it appears to the foster parents that Angela still has grave difficulties.'

These were glowing tributes not only to the decision made to foster the children out but also to those foster parents who had added Angela and Vera Dixon to their own home. It meant that the foster parents had five children around them, all of them young, all of them happy, all of them enjoying a full family life with noise and bustle and a sense of security as well as contentment. The foster parents too had the assurance of knowing that Dr Higgs, having made the original diagnosis of sexual abuse on Vera Dixon, had not taken her eye off the child since. Such was her interest that in addition to the regular medical check-ups and surveillance of social services, Dr Higgs had personally seen the child twice since those events in July when she and her sister had been taken from their parents.

In fact, Dr Higgs personally visited the home of Matthew and Ruth Allan in September 1986. She could not recall the exact date, but she had been to a case conference about the Dixon family (of which the Dixon family would learn nothing) and she had called into the foster home on the way back in order to meet the children again and see how they were progressing. And upon taking up her post at Middlesbrough, Dr Higgs had seen Vera Dixon again at her out-patients' clinic. This was on 9 February 1987. She noted that the child had no problems but that she did not mention her parents. And even when she did utter the word 'daddy' it was in relation to the foster father. The child apparently had no recollection of past events, although she could chat happily about events in the foster home. Dr Higgs found it equally significant that while Vera had been to jazz band concerts with her own mother and father, when she was taken by the foster parents she made no mention of these earlier outings.

Vera had been booked into nursery school after Easter and Dr Higgs found her not so dependent: she felt Vera used to be very protective towards Angela, her young sister. She was equally satisfied to learn that Angela was seeking comfort from her foster parents rather than her sister and although they fought over toys and the like Angela was now starting to talk – that is, string words together. Dr

Higgs was not to see Vera Dixon and her sister again until 30 April, when again she asked for both of them to come to the outpatients' clinic.

Matthew Allan recalled that on 29 April he received a call to say that Dr Higgs wished to see Vera. He was told by a social worker that the police surgeon who had originally confirmed a diagnosis of sexual abuse had recanted. In fact this information was false, for Dr Ellis Fraser had stuck by her original report. As she wrote to a solicitor on 28 May 1987: 'I have not changed my opinion as to the cause of dilatation of the anal sphincter in my second examination. It is still my opinion.' Who then had asked to see the children again? It was Dr Higgs herself, for as her case notes showed, she had 'seen the children as a follow up because of sexual abuse July 1986 prior to court hearing next week'. The court had now set 4–6 May for a full custody hearing on the Dixon children, and with this in mind, Dr Higgs wished to see the children again.

It was to be a fateful trip to Middlesbrough General Hospital for Matthew and Ruth Allan.

10

A week after she had seen Vera Dixon at her outpatients' clinic on 9 February 1987, Dr Higgs received another patient. This was Alma Smith. Alma had been born in 1980, the daughter of Tony and Liz Smith. They lived across the river from Middlesbrough. Tony was a blue-collar worker with a steady industrial job. His wife had no settled job but she had worked at a local factory and, from time to time, for a retail food outlet. The Smiths had two children: Kenneth born in 1984 and Alma. Alma had been born prematurely and had weighed only two and a half pounds. Tony would recall that he could hold the fragile young body in his hand and it would lie there listless.

It was one of the success stories of the Smith household that, by the age of three, Alma was beginning to thrive. Mentally she was advanced for her age and neighbours and friends thought she had the intellect of a five year old. There were no problems with Kenneth. The Smiths lived in a small respectable house that they had bought on mortgage; they were not short of drinking money. In the case of Tony, however, his mundane Sunday pleasure was watching football on television, and while he would go to his in-laws for his Sunday lunch he liked to nip back home for the match: besides, he never did like the chit-chat at the in-laws' home.

If Tony Smith did not get on well with Liz's mother and father, the truth is he did not get on well with Liz either. He had a jealous side to his character. His mother, Arlene Smith, would say that he had no reason to be jealous of his wife, there was no indication that she was unfaithful; but he was also possessive, and the combination of the two would prove lethal to the long-term future of the marriage. The years had slipped away beyond the seven-year itch and Liz felt the constraints of her husband's temperament so overwhelming she asked for a divorce. This was in 1986. Tony, however, had nursed for too many years his prematurely born daughter and he loved his young son Kenneth. Which father will not love his son and look forward to football matches in his company, complete with club scarf and hat and rosette? And he had not yet fallen out of love with his wife. Their difficulties were therefore papered over, Tony eased up on his jealousy, his wife felt him less intolerant, and they were back to enjoying themselves on a Saturday night in the local clubs.

On the night of 14 February 1987 their regular babysitter was away and therefore, not for the first time, Liz's father Oliver offered to babysit in her stead. He came along with crisps and sweets for his grandchildren. Tony Smith did not think this remarkable, except that his father-in-law had never before brought crisps and sweets into their home. The Smiths went to their local club and because they were socializing on the Sunday evening as well, Grandfather Oliver was to babysit again. On Sunday morning, 15 February, when dressing Alma and putting on her tights, Liz Smith noticed a mark to her vagina. The child made no particular fuss about it.

'See if it's there when she goes to bed,' Tony Smith said.

The 'mark' was a reddening of the vagina and, since it did not go away, Liz Smith took her child to the local medical centre. This was on Monday morning. She took her daughter by the hand and walked up the road and into the town centre. She had never had any undue worries about the health of her eldest child. Alma had been treated in 1984 for cystitis but only by her local doctor and in December 1986 she had had a vaginal discharge. This had been so minor that she had sought no medical advice.

She was anxious to get her child to the local medical centre this

Monday morning because she knew that a female doctor would be in attendance. She had a mother's embarrassment about male doctors looking at her child. She explained to the doctor that the day before she had noticed a redness around Alma's vagina and what appeared to be a scratch on the inside. Although the female doctor was also on the police list, she had no experience in child abuse, alleged or otherwise, and she therefore called Mrs Richardson, Cleveland county's child abuse consultant. Mrs Richardson was not available that day and it was only on the following day that the doctor was able to speak to her. A local police inspector was also contacted. This was Inspector Michael Whitfield of Cleveland Constabulary.

He was called by Mrs Richardson on Tuesday 17 February, who stated that Alma would be examined by Dr Higgs. As Inspector Whitfield recalled: 'I informed Mrs Richardson that if sexual abuse was suspected, I required an examination by a police surgeon.' However, notwithstanding that the medical centre doctor was on the police list, Inspector Whitfield knew she had little experience in matters of child sexual abuse, and therefore asked for Dr Alistair Irvine. It was his intention that Dr Irvine should oversee the medical centre doctor. The examination was to be conducted at North Tees General Hospital and subsequently all three doctors met.

This was to be the first confrontation between Dr Marietta Higgs and Dr Alistair Irvine. Prior to the arrival of Dr Higgs to take up her consultancy, there had always been a close cooperation in matters of alleged child sex abuse between the social services, the health authority and the police. This was known as a multi-disciplinary approach. There had been various methods of referral. One method would be for the police to call in a police surgeon and ask him to examine a child about whom an allegation had been made. Another would be through the paediatric service at North Tees or Middlesbrough General hospitals, where a paediatrician would ask for a police surgeon to attend. Or a call would come from the hospital directly because the child was actually admitted. Should the request come directly from the police the examination would take place in the police surgeon's own surgery.

Dr Alistair Irvine had been appointed a police surgeon thirteen years ago and was made senior police surgeon in Cleveland Constabulary in 1982. He also practised as a doctor with his own surgery and patients. He was a member of the Association of Police Surgeons and for the last six years he had lectured on a national course run by Durham Constabulary on such technical subjects as the role of the police surgeon, forensic medical examination and diagnosis. He was highly respected by Cleveland Constabulary. With this background, Dr Irvine was no stranger to child sexual abuse and assault. In his thirteen years as a police surgeon he had examined what he described as 'an increasing number of child victims' and during the eighties he estimated that he had examined something in excess of fifty cases a year. Up until the early part of 1987, the vast majority of requests came from the police to examine some form of complaint, either from the child or from someone close to the child: this was the classic route into child sexual abuse.

'On occasions,' as he recalled, 'a teacher or relative may have noticed something about the child's behaviour. In essence, therefore, I was asked to carry out an examination in order to corroborate evidence or a suspicion that was already present. Until this year I have never experienced a case in which a child had gone to hospital for some entirely unrelated condition and was then diagnosed as being sexually abused.' Dr Irvine had enjoyed good relationships with other medical practitioners in the county: 'In relation to my work as a police surgeon, I never encountered any problems in the management of cases in which paediatricians might be involved.'

Within weeks of Dr Higgs taking up her appointment, he felt this was to change. The call he had received from Inspector Whitfield had been of a routine nature and he had gone along to North Tees General Hospital where he had met the medical centre doctor. They met in casualty. 'We discussed the case and then went together to the children's outpatients to examine Alma. When we got there Dr Higgs was already present and as I did not feel it was appropriate for three doctors to be present during the examination I gave the medical centre doctor advice on the taking of forensic swabs and offered to lend her any equipment she might need. I knew nothing of Dr Higgs at this time and due to the good relationship I enjoyed with other paediatricians I saw no reason to do other than I did.'

There was something about the atmosphere, however, that Dr Irvine had not liked and when he reported to Inspector Whitfield he said that he felt there had been 'diagnosis by committee', which is why he had not stayed. He had found a coldness about the meeting that he had never before experienced. He had been introduced to Alma Smith and also her parents, who had accompanied her to the hospital. They then went into the consultancy room where they met Dr Higgs.

As Dr Irvine recalled: 'Dr Higgs did not speak to me. She did not look at me. I felt terribly unhappy.'

Given what he felt to be the unfriendly atmosphere, Dr Irvine simply said that the two doctors knew what they had to do, and if they wanted his advice they could give him a ring. Certainly if anything went wrong. On this sour note he left. The Smiths, of course, knew nothing about any professional discord. Tony Smith had readily agreed to have his child examined at the hospital and on this 17 February, at lunchtime, he and his wife had taken their six-year-old daughter to the casualty room.

'I sat in the assessment room,' Tony recalled. 'I was there for forty to fifty minutes. Alma had been weighed and measured and then the receptionist took the child to see Dr Higgs. I waited for an hour. Finally, they called me in. Dr Higgs said the child had been sexually abused. I said: "Are you sure?" She said there was no doubt about it. She was gabbling on about these things but they went completely over my head. How could our child have been abused?'

Dr Higgs had made her first diagnosis of child sexual abuse in Cleveland. This was February 1987.

With Dr Irvine gone and the medical centre doctor in attendance, Dr Higgs examined Alma Smith. She found before her a six-year-old child whom she would later describe as 'a happy, friendly, confident' little girl, and whatever the diagnosis Dr Higgs would make of the mark on the child's vagina, she was clear about the examination of the child's anus: there was reflex dilatation to the extent of approximately one centimetre. This was 'consistent with sexual abuse' and this was the information that was imparted to Tony and Liz Smith. They had gone to a hospital worried about their daughter's vagina. They would leave it with a diagnosis of anal penetration.

Alma was admitted to ward sixteen of the North Tees Hospital and the police were called. Tony Smith had no objection. How could he? 'Fair enough' were the words he used. He and his wife stayed in a small room at the hospital for two hours until a policewoman arrived. He thought the policewoman had no car and offered to drive her to the police station. The policewoman said there was no hurry. He and his wife could come in the following morning. Tony therefore went to the police station at nine o'clock on 18 February. He explained that over the past few days he had spent only an hour or so with his children. When the police asked who else had been in the house he replied that his wife's father had been babysitting.

Had he noticed anything unusual?

Only that his father-in-law had brought along crisps and sweets. How was that unusual? Because generally, while he was generous with the children, he had never brought sweets into the house before. These remarks, however, found an echo with the police; for when Alma had been interviewed by a policewoman, in the presence of Mrs Smith, and when asked who had hurt her, she replied: 'Grandad'. She had refused, however, to go into further detail. Just as the police surgeon had walked out on his first case with Dr Higgs and would live to regret it, so the policewoman was now called away and she would live to regret that too. For in her absence, according to the social worker who was alone with the child at the time, Alma gave substantial details of allegedly being abused by Grandfather Oliver. This allegedly consisted of digital penetration and would enable Dr Higgs to say that the diagnosis had been followed by a disclosure from the child.

Armed with the diagnosis of Dr Higgs and the statement of the social worker, the police swung into action. Grandfather Oliver was arrested and interviewed at length. In the words of Inspector Whitfield, 'there appeared to be a fair amount of circumstantial evidence and the decision was taken to charge Grandfather Oliver'. The alleged perpetrator now in police custody, a case conference was held at a hospital in Middlesbrough on 19 February, where it was decided that Alma could be returned to her parents because she was no longer at risk.

Grandfather Oliver had managed to get through his whole life without any brushes with the law. He was an ordinary working man who had lived in an age where blue-collar industrial workers like himself had been able to work their full term without threat of redundancy. He felt he had earned his pension. Now in his seventies, he had to endure the mortification of being charged with indecently assaulting a grandchild whom he dearly loved. The story of the crisps and sweets was related to him, thus destroying for all time his fragile relationship with his son-in-law; and if the child had been abused at all he knew most assuredly it was not he who had been the abuser. But being duly charged he was remanded to a bail hostel well out of the way of his granddaughter.

Both the Smith children had been admitted to hospital, as a precautionary measure, and Liz Smith had slept on a campbed on the floor beside them. The nurses did not realize at the time that this would become a regular feature of hospital life across the river in Middlesbrough. They felt sympathy with the children, sympathy with the distracted mother, and they too were glad to hear the news that the alleged perpetrator had been arrested. They were also impressed with the diagnostic skills of Dr Higgs. No one wanted children to be the victims of sex attacks or abused in their own homes: everyone wanted children protected and perpetrators behind bars.

Dr Higgs was clearly going to be an asset in Cleveland's fight against child sex abuse.

A sense of normality was restored to the Smith household. It was upsetting to know that another condition of his bail was that Grandfather Oliver could not stray beyond the outskirts of the town nor make any contact with his grandchildren, but the children themselves were settled back to their home life and when the social worker visited the house and noticed Tony, who worked shifts, playing with his children, she remarked: 'That's the kind of family life I like to see.'

There was one peculiarity, however, that could not be explained. The child still had the mark on her vagina. This required yet another visit to the outpatients' department. It required yet another examination by Dr Higgs. This took place on 10 March. Dr Higgs noted that Alma's anus was still dilated, suggesting further sexual interference. To the consternation of the parents, the child was readmitted to North Tees General Hospital and again the campbed was brought out so that her mother could sleep by her side, albeit on the floor. A wave of shock passed through the health and social services community with the news that a child who had been abused, whose alleged abuser was in a bail hostel, should now be abused again by someone else.

Did the police have the wrong man?

Inspector Whitfield became understandably nervous. There was such a thing as unlawful arrest and false imprisonment and if indeed they had the wrong man some explanations would be required. Dr Irvine had not been present at the 17 February examination. Could he now examine the child and clear up once and for all whether she had – or had not – been abused? 'As I recollect,' Dr Irvine recalled, 'the inspector had approached Dr Higgs and Dr Higgs had said she did not feel there was any need for a second examination.' Dr Irvine suggested that he should speak directly to Dr Higgs, which he did. Dr Higgs was very firm in her opinion that she did not consider a further examination necessary.

In the words of Dr Irvine: 'I therefore telephoned Dr Higgs. She asked me what was wrong with her diagnosis. I expressed my reservations about her diagnosis being based solely on the presence of reflex anal dilatation. She was rather abrupt and told me that she had no doubt at all that reflex anal dilatation was in itself indicative of sexual abuse. She refused to allow me to examine Alma.' Dr Irvine wanted to make clear that this was not a re-run of the 17 February examination where sexual abuse had *first* been diagnosed; it was to seek confirmation of the 10 March diagnosis where sexual abuse had been alleged a *second* time.

Dr Higgs had a different recollection of these events: 'I do not recall discussing physical signs and their interpretation either in general, or in relation to this particular case, during this telephone conversation. Nor was I abrupt. We did discuss physical signs and their interpretation both in this case and generally at the case conference.' She recalled there had been no slide-viewer at the case conference but she could not remember Dr Irvine commenting that he had difficulty in seeing the slides clearly before saying that he disagreed the anal signs could be due to sexual abuse. He said that they could be 'normal'.

Faced with this stalemate in medical opinion, it was agreed that the child should remain in hospital. On one thing they were agreed, as Dr Higgs recalled. This was that the mark to the vagina of the child was 'consistent with sexual abuse'. And while their interpretations of events might be different, there was to be no second examination of Alma by Dr Irvine. In the words of Inspector Whitfield: 'Dr Higgs was categoric that Dr Irvine could not physically examine Alma.' Indeed, Dr Higgs would later accept that she had kept Dr Irvine out: 'The only police surgeon who ever approached me directly to request a second examination of a child was Dr Irvine in a telephone conversation in the case of Alma. However, since a police surgeon had jointly examined the child with me already, taken specimens and provided a statement to the police, I did say that I did not consider a further examination appropriate, particularly since the child had begun disclosure work.'

Dr Higgs had not experienced police opposition before, but then she had never before been a consultant in her own right diagnosing child sexual abuse. She recalled that before coming to Cleveland she had had little contact with police surgeons, though while she had been at Gateshead she had made contact with Dr Ellis Fraser, 'a member of the Northumbria Women Police Doctors Group, which was well known locally'. Colleagues had spoken highly of Dr Fraser as having a particular experience of, and interest in, child sexual abuse. It had been for this reason she had been asked for a second opinion in the case of Vera Dixon.

Dr Higgs had attended some meetings of the Women Police Doctors Group and had also asked members to let her know when they had been asked to examine children suspected of sexual abuse, 'so that I could be present at their examination and thereby gain experience'. As a result, she attended a number of such examinations and since all concerned girls this increased her knowledge of what she described as 'abnormal hymenal findings'. However, in Newcastle it had not appeared to her to have been the practice for some years for children to be examined by police surgeons 'whether for the purpose of obtaining specimens or otherwise'. Instead, according to Dr Higgs, in cases in which she was involved, 'it had been police custom to indicate to the paediatrician what specimens were required and for the paediatrician to take them'.

Dr Higgs had not anticipated having any close contact with police surgeons in Cleveland, since 'it seemed to me that so far as the police investigation was concerned, there was no difference in principle between the role of the police surgeon and that of the paediatrician in cases of child sexual abuse'. Perhaps, with hindsight, this was where Dr Higgs would fail in Cleveland: 'In retrospect, I feel that it might have been helpful to try and build a relationship with the police surgeons at the outset, as I did with representatives of other professions, so that the difference of opinion between myself and the senior police surgeon might have been recognized in advance and discussed before it led to us taking opposing views in a particular case.'

If failure this was, it would take place only six weeks after her arrival in Cleveland.

Matters would become even more complicated following the case conference decision to allow the child to remain in hospital. Alma Smith, in fact, was now about to enter medical history. For on Monday 16 March she was again examined by Dr Higgs. Again Dr Higgs diagnosed anal abuse. Further, this abuse was so recent that it could only have happened while the child was in hospital. Tony Smith had been present at the hospital with his wife Liz on both 11 and 12 March. Mrs Smith did once or twice leave Alma with Tony while she had a cigarette or went for a cup of tea. Alma was examined again by Dr Higgs in the late afternoon of Thursday 12 March and, according to Inspector Whitfield, 'nothing of any significance was found'. But since sexual abuse had been diagnosed on 10 March all male visiting would be stopped.

'Recollections by Dr Higgs then became somewhat clouded,' Inspector Whitfield recalled. 'But she remembers seeing Mr Smith in the hospital buildings shortly after issuing the instructions in respect of male visitors. Mr Smith in the course of his employment visits the hospital. It was put forward as a theory that Mr Smith may have sneaked back into Alma's room later that afternoon and in a very limited space of time, while Mrs Smith was out of Alma's room, abused her.' According to Inspector Whitfield: 'Following the medical examination on 16 March 1987, Mrs Smith in my opinion was under extreme pressure from the psychologist to come up with an explanation, in that the finger of suspicion must now point at her or her husband, and I believe that this was in a roundabout way put to her by the psychologist.'

Liz Smith duly followed that finger of suspicion and stated that at approximately eleven o'clock on the night of Tuesday 17 March, whilst kissing Alma goodnight, Alma opened her mouth and put her tongue out and kissed her mother. She asked Alma who had taught her to kiss like that. By going through the alphabet with her mother letter by letter Alma spelt out D–A–D–D–Y. Liz Smith then stated that she now recalled that Alma had tried to do this in the past, but she had given the matter no thought. The following night, Wednesday 18 March, Liz Smith decided that she would try and trick Alma into telling her more. Alma, after a great deal of pressure, reluctantly again spelt out D–A–D–D–Y, and said: 'Why did Daddy hurt me?'

Inspector Whitfield pointed out that there was no corroboration for this conversation.

Dr Higgs, however, would have a vivid recollection of the incident. It was true Alma had been readmitted on the tenth: 'I was concerned that the dilatation at that stage had been much worse, which was why I examined her, I think, two days after that. The dilatation improved markedly and stayed improved over that forty-eight-hour period.' Liz Smith had been present at both examinations. She was also present on 16 March. As Dr Higgs described it: 'I remember that her face really was quite ashen when she saw the appearance of the anus on the sixteenth and in fact looked at me and said: "*You are going to accuse me now?*" to which I clearly replied that it was something that we needed to consider further and look into. But mother herself recognized that signs had got much worse from having improved the previous week during the period in hospital.'

The marriage of Tony and Liz Smith had been even more fragile than Tony supposed. There was in the comportment of Liz Smith none of the resilience of Norma Yardley or Mary Dixon. Neither of them believed for a moment that her husband had abused her children. Liz Smith, however, alone in the hospital, on a campbed on the floor, in the uneasy, shuffling silence of a ward, in that dim glow that is never obliterated, felt not only uneasy but frightened. At three o'clock in the morning she got up and asked to see the doctor. In the words of Dr Higgs: 'Something had clearly upset her and at quarter to three in the morning – that is, in the middle of the night – she had felt the need to talk to a doctor because she was worried that this six year old had been trying to tongue-kiss her in what she felt was an adult way.'

Tony Smith was acutely conscious that the finger of suspicion pointed in his direction. He received the following letter from his solicitor: *Dear Mr Smith: It is more than likely, in view of Wednesday's* [court] *hearing, that the police may arrest you and might charge you. It is most important that you say nothing to the police without your solicitor being present. In the circumstances, should you be arrested you are entitled to have your solicitor present should the police wish to question you, and you are allowed to telephone me to request me to attend with you. My numbers are as follows: . . .*' The solicitor then gave his personal and professional telephone numbers.

In fact Tony Smith never did hear from the police, either at the time when sexual abuse was diagnosed a *second* time, or a *third*, or at any time later. His wife, however, did not return to the family home; nor was he to see his children again till another year had passed. Access was denied. His daughter Alma was detained in hospital but Liz took Kenneth to stay with Tony's brother, who also refused to speak to him. Thus his own family became irredeemably split. Word got out where he worked and in the local clubs he and Liz had visited; his foreman had him in to describe the men's distress at working with 'a child abuser' and at the club there was many a time Tony would round on a fellow clubman for a remark that linked him to child abuse of his daughter.

Within the space of weeks his life had collapsed in ruins. His marriage had broken apart, his children were gone, his job was in jeopardy, his mates refused to speak to him, his brother too, and only his sister and mother would stand by him. Even his mother refused to speak of the events which led to the two children being taken from him, for she had now lost her precious grandchildren. At this time, in February and March 1987, there was no knowledge of Dr Higgs, no knowledge of the breakdown between Dr Higgs and

Dr Irvine, no knowledge of the deep unease that had crept into the police attitude towards Dr Higgs, no knowledge of Joseph and Mary Dixon who, elsewhere in the county, were equally suffering.
The human costs in Cleveland were beginning to mount.

11

On 17 March Grandfather Oliver appeared before a magistrates' court. The prosecution told him that they had no evidence of indecent assault, and that the case would be dropped. So outraged, however, was the old man that he insisted on being prosecuted. He had been charged with the sexual abuse of his grandchild; at his age, he had been bailed to a hostel with instructions not to visit either his family or the town where he had lived all his life, apart from the war years; and he too had hanging over him the gossip of friends and neighbours who would not understand his provisional incarceration. Grandfather Oliver wanted justice done and he wanted it done in open court. The prosecution offered no evidence and a not guilty verdict was returned. Grandfather Oliver walked out of the court a free man, but there was anguish in his heart.

For Tony Smith the shock of losing his wife and children was one thing. The actions of his wife were another. While there would be no police enquiries, let alone charges brought against him, nevertheless Liz obtained a court order that ousted him from the family home, claiming he had abused their child, and it was consequent upon this order that the solicitor warned Tony he might be arrested. He was now a pariah in the town. Within months his wife was able to divorce Tony and he was obliged to start again in a small flat arranged for him by his employers, who notwithstanding the anxieties of the foreman had decided to stand by him. How was his wife able to divorce him so quickly? 'I did not have a great deal of option,' Tony recalled, 'I was accused of being a child molester, my wife wanted a divorce and I went along.'

The courts too would provide a battleground for Tony Smith. He would fight to gain access to his children; and he would fight to clear his name as a child molester. He had found comfort in his work but the weekends he found terribly empty, with no children, no wife, no more socializing in the clubs. He began to take an interest in the local football team and on Sundays he involved himself in car-boot sales. In this way, Tony was able to fill in the empty spaces and maintain his sanity.

With the assistance of his solicitor and legal aid, Tony obtained independent medical opinions on Alma which showed that the child suffered a rare form of disease known as lichen sclerosis: this would explain why, months after the events of February and March, the mark to the child's vagina was still there. The child psychologist who spent some time with Alma wondered if she might have injured herself at the front because of the mark. In the words of Dr Higgs: 'I think she described her either in hospital or somewhere as straddling across a bedpost or a piece of furniture, and that certainly is a possibility for the bruising. The child also has a skin complaint of her genitalia which I understand does make that area quite easily traumatized, so the possibility of her having caused the bruising herself may be reasonable.'

It might be news to Tony Smith, but it had never been the mark, or 'bruise', as Dr Higgs described it, to the vagina, that had concerned her: it had been the dilating anus which, to her mind, showed signs consistent with anal abuse. Had she read an article in the *British Medical Journal* for 30 May 1987 headed 'Lesson of the Week'? The lesson was that the features of lichen sclerosis may be mistaken for signs of sexual abuse in children: 'All medical staff should learn to recognize those other conditions that may mimic sexual abuse.' Dr Higgs admitted that she did not read this article on publication, though she agreed she read it probably some while later.

Unknown to Tony, however, settling down in changed circumstances and a changed environment, the saga of Alma had only just begun. At another case conference on 20 March, attended by Inspector Whitfield and another detective inspector, it was indicated by the police that they did not have sufficient evidence to arrest or to charge Tony Smith. The police also wished it to be noted that Grandfather Oliver could not have had access to Alma either in the home or at the hospital and therefore could not be suspected of the further abuse.

Alma was now in the hands of professionals who saw it as their job to obtain a disclosure to back up the diagnosis. There was in fact nothing wrong in this approach: Dr Higgs was the consultant paediatrician. She had made the diagnosis. She must be presumed to know what she was about. And child sexual abuse was a serious thing. Nevertheless, this would put Alma under serious strain. She was interviewed by a child psychologist and during the first session, under the persistent questioning of the psychologist, she repeated some of her initial allegations against Grandfather Oliver. Since that first interview, Alma had been seen by the psychologist on several occasions and the best that was obtained was that, in answer to several leading questions, she wrote down DADDY. Strangely, when interviewed by police officers perhaps more skilled in questioning and more wary of leading questions, the child did not repeat any of her allegations, against either the father or grandfather.

In the words of Inspector Whitfield: 'The psychologist is of the opinion that Alma has been subject to recurrent and intrusive sexual abuse over a considerable period of time, and that it might take months for Alma to disclose the circumstances of the abuse with the distinct likelihood that Alma may never disclose.' It was Inspector Whitfield's understanding that Tony Smith arranged for Alma to be examined by a psychologist from Cambridge, 'hoping that he would be able to use the psychologist's evidence to gain access to Alma at a "care hearing" at which social services would oppose access'.

Inspector Whitfield also understood that Alma presented as a very disturbed child at the examination and 'the social worker who accompanied her informed me that Alma could not have performed better as a sexually abused child if she had in fact been coached to perform'. Meanwhile, having allegedly been abused at home and her grandfather charged, having allegedly been abused at home and her father suspected, having allegedly been abused in the hospital with her father suspected again, it was clear that social services must devise a place that was safe where the young girl would be protected. The decision was made, therefore, to place Alma with foster parents, and not with Liz Smith who had now cleared herself of any suspicion.

This unusual number of diagnoses, all on the basis of reflex anal dilatation, and coming within weeks of her arrival on Teesside, preoccupied Dr Higgs. She did after all genuinely care for her patients. She was greatly concerned for this little girl. She had been 'a great worry' to her.

The consequence for Alma Smith was that she would endure *eight* physical examinations between 16 February, when she first visited the health centre with her mother, and 16 March when for the *third* time she was diagnosed as having been sexually abused. Why had there been so many examinations? Dr Higgs explained that she wanted to see whether the signs were 'resolving'. She thought it important to follow up children to see whether the reflex anal dilatation disappeared: 'I think there is much that we still need to know about this problem in terms of resolution.'

But did she not believe in keeping examinations to a minimum?

'I think one should probably keep examinations to a minimum, but on the other hand, we need to know about this problem. This is a new field and we need to educate ourselves about it. One thing that I need to try and understand is how signs resolve and I think it is also important, from the child's point of view, to reassure them when things are looking better.' This might advance knowledge and science generally, but Dr Higgs was asked: 'Can you imagine the effect on a six-and-a-half-year-old child, of having her anus and vagina repeatedly examined, the labia parted, her legs spread, photographs taken?'

Dr Higgs acknowledged that Alma had been a little embarrassed: 'Clearly, had she been distressed or objected in any way, I would not have conducted the examination. I asked her permission each time. I asked her if she would mind if I looked at her bottom and she did not object.' The hospital notes, however, referred to Alma's 'reluctance'. 'She was a bit embarrassed,' Dr Higgs acknowledged, 'but she agreed to my request. There was no force or coercion. She certainly was at times embarrassed about having that done.'

Alma had been described by Dr Higgs on 16 February as 'happy, friendly and confident', but by 3 April a child psychologist would describe her as 'seriously disturbed'. Had this anything to do with the repeated examination and photography of the child? Dr Higgs did not think so. As she recalled: 'She presented as a very bright and happy little girl. That was the way she presented to the world and I certainly saw her and was witness to one of the disclosure interviews at which she, with great difficulty, described her abuse.' It was impressive that the consultant paediatrician should attend such sessions and later actually participate in them.

Dr Higgs went on: 'There was a transformation of that little girl. She regressed and was very upset and disturbed at talking about her abuse. As soon as it was over, it was like a switch. She immediately went back to her bubbly, bouncy self in the ward and played with the other children, so I think she presented one face to the outside world and another in the course of talking about abuse.'

Dr Higgs recalled that at some point the child psychologist had described Alma as 'quite brittle' and Dr Higgs felt this to be a good description. It was not Dr Higgs, however, who had pointed the finger at the grandfather: 'The initial disclosure that the child made was that it was the grandfather. That was within a couple of days of being admitted on the first occasion, so that it was worrying that, when she went home and the signs appeared to get worse, with no access to the grandfather, the situation did need looking into further.'

This was when professional suspicion fell upon the father.

'I cannot begin to nominate who the abuser may be,' Dr Higgs declared. 'All I can do is comment on the signs that I find, interpret them and be concerned about them. Certainly after the second admission there was further work done with this child and she, with great difficulty, nominated her father as the abuser.' Was there not another consideration for Dr Higgs in these February days? She was new to the rank of consultant. Her experience with regard to this diagnosis did not rest on any extensive medical training but rather on a two-day seminar that she had attended which was of a quasi-medical nature. In all of these circumstances, did it not behove her to move more cautiously, more circumspectly? Would it not have been more sensible to carry the problem to older heads, heads who had had years of experience in paediatrics? Share her problems with them and say: 'What do you think about it? Am I on the right course?'

Dr Higgs conceded that this was 'a possibility, although one of the difficulties of medical findings in sexual abuse is that years of paediatric experience do not necessarily help you with this problem. It is new information and I tended to use the people that I thought either were experts or had developed an expertise, such as the Leeds team, and this is in real terms, not with this particular patient, but in trying to get the feel of the findings, talking to other consultants who had started diagnosing children and sexual abuse. I think at the end of the day, as a doctor, you still have to make up your mind when you have got the patient in front of you, and if you have grave doubts then naturally enough you either temporize and wait or you seek a second opinion.'

But how could one explain the *third* diagnosis in the hospital? Was this not comparable to the case of Joseph and Mary Dixon and their child Vera? Had she not been diagnosed as having been abused in hospital? 'I think that needs to remain a possibility and I could not think of any other explanation at the time. I think I do not have any other explanation. I think I do not have many reservations anyway about the sign of reflex anal dilatation, but certainly trying to explain why it seems to be worse and better at times is a difficulty. I think the important thing that does need to be excluded is that re-abuse has occurred.'

Would she not accept that there had been enormous consequential problems and difficulties, not only of a medical nature but also of a social and legal nature? Would she agree that the sign of anal opening and the consequences and conclusions to be drawn from its apparition are extremely complex and as yet by no means definitively established in science and medicine? 'I think the sign itself is a very important sign. I believe that it is a good indicator of sexual abuse and that is the diagnosis that we need to look into very carefully. I think it does highlight the importance of making sure that assessments of these children and their families become broadened outside the medical sphere. The resolution of the sign certainly is a difficult area, but I think the sign itself is important and I believe it to be an important sign in this diagnosis.'

Dr Higgs again shared her thoughts with Dr Jane Wynne. Just as she had discussed on the telephone with her the first diagnosis of child anal abuse, so now she discussed with her the second. When Dr Higgs had met Dr Wynne for the first time in March 1987 at a lecture in Northumberland, they had discussed the resolution of signs, whether or not, once the dilatation started improving, it could become worse. It seemed to be Dr Wynne's view as well, at that time, that once it started improving it should continue to improve, but according to Dr Higgs, 'I think it is at an early stage and I think we need to look at the resolution of this sign carefully, but as to the sign itself, I think it has to be taken very seriously'.

And so it came to pass that little Alma Smith, like Elaine, Susan and Anne Yardley, like Vera and Angela Dixon, and like the twins examined at the request of Dr Wyatt, would find herself fostered out under the auspices of Cleveland Social Services. Would Dr Higgs, herself a mother of five children, agree with the late Dr Christine Cooper, who had declared it had been her long-term objective to keep the family together? Of course she would agree with that, but Dr Higgs would add an important rider: 'Although I think sometimes difficult decisions have to be made in the interests of the child if the family in which the child lives is unable to provide good enough parenting, which is the phrase that is used, such that the optimum development of the child is being impaired, then maybe alternative care for the child needs to be arranged. But on the whole it is far more satisfying to all if optimum parenting of the child can be encouraged by improving the natural family. I would certainly agree with that wholeheartedly.'

However, when it was put to Dr Higgs that Mrs Richardson believed in an authoritarian approach by the local authority for the best management of the child – which meant a place of safety order followed by an interim care order – would she go along with that? she replied: 'The professionals involved do need to have control of the situation and if parental cooperation was not there then it would be an appropriate situation. There is one child that I can think of where in fact the mother very much allied herself with the child at the beginning and it really was not necessary to have a place of safety.'

Liz Smith had indeed cooperated and agreed that her child should remain in hospital, but despite her cooperation a place of safety order had been signed as well as an interim care order. Alma was also made a ward of court. As Dr Higgs recalled: 'There was work done with the mother, with the child, both resident on the ward, and that worked very well. But I think in a lot of cases where one cannot have that cooperation, then the professionals need to take control of the situation.'

As we have seen, the decision was ultimately taken to foster Alma out so that she might now come to terms with her past, might find comfort in her new environment, might be allowed to settle, might be able to forget the trauma of examinations, physical and mental, disclosure sessions with both Dr Higgs and a child psychologist, case conference appearances, special appearances before the court. A new world had opened up to her of disinfected corridors, grey walls, strange people wearing collars and ties and looking serious, women primly and professionally dressed. A world without mummy and daddy, nanas and grandpas: a world strange and hostile to her, sadly lacking in love and affection.

Three months later, on Tuesday 24 June 1987, at the outpatients' clinic at North Tees General Hospital, there was the usual quiet milling of mothers and children. There were the usual anxious faces, clutched hands. There was the usual queue, the usual wait, the usual resigned patience of those who have placed their medical destinies in the hands of the National Health Service. There was also some apprehension, outweighed only by concern for a child's health. For there had been stories in the newspapers about 197 children taken into care over a period of weeks; there were reports that they had been made subject to place of safety orders under the diagnostic recommendation of Dr Marietta Higgs and Dr Geoffrey Wyatt. There had been local television reports and headlines in that day's national newspapers. National television networks would make Cleveland child abuse their leader in evening news bulletins that very day.

All these things, of course, happened to others; not to the mothers and children waiting patiently this day. Five such mothers and their children would learn differently. One mother who waited patiently to see Dr Higgs was in fact a foster mother: she held the hand of a little blue-eyed child who had been fostered to her on 20 March. The foster mother, who had two grown-up children of her own, did not know that her own family life was under threat; that she would be warned by social services to expect police investigations; that social services themselves would anxiously worry about what to do with her own children; and that only the fact they were grown up would make examinations of them 'inappropriate'.

The only thought that went through her mind was that the little foster child held her hand tightly, that she sat straight but taut, that she watched carefully as each mother and child went into the examination room. What was the expression in her eyes? Was it one of wonderment? Or one of apprehension? Can a six and a half year old know what is going on in the adult world? Does she have the instincts to know danger or fear? Or is it just curiosity that suddenly tightens the muscles in her young cheeks and makes her extremely alert?

Who can guess the thoughts of Alma Smith as she waits to see Dr Higgs? Perhaps she knows what others do not. That again, for the *fourth* time in her tender years, she is about to be diagnosed as having been sexually abused.

12

Dr Geoffrey Wyatt, in a style which had much to commend it for lucidity and brevity, wrote: 'After Dr Higgs took up her appointment in Middlesbrough, the first children I saw who had been sexually abused were the Ames children, who were seen by Dr Higgs on 19 and

20 March. I remember that Dr Higgs called me over to have a look at one of the children and she demonstrated to me the anal findings. By that time, because of the diagnosis in the case of the Dixon children, I was beginning to be aware of the problem of child sexual abuse.'

Dr Wyatt was of course bold to describe the Ames children as having been sexually abused, rather than the more cautious approach of Dr Higgs, who in a similar situation would have said that she had 'detected signs consistent with sexual abuse'; and although the Dixon children had been his patients he seemed unaware that only one of them had been allegedly sexually abused. Dr Wyatt had several months to prepare this statement but nevertheless managed to get it wrong. In an earlier paragraph, Dr Wyatt made the same mistake: 'In July 1986 the Dixon children were referred by social services to Dr Hans Steiner in Newcastle but he was on holiday and, in Dr Steiner's absence, the children were seen by Dr Higgs who found abnormal anal signs and diagnosed sexual abuse. The children were taken into care.'

Dr Wyatt might have cut a dashing figure in the Cleveland child abuse drama, with his dark hair and debonair appearance. He was thirty-seven years old. He was married with three children of his own. They were all boys – eleven, nine and six. His wife was also a doctor and he himself had qualified in 1973. This had been in Liverpool and he had taken an early interest in paediatrics. He had gone to South Africa as a student where he had worked with children in a hospital. He had returned to the United Kingdom in 1976.

His first appointment was in Manchester, specializing in neonatology. Then he had gone to Portsmouth, where he joined the neonatal intensive care unit and also did paediatrics. Then he worked in Southampton in the oncology service – the study of tumours. And in 1983 he was appointed as a consultant paediatrician with a special interest in neonatal care. The appointment was made by the Northern Regional Health Authority and sent him north again, this time further north, to Middlesbrough General Hospital, where over four years he built up a reputation as a caring doctor.

Upon his appointment, a sense of anticipation and excitement had run through the Teesside health community: a young doctor, only in his thirties, with obvious enthusiasm and commitment, had come to grace their hospital service. He became involved in a burns unit and did work on his own in child nutrition. He impressed parents because he listened to what they had to say. One parent was astonished that he took her home and introduced himself to her husband, another that he showed so much concern for a child's chest infection that he did not get home for dinner: 'In fact, there were times when nurses had to pass on messages from his wife that his meals at home were ready.' These were the words of one grateful mother. 'Though my stay covered the Christmas period there was only one day that he did not appear in the wards.' Another parent wrote that Dr Wyatt was 'among the most caring, dedicated, hard-working and child-centred doctors I had ever met'.

But if Dr Wyatt had qualities which endeared him to patient and parent alike they had the opposite effect on some of his colleagues in the health service. They disliked the 'disruptive' hours of his practice. They saw it as 'a lack of discipline' that he should be on the wards at all hours, as they conceived it. They felt that this created friction and tension. As Mr John Urch, Secretary of the South Tees Community Health Council, remarked: 'His attitude seemed to be "I'm the captain of this ship. You swim in my wake or you don't swim at all. You are irrelevant."'

The unease that the South Tees Community Health Council felt at the atmosphere created in Middlesbrough General Hospital had been reflected in the council's 1986 report: 'Multi-disciplinary commitment to child health is essential, and an integrated service can only be achieved by inter-unit activity. Therefore, managerial accountability is of paramount importance and requires there to be no artificial distinction between professional and managerial issues.' In plain English, this was a plea for harmony within the paediatric service and in relation to the other hospital disciplines. The plea was bolstered by a hope, the hope that the appointment of Dr Marietta Higgs, of the same age as Dr Wyatt and sharing the same dedicated, enthusiastic outlook, would not only strengthen the service but enable it to settle down.

Enthusiasm and dedication were the hallmarks of Dr Wyatt. He displayed these qualities not only towards his patients, but towards the administrators as well. It was not always to their liking. Thus on 18 September 1986, when he, Dr Higgs and Dr Morrell wrote to the South Tees Health Authority complaining of 'asset stripping', he was in turn berated by the district general manager, Mr Ian Donaldson, who described the letter as 'a mixture of fact and serious misunderstanding', or 'fantasy in other parts'. Dr Wyatt later admitted that he might have expressed himself differently, though he pointed out that it was only natural for him to put forward a case for more consultants, 'as can anyone who wishes to improve the service to the patients'.

Dr Wyatt took his case to a meeting of the local medical advisory committee on 21 September 1986 – known as the 'cogwheel group'. He presented a paper entitled 'Skimping on the Care of the New Born'. At another similar meeting in November he expressed himself so strongly that some of the members walked out. Later, three of his consultant colleagues asked to come and have a private chat with him. He told them that it was his view there should be a coordinated child health care service run by paediatricians. Or as he later put it: 'I think integration of a child health service is topical and desirable.' What Dr Wyatt had in mind was an integrated child health service which included the 'notion that each paediatrician takes on responsibilities in the hospital and in the community'.

If Dr Wyatt erred, surely it was in the right direction: towards an improved paediatric service, improved health care for children, improved facilities, more consultants. It was all perhaps part of an impossible dream, the dream of an ever-growing, ever-expanding National Health Service whose resources were infinite. Perhaps some who listened thought that it was a pipe dream, incapable of fulfilment in a bureaucratic, top-heavy health administration that was always going to be strapped for cash. Such criticisms left Dr Wyatt unruffled: 'I simply sought to make sure that I put my views forward, along with others, so that those with authority who were taking decisions could be as informed as possible.'

It was not administrative battles that preoccupied Dr Wyatt in the early months of 1987. There was a curious incident at Middlesbrough General Hospital that would have some impact on future events. On Thursday 19 February Robert and Joan Hitchins took their seven-year-old daughter Ethel to the casualty department of the hospital with a foot injury. As Robert Hitchins recalled: 'She had been playing with her elder brother trampolining on her bed on Tuesday 17 and had fallen off the bed.'

It had been painful for Ethel at the time but the Hitchins surmised that the foot would get better. 'On the Wednesday she was in some pain but was able to get around and was perfectly happy after my wife put a crêpe bandage on the foot. On Thursday morning it was obvious that this was not simply bruising or a strain and we therefore took her to the casualty department.' On being admitted, Ethel was examined, X-rayed and diagnosed as having fractures of the second and third metatarsals.

Joan Hitchins was informed that her daughter was to have her foot put in plaster and she was to be kept in hospital for observation. Ethel was subsequently transferred to ward nine and admitted at three o'clock in the afternoon. Shortly after admission she was examined by a doctor who suggested that the breakage she had sustained 'should not have happened in the circumstances' the Hitchins had described. 'We interpreted this later as meaning she had some possible bone disorder,' Robert Hitchins recalled. 'My wife asked why she could not be discharged and the doctor gave no answer to this question.'

Robert Hitchins was by this time at home, following a day at work, but expecting his wife and daughter back and puzzled by the delay, he telephoned the hospital. He was told his daughter would be released 'after she had been seen by the consultant'. The consultant was Dr Geoffrey Wyatt. He came on the ward and examined Ethel Hitchins at ten-thirty that evening. 'He asked how the injury occurred. The explanation was given again and Dr Wyatt said: "You can stop worrying that we think you did it."'

This response floored the Hitchins. 'My wife was absolutely devastated, she had thought something was amiss, and could not understand why she could not observe our daughter at home, but the suggestion that we had somehow caused the injury was just too much.' The following day, 21 February, Ethel Hitchins was seen by a doctor and discharged from ward nine. The Hitchins spent the weekend in a state of shock. It 'terrified' both of them to think that they had been suspected of causing an injury to their daughter.

Robert Hitchins wrote a letter to Dr John Drury, general manager at Middlesbrough General Hospital: 'We both feel humiliated by the thought that we spent three days in the hospital being observed by every member of staff. Understandably we feel very angry at the way we have been treated and that even though a doctor has declared that the injury was accidental there still hangs over us a cloud of suspicion.'

When their daughter had been admitted to ward nine Joan Hitchins had been given no information about visiting hours or facilities available in the hospital. Both she and her husband found the ward 'inadequate for the care of young children. Generally, the ward seemed in a poor state of cleanliness and repair; the conditions certainly felt overcrowded and the atmosphere was not in our opinion conducive to the care of sick children. We did not feel that the staff were very cooperative, but obviously we are not sure whether our daughter's confinement for "observation" was the underlying reason for their uncooperative attitudes.'

Robert Hitchins, in his letter of 23 February 1987, would add some prescient lines: '*We are concerned about the procedures in cases like ours because they seem wholly inadequate, discovering that you have been under suspicion is a devastating experience. We would be very interested to know what guidelines and provisions there are in such situations. We would not like to think that every week parents leave Middlesbrough General Hospital in the distressed state we find ourselves.*'

Dr Drury made profuse apologies, but left the Hitchins with the impression that, as a result of the injury, Ethel might now be on the abuse register. He suggested that the Hitchins meet Dr Geoffrey Wyatt personally. Dr Wyatt visited the Hitchins home. As Robert Hitchins recalled: 'He was genuinely apologetic and admitted that a mistake had been made. He also dismissed the suggestion that our daughter was on the register.'

During his first years as a consultant Dr Wyatt had constantly been aware that Middlesbrough was 'a very demanding environment where the existence for many children was a hard one'. Before the arrival and influence of Dr Higgs, he felt children who were being sexually abused in the Middlesbrough area received scant attention and help. 'I had been investigating for some time without much success a number of children recently diagnosed as sexually abused,' Dr Wyatt recalled.

These were sweeping statements made with conviction. How did one know there were children out there being abused but receiving 'scant attention and help'? Dr Wyatt's first involvement with a sexually abused child came only two months after he had taken up his appointment in 1983: 'A baby of six weeks was brought in with a vulval tear and I interpreted this as non-accidental injury of the genitalia rather than as sexual abuse *per se*, a concept of which at that time I knew very little.' A man was later charged and prosecuted. He was convicted and sent to prison and Dr Wyatt well recalled the police telling him the perpetrator had confessed that he had had 'a sudden urge' and pushed his finger into the child's genitalia.

'This case, which is not in fact characteristic of the majority of recent cases which we have considered, typified my perception of sexual abuse at that time, namely that it was part of non-accidental injury; in other words, I merely thought that non-accidental injury occasionally had a sexual dimension.'

All this would change for Dr Wyatt on the night of 19 March 1987. On that evening, little Malcolm Ames, aged two, had been admitted to Middlesbrough General Hospital as an emergency following a long-standing bowel complaint and constipation.

The constipation was considered to be acute but this was not the view of Dr Higgs when she examined the child: 'I think he had had a problem for several months with difficulty in opening his bowels. He was very distressed at the time, but it was not acute constipation.' The local doctor had described Malcolm as being 'acutely distressed' but Dr Higgs pointed out that the distress came more from within the family: both mother and father were anxious at seeing their young child in pain and in difficulty and it was consequent upon this that the local doctor had decided upon an immediate referral to Middlesbrough General.

Malcolm Ames was to have the attention of more consultant paediatricians than he had bargained for. In all, there were four who examined his anus. The first was Dr Higgs, who saw the child at half past five. Next there was Dr Morrell, who came on the ward at half past eight.

Prior to the arrival of Dr Higgs at Middlesbrough General Hospital in January 1987, Dr Morrell had diagnosed few cases of child sexual abuse. He felt there were two reasons for this. He had not been aware of the Leeds experience until Drs Wynne and Hobbs published their article in the *Lancet* on 4 October 1986. And then there was the arrival of Dr Higgs: 'She brought undoubted expertise to Middlesbrough, and this made me more confident in my diagnosis of the condition.'

Dr Morrell's personal involvement in child sexual abuse in Cleveland would be limited to some fifteen cases. His own handling of suspected cases consisted of an initial consultation with the parents which involved taking a detailed history from them, followed by a complete examination of the child. 'This consultation would last probably about one hour. If child abuse was suspected then this would be discussed with the parents.' Social services would be informed and also the nursing officer for child abuse. In the case of Malcolm Ames, however, the question would be asked: why had Dr Morrell been called in at all? The child was obviously the patient of Dr Higgs.

'I wanted to have a second view of what I had found,' Dr Higgs recalled. She wanted to be sure 'what the possible causes' were: 'Although I felt that the findings were consistent with sexual abuse, I wanted a colleague to see the child.' Dr Morrell's own case notes referred to the fact that he felt the child's anus to be 'abnormal'. He also recalled how, in dealing with the Ames parents, Dr Higgs had been 'gentle and sympathetic'. But in accordance with his own practice, once sexual abuse had been alleged, the police would be called in, and this procedure was followed in the case of Malcolm Ames.

Yet there had been no history or suspicion of sexual abuse when Malcolm had been brought to the hospital; there was every indication that the child was properly cared for. He came from middle-class parents and his father was in a professional job. Even Dr Higgs agreed that Malcolm was 'a very nice little boy'. She realized it would be a difficult case in which to come to a firm conclusion and this was why she wanted a colleague such as Dr Morrell to look at the child. She had taken a short case history, in the presence of Malcolm's mother, Jennifer Ames, and then had made an initial examination. She had requested that Malcolm be kept in overnight for observation.

This had relieved Jennifer Ames. She and her husband Bryan had three children: Malcolm aged two, Carol aged nine, and Nigel aged eleven. While Jennifer had professional qualifications of her own, she was a full-time mother. She was often in fragile health herself but she worried about Malcolm. His bowel complaint was of long standing. This was why she had urged her family doctor to have the child examined at Middlesbrough General Hospital. When the consultant paediatrician told her that the child should be kept in overnight 'for observation', therefore, this pleased and satisfied her. Perhaps now, under hospital treatment, a cause and remedy would be found for the bowel complaint.

Such was Jennifer Ames' anxiety that she too signed herself into the hospital. She would stay the night on ward nine. Following the initial examination by Dr Higgs, she settled the child down but was surprised later to see Dr Higgs back on the ward. This time she had brought a nurse with her. The explanation was that they wanted to take the child away and have another look at him. Malcolm was taken from his bed and into the examination room. When he returned the nurse asked Jennifer Ames to follow her into the examination room, where Dr Higgs wanted a word with her.

Dr Higgs asked Jennifer Ames whether she had ever noticed any other problem with Malcolm's anus, whether he had been bleeding, or whether she knew of anything that might have been pushed up his bottom in terms of suppositories and so on. The attitude might have been gentle but the conversation nevertheless unsettled Jennifer

Ames. The news she brought home to her husband the following day was not good. She was puzzled about the allegation that something had been stuck up her child's bottom. This equally disturbed Bryan Ames. He decided to accompany his wife to the hospital next day and accost Dr Higgs.

Unbeknown to the Ames there had been a third paediatrician on duty at Middlesbrough General Hospital that night. This was Dr Geoffrey Wyatt. Dr Higgs had called Dr Wyatt over to look at the findings. In the past he had been impressed by her work with the Smiths and of course the Dixons, where he had had 'a long experience'. Now he was to discover for himself the signs that so perturbed Dr Higgs. Malcolm was in the knee–elbow position, his buttocks were parted; the anus was apparent and as one watched it, the anal canal opened from the outside inwards. This proceeded for some time until the anal canal was open and one could look into the rectum.

This was a classic case of reflex anal dilatation.

This Dr Wyatt had never seen before. It made a startling impact upon him, but then it made a startling impact on any doctors when they saw it for the first time. The sign could be elicited within a space of thirty seconds; all the doctor had to do was hold the buttocks apart for half a minute, or thereabouts, and if the anus dilated this was a sign consistent with sexual abuse. Or so it was said by those who believed in it. Nevertheless, it would open new medical avenues to those paediatricians like Dr Wyatt who had struggled with poor health among an ill-nourished child population whose greatest difficulty, for those whom he saw as outpatients or inpatients, was failure to thrive.

Because if child sex abuse could be linked to failure to thrive then many inexplicable health problems of children would now suddenly become explicable. This would be an enormous breakthrough. Dr Wyatt would not be convinced by the case of Malcolm Ames alone. He would perceive reflex anal dilatation in three other children who equally failed to thrive. But once he was convinced, for him there was no going back. He made his own first diagnosis on 7 April. On the same day he saw another of his girl patients and wrote to the family doctor on 1 May saying that the child had much improved following her discharge from hospital. The child had suffered from a multiple food allergy. A month later, however, when he saw her again, he diagnosed sexual abuse on the grounds of reflex anal dilatation.

What had happened to the earlier diagnosis of the multiple food allergy?

That particular child, along with her brother, was taken into care and seen to 'thrive'. Dr Wyatt did not see the child very often after his diagnosis of sexual abuse but believed that she was well and, as he described it, under these circumstances, and in his view, 'that child has recovered from the effects of child sex abuse'. When challenged to explain why his present diagnosis of child sexual abuse should be given any greater weight than his original diagnosis of food allergy, Dr Wyatt replied: 'There is no other explanation that I know for the physical signs of reflex relaxation and anal dilatation. On going into care the children gained weight.'

There had been no allegation that the second child had been abused, but it too was evidently benefiting from being taken from its natural parents and placed in a foster home. And if taken from its parents, who allegedly had abused the first child, this would prevent them from abusing the second. Dr Wyatt knew that the diagnosis of reflex anal dilatation was novel, but he did not stop to consider whether it was controversial. Unlike Dr Higgs, who at least had the benefit of a two-day seminar, and a talk with the pioneer Dr Jane Wynne, all Dr Wyatt had to go on was the experience of his own eyes and his intuition that linked it to failure to thrive.

He had not read any of the literature, which by this time had filled several columns of the *Lancet* for many months. He did not know there were those who contested the value of reflex anal dilatation as a definitive indicator of child sexual abuse. He made no enquiries. He was not even aware that if there were those who disputed the diagnosis there were others – like Dr Higgs – who believed in it and that it was gaining prevalence among fellow paediatricians. The writings of Drs Wynne and Hobbs were unknown to him. He would catch up with them only in June, when the Cleveland child abuse drama had overtaken him. In these latter days of March he had made himself, as he would later acknowledge, entirely dependent upon the oral tuition of Dr Higgs and 'the observations that any clinician makes on his activity'.

Having embraced the diagnosis as his own, however, Dr Wyatt would sooner or later have to consider its ramifications. Much to his own misfortune, and the impact on his paediatric career, it would come later rather than sooner. What, for example, was the extent of the dilatation? What was its fluctuation range? Over what period of time? On what number of different inspections? Was it greater than on the first occasion he had seen it? Or on some other occasions was it smaller? More precisely, did Dr Wyatt ever consider whether there was likely to be a fluctuation range in the area of dilatation, or did he assume that once he saw it, it would remain?

'I knew early on that the sign would disappear if the child was in a place of safety,' Dr Wyatt declared. 'I knew of Dr Higgs' concern about fluctuating signs, but this was not a personal experience early on, and I cannot remember an instance where I was involved with a child which, if you like, was my child where that happened.' Did Dr Wyatt distinguish between reflex relaxation and anal dilatation? The one, he observed, followed the other. Did he feel guilty that he had not understood the attributes of reflex anal dilatation earlier? No, though he regretted that he had not done more for his patients in the past.

The venture on which Dr Wyatt had now embarked would have significant consequences for many Cleveland families who worried about the health of their children, for now there were *two* doctors at Middlesbrough General and North Tees hospitals diagnosing sexual abuse on the basis of an anal test. More: because the test was linked to failure to thrive, it meant children who were under no suspicion of sexual abuse, but suffered generally poor health in an area of acknowledged deprivation, could also have their bottoms examined. This would, unfortunately and unhappily, extend to handicapped children. Nor did it matter from which class of people the children came: rich parents, poor parents, working- or middle-class, employed or unemployed, educated or otherwise. All they had in common was that they used the National Health Service.

The diagnosis of reflex anal dilatation would be made upon the children of them all.

13

This advance in medical science was lost on Bryan and Jennifer Ames.

At the hospital on 20 March Bryan Ames wanted to know what Dr Higgs had meant when she had suggested 'something' had been pushed up Malcolm's bottom. If Jennifer Ames was fragile in health and temperament – though she would show remarkable resilience in the months to come – Bryan was reflective and rational. He was courteous at all times with Dr Higgs, as indeed she would be with both the Ames. As Dr Higgs recalled: 'In fact, I think I actually showed them what it was that I was concerned about. We had a conversation about possible things that might have gone up. In the end, having spoken to them about other possibilities, I said I was very sorry but I thought that he had been interfered with.'

A case conference was held immediately and the Ames' own family doctor called. From the case conference notes it was acknowledged that Jennifer Ames had been so concerned about Malcolm that she had asked for him to be brought to the hospital. Following the case conference, Dr Higgs told the Ames that she would need to notify the police and also see the two elder children, though it would not be necessary to bring them from school. The Ames were a gentle couple, slow to rouse, both of them sensitive, stunned by what they had been told and not entirely sure what their position was. They agreed to return to the hospital later that day with their children.

In one sense, the Ames were lucky. They knew why their two other children were being called to the hospital. Other parents with siblings would not be so fortunate, for as Dr Higgs explained: 'I took the view that siblings were potentially at risk of abuse and needed to be examined very quickly, probably before the abuser had a chance to reinforce a threat not to tell. It was only very rarely that I could give the parents a reason for bringing their other children in to be examined.' Thus it was that many an anxious parent would round up siblings of a child taken to the hospital and in one case do so in the belief that all of them were suffering from a hereditary complaint.

Bryan Ames waited for his children outside their school rather than plucking them from the classroom. Carol and Nigel were not taken home, but directly to the hospital, riding in their daddy's car. They had, of course, complete confidence in their loving father. There was no sense of apprehension on their part. They were driven across town from the school to the General. They found their mother waiting for them there. Perhaps she was tenser and paler than usual. But she retained her composure, as did their father. For the children, curious to know why they were in hospital, there was no premonition of what was likely to be in store.

Dr Higgs was so busy that she was unable to see them immediately. After a while, as his children grew restless, Bryan Ames returned home with Carol and Nigel while Jennifer stayed and minded Malcolm on ward nine. Dr Higgs arrived at seven o'clock and wanted to know where the two siblings were. Jennifer Ames therefore phoned home, Bryan bundled the children into the car and they were all back at the hospital within half an hour. The two elder children were then examined in the presence of their mother. Dr Higgs diagnosed Carol as having been abused anally and vaginally, Nigel had threadworms and upon her examination, though she found no reflex anal dilatation, she did mention scarring and an area of thick skin that she felt was consistent with *past* sexual abuse: 'My view was that the findings were consistent with old abuse, not recent, because of the scarring.'

Dr Higgs asked Jennifer Ames if she could see the children alone? The dutiful Ames let her get on with it, though later they came to regret this. The children were therefore seen separately by Dr Higgs and so far as the Ames are concerned, there was no record of anything that was said. It was now half past ten at night. The Ames were given a cubicle on the ward but no provision was made for the parents, only their children, and therefore if they wished to stay the night there would be nowhere for them to sleep. With three children in the hospital, all in the same cubicle, there was clearly no room for the parents.

Notwithstanding the lateness of the hour, Dr Higgs asked to see Mrs Ames on her own. She said she had spoken to Carol, who had been able to tell her that she had been sexually abused by her father. The nine-year-old Carol was in the room but said nothing, only that she did not know what anyone was talking about. But the police, having been alerted by two calls made to them that night, one at half past eight and another at half past ten, arrived at eleven-thirty. The officers said they wished to see Bryan Ames at the police station the following morning. The family doctor also arrived, making it all extremely busy on the children's ward of the hospital, with police officers and a family doctor arriving, and two anxious parents hovering around the bedside of their by now equally anxious older children, Nigel and Carol, who had reached the age of reason.

The family doctor had a long conversation with Dr Higgs. He was a family friend of the Ames. His wife was a social worker, also a friend of the family. Neither could believe what was happening. The doctor persuaded Dr Higgs that the two elder children need not stay on the ward that evening and while she agreed with this it was on condition that they should return the following evening, and that they should stay in hospital over the weekend. The family doctor did not know it, but in this conversation he was hearing the development of another of Dr Higgs' tendencies: the need to have children in hospital for observation and assessment.

Or as she would later explain: 'The hospital ward was a safe and neutral place. It also enabled parents to be able to stay with the child, particularly if the child was small, or to be able to have access and be round the child. I think in some instances that naturally was not very helpful because I am not sure some children were not silenced by that practice.'

Bryan Ames had earlier that evening wanted to go home but he had been told that the police were on their way, that he would be detained, and he therefore stayed until they arrived. The following day, appearing at the local police station, Bryan Ames spent most of the day being interviewed. The two older children returned to Middlesbrough General Hospital and they too were interviewed by police. On Sunday 22 March the police advised Bryan Ames that they were withdrawing from the case and he would not be hearing from them again. The children too were not seen again by police.

The anxiety of having grave criminal charges over Bryan Ames' head was now removed and such was his relief that he had difficulty focusing his mind on the plight of his wife and children. The bewilderment was shared by his wife. Neither of them knew to whom they should be turning for help. Jennifer Ames was particularly upset that her children had been interviewed by police without her present. She felt that at least a social worker should have been there to protect the children's interests, if not those of the parents. They had also presumed that some help would be available to provide support and family advice.

The family doctor, however, had not been inactive this weekend of 21–22 March. Being more objective than the Ames were able to be, he saw that what was needed was a second opinion that would confirm or reject that of Dr Higgs. He himself was not aware of the additional opinions of Drs Morrell and Wyatt. He put himself in touch with Dr Hans Steiner, of the Steiner Unit, who on Saturday agreed to see the children the following lunchtime at the Steiner Unit in Newcastle. In fact, following a telephone conversation with Dr Higgs, these arrangements were cancelled.

Dr Higgs would not recall who had called whom over that weekend, whether it was Dr Steiner who had spoken to her or whether she had spoken to Dr Steiner: 'I certainly remember discussing the case with him and explaining that it was an extremely difficult situation. I think during that phone conversation he said that he would concentrate on the youngest child's problem, and that was what the referral had been made to him for, and that was what he would be dealing with.' Dr Higgs would later accept that, in the case of Malcolm Ames, she never did carry out any medical investigation into his constipation, believing it would clear up once he was in care.

The upshot of the talk between Dr Higgs and Dr Steiner was that a call was made to the family doctor at eight o'clock on Sunday morning, 22 March, cancelling the arrangements to see Malcolm Ames. Had it been proper for Dr Higgs to interfere? 'I did not realize that I had done that,' Dr Higgs explained. 'As I said, the discussion that I had had with him was to explain the difficulty of the situation with that family and I remember that he felt that he had been asked purely for an opinion on the bowel problem of the youngest child, and that was what he would be concentrating on.'

Dr Higgs acknowledged that the status of the Ames created a 'difficult' situation. 'It was a professional family. The family general practitioner was also a family friend, as was one of the consultants at the hospital.' This consultant disbelieved the diagnosis. 'It was a very complex situation. The wife of the general practitioner was also a social worker. I think there was a lot of communication, certainly between the general practitioner and the social services that I was aware of.'

The family doctor persisted in his endeavours to have a second independent opinion on behalf of the Ames and wrote to Dr Higgs telling her so. Dr Higgs then telephoned the doctor. She advised him it was her firm opinion that the youngest child Malcolm should not have been referred for a further opinion. It was her view that the doctor had already made a referral to her; that there might well be 'a defensive conspiracy' developing around the Ames family. Or as Dr Higgs described it: 'I did warn him about the problem of collusion and disbelief when this diagnosis is raised in someone you know very well.'

It was fortunate that the family doctor was seeking to act in their interest, for events were moving far too quickly for either of the Ames to exercise any rational thought. A case conference decided on Monday 23 March that all three children should be taken immediately to be seen by Dr Jane Wynne. This was in order to obtain a 'second' opinion. But in reality this would be a *fourth* opinion, for there had already been the diagnosis of Dr Higgs confirmed by Dr

Morrell, and there had been the 'sighting' of Dr Wyatt, which in the eyes of the Northern Regional Health Authority would constitute a third opinion. So why was a *fourth* necessary?

Was it because Dr Higgs needed the opinion of Dr Wynne, of whom she thought so highly, to buttress her own? Did she have any doubts? There was after all no Dr Christine Cooper to turn to. Was the disciple turning to the pioneer in search of the imprimatur of a confirmed medical diagnosis? There was no legal reason for the *fourth* opinion. The police had withdrawn from the case. They would not be coming back regardless of whether a fourth opinion confirmed the other three. Social services had confidence in Dr Higgs and were prepared to act on her diagnosis alone; but even if this had not been so, they had as a back up to Dr Higgs the medical opinions of Drs Morrell and Wyatt.

It was rather curious that Dr Higgs should have held out so steadfastly against a second opinion on behalf of the Ames when she had in fact arranged three additional opinions to that of her own. It was one thing calling upon colleagues to confirm her diagnoses; it was another for a family to seek an independent opinion. Dr Higgs accepted that at the time she had made the diagnosis on Malcolm Ames she was still feeling her way: 'Initially, when I encountered the first case of child sexual abuse from Middlesbrough, and before I was confident that the signs I found were consistent with sexual abuse, I sought a second opinion on the case. I chose to refer to Dr Jane Wynne, since she had a particular interest in the subject and was the nearest consultant who I thought had particular expertise in it.'

There were logistical difficulties in transporting the entire Ames family to Leeds. On this Monday morning, 23 March, a social worker arrived at the hospital. She introduced herself to the Ames and declared that her job was to accompany the family to Leeds where a 'second' opinion would be given by Dr Jane Wynne. The name meant nothing to the Ames. The distressed family had before them an embarrassed social worker who readily admitted that she knew nothing of the Ames, had nothing to do with their case, and in fact was simply a minder. Her job was to transport all of them to Leeds in her Metro. Bryan Ames pointed out that the vehicle appeared on the small side and did not seem to be properly equipped for the transportation of a two-year-old boy.

Where, for example, was the baby seat?

And how were three adults and three children to fit in comfortably for what was after all a two- to three-hour journey? In a spirit of cooperation, he suggested that they use his own car, since this was properly equipped with restraints for all of the children. The trip to Leeds was therefore undertaken in the Ames' car and they would spend five hours with a social worker who knew nothing about their case when they themselves were confused and extremely upset. As Jennifer Ames recalled: 'We were with someone who was not going to be involved with our situation and was therefore unable to offer support or guidance.'

All three children were diagnosed by Dr Jane Wynne as having been sexually abused. Dr Wynne did not take a history from the children but she talked to Jennifer Ames about each child, though she did not discuss her findings with either parent. By this time Malcolm Ames was two years and two months old. Dr Wynne found that he had been chronically sexually abused and there were signs 'consistent with repeated anal penetration over a prolonged period'.

In the case of Carol Ames, Dr Wynne found vaginal abuse, though she carried out no internal examination. She also found abnormalities to the child's anus and reflex dilatation. However, when she was asked whether she was clinically certain or only probably certain that this child had been abused, Dr Wynne would say only 'on the balance of probabilities'.

As to Nigel, Dr Wynne agreed there was evidence of scarring as well as threadworms. Did Dr Wynne talk to the two older children about what she was examining for and how she viewed the findings? 'I think it is very difficult,' Dr Wynne recalled. 'I do not think it is appropriate for a series of professionals to talk. When I am asked to give a second opinion on physical signs, I try to be pleasant to the children, make them feel as relaxed as possible, but I do not think it is appropriate for me to start to form a relationship with them in that sense.'

On Tuesday 24 March, at approximately ten-thirty in the morning, two people walked into the Ames cubicle at Middlesbrough General Hospital, introduced themselves as social workers, and said that they intended to obtain a place of safety order for their three children. They said they would be back within the hour. What shocked the Ames, if they were capable of being further shocked, was that this conversation took place in front of their three children, two of whom were eleven and nine respectively and fully aware of what was going on.

'We were perfectly appalled at the lack of sensitivity displayed by these two persons, who could easily have asked us to step outside and spoken to us privately. This intrusion served to completely wreck any and all previous efforts to calm and comfort our children in the preceding four days. During that time we were in desperate need of an agency concerned with explaining our position, advising us of social service procedures and supporting the family.' Information now coming to the Ames was of a technical nature: the two elder children would be placed separately in council-approved foster accommodation. This would take place the following day. A decision would be made as to whether the youngest child would be placed with the family doctor and his wife. The Ames had no thought of themselves: they were still thinking of their children.

How could they prepare them for this traumatic separation?

As Jennifer Ames described it: 'Needless to say, they were extremely upset. However, we tried to reassure them and promised that I would go home and prepare cases with clothing and special items that both of them wanted to take with them the following day.' That night, at half past seven, when Nigel and Carol were both in their pyjamas and somewhat calmer, 'though exhausted', the Ames were told that Dr Higgs wanted to see them. She told them, in the presence of a social worker, that there was an acute shortage of beds on ward nine and that the children would be taken away that night. The social worker raised no objection.

One question that would be asked was why, in the case of eleven-year-old Nigel, he should have been taken and placed in any safety at all. Dr Higgs had not diagnosed recent abuse, only old abuse. Surely he too could not be considered at risk? Had it not been the case, for example, that when Dr Higgs had examined him he had been fit and healthy; the general examination had been normal? And if he suffered from threadworms, as indeed he did, could not this have accounted for the scarring that Dr Higgs had interpreted as reflecting past anal abuse?

So why had he been made the subject of a place of safety order? As Dr Higgs explained: 'On that day all three children were admitted to hospital. Mother was resident. I think the father also became resident. He was around on the ward. The decisions about foster placement came after a second opinion from Dr Wynne, who agreed the signs on the children, and a case conference decision.' But the place of safety order had been taken out *before* the case conference. What was the danger to the eleven year old that required a place of safety order designed only for emergencies and which would take him from the family home?

Dr Higgs was adamant that place of safety orders were not her responsibility. Where parents cooperated in their child remaining on the ward she would not advise social services that she thought a place of safety order appropriate. But generally social services did not ask for her opinion. In the case of the Ames, Dr Higgs was not sure why anyone would call it an 'emergency' place of safety order, since the children were already in hospital: 'I am not sure why social services took the place of safety order out that morning. It may have been to do with Dr Wynne's opinion as well as mine and Dr Morrell's.'

Emergency or not, it was now for Bryan and Jennifer Ames to explain to their children there had been a change of plan. They had to be dressed, put back into their dirty clothes, their pyjamas put in a carrier bag. The parents left the hospital in the full knowledge that if they returned the following morning two of their children would be there no more. 'We consider this action to have been brutal and heartless on the part of Dr Higgs,' Jennifer Ames would declare. For by now both Bryan and Jennifer Ames were truly angry. They laid the blame equally at the door of Cleveland Social Services: they felt their social worker had done nothing to prevent it. The Ames were still looking to their social worker for some sort of succour in this situation, as someone who understood these matters and would handle them with delicacy and diplomacy. They were not yet looking upon her as an enemy.

Nor did the social worker tell them where the children were going. 'She did not ask for any details about them, either general or medical. This we felt was negligent on her part, particularly since Carol has a medical condition that should have been discussed.' Their two eldest children having now been taken from them, the Ames spent all the following day, Wednesday 25 March, with Malcolm. They had no word from anyone. They waited to hear the decision on his placement. The first they knew was when the family doctor's wife arrived at four o'clock. She had agreed to foster the child. She thought that the decision had already been communicated to Jennifer and Bryan Ames. The Ames were happy that their youngest child should go to someone they knew, but thought it particularly 'heartless' that no one should properly inform them that the arrangements had been finalized.

As they would later write to social services: 'You know how very anxious we were that Malcolm be placed with someone familiar to him. Is it too much to hope that social services would have wanted to relieve us of that anxiety as soon as possible and therefore would have informed us of their decision immediately?' The Ames did not entirely realize it, but with Malcolm gone too they were now alone in the hospital. All three children were now taken from them. There was no point in their hanging round any longer. They therefore shook the dust of Middlesbrough General Hospital from their feet and returned home.

'We were left totally alone, not knowing what was happening, and not having been told of any future contact with the social services, let alone when we would see our children.' The Ames were still not aware that they had entered a twilight zone where nothing was as they might expect it. They did not concentrate their ire on the doctor who had diagnosed child sexual abuse, nor on the police who had done the interviewing before withdrawing from the case. They directed it at Cleveland Social Services in the view that they were there to help families as well as children. They would be sadly disillusioned.

They were so distressed that the family doctor called social services himself and arranged an interview with a social worker the following morning at quarter to nine. The social worker arrived twenty-five minutes late. She did not apologize. She took the couple to an interview room. She did not introduce herself. Jennifer Ames therefore asked if she was the person they were supposed to see. She still did not own up to being the social worker who had been allotted to the Ames: 'She was extremely reticent and unresponsive to our questions about access and communication with our children. She gave few details about them and none about their placements. Although the appointment had been arranged, she did not appear to have any information at her disposal. To this day – this was written 28 June 1987 – we have not been officially informed of Nigel and Carol's whereabouts and the names of their foster parents.'

Jennifer Ames felt that the social worker showed no compassion and displayed total indifference towards both the Ames and the predicament in which they found themselves. 'We had expected a greater degree of empathy from the social worker appointed to work with our family and the total lack of this, in our view, prevented any good relationship between us as parents and the social worker developing. We did not see this in terms of a personality clash but as total prejudice against us. We would not accept that her attitude was in line with placing "the interests of the children first".'

The social worker informed them that an extensive social history would be required from both the Ames but in fact none was called for until some months later. On 7 April the Ames were asked to a meeting and since Jennifer Ames had been admitted to the Fleming Hospital in Newcastle she would leave her hospital bed and come down to Teesside specially for this meeting. There was now the original social worker and two colleagues, both women. Bryan Ames said that he could not understand why they had been 'treated like lepers and was amazed that no one from social services had visited us in our home to make any kind of family assessment'.

One social worker replied: 'We do not come to you. You come to us.'

They would be willing to work with them but until the Ames accepted responsibility for what had happened they would not do so. The Ames denied all knowledge that anyone had abused their children. They did not believe sexual abuse had taken place. At this, according to Jennifer Ames, the social worker who had spoken earlier said: 'You are in a no-win situation and until you accept responsibility you will not get your children back.' The implication, for the Ames at least, from that moment onwards, was that their children had indeed been abused, both parents knew it, Bryan Ames was the perpetrator and Jennifer Ames was a bad mother.

The penny had at last begun to drop.

14

Inspector Whitfield completed his report on Alma Smith in the following laconic fashion: '*After leaving hospital Alma was placed with foster parents and the situation remained stable until 23 June 1987 when Alma was again routinely examined by Dr Higgs. Further sexual abuse was diagnosed with reflex anal dilatation and similar bruising to the vaginal area. The suggestion therefore was that Alma has been sexually abused while in foster care. This of course was beyond belief and initially the divisional director of social services wanted her examining by the police surgeon. Events then overtook us and Alma was made a ward of court and the further examination was refused at a senior level in social services. Alma has since been returned by the High*

Court to her mother's custody under a supervision order.'

Inspector Whitfield's reference to being overtaken by events arose from the fact that there was by now a national outcry at events in Cleveland; but the question that remained to be answered was how it had come about that Alma had been diagnosed a *fourth* time? And while the child had been subjected to eight examinations between 17 February and 16 March there would be five additional examinations leading to 23 June. Had Dr Higgs been carrying out general research on Alma? 'No,' was the firm response. 'It was to keep an eye on this little girl to see whether there was a resolution of the signs.' Following the examination on 23 June, Alma found herself back in hospital for observation and assessment and more photographs were taken.

She had been taken from her own home because it was not safe; she had been discharged from a hospital to a foster home because the hospital had not been considered safe, with all male visitors refused; and now she had to be removed back to the hospital because the foster home was no longer safe. There would have to be an examination of all the other children who had been in the foster home. Had they been abused too? A social worker was sent to the home of the foster parents. He did not bring tidings of great joy but rather the news that Alma had been abused in their home and that explanations were demanded. Belief in the diagnosis of reflex anal dilatation ran deep within Cleveland county.

The foster parents were 'shattered' when it was put to them that Alma had been abused. The foster father was 'absolutely devastated' and the foster mother was left feeling 'physically sick' and expressed her disbelief that 'this could have happened'. Even the child psychologist, who had followed Alma from the early days of February, began to wonder. She penned her thoughts to Dr Higgs. So what had been the grounds for the *fourth* diagnosis? As Dr Higgs explained: 'My concern was that her anal dilatation, which had been resolving and was very slight when I had seen her a month previously, was now much more marked and there had also been a return of the bruising which had resolved.' It was clear that neither Grandfather Oliver nor Tony Smith could be responsible for abusing Alma in the self-same fashion and in an identical manner; but whoever had effected the abuse had used the self-same technique and, frankly, indulged in the self-same buggery.

Or was there not some other message being conveyed by the sad plight of Alma? Did not her case illustrate 'the difficulties and dangers' in coming to an 'early and firm' conclusion simply on the basis of physical examination? Was there not a lesson to be drawn of the dangers of jumping in with an early diagnosis and sticking to it through 'thick and thin'? Response of Dr Higgs: 'I would not use the word dangers. I think it is important to make this diagnosis where you can in children. I think what certainly does need looking at is subsequent management and how that can be handled better, and certainly there are a number of cases where management has been far from satisfactory. But I still feel that it is a situation that does need looking into when there are physical signs.'

But what would this mean for Alma and her family? Would it not be 'extremely serious' and would this not have long-term effects for the child if it proved that she was the object of a mistaken diagnosis? As Dr Higgs recalled: 'Well, with this particular child, she actually has been able to disclose her abuse, having gone through the process of assessment and evaluation. She is now living with her mother and her brother and with a mother who is very supportive of her and who has aligned herself with her child and the little girl seems to be doing extremely well at the moment.' What Dr Higgs did not say, of course, was that the mother and child had been reunited as a result of a court order, and that in the disclosure sessions as revealed by Inspector Whitfield the child did not make confessions of alleged sexual abuse.

If the police had, as it were, been caught out by mistakenly arresting Grandfather Oliver in February, they had since been determined to follow procedures that would provide for them the best evidence of alleged child abuse that would lead to prosecutions in courts of law. They were particularly on their toes on 2 March 1987 when another case was referred to them. This involved the suspected non-accidental injury of a female child. A diagnosis of sexual abuse was made by Dr Geoffrey Wyatt. This was not anal abuse but the police immediately began investigations with the parents, who were interviewed at length. Officers were distinctly uneasy, for all the evidence centred upon the diagnosis of a paediatrician alone; and, aware of the controversy around Alma Smith, they immediately asked social services to arrange for a second medical opinion through a police surgeon. This request was refused.

In fact, police had noticed changes in emphasis going back to the latter part of 1986. Police officers would later attribute this changed emphasis to publicly stated opinions of various child abuse experts and the introduction of novel investigative techniques such as anatomically correct dolls and video disclosure sessions. The police could reconcile neither with their task of preparing evidence in criminal cases. Senior officers felt the new techniques should be treated with circumspection: after all, they had to handle the evidence for a court of law and juries had to be persuaded beyond reasonable doubt.

Dr Higgs had confronted the police with a major and even phenomenal problem that had nothing to do with dolls or videos but everything to do with medical diagnostic technique. Behaviour patterns of sexually abused children, notification or warnings from school teachers, members of a family, members of the public, reports from the NSPCC, were no longer to be the source of information that would lead to the rooting out of child sexual abuse. A medical diagnosis would reign supreme. The child's disclosures would come later. However, the diagnosis was not followed up with disclosures which had, in the eyes of the police, any validity: there were too many leading questions, the children were not disclosing, and if the medical diagnosis was suspect in the eyes of the police the corroborative evidence was woefully unhelpful.

The police then began to discover that the medical diagnostic technique itself was controversial: it was not accepted throughout the medical profession. What prospect was there for a jury to convict on a medical diagnosis alone if the defence, as they would, could call upon other consultant paediatricians who were prepared to rubbish the technique? These were dilemmas for the police but they were dilemmas that could be handled. All cases could be investigated even if caution was necessary. However, this brought about a counter-reaction from social services. For if the police were sceptical this, in the eyes of social workers, was translated as a failure to investigate properly.

This build-up of mistrust, or lack of confidence, was highlighted in the case of the Ames children. On 19–20 March, Dr Higgs made her diagnoses that the three children had been abused: the daughter Carol, aged nine, had been diagnosed as vaginally and anally abused; the elder boy Nigel, aged eleven, as anally abused in the past. Malcolm, aged two, had also allegedly been anally abused. On 20 March Dr Higgs asked a detective constable who was also a police photographer to photograph the vaginal area of Carol. There had, however, been no medical examination by the police surgeon as part of the police general investigation.

This seemed to be a breach of proper police procedures and the detective constable initially refused. However, Dr Higgs insisted on the photographs being taken and reluctantly the police met the request. The doctor herself was reluctant to take the forensic samples that the police required as part of their own evidence in any eventual prosecution. Later that same day, Dr Higgs requested the detective constable to take further intimate photographs of four children who were also in hospital suspected of being sexually abused, but on this occasion he firmly refused. Dr Higgs was nonplussed at this attitude of the police. She was also surprised at the slow response of social services. She made her views known to child abuse consultant Mrs Richardson. The police would in fact interview both Bryan Ames and two of his children over that weekend, but the manner in which these interviews took place raised the ire of Mrs Richardson. The police had apparently spoken first to Bryan Ames and had his authorization to be firm in their interviewing of the two children, while the approach of social services would have been to take the session more gently, thus obtaining what for them would be valid disclosure.

Mrs Richardson took up Dr Higgs' complaints with Inspector Whitfield on 23 March, but Inspector Whitfield sharply reminded her of the consequences of police involvement with Alma Smith, where the wrong man had been arrested. The language of Inspector Whitfield was blunt: 'The police had been left with egg on their face', as Mrs Richardson recalled. She had a further discussion with a detective inspector on 25 March, with Dr Higgs present, when much the same point was made.

On 26 March, Mrs Richardson went to Leicester to see a detailed presentation by Dr Hobbs from Leeds, who was present with Dr Jane Wynne. She took the opportunity of broaching the Ames case with Dr Wynne directly. Mrs Richardson had taken to heart the criticisms of Dr Higgs in relation to the slowness of social services; she had been preoccupied that no place of safety order had been taken out on the Ames children until after the second opinion had been obtained from Leeds. The medical evidence, in her eyes, had been 'unequivocal': there had been the opinions of Dr Higgs and Dr Wynne. She did not know about the opinion of Dr Morrell and the 'sighting' of Dr Wyatt.

In the view of Mrs Richardson, any second opinion in the Ames case had been unnecessary because 'Dr Higgs was sure of her diagnosis. But because of the difficulties surrounding the case and the conflicting views on the matter from the police, she felt it proper to get a second opinion, although she was confident of her diagnosis.' The 'unequivocal' medical evidence was bolstered by her conversation with Dr Wynne in Leicester. As Mrs Richardson would later write, Dr Wynne expressed the view that she strongly suspected the father was the perpetrator. But had she given a basis for that view? 'I am not sure how much information she had about the family that led her to make that remark,' Mrs Richardson recalled. 'My impression was the nature of the abuse indicated someone within the family.'

With no place of safety order issued on the Ames children, Mrs Richardson had called the social worker in charge directly. She wanted to find out what he was doing with the case. 'He told me that he had already made arrangements, he had a worker standing by to take a place of safety order if Dr Wynne confirmed the findings.' The place of safety order had been taken out on 24 March but the ire of Mrs Richardson at the way the Ames matter had been handled did not ease: there would never again be sluggishness on the part of social services in getting place of safety orders signed. As to the police, their conduct was raised at the next case conference, when she made clear her disapproval of the manner in which the police had interviewed one of the Ames children: 'Police did not share the same understanding as myself and Dr Higgs,' she would write, 'that disclosure of sexual abuse takes time, is unlikely under conditions of pressure', and that the 'alleged behaviour [of the child] is indicative of having been abused'.

It was Mrs Richardson's view that once a diagnosis of alleged sexual abuse had taken place then the disclosure from the child would follow, though not necessarily in the way that the police had gone about seeking a disclosure in the case of the Ames children. For her, the medical evidence being 'unequivocal', it would only be a matter of time before the child disclosed. 'I would have thought in that kind of situation [children] would need a lot of work, a lot of help, and that it would be quite valid to continue over a period of time with the kind of sessions that would be designed to help them, and if necessary to disclose, if that was what they felt able to do. But I wouldn't see that as a kind of interrogation sort of disclosure session.'

In these circumstances, how much pressure did Mrs Richardson feel ought to be placed upon a child who was saying that it had not been abused? Was the child saying that in order to protect someone? Or because the child did not want to give an answer? Response of Mrs Richardson: 'I don't think any pressure should be placed on children at all, but I do think they sometimes need to be given permission by making it clear what your view is as an adult.' But since the police had no faith in the medical diagnosis it was apparent that they were not certain what weight to put on any subsequent disclosure, if any at all. And their experience with Alma Smith was such that not only had they seen the defectiveness of the diagnosis in evidential terms, but, equally, the leading questions put to the child had evoked conflicting answers implicating two different suspects.

It was for this reason that Mrs Richardson, in the case of the Ames children, assigned to their case a child psychologist who would take the medical diagnosis as it stood and seek disclosure on that basis. The child psychologist had already been at work with Alma Smith and would wonder in writing whether the *fourth* allegation of sexual abuse on this child was valid. She too would later become the subject of much comment and, indeed, hostile criticism. At the time, however, Mrs Richardson felt that 'the police at that stage were not in a position or were unprepared to continue their investigation, and had not been able to corroborate the medical facts as we understood them. So, therefore, another approach needed to be taken to see what protection the children needed.'

In the case of the Ames this had meant getting them away from the family home as quickly as possible because the parents were saying that their children had not been abused and that they were in no way responsible for abuse. However, even when in foster care, the Ames children would deny they had been sexually abused. Was this usual? 'That is certainly not unusual because the bonds of loyalty to the parents are still there,' Mrs Richardson would state. The possibility of a misdiagnosis 'never occurred to' Mrs Richardson. It was not just a question of following a medical diagnosis because it was there, because social services had no option, because Dr Higgs and Dr Wyatt were consultant paediatricians, because Dr Higgs was a child abuse expert with special skills in relation to sex abuse: *it was that Mrs Richardson also believed in the diagnosis.*

As she would say: 'I cannot deny that the damage in separating children from their families is awful.' But, 'if I had to choose I would say that the damage done by sexual abuse is far, far greater'. With such certainty in the diagnosis, however, each case of reflex anal dilatation and its subsequent diagnosis of sexual abuse would be another stage on the way towards the Cleveland crisis of May and June. Alma Smith had opened the eyes of the police. They could not be convinced that the diagnosis had any evidential value. The case of the Ames children would convince Mrs Richardson that there had been tardiness on the part of social services. Dr Higgs' disappointment with the police was so great that she had raised it with Mrs Richardson and she had raised it at joint consultative meetings with the police.

Equally, following her conversations with Dr Jane Wynne in Leicester on 26 March, Mrs Richardson had agreed to closer cooperation between the Leeds team and her own social services. She had not liked the idea of a 'second' opinion from anywhere but should one be required there was no doubt that Dr Jane Wynne would be eminently well placed to provide it. Also, since the police had not been on the same wavelength and the Ames children had been handed over to a child psychologist for disclosure to be effected, all of the parties in the Cleveland drama began to take fixed positions without consciously knowing it. The consensus was eroding.

There would be the police on the one hand and Dr Higgs and social services on the other. The police were sufficiently concerned to raise the dilemma at a meeting of the Force Scientific Aids Photographers on 28 April. The force policy of not undertaking intimate photography unless there was an observable injury was spelled out. Instructions were in effect being given and they would shortly be needed. On 30 April, Dr Higgs asked a detective constable to take photographs of the anuses of two small girls who were being detained at Middlesbrough General Hospital. The request was refused.

Fifteen days earlier, on 15 April, a two-year-old girl had been admitted to the same hospital suffering from non-accidental injury. Her brother and sister were examined and found to be in good health and not subject to abuse. All three were taken into care. While the interim care order was still in force the children were returned to their parents, but on 17 June Dr Higgs re-examined the children and diagnosed reflex anal dilatation. The case was investigated by the police but a request for an examination by the police surgeon was refused. There would be no police investigation and no prosecutions.

On 6 May Dr Higgs examined a twelve-year-old girl for a stomach complaint, and diagnosed chronic anal fissuring and vaginal damage and infection. The girl's sister, aged two, was consequently examined and anal dilatation was diagnosed. Both children were taken into care but requests by the police for examination by a police surgeon were refused. There was insufficient evidence to charge any person with an offence. The following day, 7 May, a ten-year-old girl was examined by Dr Higgs following a suspected injury to her vagina. A written statement was not received by the police until three weeks after the examination, so that no enquiries could be made; and a request for an examination by a police surgeon was refused.

The refusal came from the social services department.

Again, on 26 May, two children, Annie and Beatrice Townend, aged five years and sixteen months respectively, had been referred by Cleveland Social Services to Middlesbrough General Hospital for examination by Dr Higgs. As Inspector Colin Makepeace recalled: 'Her findings were anal dilatation on each of the children who were then made the subject of a three-week place of safety order.' A policewoman had been detailed to investigate the referral and in order to do so telephoned the social worker: 'At this time she requested some form of written statement from either herself or Dr Higgs in order that a full investigation should commence. The social worker stated there was no immediate rush for such a statement as "there is a three-week place of safety order on the children".'

The policewoman stressed the need for urgency and later the same day personally contacted Dr Higgs. She agreed to prepare the statement for collection, but despite frequent personal requests it was not until 8 June that the policewoman was actually able to collect it. Also in relation to Annie and Beatrice Townend, the police arranged with social services for a second medical examination by police surgeon Dr Alistair Irvine, but shortly before the appointment, according to the chief constable, 'a social worker telephoned to say that social services were not now consenting to the second medical examination'.

There would be police protests at this to senior staff within social services, and these protests also referred to the policy towards police surgeons, but social services refused to consent to any other examinations. As the chief constable concluded: 'No other corroborative evidence could be found to substantiate the allegation by Dr Higgs. No prosecutions are pending.'

Perhaps the real breakdown came on 1 May 1987 when Dr Higgs met with Inspector Alan Walls, in charge of Cleveland Constabulary Scientific Aids Department.

Following the 28 April meeting of the Force Scientific Aids Photographers, Alan Walls thought it prudent to come along and explain police policy in relation to photographs. The opportunity had presented itself when Dr Higgs had called to ascertain what the procedure was for obtaining photographs. Walls invited himself along rather than discuss the issue on the telephone. The meeting was arranged for seven o'clock on the evening of 1 May on ward nine of Middlesbrough General Hospital.

The police officer was obliged to wait for half an hour, but he was able to speak to Dr Higgs at half past seven. In view of the delicate nature of the subject to be discussed, Walls asked to see her in a private room and they therefore went into an examination room on the ward. As Walls recalled it: 'I asked Dr Higgs how I could be of assistance. She said that I could supply her with photographs of children which she had requested to be taken. I asked her if she could explain what the photographs showed and she told me they showed a ruptured hymen and reflex anal dilatation.'

Walls, who knew nothing of the technicalities of the medical diagnoses, asked for an explanation as to what all this meant. Dr Higgs patiently explained. 'I told Dr Higgs that it was not our policy to photograph genitalia, only injuries which may be present in the immediate area, and that her verbal description of the injuries to the vagina and anus would be acceptable evidence without putting a child through the trauma of having a photograph taken, and we had always considered the emotional effect it could have on the child.' But if the verbal description would be adequate why was it that Dr Higgs wanted the photographs in the first place? As she explained, she wished 'to educate the magistrates in child abuse'.

'I asked Dr Higgs if she reported the child abuse cases to the police and she told me that she did not consider it necessary to involve the police in every child abuse case, as the matter would be dealt with by herself and social services,' Walls recalled. 'I told Dr Higgs that if a child had been sexually abused, not self inflicted, then it must be a criminal offence and as such reported to the police for investigation. Dr Higgs again stated she did not feel it always necessary for the matter to be resolved by a police investigation.'

Walls therefore explained the agreed procedures as he understood them. These were that when a paediatrician for the health authority diagnosed or suspected child sexual abuse the police would be notified. 'A police surgeon would then examine the possible victim, obtaining swabs for forensic examination and then by taking vaginal and anal swabs this could produce corroborative evidence for the medical diagnosis. Dr Higgs told me again that she did not consider it necessary for police involvement and that included forensic corroboration and examination by a police surgeon.'

Walls then came to the decision of 28 April: 'I told Dr Higgs that as far as my officers were concerned I had instructed them not to take intimate photographs of persons of any age, only sites showing injuries, and that these would be taken on the request of the senior police officer investigating a criminal offence. Dr Higgs informed me that she had the authority of Chief Superintendent Bruce for the photographs to be taken. Dr Higgs told me that she required the photographs already taken by police officers at her request. I told her that I was in possession of the photographs and negatives and that I would not allow these out of my possession. The photographs did not assist in proving any criminal offence.'

Was it frustration that drove Dr Higgs to tell Walls that she considered it pointless carrying on the conversation any longer? Was it out of her distress that the children who had been confined to her care, either by referral from social services, or from family doctors because the children had ailments that required hospital treatment, were not going to be taken into the hospital for assessment on allegations of sexual abuse? Was it because the police officer was unsympathetic? Was it because he was standing in the way of protecting children?

Or was the deep-seated anxiety that Dr Marietta Higgs felt that evening actually for the children of Mary and Joseph Dixon? The children she had first diagnosed as having been sexually abused in July the previous year in Newcastle? The children she had seen in the foster home in September and again in an outpatients' clinic on 9 February? The children whose case was about to come up before a magistrates' court after the upcoming bank holiday weekend, when the interim care order would be brought before the law? Is that why she had said to the police officer that she wanted to 'educate the magistrates in child abuse'?

Vera and Angela Dixon were at this moment on ward nine of Middlesbrough General Hospital, again in the direct care of Dr Higgs. Was it because of them she wanted the photographs from Inspector Walls? Were these the photographs and negatives which he had in his possession? Could this be the concern that so distressed Dr Higgs that when the police officer refused she asked him to leave her hospital ward? What were the thoughts that went through the mind of Dr Higgs this May evening as she prepared to return to the ward? Was she worried about the court proceedings the following week? Or was she simply turning her mind to the next patients, the Allans, the foster parents of Vera and Angela Dixon, who were due about now with their own three children?

Tomorrow would be the Saturday of the bank holiday weekend. It was the last bank holiday before the calling of a general election. There would also be district elections on the first Thursday of the month. If public opinion could be said to have any concerns at all, it was that Margaret Thatcher would go again to the country and seek her third successive win. Many people in this month of May stood on the brink of important events; but none stood closer to the brink than Marietta Higgs. Her life was about to undergo a seismic change that would alter its pattern for all time. Equally, she was about to alter the pattern of many other people's lives – parents and children – for all time.

Did she know this as she saw the police officer off the premises? Did she think this would be the end of police cooperation? Was she disappointed that while she worked so hard others gave so little; that while she diagnosed sexual abuse others looked upon her askance, would not investigate, or did so half-heartedly; and now would not give her the negatives or take the photographs so vital to her diagnosis? For reflex anal dilatation without back-up photographs was worse than useless, a mere verbal or written description of a medical technique. It would be the photograph – the gaping anus – that would underpin the practitioners' case in courts of law.

However, as this first day of May drew to a close, there was work to do on ward nine. At any minute now Matthew and Ruth Allan would arrive with their three children. They would be the first of the hundred and more children who in the months of May and June would be diagnosed as having been sexually abused. The Allans, parents in their own right, foster parents and childminders, lovers of children, had their own forebodings as they drove into the forecourt of the hospital and looked for a parking space.

The Allan family too were about to embark upon a venture they were not likely to forget.

15

Ruth Allan described thus her family and extra-family activities: 'My husband and I adore children and we like to look after them. I also realize there are a lot of children who are less fortunate than my own children and we wanted to see if we could do something to help them and give them a happy home.' There had never been any complaints about their fostering or childminding capabilities: social services regularly visited their home and they were well known to both health visitors and social workers. There were also, of course, solicitors and guardians *ad litem* who would come by on professional business dealing with the children in care.

Matthew Allan had a steady white-collar job but nevertheless helped around the home whenever he could. He described himself as 'supportive' of his wife. They had a large rambling house, with four bedrooms, one downstairs, three upstairs; there was also what Matthew Allan described as a 'granny flat', where his mother lived, a large living room, a kitchen and dining room. The granny flat was self-contained and his mother had lived there with the Allans since the early eighties. She did not mind the noise and, like her son and daughter-in-law, she enjoyed the children's chatter, their commotion, with the house big enough to absorb it, so that they could all jolly along and appreciate each other's company.

Matthew and Ruth Allan had already met Dr Higgs. Although in September she had come unannounced to their home, she had nonetheless been welcome. She had come to see Vera and Angela Dixon. Vera was, after all, her first diagnosis of sexual abuse and it was right that she should visit them in their new foster home; right that she should look through the Allan family album; right that she should take with her some photographs of the Dixon children which had been taken upon their arrival; right that she should want some later photographs, to be taken at Christmas-time, when the festive season had settled upon the foster home.

The photographs reflected Dr Higgs' satisfaction with the development of the children, and she also needed them for the forthcoming court case where the interim order would have to be taken to a full hearing. Dr Higgs was garnering her own evidence for these proceedings. She wanted to show the contrast between the children upon their arrival in foster care, when they had been 'withdrawn and miserable', as Ruth Allan recalled, and later when they had visibly 'improved' in care. The children had also put on weight, a fact noted in the regular checks by the health visitors.

There had been the visit to outpatients' on 9 February. And then on 30 April, with the court case only a few days off, there was another appointment at Middlesbrough General Hospital. On this day Matthew Allan's car was being serviced and he was therefore unable to take his wife over to the General; Ruth took the children in a taxi. Dr Higgs carried out her usual thorough examination. She examined the bottoms of both Vera and Angela. She said both bottoms were 'abnormal'. This would have caused considerable surprise to Mary and Joseph Dixon, had they known or been told; for while there had been a diagnosis of sexual abuse to Vera there had been none made on baby Angela. Now Angela, approaching her second birthday, was also discovered to have an 'abnormal' bottom.

'Do you want me to show you?' Dr Higgs asked.

She showed Ruth Allan the child's bottom.

'But when I saw Angela her bottom did not look abnormal,' Ruth Allan recalled.

Did she know what she was meant to be looking at?

'The anus was supposed to have been dilated.'

Ruth Allan was told that the children would have to stay in hospital overnight. The following day, 1 May, she returned to Middlesbrough General Hospital with her husband. They had come to see the foster children but also Dr Higgs. On this occasion, Dr Higgs was more emphatic than she had been the evening before. As Ruth Allan would recall: 'She told us that while in our care they had been sexually abused.' There was no indication as to *how* they had been abused, only the diagnosis that their anuses were dilated. Ruth Allan pointed out that when she had seen Angela's bottom the previous day there had been no dilatation and the bottom looked normal.

'Well, it did later on,' Dr Higgs replied. 'And I did not have her in the right position.'

Having the matter put to them as bluntly as this, the Allans staggered from the hospital in a state of shock. The Dixon children had come to them 'frightened, a bit cowed, timorous' as Matthew Allan recalled, but they had developed well, they had come out of their shells and after a while they had become normal children, getting up to all sorts of childish pranks in the Allan household. There were even plans for adoption: 'It was our understanding that the [county] council wished us to adopt them and we said that we were more than happy to do that because we said that we wished to continue to work with these children.'

The Allans even had a good working relationship with the children's guardian *ad litem*. But that 1 May in the hospital, on being apprised of the true extent of Dr Higgs' diagnosis, as Matthew Allan recalled: 'We tried to explain to Dr Higgs that these children had come to us in the state that they had, and how they had progressed mentally and physically, and the way in which the elder child's speech had improved dramatically, but to no avail. It was just of no consequence.' The shock also turned out to be too much for Ruth Allan: 'She burst into tears,' her husband said. 'We were both very depressed. Dr Higgs seemed surprised that we had been upset by the allegation. The two foster children were very distressed because they had never been left with anyone since they came to us, such was the state they were in.'

Having lost their foster children, the Allans were still in a daze, pottering about their own home, when at four o'clock that afternoon there was a knock on the door. Two social workers stood there. They were the fostering officer and the child abuse officer. There had been a case conference that morning and it had been decided to remove Vera and Angela Dixon from the foster home. Worse was to come. The conference had decided their own children should be examined 'as soon as possible'.

The Allans had no objection to their children being examined, but they became distinctly queasy when they learned the examination would be by Dr Higgs: 'I did not want Dr Higgs examining them because I felt she had made a grave mistake with the Dixon children and, although I had nothing to hide, I did not want her making the same mistake with my own children,' Ruth Allan recalled. One social services officer said she did not want too many doctors involved. Besides, there was only one doctor on Teesside qualified for 'that sort of examination'. The social services officer had ungraciously left out Dr Geoffrey Wyatt, but it was made plain to the Allans that their children would be required to go to Middlesbrough General Hospital and submit to Dr Higgs. Otherwise a place of safety order would be taken out on their children.

Matthew Allan, in desperation – fully aware of the consequences of a medical diagnosis of sexual abuse – called the family solicitor. It turned out he was unavailable and so another solicitor was contacted. The first safeguard that crossed the mind of Matthew Allan was that he would need his own family doctor present at any examination;

and the solicitor added a proviso of his own – that he should be made aware of any future developments. The social services officers, however, were adamant they did not want too many doctors involved but eventually relented 'as a special concession'. They did agree that no action would be taken in respect of the Allan children unless the solicitor was first informed.

The promise was not kept.

The Allans were asked to take their children to the hospital that very evening, but prior to their departure a friend of the family came along. This was Marlene Taylor, a single mother who had brought her two children with her: Mandy aged six and Luke aged thirteen months. The Allans had fostered Mandy while Marlene had given birth to Luke. She had called by that evening because, this being a Friday, Matthew Allan would take her daughter to the Girls' Brigade, along with his own children. This had been their regular routine since the Allans had ceased fostering Mandy. But there would be no going to Girls' Brigade that evening; and with the Allan children being hurried and packed in the car, which was now back from the garage, there was little Marlene could do but stay with her own children in the Allan household and await their return.

At the hospital the Allans were met by their own family doctor and another social worker. All three children were then examined by Dr Higgs in the presence of the family doctor and the Allans. The examination was extremely thorough. Dr Higgs found Selina to be 'friendly and cooperative', although on the heavy side; Rebecca was generally well, though she suffered from asthma. Eleanor also had asthma, for which she received regular treatment: 'She had also been under care at North Tees General Hospital because of failure to thrive and diarrhoea for which no medical cause had been found.'

She then turned to an examination of the lower parts. She found that Selina, the eldest child, had an anal verge thickened, and fissures, and the hymen had an irregular scarred edge; she found Rebecca, the middle girl, with gross reflex relaxation and dilatation, and a hymen that was swollen and slightly reddened, with a scarred hymenal edge. Eleanor, aged two, she found with reflex relaxation and dilatation of the anus. As the doctor wrote, the hymen was not 'visualized'.

In her paediatric report, Dr Higgs wrote: 'My conclusions were that all three girls had signs consistent with sexual abuse. All had reflex relaxation and dilatation of the anal sphincter which has been consistent with anal abuse.' The family doctor who had assisted throughout the examinations was rapidly overawed by this examination and its findings and felt he could not disagree with a consultant paediatrician whose skills were so apparent. The parents, meanwhile, sought to calm their nerves. They had faith in their family doctor. Besides, even Dr Higgs could not diagnose sexual abuse where none had existed.

According to the Allans, Dr Higgs told them: 'I have examined your children and there are signs of sexual abuse. If you tell us who has done this we can help you with counselling.' Or as Dr Higgs reported the conversation: 'I expressed my concern regarding the findings to the parents in the presence of their family doctor, and also told the two social workers accompanying the parents, and the decision was made to admit the girls while further assessment of the situation took place.' She denied asking the parents who had done it. 'I do not ask parents that. It is not something I do.'

The children were led away on to ward nine and as Matthew Allan recalls: 'We were not guilty and we discussed the matter. Dr Higgs would not tell us what the grounds for her opinion were. She refused to give any details other than that. We begged and pleaded to see our children and we were refused. We were removed from the hospital because we refused to go. The reason given for our not seeing them was because we might upset them.'

As Dr Higgs recalled: 'When I said to Selina and Rebecca that they needed to stay in hospital because it looked to me as though something had been poked up their bottoms, Selina's reply was: "It must be hairs. It felt like hairs and they could have come from the sponge that daddy used!" She described how she had seen him using the sponge and then when she used it "some hairs must have got caught up her bottom".' Despite the fact that the police officer in charge of photography had now left the premises the police were called and advised of the allegations of sexual abuse. Cleveland County Council's child abuse consultant, Mrs Richardson, was also advised.

Dr Higgs interviewed the children again.

She recalled her discussions with the middle child, Rebecca, aged eight: 'After an initial discussion about family routine, including various children and adults who regularly passed through the household, discussion about Rebecca's bottom resumed. She offered the explanation that perhaps she had sat on a pencil case and a pencil might have hurt her bottom and so was asked what her bottom felt like when it was sore. She replied: "Like a stitch, a running sort of stitch." When asked to point out where it hurt, she demonstrated, on herself and on an anatomically correct doll, how it started at her right hip and then travelled to her vagina, stayed there a while then up inside and around the back to the bottom and up inside.'

Prior to their departure from the hospital, Ruth Allan told Dr Higgs how 'ridiculous' it was for her to say that their children had been abused: 'I remarked to Dr Higgs, "Look at them, how can you say they have been abused?" She said, "No, they are beautiful, well-grown girls, but they have still been sexually abused."' As for Matthew Allan, he felt the behaviour of his own doctor incomprehensible. Had he agreed with Dr Higgs or had he not? 'After the examination, of course, Dr Higgs left the room and my wife and I were left alone for quite a long time. Then the family doctor returned and we discussed the diagnosis with him. He was astounded.' He had, however, gone along with the diagnosis and when confronted with this fact some two weeks later, would say: 'I'm sorry, the events of the evening are a total haze to me now.'

On Saturday morning, 2 May, the Allans went to Middlesbrough General Hospital to see their children. As Matthew Allan recalled: 'I turned up with some clothes for the children and attempted to walk into the ward. I could see the children behind a glass screen. I went to go in and a nurse physically stopped me. I asked her why and she said: "I'm sorry, Dr Higgs won't let you in." I left the clothes and then I could see the children were visibly distressed by my presence, so I left quickly.' The Allans returned home. The social worker whom they had seen that morning at the hospital called at the family home at lunchtime. He brought with him the dreaded place of safety order.

Within the space of two days the Allans had lost five children, three of their own and two foster children. It was clear that their elder children were now also being subjected to interview at Middlesbrough General Hospital. The interviews were being conducted by Dr Higgs herself and a woman police constable, who had spoken to Selina and Rebecca individually. Another representative of social services had been called in. This was none other than Mrs Richardson, head of the child abuse service.

She had been called in by a divisional director of social services because it was a bank holiday weekend and he wished her to stand in pending the allocation to the case of an experienced social worker. This was explained later by Mrs Richardson.

Notwithstanding the fact that the children had only been in

hospital a few hours, that they had been deprived of their parents, that they had spent the night in strange hospital beds, Mrs Richardson later wrote: 'Dr Higgs was present because the children had clearly formed an attachment to her.' Mrs Richardson found the picture that Selina painted for her was of a happy family life with her parents, her sisters, two foster children and her grandmother. Uncle Sam had lived in the house till his marriage the previous August, but he still visited and played games with all three of the children.

The weekly routine in the Allan household consisted of piano lessons on Monday, the St John Ambulance Cadets on Tuesday, shopping with her parents on Wednesday. Thursday was a night in, and there was the Girls' Brigade on Friday. Household duties consisted of bathing, washing-up, preparing breakfast, and laundry. This description of everyday life in a Cleveland home, with a mix of indoor and outdoor activities, with no mention of television or radio, may no doubt gladden the hearts of future sociologists.

But the painful, distressing subject of anal abuse had now to be taken up by Dr Higgs, for whom the children had formed 'an attachment'. Selina repeated the earlier statements she had made to Dr Higgs – about hairs on the sponge, the stitch. Selina, however, made no disclosure of sex abuse: 'Selina told us she did not want anyone to get into trouble. She stated that something had happened to her several times. She remained distressed as she spoke to us. She was unable to tell us who may be responsible for the "horrible" feelings which she had. In order to assist Selina, it was suggested that she write a name for us. Selina agreed to this and left the room to go to the toilet. On her return, she wrote: "It's nobody." The interview had now been going on for two hours. As Mrs Richardson succinctly wrote: 'Selina was obviously reluctant to speak with us.'

It was now the turn of Rebecca, aged eight. Mrs Richardson found Rebecca 'bright and talkative'. She too, it seemed, enjoyed a normal household routine. The foster children would go to bed first, followed by Rebecca, followed by Selina. Baby Eleanor, aged two, would go to bed at different times, depending on how easy it was to settle her. Both Selina and Rebecca, however, were describing family lives that had been destroyed. The foster children were no more. Never again would they set foot in the Allan home. And if Uncle Sam had popped in to play games with his delightful nieces, that part of his life would change too, for in the months to come he would not even know where his nieces were, let alone play games with them in the Allan household.

What this disclosure session was doing was dismantling the happy home life of a series of children and grown-ups. There was never any doubt in the mind of those doing the interviewing that they were right. Nor did anyone find it strange that while Mrs Richardson had been brought along, until such time as 'an experienced child worker' was available, it was the consultant paediatrician who asked the social worker's questions. As Mrs Richardson recalled it: 'Following the break, Dr Higgs directed the conversation towards abuse. Rebecca had previously told Dr Higgs that she had sat on her pencil case and that a pencil had stuck up her bottom [the record of Dr Higgs stated that *Rebecca had offered the explanation that she had perhaps sat on a pencil case and a pencil might have gone up her bottom*]. Dr Higgs explained that that could not account for the appearance of Rebecca's bottom. Rebecca described suffering considerable pain. She said that there was pain in her back and front bottom like a stitch, as if she had been running.'

Mrs Richardson: 'She told us that one night when she was watching television the "stitch" hurt her very badly. The pain remained until the following day, such that she was forced to tell her parents.' Rebecca described the stitch as overlying her right hip, then moving towards her front bottom, that is, her vagina: 'She said that the "stitch" remained in her front bottom for a while before moving to the back and staying there for a while. The pain had been inside her front and back bottom.' Rebecca then described how her father applied cream to her front and back bottom after a shower. She had been wearing a vest and dressing gown. She had gone with her father to her parents' room: 'Her father checked that the other children were asleep. He left the bedroom door open.'

According to Mrs Richardson: 'Rebecca described lying on her back. Her father rubbed cream around and inside her front bottom with his finger. Rebecca then described lying on her front. Her father rubbed cream gently around her bottom with four fingers. The cream was also rubbed inside her bottom. Rebecca clearly stated that it was "the stinging" which hurt her – her father did not hurt her.' After her father had rubbed in the cream she got dressed and went to bed.

Rebecca, however, could not remember when such incidents had occurred, except to say it was a long time ago, although 'it had happened on several occasions. Rebecca could remember an occasion when her father had rubbed cream on to her bottom when it was not hurting, in order to make sure it did not hurt.' The youngest child, Eleanor, was not of an age to make disclosures; but her eight-year-old sister was able to claim that she recalled Eleanor in some pain, 'crying and pointing to her front and back bottom'.

Rebecca had used anatomically correct dolls to describe the cream-application process to the interviewers. There was now no doubt in the mind of Mrs Richardson that all three children had been abused. She was also clear that Matthew Allan had been 'implicated'. Notwithstanding the length of these interviews, the process was to be repeated the following day. This was so that the 'disclosures' of the children could be committed to video for evidential purposes. There were, however, difficulties, for Selina, who had made no disclosures, became 'tearful and distressed throughout'.

The 'attachment' which the child had formed for Dr Higgs had clearly run its course. On this day, a Sunday, the trio of Dr Higgs, Mrs Richardson and a woman police constable was present again, with another social worker to operate the video. The reason for Selina's upset soon became clear. She had had enough of hospitals and interviews, of anatomically correct dolls, and wished to go home. She disliked being separated from her parents. The trio had therefore to explain why it was she could not go home. All that Selina knew was that there had been hairs on a sponge. Her distress and reluctance did not dissipate and the only fresh information the trio were to obtain was that 'Mr and Mrs Allan had family rules preventing the children from going upstairs without permission and from going into the parents' bedroom'.

As Mrs Richardon recalled: 'Selina clearly regarded her home as a safe place. She stated she trusted the people speaking with her but was unable to perceive the need for herself to be protected.' There would be a better response from Rebecca. She told the trio that her father had applied cream over a period of time: 'Rebecca had put her nightdress over her face so that she was unable to see what happened.' Her mother had only applied cream once, 'though she did it differently'. Her father had the job of doing so 'because he did it better'.

The unease of Selina was quickly communicated to Rebecca, two years her junior. She too remained disconsolate. Both children were homesick. There is no record of what the two year old felt. As Mrs Richardson reported: 'Rebecca remained unable to connect the pain with her father's behaviour. She repeated that her father had not hurt her.' That evening a planning meeting was convened to discuss the future of the children. The Allans were not invited. In fact they were not to know it had taken place until many months later. Decisions were made on the future of their children: that wardship proceedings should be deferred pending further investigation.

The social worker who could handle the disclosure sessions was now available. This was BASPCAN member Mrs Madge Bray. Cleveland Social Services would find enough to keep her busy and in the next weeks she would find herself involved with the children of *six* families. In fact, there would be so much work that Mrs Bray herself would complain: 'At the time I was involved in Cleveland,' she recalled, 'I was very aware of the appalling problems with regard to lack of facilities.' She also remembered walking through the full and hectic children's wards at Middlesbrough General Hospital and being accosted by social workers who 'desperately' wanted her to interview those children under their care who allegedly had been sexually abused.

Ironically, though the irony would be lost to those in Cleveland Social Services who made the decision, Mrs Bray would begin where she left off. For having visited the Allan household but a few weeks earlier, having written a report on their care of the foster children, Vera and Angela Dixon, now she was called upon to interview not only Vera and Angela Dixon yet again in their second foster home, but also the Allan children and their former playmates, Rebecca and Selina.

16

Other monumental decisions were taken this May weekend. For if Vera and Angela Dixon had been abused in the foster home, if Matthew Allan had abused his own three children, how many more had he interfered with in the course of his years with social services as a foster father? A trawl would therefore be made of all those children who had been in his care over the past few years. This required more than a peep at the social services' records; it required police assistance and involvement. The breakdown with the police had not yet become total, and with the help of their records Cleveland Social Services were able to put together a list of all those children they had fostered out to the Allans and who should now be brought in for medical examination.

The list fell into two categories: those who had been fostered on a residential basis, such as the Dixons, and those who had been there on a daily basis, when the Allans had acted as childminders. Over the past year, only three children had fallen into the first category, but there were difficulties with those children minded on a daily basis – some eight or nine of them. A bush telegraph became operative. One mother took her child to see her own local doctor, who diagnosed no abuse, and others promptly declined any invitation to have their children examined by Dr Higgs at Middlesbrough General Hospital.

Among the children who fell into the first category was young Peter Chapman who had been with the Allans for about a year. His mother had one other child, but she had been unable to cope as the head of a single-parent family. She therefore placed Peter into voluntary care. He was fostered to the Allans and she had regular access. The child was three years old in April 1987. He had been fostered to the Allans when he had been ten months old and had spent six months in their care. This was before the birth of the Allans' third child, Eleanor. Peter returned again for six months and then in February and March 1987 he was to stay again with the Allans, after which time he was returned to his mother.

Peter, having been traced through his mother, was now diagnosed as having been sexually abused. His mother was told that her child had been abused while in care. As one divisional director of social services put it: 'I think the reason for wanting to inform parents and to ask for their cooperation in terms of medical examination, and talking to the children, was mainly that, if they had been sexually abused while in our care, parents should know about that and that was an important aspect of our making the decision to go further rather than to just leave the possibility that children may have been abused in our care.' There was the additional implication that, if the children had been abused, there would be subsequent behavioural problems.

It was energetic and efficient of the divisional director to want to tell parents that their children might have been abused while in care because there might be a problem of 'unexplained behaviour'; but no one in social services appeared to grasp that of all those children now being examined and confirmed for alleged sexual abuse none had behavioural problems *before* they went to the hospital. None had been reported. None had been noticed. The divisional director, however, was doing the best he could with the information that he had. Therefore with no one from social services challenging the merit of the diagnosis, or urging caution in the handling of child sexual abuse, the trawl went on.

Another child who had been in the Allans' care was Kathleen Daily. Her mother, Arlene Daily, had an elder child who was jealous of the newborn. Arlene was an unmarried mother, and in a state of confusion and quandry had not known what to do with her child. The Allans had fostered the child for just a week. Later, when the mother settled down and wanted her child back, the Allans returned Kathleen on 25 July 1986. This child too was now examined and diagnosed as having been recently sexually abused. But there was a problem for social services. A problem that had not been anticipated when the decision had been taken to trawl the foster children who had been through the Allans' home.

The problem was this: *since Kathleeen Daily had been only a week with the Allans, and this in the summer of 1986, it could hardly be claimed that the Allans had perpetrated this new sexual abuse on a child whose whereabouts, in May 1987, were clearly unknown to them. The child had in the meantime been fostered to another home. Therefore, the child must have been abused in this second foster home. A diagnosis of sexual abuse having been made, Cleveland Social Services felt they now had to check out the children of this foster home. This they did. Perhaps it came as no surprise to Cleveland Social Services that another child there was diagnosed as having been sexually abused, but since the child was now back with its own mother no place of safety order was taken out.*

There was also the third child who had been fostered by the Allans. This was the child of Marlene Taylor. Marlene was the family friend who had stayed with the Allans to help them through the trauma of these first days of May. It had not occurred to her that her own children might be in danger of being called to Middlesbrough General Hospital for examination. But then it had never occurred to her that Matthew Allan might be a child abuser, a molester, and therefore she had felt perfectly comfortable staying with the Allans over these few days, her own children with her.

Her anxieties for the Allans would now be converted into anxieties for herself.

On 6 May there was another knock on the door of the Allans' home. There were two more social workers on the doorstep. This time they had come calling upon Marlene Taylor. One of the social workers was known to Marlene Taylor and the other was a team leader. Six-year-old Mandy Taylor was at school at the time, so Marlene was in the Allan house with thirteen-month-old Luke. Was Marlene Taylor aware that her children were in moral danger? They must be taken to Middlesbrough General Hospital immediately. This panicked Marlene Taylor: the sort of blind panic that can overwhelm a mother when she fears that her children are about to be taken from her.

She refused the request of the social workers point blank. As she would later recall: 'I said, "No, you can take them to see anybody you like, any other doctor in the country. I do not want Dr Higgs examining my kids." They said, "If that's your attitude, I'll go back to the office for a place of safety order and we'll take them that way."' In the face of such a threat, Marlene Taylor yielded. The knock on the door had come at half past eleven in the morning. Marlene therefore collected Mandy from school and the two children were at Middlesbrough General Hospital to be examined at around one o'clock.

There was a long wait before Dr Higgs arrived.

Sitting waiting for the doctor, it had not occurred to Marlene Taylor that Dr Higgs would wish to examine *both* children. She had understood that only the eldest, Mandy, would be looked at, for it was Mandy who had been fostered by the Allans. She became completely 'shocked and distressed' when she learned that Dr Higgs proposed to examine not only Mandy but Luke as well. 'I explained that Luke had not been fostered and had never been alone with Mr and Mrs Allan, whom I knew anyway as friends.'

It was the understanding of Dr Higgs, however, that the Taylor children had been regular visitors to the Allan household and had stayed overnight more than once. Marlene Taylor was looked upon as an 'over-anxious' parent who regularly brought her children to the outpatients' clinic for attention. She seemed to be 'a very caring mother'. First Mandy was examined. She lay first on her side and was then put on all fours. The response of Dr Higgs, according to Marlene, was that 'Mandy had definitely been sexually abused anally'. Now it was the turn of Luke. As Marlene recalled: 'By this time I was so distressed I was unable to protest other than to repeat that he had never been fostered and that he had been with me all the time since he was born.'

Upon examination, Dr Higgs said that Luke 'had also been sexually abused, probably, but I could not be absolutely sure'. Marlene

Taylor recalled that Dr Higgs then took the children to be admitted, although she did not want them admitted: 'Dr Higgs made me believe that admitting them was compulsory, but I later found out that as they were not subject to a place of safety order, I could have refused to let them stay.' No one told Marlene Taylor this at the time. The effect was the same. Marlene Taylor now had her own children taken from her too.

Within the space of six days, therefore, Vera and Angela Dixon would find themselves reunited with their playmates and foster sisters Selina and Rebecca and Eleanor; and now they would be joined by their playmate Mandy, who went with them to the Girls' Brigade, and her baby brother Luke. None of them would be lacking in company. And if they wished to find new playmates on ward nine of Middlesbrough General Hospital this would not be difficult. Nor would they need to bother those children who were on the ward because they were casualty patients; they need only step around the ward to find others, like themselves, suddenly taken from home, deprived of their parents, all of them well children, but all of them subject to the same diagnosis of reflex anal dilatation that confirmed they had been allegedly sexually abused.

In the first few days of May some eighteen children would be so diagnosed; the figure quickly became twenty-five, and from there it would move rapidly towards the hundred mark. Why had all this come about in the months of May and June? Was it because Dr Higgs now had sufficient confidence in her own diagnosis? After all, she had had it confirmed by Dr Morrell, by Dr Wyatt – who was now convinced that this was a new method of detecting child abuse – and she had had it confirmed by none other than Dr Jane Wynne. If there had been doubts before they were swept aside.

Or was the trigger the Allan family, and the fact that not only the Dixon children but their own, and then the Taylor children, and then other children such as Peter Chapman and Kathleen Daily, had all been diagnosed as sexually abused, thus suddenly pushing up the numbers? Or was this the tip of an iceberg that was rising in the water, that was predictable, that was inevitable, and that with the improved diagnostic technique of Dr Higgs made this a phenomenon of our age? Dr Higgs would say it came about because of referrals from social services. Social services would say it came about because of the influx from the Allan foster home.

Others would note that the increased numbers of children diagnosed as sexually abused had in fact presented themselves at outpatients' clinics with routine ailments such as croup and asthma and infection; one would go in with a bump on the head. So many would be diagnosed, however, that not even the authorities knew how many had come into their hands, and on one evening there was a head count on ward nine of Middlesbrough General Hospital to ascertain the true numbers. Getting the figures right might be a bit frustrating, but for Mrs Richardson there was no doubt that the children would keep coming in and she fully anticipated ten, twelve or even eighteen diagnoses a week.

'I thought we would have to be prepared for that kind of number,' she stated. 'I think in Leeds, for example, where even though their immediate upsurge has levelled off, I understand that it is not unusual for them to receive an average of ten referrals a week.' Whatever the figures, whatever the diagnosis, whatever the enthusiasm for place of safety orders evinced by Cleveland County Council's social services, whatever the doubts of the police and other doctors and paediatricians, whatever the anguish of parents and mystification and distress of children, whatever the sincerity of all the participants, whatever motivated their drive and enthusiasm, whatever were the real issues, as to who had ultimate power over children – bureaucracies or parents – those first few days in May saw a rising tide of human distress that would soon engulf not only hospital authorities and social services alike, but the whole population of Cleveland.

The great child abuse drama of 1987 was on.

Book Two

THE ROAD TO SALEM

17

Mrs Sue Richardson had been appointed child abuse consultant of Cleveland County Council's social services on 1 June 1986.

She had been appointed in the wake of the report on the death of little Jasmine Beckford, who had been killed by her stepfather, Morris Beckford, in a suburb of London. There had been a public outcry at her death because it was revealed that she had earlier been removed from her family because of suspected physical abuse but allowed to return home by Brent Social Services. Such was the sense of public outrage that a general enquiry ensued and a final report was submitted to Brent Borough Council and the Brent District Health Authority. The enquiry laid no blame on any one individual, but criticized the lack of explicit procedures and the general level of awareness of child abuse among the variety of agencies which had responsibility in this field.

Morris Beckford was convicted of manslaughter at the Old Bailey on 20 March 1985 and sentenced to ten years' imprisonment. Jasmine's mother, Beverly Lorrington, pleaded guilty to child neglect and was sentenced to eighteen months' imprisonment. The enquiry suggested improvements in the general area of child care law that were taken to heart in Cleveland. Their response was to appoint Mrs Richardson as child abuse consultant – the first county to create such a post. Sue had been with Cleveland Social Services since 1975 and had been specializing in social work for some fifteen years.

She had first met Dr Marietta Higgs through the British Association for the Study and Prevention of Child Abuse and Neglect, BASPCAN. Such was her enthusiasm for this organization that she was arranging its regional conference in June 1987. Mrs Richardson had met Marietta on only two occasions prior to her arrival on Teesside, and had spoken to her on the telephone. Nevertheless, the future consultant paediatrician and the child abuse consultant were sufficiently friendly to be writing to each other as *Dear Marietta* and *Dear Sue* some months prior to Marietta taking up her appointment.

One such letter was written in October, another, which consisted of a compliments slip, was dated the end of October and a third letter was written in November. Mrs Richardson had specialized in working with children and families throughout her career. In her new job she was the custodian of the child abuse register and handled case consultancy, advice, preparation and planning. It was

Mrs Richardson who persuaded her superior, Mr Mike Bishop, to hire Ms Deborah Glassbrook, who had worked with *Childwatch*, the television campaign opened by Miss Esther Rantzen.

The BBC *Childwatch* programme was launched by Miss Rantzen on 23 October 1986. The programme, as Miss Rantzen explained, was about cruelty to children. 'Our aim', she said 'is to find ways of protecting children, of saving them from suffering.' This was more than a television programme. It was also an opportunity to launch a brand-new campaign in the United Kingdom in the style of similar campaigns in the United States, Holland and Sweden.

Miss Rantzen had in mind a free national helpline to be called Childline. This was not to be an investigative agency nor a body which attempted to solve children's problems. As its own documents pointed out, Childline was rather about offering a confidential telephone counselling service offering care, support and concern for *all* children and for *all* purposes: 'Childline exists because there are large numbers of children with problems.' The children should be listened to, comforted and offered confidentiality.

The *Childwatch* programme had an important impact on professionals in some counties. Social services in Lothian, Scotland, mobilized thirty-six social workers to handle what was expected to be a flood of referrals when the first free calls came to be made to Childline. There was a similar mobilization in Cleveland. It was expected that children would respond by telephoning their distress to the new Childline numbers and that Childline would then make referrals to social services. In fact, while 3395 children used the free telephone there were only seventy-six referrals to social services nationwide.

Dr Liam Donaldson, regional medical officer of the Northern Regional Health Authority, employers of Dr Higgs and Dr Wyatt, was impressed by the *Childwatch* programmes of 23 and 30 October 1986, and wrote: 'After seeing the Childline television programmes, I had become aware that the problem of child sexual abuse was a growing one.' He gave 'serious consideration' to widening the scope of the regional health authority into this area but felt that essentially it was a matter for district rather than regional authorities and there were a number of other 'national priorities' yet to be taken up by the authority. National guidelines were also awaited.

Of her relations with Dr Higgs, Mrs Richardson had this to say: 'Dr Higgs' appointment in January 1987 was welcomed by the department, since she was known within the region to have the interest and expertise of which the department was in need. I was also aware of Dr Higgs' work via BASPCAN North East, where I knew she was respected by colleagues from a range of agencies, including members of Northumbria Constabulary, with whom she had worked closely. Cases were identified within the department prior to Dr Higgs' arrival in readiness for her assessment.'

What was not known to Mrs Richardson was that Dr Higgs had been appointed to Middlesbrough as a neonatologist. How had it come about that there were cases already prepared for Dr Higgs prior to arrival? Did this mean that children in care for a variety of reasons were to be escorted to Dr Higgs for 'assessment'? Did Mrs Richardson mean that any child on the child abuse register would equally be an obvious candidate for such 'assessment'? Mrs Richardson was quick to point out that none of these cases prepared in advance was of sex abuse: 'Some of the new cases were rather difficult cases of physical abuse, or failure to thrive, which the department was having difficulty taking a decision on.'

Prior to taking up her post, however, Dr Higgs had made contact with her fellow BASPCAN colleague in her role as child abuse consultant. She was asking for background information, such as procedural documents, as part of her preparation for coming to the area. Mrs Richardson provided these documents and considered this to be 'a positive initiative'. But these documents had nothing to do with neonatal care, a subject not within the purview of Mrs Richardson; nor were they documents of a procedural or background nature only. Their orientation was clear: they were about child sexual abuse in Cleveland.

For what Mrs Richardson sent up to the private address of her friend Marietta in Newcastle were full details of Cleveland's child abuse register as it stood on 30 June 1986, with the numbers of children who had been removed from April to June 1986, how many from April to June were new cases, and a total at the end of March, with another total for the end of June. Some of this information was actually typed by Mrs Richardson personally. There was also an indication of the number of families involved and where referrals came from. Past year figures were also communicated, and so even before setting foot in Middlesbrough General Hospital Marietta Higgs had a profile of Cleveland: a profile that covered physical injury, physical neglect, emotional abuse, failure to thrive.

And sexual abuse.

Towards the end of the month, on 24 October 1986, Mrs

Richardson was in touch with Marietta again, this time sending her a report of a working party on the identification and management of child sexual abuse that had been published some five months earlier, in May 1986. This was a twenty-nine-page document on the front of which Sue wrote: 'I would be interested in your comments on attached working party report re sexual abuse (not all of which I agree with).' She signed herself: *Sue R.*

Mrs Richardson would later state that she never heard from Marietta about this document, but on 7 November 1986, after an exchange of telephone conversations, further documents were sent to Marietta. There was a briefing document prepared in anticipation of the first *Childwatch* programme. There was a briefing document on residential family assessment in line with the wishes of Marietta to establish a Steiner-type unit on Teesside. There was another document entitled 'Child Sexual Abuse Management and Disclosure'.

And there was yet another entitled 'Notes for Managers re Child Sexual Abuse; Particular Questions to Ask a Sexually Abused Child in an Investigative Interview; General Conditions for the Interview with the Child; How to Talk to a Child who has been Assaulted', and a note from the child abuse assessment team. All of the blueprints were there on how to deal with sexual and physical abuse in Cleveland, and all of them were sent to Marietta Higgs at her home address some months before her arrival at Middlesbrough General Hospital.

This did not mean Mrs Richardson knew Marietta 'particularly well' before her arrival. She knew of her reputation and she also knew of her interests. Marietta took an early opportunity to visit the social services department in Middlesbrough and meet Sue's bosses, Mike Bishop, director of social services, and his deputy Bill Walton. According to Mrs Richardson, Marietta had made her own arrangements to visit the office. The visit took place on 23 January. Marietta made it clear that she wished to work as part of a 'multi-disciplinary team'. According to Walton she was welcomed because of her expertise in the field of child abuse: 'I think my staff were aware of the work of Dr Higgs because she had been involved in cases in the Cleveland area before she arrived.' The case that Bill Walton had in mind was that of Vera and Angela Dixon.

It was the recollection of Bill Walton that Dr Higgs had worked with Dr Christine Cooper, who in her own time had been of some assistance to Cleveland County Council's social services department.

Mrs Richardson explained: 'Dr Cooper offered assistance to professionals dealing with child abuse by providing consultancy, advice or diagnosis for any child about whom the department was concerned.'

Marietta expressed an interest in developing resources for the residential assessment of children with their families. Now that she was on Teesside she wished vigorously to pursue the Steiner-Unit concept that she had brought with her from Newcastle. Again, in the words of Mrs Richardson: 'From the time of Dr Higgs' appointment, therefore, much closer contact was established with paediatricians in Middlesbrough and a fruitful working relationship began to develop with Dr Higgs contributing to multi-disciplinary assessment with other professionals, particularly social workers, sometimes via membership of core groups.' In fact, such a relationship had already been established the previous year.

An example of this 'fruitful working relationship' could be seen in the case of Anne Thomlinson, aged seven and suffering from 'thrush'. The 'thrush' had been caused by an accident when Anne had slipped getting out of the bath. She had cut the inner wall of her vagina. The 'thrush' had appeared shortly afterwards and had stayed with the young child ever since. She had had a series of visits to doctors and paediatricians and the 'thrush' had been kept under control with the use of prescribed creams.

In 1984, when Anne was five years old, the Thomlinsons lived in the country and Anne attended the local village school. As Bill Thomlinson recalled: 'It was on one afternoon as my wife Kim called to collect Anne from school that Anne's teacher informed her that the head teacher would like to see her. A meeting took place during which the head teacher told Kim that Anne had been "masturbating" in class. Kim's initial reaction was one of shock, but she quickly reviewed what the teacher had said and pointed out that Anne was more likely to have been scratching herself to relieve the irritation caused by a vaginal disorder called "thrush".'

The head teacher confessed herself 'totally ignorant' of 'thrush', what it constituted, what kind of infection it was, how it could spread, or if it could spread at all. The head teacher's ignorance was quickly passed to the school nurse who brought Anne home the following day, saying that she should not be at school with such a complaint, that other children might catch it through the use of school toilets. As Bill Thomlinson would say: 'Once again a professional person proved herself to be totally ignorant of what we had been told by hospital consultants and general practitioners was a quite common ailment, and not infectious in the manner in which the nurse was implying.'

The health visitor made regular visits to the Thomlinson household. They had welcomed these visits and they had regularly discussed the progress of Anne. What they were not aware of, and would not become aware of, until two years later, was that the health visitor was making her own secret assessment of the family for possible child abuse: 'The health visitor got together with the head teacher of Anne's school and also the school nurse, and between them they compiled a report which was sent to a local paediatrician, who was then the paediatrician at Middlesbrough General Hospital.' This paediatrician had since left.

The paediatrician made an appointment to see the Thomlinsons at the hospital with their daughter Anne. The paediatrician related, in a general way, the observations and conclusions of the health visitor in her report, and directly asked if the Thomlinsons had in any way interfered with their child. As Bill Thomlinson recalled: 'I was shocked but at the same time I was impressed that the procedure dealing with this type of problem was as quick as it appeared. My reply satisfied the paediatrician and I thought the issue was resolved.'

All this happened in 1984, but two years later, in the winter of 1986, the Thomlinson family moved into the heart of Middlesbrough, and while they thought this file on their child was closed, it was actually following post-haste behind them. By an oversight on the part of his new family doctor, Bill Thomlinson was handed his own and family's medical records, and while he knew these were confidential he could not resist having a peep inside. He was startled to read a letter from the paediatrician at Middlesbrough General Hospital to his former doctor giving his conclusions after the interview with the Thomlinson parents. It highlighted a statement made by Anne to the health visitor which had apparently motivated the health visitor into making her report in the first place.

The statement read: 'I like my daddy to tickle my back in bed when Mummy is at her crystal parties.'

This innocent remark had been capable of sinister interpretation, but there was another which was equally damaging. This was a whispered remark by Anne to a friend of the same age at school. This girl, too, was aged seven. But it had nevertheless triggered off the investigation into child sexual abuse within the Thomlinson household:

'I've seen my daddy's willy. Have you seen yours?'

Anne's school friend told her own parents of this whispered conversation and her father passed it on to the headmistress at the village school. The headmistress would later deny that she had passed it on to the health visitor, but, whoever had passed it on, it was there in the file, in the medical records, and this had been the true reason why the health visitor had written to the paediatrician, the paediatrician had called the family in, and then written to the family doctor that he was satisfied there was no sexual abuse in the Thomlinson family.

This, in a sense, was an everyday story of countryfolk: the desire to protect a child, a child's chance remarks given a sinister meaning, a health visitor and head teacher and paediatrician all doing their duty; but a dark cloud of suspicion settled upon the family and eventually a record was made that would fall into other hands at a later date. That 'later date' would come at the end of April when, at their Middlesbrough home, an appointment card came through the letterbox requesting that Anne Thomlinson be taken to Middlesbrough General Hospital for an examination by Dr Higgs.

Would this be one of the cases which Mrs Richardson had 'identified within the department prior to Dr Higgs' arrival in readiness for her assessment'? Why was it that out of the blue there should be a referral to a paediatrician of whom the Thomlinsons had never heard? Was this a part of the 'fruitful working relationship' that was beginning to develop between social services and Dr Higgs? In their innocence, the Thomlinsons assumed that this request to visit the outpatients' department was linked to a kidney scan which had been discussed when Anne had last seen Dr Morrell.

In this, however, they were wrong.

18

The real behind-the-scenes story would have perplexed the Thomlinsons, had they known it.

Their former paediatrician had handed over his case notes and file to Dr Peter Morrell at Middlesbrough General Hospital in

November 1986. The case notes indicated that in the opinion of the departing paediatrician Anne had not been sexually abused. However, the child was then examined by Dr Morrell on 28 November. Dr Morrell might be said to be the third paediatrician in the Cleveland child sex abuse drama. He had been appointed to Middlesbrough General Hospital as a consultant paediatrician in 1985. He had more knowledge of child sex abuse than did his colleague, Dr Geoffrey Wyatt, for he had worked for six months in Newcastle upon Tyne with Dr Hans Steiner.

As he himself recalled: 'I was working full-time and the rest of my work in general paediatrics has involved a lot of exposure to child abuse of all kinds.' Again, unlike Dr Wyatt, Dr Morrell had attended several seminars on child abuse, but all of them when he was working out of Newcastle, none when working out of Middlesbrough General Hospital. He would not say that he had a great deal of experience of child abuse until 1987. However, as 1986 came to a close, he had become aware of the literature on child sexual abuse. And he had no hesitation in accepting that for him it was 'a major event' to read the *Lancet* article in October by Drs Wynne and Hobbs dealing with their diagnosis of reflex anal dilatation.

He was also impressed by the arrival of Dr Higgs: 'She came with particular expertise in child abuse and I have learned a lot from her,' he would say later. In 1987, he examined some fifteen children for sexual abuse, children who had been referred from a variety of sources: general practitioners, social services, casualty department, and emergency admissions to the paediatrics ward. Imbued as he had been with the diagnostic techniques of Drs Wynne and Hobbs, he had looked at the bottom of Anne Thomlinson when she had presented on 28 November.

He had not advised the parents of this fact but he had noticed some dilation of the anus. As to the diagnosis itself, Dr Morrell would have this to say: 'I believe that it is a good indicator of sexual abuse. I have looked for it in children where sexual abuse has not been suspected and have not found any signs of dilatation.' But there was no follow-up to his examination, except that when Dr Higgs arrived at Middlesbrough General Hospital he would discuss with her his findings. He had shown her the medical records and asked her opinion on the events related by the Thomlinsons that were in the file and which were described as 'past medical history'.

Dr Higgs knew all about the Thomlinsons and their daughter long before the Thomlinsons heard of her, or before the appointment card bearing her signature fell upon their doormat. Dr Morrell would have this to say of Dr Higgs: 'I have known Dr Higgs for quite some time because I worked with her in Newcastle and my opinion has not changed since she came to Middlesbrough in January 1987. I feel that she is a competent and extremely dedicated paediatrician, and I have no problem in her clinical ability. I would never doubt her clinical ability in any field of paediatrics. I recognize her special expertise in the field of child sexual abuse in all forms.' The fact that, of her own admission, Dr Higgs' knowledge of reflex anal dilatation had come from the attendance at a seminar in Leeds the year previously had eluded Dr Morrell, as indeed it would elude many others.

Unbeknown to the Thomlinsons, a case conference on their daughter Anne was held on 29 April. Social services were now getting round to past files. But why the delay from 28 November 1986 to 29 April 1987? Dr Morrell would explain it thus: 'The reason, in fact, for that is that I was concerned in November and because of that concern I wrote to the social worker. I then arranged some medical investigations to try to exclude any physical illness and for some reason the medical investigations were not done.'

The Thomlinsons had known nothing about this. Dr Morrell explained: 'The notes were put back into the file and were not brought to my notice, and there was rather a large gap therefore of three to four months before it was again brought to my notice when I was invited to a case conference.'

The case conference had been set for 29 April. But there was another paediatrician who, knowing the child's case history, and having read the medical records, decided to go ahead and allocate for her a bed at Middlesbrough General Hospital. This was Dr Marietta Higgs. Mrs Marjorie Dunne reported that Dr Marietta Higgs 'had arranged a bed at the hospital the day of the conference'. 'I can only assume that Mrs Dunne had spoken to Dr Higgs and Dr Higgs had looked at the case records,' Dr Morrell recalled. The bed was already available at the hospital even before the Thomlinsons received their appointment card, even before they had set foot over the threshold of the outpatients' clinic. Dr Higgs was invited to this conference on 29 April but she was unable to attend. Nevertheless, a decision was made to have Anne Thomlinson brought to the hospital for examination.

The appointment was made for 5 May, which was a busy day at the outpatients' clinic for Dr Marietta Higgs. Over the 5, 6, 7 and 8

May some *fourteen* children would be diagnosed as having been sexually abused. So busy was Dr Higgs that she was unable to see Anne Thomlinson immediately and she was therefore examined by the paediatrician whom she had already met on 28 November. This was Dr Morrell. Although the appointment card had been sent by Dr Higgs and the appointment was with her, Dr Morrell would later claim that the appointment had been with him all along. He carried out an examination upon Anne, but then Dr Higgs arrived and converted the examination into a joint examination. In the words of Bill Thomlinson: 'They left the room and returned some time later saying that they felt Anne should be admitted as soon as possible for tests.'

Or as Dr Morrell recalled it, he found Anne Thomlinson suffering from vaginal discharge and when her bottom was examined the anus dilated easily. At this point Dr Higgs came into the room and also conducted an examination. Dr Higgs confirmed her colleague's findings. The bed would be called for after all. But this upset the seven-year-old Anne. Why did she have to stay in hospital? Many children would make the same unscripted, unprompted plea. In order to calm her down and at the same time meet the wishes of the two consultant paediatricians, the Thomlinsons suggested that they take Anne home for that evening and that they return with her the following day. This was agreed and the Thomlinsons arrived back at nine-fifty on 6 May. Nothwithstanding the agreements made the previous day and the allocation of a bed for Anne Thomlinson from 29 April, there was no bed available and two and a half hours would pass before a bed could be found.

No one had told the Thomlinsons why they were required to bring their daughter back to the hospital, but during the long wait the parents became aware of something which they found peculiar: the hostility of the hospital staff. It was something they could not understand. A social worker arrived and said that it was 'normal practice' to interview children who were admitted into hospital. Would she mind therefore if Anne went along with her for a moment or two? It did not occur to the Thomlinsons that this was rather a strange procedure: a child entering hospital being interviewed by a social worker.

The Thomlinsons, as they sat patiently awaiting the return of their own restless daughter, were not aware that like many other parents they were now in a twilight zone where things were done differently. The interview with the social worker actually lasted two hours and

Bill Thomlinson had no alternative but to leave to collect their son Allan from school. In the absence of Bill Thomlinson, Anne returned, and her mother Kim was now asked to see Dr Morrell, together with the social worker. They told her that the opinion of both doctors – Morrell and Higgs – was that there was reflex anal dilatation and that there were signs consistent with sexual abuse. In the view later expressed by Dr Morrell there was 'vaginal abuse and probable anal abuse'.

As Bill Thomlinson recalled: 'Kim completely rejected these suggestions and insisted that Anne was not being uncooperative because there was nothing for her to be cooperative about. Nothing had happened to our little girl.' Kim challenged the diagnosis of Dr Morrell. She wanted to know whether, in his view, the trauma had not been created by Anne's continual scratching to relieve the irritation caused by 'thrush'. This would worry Dr Morrell but it was clear that the only person who knew the answers to any of these questions, as they all agreed, was Anne herself.

As Kim was the closer of the parents to her daughter, it was agreed that she should talk to Anne personally in the presence of both Dr Morrell and the social worker. Perhaps this was a curious mix, a paediatrician and a social worker talking to a seven-year-old child. But it was Dr Morrell's view that, 'my experience in this area with social services is that it is an entirely joint decision as to the placement of the child, although sometimes if, say, a social service has greater experience of the family, then they will probably contribute more.'

And in the specific case of Anne Thomlinson, Dr Morrell would have this to say: 'There was a lot of information from social services and other paediatric comment about the background. So I think there was a lot of information we had in that case.' What neither Dr Morrell nor the social worker had, however, was a disclosure from the child that anything untoward had befallen her. She categorically denied that she had been abused. However, one had to accommodate the diagnosis of two distinguished paediatricians and therefore the social worker would say that 'there was a lot being kept secret'.

Dr Morrell recorded in his own notes that the police were now informed, the police would interview Anne, and that there would be a place of safety order. He was also anxious to get hold of the medical notes. The place of safety order would be swiftly issued. Bill Thomlinson had meanwhile returned to the hospital after picking up his son from school. His wife told him what had happened. They were then left on the ward for some time. Their son, Allan, played with Anne outside the hospital. At half past four, in accordance with Dr Morrell's instructions, a policewoman arrived and wanted to speak to both of the parents in the day room.

'The policewoman told me that she had been called in by social services and that she would like to talk to us both, after which she said that the social worker and herself would be talking to Anne.' Later that evening, Dr Morrell, Kim and Bill Thomlinson talked about Anne's case: 'We expressed our feeling that Anne had not been sexually abused, but Dr Morrell stated that only after a number of sessions with the social worker and policewoman would there be any definite explanation.'

The Thomlinsons therefore settled Anne into the ward for the evening and went home 'totally exhausted, both mentally and physically'. They returned to the hospital the following morning, 7 May, at half past nine: 'Anne was totally overjoyed to see us and shortly after that time the social worker arrived to take Anne for another session in which the policewoman was involved. On her return after the session, the social worker told us she had been playing with dolls and she had also been crying.' The social worker said that the session had 'gone well', although the Thomlinsons were not entirely sure what that meant.

There were further meetings with a social worker and Dr Morrell, but the fourteen-day place of safety order now materialized, dated the previous day, and the Thomlinsons were informed that 'there was nothing we could do except cooperate'. They were advised to see a solicitor, but even at this stage the Thomlinsons, unsure how to cope with this sudden crisis, felt that they could reason through their difficulties without legal assistance. They were not aware of the straits they were in and felt that the social worker was on their side and that, together with the paediatrician, they were still considering Anne's wellbeing.

They may well have been considering the child's wellbeing, but the context was somewhat different from that envisaged by the Thomlinsons: 'It was several hours after Anne had been returned to us and we felt that the social worker was not going to come to us; so we decided to take the initiative and contacted her to give us an up-to-date position on what was happening. We were then asked to go into her office. There she informed us that nothing untoward had taken place. The social worker told us that there would be a case conference on Friday afternoon, 8 May, and would we like to attend?'

The Thomlinsons were more than delighted to attend. It meant for them that the issue of sexual abuse of their daughter was not settled. It was still in contention. A point of view could still be put. The matter could still be cleared up. Again they settled their daughter down in her hospital bed. Again they went home without her. Again they consoled themselves with their son Allan. And again, after a restless night's sleep, they were back at the hospital to meet an overjoyed daughter.

'We played for most of the day and when it was time to go to the case conference a nurse took Anne for a kidney scan,' Bill Thomlinson recalled. 'We arrived at the meeting only to be told that we had to stay outside and that when the committee reached a decision the chairman would inform us of the outcome. About two hours later the policewoman came out and told us that there would be no police charges and that their enquiries had found there was nothing to worry about.' The Thomlinsons thought they were in the clear. They were about to recover their child.

This, however, was not the message forthcoming from the chairman of the case conference when he emerged from the meeting. For at the meeting the chairman had asked Dr Morrell if the child showed any of the expected symptoms of a sexually abused child. Dr Morrell replied that he was not sure. He could not really answer the question. Dr Morrell did not think there were any other interpretations apart from trauma that he was aware of. Trauma did not necessarily point to sexual abuse. There had been a finger or some similar object used. The findings of the anus were not enough to imply there was anything obvious.

Faced with this somewhat obscure and unsure opinion, the question was asked why a fourteen-day place of safety order had been taken out on Anne Thomlinson? Response of Dr Morrell: 'The medical findings point to trauma and, as I indicated, I felt that that was due to sexual abuse, taken in conjunction with the previous history.' It was this 'previous history' that would continue to haunt the Thomlinsons, although their child's accident had happened some four years ago. Part of the obfuscation lay in what the professionals described as conflicting reports.

As Dr Morrell put it: 'It is interesting that there is a slight discrepancy in the history obtained by the former paediatrician and the history obtained by the health visitor in her report, in that the history of the former paediatrician relates to an injury getting out of the bath; the health visitor relates to an injury occurring in the garden.' No one had sought to clarify this with the Thomlinsons. Then of course there were the other allegations of sexual misbehaviour at school, supposedly observed by the teacher and the school nurse, but which Kim Thomlinson had thought she had explained through the 'thrush' which made her daughter itch.

Into this cloud of suspicion and misinformation the diagnosis of reflex anal dilatation had been dropped. But the problem still remained. The child had not disclosed. Nevertheless, so great was the confusion that the case conference on 8 May, with the Thomlinsons waiting outside, felt it prudent to foster Anne out. This would allow the experts involved to resolve the problem, as the chairman described it. The reaction of the Thomlinsons to the news was different: 'This was a total kick in the teeth after being reassured so many times that there was nothing to worry about. The chairman continued that it was still in the interests of Anne, and that if we were as good a family as we insisted we were, the damage caused by our separation would soon be repaired.'

The dénouement came on 5 June at another case conference held at quarter past two in the afternoon at Middlesbrough General Hospital. What had worried Dr Morrell was that there had been no disclosures to back up either the diagnosis of reflex anal dilatation or vaginal abuse. Equally worrying, on the table was an opinion from a police surgeon that indicated there had been no abuse at all. It was here that Dr Morrell diverged somewhat from his colleagues, for while they would indicate that they felt reflex anal dilatation was an *absolute* sign, for Dr Morrell it was not conclusive without additional case work backing up the diagnosis.

It is to the credit of Dr Morrell that he took this view. As the minutes of the case conference show, Dr Morrell restated his earlier opinion that there was no conclusive medical evidence of sexual abuse: the injuries could have been caused by abuse but could also have been caused by Anne herself. There was no mention here of reflex anal dilatation, and of course there had never been any injuries other than that of some four years ago. And then there was the opinion of the police surgeon. Did this have an impact? Was this the reason why a decision was made to allow the child home? Response of Dr Morrell: 'I think probably it did make a difference.' And on this occasion the police officer reiterated there was no evidence to indicate that the child had been abused.

Child abuse consultant Mrs Richardson, who was also present, had nevertheless signed a report which included the following: 'Dr

Higgs has also seen the child and is of the opinion that she had been sexually abused.' It was the view of the meeting that this should be qualified or withdrawn from the record. Dr Morrell stepped in again to say that Dr Higgs had seen Anne in outpatients' on 5 May and had not seen her again. It was his view that the statement should be erased from the record. A social worker said that Anne had demonstrated to them how she had damaged herself, that these comments had been passed on to Dr Morrell, and that Dr Higgs had not received this information.

The fact is, however, that Dr Higgs' statement was not erased from the record and the medical evidence would stand as 'inconclusive'. One would have thought that this was the end of the matter, but it was not. It was agreed that the child should be returned home. It was agreed that there would be no police prosecutions. It was agreed that, in the interests of the child, Dr Morrell should see her from time to time to be sure. It was agreed that this medical surveillance should last six months. Those present at the case conference were magnanimous in their praise for the fine job of work the social workers had done, but there was not a mention of commiseration or sympathy for the Thomlinsons who had almost lost their child and were not, even at this stage, to regain their reputation as caring parents.

The final paragraph of the case conference minutes was grudging: 'This continues to be a case where there is both an innocent and a sinister interpretation of the history and physical condition of Anne. This ambiguity has *not* been resolved.' The Thomlinsons' joy at having their daughter back was followed quickly by resentment that any of this had happened in the first place. The professionals had run amok: 'Their discussions should, we feel, not have taken four and a half weeks to decide what we already knew from the beginning of this very traumatic experience. Anne herself had already explained from the outset of this investigation that her continual scratching had caused the effects that were under debate.'

It was now left to the Thomlinsons to try to pick up the pieces and start afresh, as they would say, hoping and praying that Anne and they as parents would never have to go through such a terrifying ordeal again. Meanwhile, the 'fruitful working relationship' between Dr Higgs and social services was to continue. Another *forty-seven* children would be taken into care by social services before the month was out.

But little did social services realize that they too would soon be called to account.

19

On Tuesday 5 May, Dr Higgs held her regular outpatients' clinics at Middlesbrough General and North Tees hospitals.

Dr Higgs had a heavy work load. She covered fifty-two beds at Middlesbrough General Hospital and, working with her colleagues, she estimated that about seventy babies a year required intensive care. She worked till eight or nine in the evening while her husband stayed at home and looked after their family; and even when she was at home she would be on call. Although still on the electoral register with an address in Jesmond, Newcastle, she had in fact moved to Middlesbrough during 1987 and lived only ten minutes from the hospital. In the days of crisis she would, more often than not, be driven in by Dr Geoffrey Wyatt who lived some seven miles outside Middlesbrough in a North Yorkshire village, but who picked her up on the way.

She also made night rounds. Sometimes these were as short as three quarters of an hour; at other times they took several hours. Some of these night rounds would provide grounds for controversy later and would give rise to protests from nurses and complaints to the South Tees Health Authority, but prior to this the night rounds would be a part of her routine. And then she had half-day clinics. Here she dealt with social problems that related to health, for she believed that the paediatrician had work to do in the community as well as within the hospital. She had a diabetic clinic, held with Dr Peter Morrell on Friday afternoons; Thursdays she would keep free for her case conferences and the like; and in addition she held clinics at the outpatients' at North Tees General Hospital.

The clinics at both Middlesbrough and North Tees on Tuesday 5 May were to be especially significant. For on this day Dr Higgs would diagnose *seven* children as having been the victims of alleged sexual abuse. Ten children in all passed through the clinics. One whom she had been anxious to see was Peter Chapman, who had been fostered with the Allans. Then came the Charlton children. One of these, a boy, Michael, had been examined on 3 May and diagnosed as allegedly sexually abused; his brother Colin would be so diagnosed on 5 May.

In Colin, Dr Higgs had found reflex relaxation of the anal sphincter. 'His bottom was not normal,' she recalled later. 'I was concerned, though I did not reach a definite conclusion. Certainly, I presented his findings as a possible to the social workers and to his mum.' Why only a possible? Was Dr Higgs doubting her own diagnosis? 'Because the signs were not as gross as the other signs that I had seen in other children. It is a clinical decision, depending on what you see at the time that you examine the child.'

There was, of course, Anne Thomlinson, whose personal drama was encapsulated in the phrase that she had attended the clinic because of 'a recurrent infection'. She suffered from 'a vaginal discharge'. Ruth Knowles, another outpatient, was fourteen months old and had come in because of a bowel disorder. She had been ill since birth with a milk intolerance. There was seven-year-old Kate Doundly: she had been brought to the hospital directly from school because she had been feeling sick and dizzy. As Dr Higgs remarked: 'She also had very poor growth, that little girl.'

Kate Doundly's two-year-old sister Edna was also there. Edna Doundly had the misfortune to be in the outpatients' department, on the knee of her mother's friend; but she too was examined and she too was diagnosed as having allegedly been sexually abused. There was Jane Foster. All of these seven children had one thing in common: none had been referred to the clinic for investigation of sexual abuse, apart from Colin Charlton, who had followed in his brother's footsteps after Michael's diagnosis on 3 May.

Was this an indication of an extraordinary prevalence of anal abuse among children on Teesside? Not at all. As Dr Higgs explained: 'You cannot extrapolate from an outpatient clinic on that day. Those children presented and the findings were made. There were many days when there were no children found to have sexual abuse and it would be equally ludicrous to extrapolate from that. On that particular day, those children presented and had findings consistent with sexual abuse.' The fact is, however, the records show that since she had taken up her appointment on 1 January 1987 there had been one case of alleged child abuse in Cleveland during the month of January, resulting in a single place of safety order being issued; none was issued in February, seven in March and eight in April.

Suddenly the figure climbed to forty-three cases in May and a further forty-seven in June. This did not mean that Dr Higgs had been looking for sexual abuse. She stated she would only look for sexual abuse where she thought it clinically appropriate. For example, in the case of two-year-old Jane Foster, a nursing officer who dealt with child abuse had rung Dr Higgs to say that she was 'a bit concerned' about the level of supervision of this child, who lived in a boarding house. Dr Higgs felt this was 'an intimation' of alleged sexual abuse. The phone call had been made at the beginning of the year, so that she could not recall whether such 'an intimation' had been imparted to her directly or indirectly, but it was sufficient to cause social services and Dr Higgs to arrange an appointment for Jane Foster at the hospital.

Of the remaining five children: 'Their clinical presentation led me to believe that one of the differential diagnoses could be sexual abuse and it needed to be looked at. One of the little girls' attention had been drawn to her bottom by her parents because they had noticed something that concerned them and I found that further worrying since when I [last] looked.' This was the case of Ruth Knowles who had been seen on 31 March. Dr Higgs accepted that since coming to Teesside she had not, in the early months of the year, looked for sexual abuse.

'But certainly, after I had seen a large number of children from that foster home, I had seen a lot of children that had signs and felt that I needed to do so when it was clinically appropriate.' She denied that she had begun 'actively' looking after 1 May, when she had interviewed the Allan children, but these seven on Tuesday 5 May would be rapidly joined by others, making a total of *twenty-five* diagnoses in the first ten days of May alone. On 5 May, however, as Dr Higgs made a series of definitive diagnoses, she had to deal with the emotional difficulties that followed in their wake.

None caused greater anguish than that of Eileen Knowles, who was a young mother of twenty-eight. She had two children: Martin aged seven and Ruth who was fourteen months old. Ruth had always been a problem child, suffering first from jaundice and then from diarrhoea. Her diet had been changed to Cow and Gate, and then to substitute milk, which was soya-based. This cured the diarrhoea but it caused instead constipation. A health visitor was called and so too was the local doctor. The resident paediatrician at North Tees General Hospital was the next port of call. When only a few months old, Ruth was extremely sluggish in her movements. Or as her mother described her: 'She just did not want anything. She just wanted to sit on my knee and was all floppy.'

At the 31 March outpatients' clinic, Eileen Knowles told Dr Higgs about Ruth's bowel problem. As Eileen Knowles recalled: 'Dr Higgs was asking us questions of how she was, what did we think was causing it, and about what kind of food she was eating, and did it happen after certain foods? It was just like a routine questions check.' Eileen also described a worrying circulation problem that often affected her child: 'Her feet and her face and her hands used to go blue.' Dr Higgs made her customary notes, consisting of a family tree and various other matters, but expressed no concern to Eileen Knowles, though when she looked at the child's bottom this upset the child 'a little bit'.

Eileen Knowles' husband Robert was at this examination and held the child throughout. He was there to help because Eileen Knowles suffered from a bad back and she also had at the time severe stomach pains, caused by strain. No comment was made on the child's bottom on this occasion: 'Dr Higgs just said she could not find anything and we had to write down a list of when she was constipated, what she had eaten at the time, and just like a routine thing of what was happening during the month.'

At the 5 May outpatients' clinic, the parents pointed to a dimple on Ruth's anus. The dimple had appeared the previous week. The child's diarrhoea had cleared but Eileen and Robert Knowles were still worried about Ruth's circulation. The child had been put back on to normal milk. But if they were happy with the child's progress they were still not aware of Dr Higgs' unease following her examination on 31 March.

She had not thought the child's bottom had been 'completely normal' but had noted that upon examination the child had been distressed and therefore she had not persisted. She made a note of this concern on her records: 'Anus rather lax; difficult to see; distressed by examination; no obvious fissures but not a good view.'

The fourteen-month-old Ruth Knowles was even less disposed to having her bottom examined on 5 May than she had been on 31 March. She was distressed and screamed. As Dr Higgs recalled: 'She seemed very frightened at having her bottom looked at, which is unusual for a child of that age, who is used to having nappies changed and so on.' Dr Higgs felt the level of distress 'rather unusual'. But notwithstanding this distress a photograph was taken of Ruth's bottom. It was also proposed to sedate the child so that it could be further examined: 'In the clinic I had seen that the anus looked quite red. She had a large skin tag which looked quite fresh and there was slight anal dilatation because the examination needed to be concluded.'

A light sedation would have been needed to settle the child down, but in fact no sedation was given because Dr Higgs had not been able to return to the North Tees that evening. She had held a clinic in Middlesbrough and had not got back across the river. As Robert Knowles explained: 'She was supposed to come back on 5 May, the evening to do, like, the operation or the examination under sedation and she failed to turn up. So the following morning the sister in charge contacted Dr Higgs at Parkside [maternity unit] and she bleeped and there was no answer.' Ruth Knowles was nevertheless admitted on 5 May to the North Tees and the Knowles caught the resident paediatrician doing his rounds at eleven o'clock.

As he saw it, there were three options available to the Knowles: their child Ruth could stay at North Tees, they could go home and take the child to their local doctor, or they could transfer the child to Middlesbrough General Hospital. The Knowles were about to go on holiday but now they had a deep anxiety about the health of their baby Ruth. They decided to accept a transfer to Middlesbrough General Hospital. This was arranged for three o'clock that afternoon. By this time Eileen Knowles, the uncertainty gnawing into her, was beginning to imagine a whole series of deadly diseases that would require her child to be kept in hospital.

'I was thinking maybe Ruth had cancer of the bowel or something, the way her bowel condition went from being born and the way she was going. Then we could not find out what was going on.' Eileen Knowles met Dr Higgs on the stairs between wards nine and ten at Middlesbrough General Hospital. She had by this time been joined by her mother-in-law, Ruth's grandmother, Caroline Knowles, who was equally concerned about what was wrong with her grandchild. 'Dr Higgs could not speak to us fully because she had to work, and she said she would come back later that night.'

Dr Higgs told them both she was not sure at this stage and she would be asking for a second opinion.

Caroline Knowles asked: 'Is it serious with Ruth?'

Response of Dr Higgs: 'Yes.'

'Will an operation cure it?'

Dr Higgs preferred to defer to the second opinion, but as Dr Higgs recalled: 'That made the mother more upset and I said that I would come back and speak to her later after I had seen the child that I was on the way to see. So I saw them later on that evening. I think it was earlier than eleven o'clock. That was when I re-examined the child, but I had quite a long time earlier on in the evening with both parents.'

Perhaps Dr Higgs was not aware that Ruth Knowles had been

examined by a resident paediatrician at North Tees. Caroline Knowles had been at this examination with her granddaughter on the morning of 6 May and there had been no mention of anal abuse, she would therefore be flabbergasted to learn later that the resident paediatrician would say that he had suspected child abuse. There was therefore a re-examination that night. According to the records, the anus of Ruth Knowles was examined while the child was asleep. Whether this counted as an official or unofficial examination, baby Ruth would be examined *four* times at least within the space of two days, 5–6 May; the examination had been by two paediatricians, but the fact that another 'second' opinion was in the offing simply perplexed Eileen Knowles even more. Second opinion for what? No one had yet let her into the secret. As Dr Higgs recalled, by this time the mother was pressing very hard: 'The parents thought their child had some fatal cancer or other illness.' Therefore Dr Higgs told the mother what her diagnosis was and why she needed a 'second' opinion.

Eileen Knowles fainted.

Although there had been seven admissions for alleged sexual abuse on 5 May there would not be seven arrests, let alone seven convictions. The police attempt to investigate the alleged abuse of Kate Doundly and her stepsister Edna illustrates why this was. Kate had been brought from school because she had felt 'sick and dizzy'; Edna Doundly, aged two, was there because she had accompanied her stepsister. It was the recollection of Dr Higgs that Kate was referred by her family doctor because of poor growth. It was for this reason she found herself at the outpatients' clinic at Middlesbrough General Hospital on 5 May.

Dr Higgs acknowledged that on taking a history from Kate's mother, Jane Doundly, teachers at school were worried and were sending Kate home because she felt sick at school and her general practitioner was worried because Kate was small. She had no serious illnesses, except that she was 'a very poor eater'. Kate Doundly was old enough to describe to Dr Higgs her dizzy sick feeling which came on suddenly: 'She tries to be sick but usually nothing comes out. She occasionally had headaches but not associated with these symptoms. On the Sunday before being seen in clinic she was walking to church with her sister when she suddenly felt dizzy and sick and started to cry. She cried for about twenty minutes. She didn't know why. Someone in the church choir looked after her.'

Following a physical examination, Dr Higgs explained to Jane Doundly that she thought Kate had been interfered with and that she thought she should be admitted to hospital 'until things were sorted out'. Jane Doundly was, in the words of Dr Higgs, 'very shocked by this', but felt that 'the most likely person was probably Kate's half-sister's boyfriend, as Kate often stayed at their home'. This was the reaction of a mother faced with the consultant paediatrician who told her a seven-year-old child had been interfered with. It was, however, taken as confirmation that the abuse had indeed occurred. As she blurted out this statement, Jane Doundly did not realize it might equally have significance for her two-year-old daughter, sitting patiently in the outpatients' department, on the knee of a friend who had come along to look after her.

Dr Higgs asked to examine this child as well. Edna was therefore brought into the examination room and given the same thorough investigation. As Dr Higgs herself acknowledged, Edna Doundly had no major illnesses and her development was satisfactory: there was no question here of a failure to thrive. Jane Doundly described Edna as 'a lively child'. Her husband, Charles Doundly, would take Edna to the garage 'to play with the rabbit' while he 'messed on' in a shed. Whatever the significance of this, or if it had any significance at all, the fact is that a general examination of Edna showed that the child was normal 'apart from her anus which demonstrated reflex relaxation and anal dilatation and there was perianal reddening'. The opinion of Dr Higgs was conclusive. 'My opinion was that Edna also had signs consistent with sexual abuse.'

Both Doundly children were therefore admitted to Middlesbrough General Hospital, at which time the duty officer of social services was brought into the picture and place of safety orders were issued. While at the hospital, the nursing staff recorded that Kate Doundly remained 'very quiet and made no attempt to mix with the other children on the ward'. The child had gone to hospital because she felt 'sick and dizzy' and she was now kept in for alleged sexual abuse. Both children were discharged to foster care on 15 May but they would be back again at the outpatients' clinic on 20 June.

In the words of Dr Higgs: 'Kate said she had been well apart from an episode of feeling sickly and dizzy on the day she had been speaking to a policewoman. She also said that she was very happy where she was and wished to stay there and she felt that Edna was also getting on well.' The moroseness the hospital staff had noticed had clearly dissipated, the child actually preferred a foster home to her real home, with her mother and father, grandmother and grandfather. As with so many other children who would be fostered out, Dr Higgs would be gratified to see how well they were doing in what must have been for the children a strange environment.

Dr Higgs was pleased to note that upon examination the conditions of both girls were much the same as on admission to hospital, 'except the perianal redness on Edna was resolving and the anal verge skin was almost back to normal'. The police had eventually managed to interview Kate, according to the records of Dr Higgs. But in their attempts to interview those who might be described as interested parties, and to garner the best available evidence as a whole on either of the children, let alone on the alleged perpetrator of these offences, the police had encountered some difficulties. A policewoman had been allocated to the case on 6 May, the day after the diagnosis had been made, but there was no follow-up until some days later.

The policewoman made the following note: 'My first involvement with this case was on 11 May when I telephoned Dr Higgs regarding obtaining a statement from her outlining the medical diagnosis in relation to the allegation of sexual abuse. I was informed by Dr Higgs that she would try and sort something out that evening. I was asked to contact her the following day, which I did, but I was unable to speak to her.' Messages were left for Dr Higgs and finally, on 27 May, the policewoman called Dr Higgs' secretary.

She was informed that Dr Higgs was away. The policewoman therefore left an urgent request for statements that would assist the police with their enquiries. A case conference was held on the Doundly children on 28 May which the policewoman attended. Dr Higgs unexpectedly appeared in person, and as the policewoman recorded: 'After its completion, I personally spoke with Dr Higgs regarding obtaining a statement from her in relation to these children. I was told by her that she had no time to do statements. When I explained to her that the initial case conference on this family was at four o'clock that day, and as a result of the absence of her statement no police investigation had ever commenced, she made no comment, but turned away from me to continue a conversation with another member of the group.'

Dr Higgs would not recall such a conversation with the police officer, although she knew that the pressure of work was so great that she was often late making such statements: 'I was very busy and I really cannot add anything more to that because I do not remember the conversation.' Following the case conference on 28 May, Dr Higgs did in fact get round to making the statement, but on 28 May momentous events took place which were way beyond the scope of the policewoman and even Dr Higgs, and which would have yet another serious impact on the crisis in Cleveland. They would lead to a total breakdown between the police and social services and set the massive bureaucracies one against the other.

None of this was known to Eileen Knowles, as she recovered from her faint, the relief that she felt because her daughter was not dying of cancer completely overshadowed by the allegation that she had been sexually abused. She was told that a 'second' opinion would be arranged for the following day at Leeds, although this in fact would be a 'third' opinion, following upon that of the North Tees resident paediatrician. Nevertheless, on the morning of 7 May Ruth Knowles was taken in a car by her grandfather to Leeds General Infirmary to see Dr Jane Wynne. Also accompanying her were her mother and grandmother, and her father, Robert Knowles.

There was not room for them all in the same car and so the hospital laid on a taxi. As Eileen Knowles recalled, when they arrived they found that Dr Wynne was 'in rather a hurry'. Apparently, 'she had a train to catch. Everybody was late for the appointment, the taxis did not turn up or something, and she was in a rush to get a train.' There was, nevertheless, what Eileen Knowles would describe as 'a very brief examination'. More photographs were taken. And then it was straight back to Middlesbrough, where there were further conversations with Dr Higgs at six o'clock on the evening of 7 May. Eileen Knowles was told that Dr Higgs' diagnosis had been confirmed by Dr Wynne. Dr Wynne's written report would say: 'This is worrying. Ruth's anus is lax and gapes; there are fissures and possibly swelling. These signs are consistent with sexual abuse.'

All that Eileen Knowles could think of, as a young mother, was the fact that her fourteen-month-old daughter was suffering from a bowel complaint, no one was treating it, she had been rushed up and down to Leeds to have the diagnosis of Dr Higgs confirmed, but she could get no one to take a genuine interest in her child's condition: 'I asked for somebody [a doctor] who knew about bowels, if we could see one. Dr Higgs said I just wanted to prove her wrong, that Ruth had been abused, and I said: "Ruth hasn't been abused. I would like somebody in." And nobody came.'

But now what about her first child, Martin, aged seven?

Could he be brought to the hospital?

Robert Knowles recalled: 'She said she wanted him the following day, but we expressed our wish to bring him immediately because it was just a ridiculous accusation she had made. So my brother went to my mother-in-law's and picked him up from there.' Following the examination of Martin, Dr Higgs said: 'No, there's nothing wrong.' This astounded Eileen Knowles. But why had it astounded her? 'She had her head down as if – I know it is only my opinion – but as if we had proved her wrong, that Martin had not been abused.' It was the recollection of Dr Higgs that she told Eileen Knowles that she was happy to tell her that Martin was perfectly all right, there was nothing wrong with him, but the impression that Eileen Knowles had received would stay with her until 23 May, when she made a statement to the police, at which time she would formally commit this impression to paper.

Such was the state of Eileen Knowles, fragile in health at the best of times, that she collapsed again and was herself admitted to Middlesbrough General Hospital. A place of safety order was brought around at six o'clock on the evening of 8 May and handed to her husband Robert. Ruth would be kept in Middlesbrough General for a further fourteen days, but the only preoccupation Eileen Knowles had was that somebody somewhere would treat Ruth's bowel complaint: 'I asked for bowel X-rays and I had called junior doctors and anybody that was on the ward. I was asking people to look at Ruth to see what could be done.'

Ruth Knowles would eventually be fostered out of the care of her parents, but this did not prevent Eileen Knowles continuing to badger Dr Higgs whenever she was on the ward. Always Eileen Knowles would ask about treatment for the bowel complaint. In the words of Eileen Knowles, Dr Higgs would reply: 'It was child abuse, there was no other explanation, and it was just a trauma, what her bottom had gone through.' She indicated that the damage would heal in about fourteen days. Meanwhile there was nothing to stop Eileen Knowles gaining access to Ruth, for the foster parents allowed Eileen to come to their home at any time. The mother was not therefore entirely cut off from her daughter and spent two to three hours with Ruth three days each week. Dr Higgs' diagnosis had already cleared Martin of any allegation of sexual abuse; but that did not mean he could return home with his parents. That did not mean he was out of moral danger. Was there now to be a place of safety order on Martin?

The fact that there was not was due to the intervention of the child's grandmother, Caroline Knowles. Caroline was well known to the hospital staff because she had once worked there and understood hospital ways. When Ruth Knowles had been admitted she had asked the ward sister to explain the reason for the admission. The sister had replied:

'We do not know. We have no notes at all.'

This lack of proper records would come back to haunt not only Dr Higgs but Dr Wyatt too as the number of admissions increased and neither doctor could keep pace with the number of children they were diagnosing as allegedly sexually abused. A note from Middlesbrough General Hospital records, dated 20 May, says that the notes on Ruth Knowles had been missing for a week, but a note would eventually surface giving abbreviated details of the admission at North Tees. This would turn out to be the least of the problems that confronted Caroline Knowles. She had been angered at the allegation of child sexual abuse and immediately challenged Dr Higgs. 'I asked Dr Higgs, if she was proved wrong and it was not sexual abuse, what would she do? She just said: "I will apologize."' Caroline Knowles insisted that a social worker be brought along immediately. Dr Higgs said that it was too late for a social worker. However, the enterprising and adamant Caroline Knowles was not to be put off; she knew from her own hospital experience that the emergency social worker would be on duty somewhere in the building.

After returning from Leeds and the confirmation of the 'second' opinion on Ruth, Caroline Knowles received a telephone call while on the ward at Middlesbrough General. It was from another social worker. He was enquiring about Martin. As Caroline Knowles recalled: 'The social worker asked me where Martin was at that precise time. I said he was with his other nana, but I was taking him from the Friday night as he was going back to school on Monday. He said that as long as he was with us or his other nana and had no contact with his parents – only if we were there – we were quite able to look after him. I used to take him up to the hospital, either myself or my husband, and let him see his mum and dad.'

There would therefore be no place of safety order on Martin, but for the next fortnight he was not allowed to spend a moment with his mother and father alone, only in the presence of his grandmother. As Caroline Knowles would later write: 'This was a harsh decision on a small child as we couldn't explain to him why this was so. At no time did a social worker come to my house or his other nana's to see if we were fit people to look after him.' A case conference held later in the month decided that Martin could go back to his parents while Ruth would be fostered out.

Truly a judgement of Solomon.

20

Of the seven children diagnosed on 5 May as having been sexually abused, two were fostered out to Elaine Evans.

Elaine Evans had two children of her own: Annette, who was almost eight years old, and Thomas, an adopted son aged four. Thomas had been adopted by Elaine and Dennis Evans and they had been fostering on behalf of Cleveland Social Services for some four years. The Evanses had a generous caring spirit and involved themselves in work with handicapped children. They had done so for some years and provided counselling and assistance to parents of mentally handicapped children. And since they loved children about them they had no hesitation in taking in Jane Foster and Colin Charlton following the diagnoses which Dr Higgs had made on 5 May. They would also take Colin's brother Michael, who had been diagnosed on 3 May.

The position was fully explained to the Evanses, that all three children had allegedly been sexually abused, that they were the subject of place of safety orders, and that these orders would subsequently be converted into care orders. The children would also be taken back to Middlesbrough General Hospital regularly to see Dr Higgs. The children had in fact been brought to the Evans home on Thursday 7 May and they would be back at the hospital again the following Tuesday 12 May. This routine did not unduly upset Elaine Evans, for her adopted son Thomas was always back and forth to the hospital.

He had had routine check-ups and then a variety of tests, for Thomas suffered from asthma and allergies and bowel problems. The consultant paediatrician looking after Thomas had been Dr Wyatt. This pleased the Evanses, for they always found Dr Wyatt understanding and helpful, and he had the gift of putting the four-year-old Thomas at ease. Dennis Evans would often accompany his wife and Thomas to the hospital, but he was unable to come along on 12 June when Thomas went to Middlesbrough General Hospital for his routine check-up.

As it happened, Thomas was not particularly well on 12 June. He was suffering from a virus infection and there was some talk about calling in a heart specialist: 'Dr Wyatt had said in our earlier appointment that he thought the child ought to see a heart specialist as well as the orthopaedic man, and so he said he would make arrangements for this to happen. We had no appointment and so I was worried about this.' However, prior to the routine examination of Thomas, Dr Wyatt called the Freeman Hospital in Newcastle which specializes in heart disease.

There was then the routine examination. Elaine Evans laid the child on the bed so that Dr Wyatt could examine his tummy. Elaine Evans undressed the child and as Dr Wyatt began to examine the tummy the telephone rang. Dr Wyatt asked Elaine Evans to answer it, which she did. In the words of Elaine: 'I answered the phone and Dr Wyatt wrestled with my child on the bed. He turned him over and proceeded to look at his bottom. Thomas was trying to crawl up the bed to get a toy and he was fighting Dr Wyatt who was trying to pull him down and hurt him. He had him under his arm like a stuck pig, trying to open his bottom.'

All the while Dr Wyatt was talking to the child but Thomas still sought to 'get away'. As Elaine Evans recalled: 'He wanted to play with the toy at the top of the bed. He did not want to be on his hands and knees; he wanted to be on his bottom to play.' There had been no suggestion by Dr Wyatt to Elaine Evans that the consultant paediatrician wished to look at her child's bottom and there had therefore been no parental consent. Dr Wyatt then parted the buttocks. Still Elaine Evans did not know what was happening. In fact, she was quite amused, for here was Thomas wrestling with Dr Wyatt, the paediatrician who had taken such good care of her adopted boy, while Elaine Evans hung on to the telephone.

It was the Freeman Hospital calling back and Dr Wyatt took the call in order to arrange an appointment for the following Tuesday. A sister walked into the examination room. Dr Wyatt asked her if Dr Higgs had been found. The actual words he used were: 'If you see Marietta ask her to call in, will you?' Thomas was then taken for an X-ray. This puzzled Elaine Evans. The X-ray, as Dr Wyatt indicated, would be needed for the Freeman Hospital. But Elaine Evans replied:

'You don't normally take X-rays up to Newcastle?'

Reply of Dr Wyatt: 'Normally you have two.'

Thomas was taken away to be X-rayed.

Elaine Evans returned to the outpatients, to await the return of her son. She was beginning to wish that her husband was here. As she recalled: 'My husband did not come because the children were meant to go to a party the next day and he changed his day off in order to accompany myself and the five children to the party the day after.' It was a long and lonely wait. Eventually she was called back into the examination room, where she found Dr Higgs as well as Dr Wyatt. Dr Wyatt said he thought Thomas had 'an abnormal bottom' and he wanted Dr Higgs to have a look at it. Thomas was then put back on to the bed and a similar examination was carried out by Dr Higgs. Elaine Evans did not know what was meant by an 'abnormal bottom'; but she knew why she had been called upon to foster Jane Foster and Colin and Michael Charlton on 7 May.

It began to dawn on her that they were now examining her own son for that self-same anal abuse. 'I thought at this stage that they were trying to suggest sexual abuse because of the nature of the examination, bearing in mind I had taken three children a month earlier and watched Dr Higgs do this, go through this process.' The doctor then left and a junior doctor appeared on the scene. Elaine Evans was now angry and starting to panic as she realized what was happening, and what she surmised the doctors were up to. She asked the junior doctor to look after Thomas while she went down the corridor 'to see what the hell was going on'.

She did not find Dr Wyatt, although she did come across Dr Higgs examining another child in another room.

'I asked her where Dr Wyatt was.'

Dr Higgs replied: 'He won't be long, Mrs Evans. I'm sorry, he won't be long.'

When Elaine Evans did see Dr Wyatt he repeated that he thought Thomas's bottom was 'abnormal'. This made Elaine Evans angrier still. Aware of the consequences of such a diagnosis, having seen the place of safety orders on the three foster children, having had to receive three morose children, all of them diagnosed as having been sexually abused at Middlesbrough General Hospital, it was as if the ground was opening up before her. She was about to lose her own child, a child she had adopted, a child she had cared for through asthma, allergy and bowel problems, a child who had needed all her care and attention to see him through a difficult childhood, a child who needed a loving home, with other children, to bring him along, to develop his personality. All this was about to be taken from her.

Elaine Evans went berserk.

She began shouting at the doctor who had been taking such good care of her child over these last four years. 'He tried to calm me down constantly, saying he was not saying that the child had been abused. He was saying that he thought he might have "an abnormal bottom". He had said by this stage that he wanted the child to go down to see Dr Wynne, and I asked him "Why?" and he said "To see if he has an abnormal bottom."'

There was an equally strong reaction from Elaine Evans at the mention of Dr Wynne. As she recalled: 'I was upset about it because I had known of this other case and what I had listened to, the parents of these other children, over the month previous, telling of court cases and various other things and Dr Wynne was in league with them and all the rest. I knew had we gone down to Dr Wynne we were only going to get the same result as we had got from Dr Higgs and Dr Wyatt.'

For again, what was being sought at Leeds was a *third* rather than a *second* opinion.

But it was one thing to refuse, it was another to face the practical consequences. Elaine Evans was told in no uncertain terms that a failure to cooperate would mean an immediate call to Cleveland Social Services. The argument between doctor and patient's mother continued and as Elaine Evans put it: 'I ended up in a kitchen with Dr Wyatt, still arguing the point. He was still trying to calm me down, still trying to tell me that he was not saying my child had been abused. He was still saying that he thought my child had an abnormal bottom.'

Elaine Evans now desperately needed to talk to her husband. However, by this time Dr Wyatt had picked up Thomas Evans and was carrying him across from a back door in the hospital towards the office of the social services duty officer. Elaine Evans again repeated that she wanted to see her husband. 'No, wait until you come back from Leeds, then you can talk to your husband,' was the reply of Dr Wyatt. Elaine Evans, feeling vulnerable now both as a mother and a woman, replied:

'No, my husband ought to know about this.'

As it happened, in the office of the social worker there was no problem in her contacting her husband. A telephone was put at her disposal. She gave him the background to what was happening at the hospital and he came immediately. The argument continued after he arrived but the situation was plain enough. Whether they liked it or not, the Evanses were destined for a trip to Leeds.

A taxi was provided by the hospital and that same day the Evanses together with the registrar of Middlesbrough General Hospital found themselves heading for the hospital where Dr Wynne practised.

Dr Wynne arrived late and Elaine Evans explained Thomas's somewhat difficult background before Dr Wynne carried out a physical examination. This examination was timed by Dennis Evans. There was the normal physical examination of chest and ears, but the anal examination took 'no more than a minute'. And that was the end of it. Dr Wynne indicated that she would speak to Dr Wyatt during the course of that day and he would speak to the Evanses directly about her findings. They then trekked back to Middlesbrough General Hospital, where they arrived at nine o'clock.

Waiting for them was a very imposing Dr Wyatt. 'He was very quiet, he looked very severe,' Elaine Evans recalled. 'He said in his opinion my child had been sexually abused constantly, persistently, frequently over a long period of time, and recently.' Elaine Evans responded by telling Dr Wyatt it was 'absolute utter rubbish and there had to be other reasons for this anal dilatation as my child is a very protected little boy. The only people who ever look after him are his parents and a babysitter.'

Elaine Evans was now beginning to realize the power of the paediatricians. After all, three of them had now diagnosed alleged sexual abuse. Her tone changed. 'I pleaded with this man at this stage to check my child and to find other reasons for these symptoms and he refused. He said: "No." In his opinion there was only one reason for anal dilatation and that was sexual abuse.' By this time Dennis Evans had joined in the discussions. He too was very upset. He knew as well as Elaine that nothing had happened to Thomas. The Evanses pointed out they had been fostering children for years; and they would not mind at all if each and every one of them was brought to the hospital to be examined. Perhaps the tone became threatening, for Dr Wyatt responded:

'I would advise you, Mr Evans, not to get violent.'

But now what about the children who had been fostered to the Evanses on 7 May because of a diagnosis of alleged sexual abuse?

There was Jane Foster. There was Michael Charlton. There was Colin Charlton. Michael Charlton had been taken by his mother to live with an aunt; but his brother and Jane Foster were still in the foster home. And so Dennis Evans, having learned at work that his own child had been allegedly abused, having rushed to the hospital, having been rushed to Leeds in a taxi, having been rushed back to Middlesbrough General Hospital to be given the forbidding news by a consultant paediatrician, now at ten o'clock at night was rushing to his own home to bring back for further verification and examination those children he had so eagerly fostered but a few weeks previously.

Although he had been a foster parent for four years with Cleveland County Council, he was not allowed to make this trip on his own. By the time he left the hospital two social workers had arrived on the scene and they too returned to the Evans home. Had it occurred to Dennis Evans that he would have to take in his eight-year-old daughter Annette? And so towards eleven o'clock on 12 June, a light night but getting dark nonetheless, in that curious half glow of the north east, the social workers, the three children and Dennis Evans arrived back at Middlesbrough General Hospital.

Annette was the first to be examined. So-called second opinions might be required from Leeds, but Drs Higgs and Wyatt would work together this night as they had done on other occasions and as they were to do in future. 'My daughter was first to be examined,' Elaine Evans recalled. 'Dr Wyatt examined her chest and tummy and then Dr Higgs took over and examined first of all her anus and then her vagina.' This was not a complete physical examination. Her chest was however examined and in the words of Elaine Evans: 'They sort of shared the examination.'

Dr Higgs mentioned 'a blemish' on Annette's vagina and tried to show this to Elaine Evans. She failed to see it. The foster children were then examined, but on this occasion only by Dr Higgs. She remarked how much brighter and healthier they looked. Their hair had thickened, they had put on weight and their bottoms had also improved. All three children were then photographed but all that Elaine Evans was ever told was that there had been the blemish; it was not explained to her what it was nor how it had come about. 'We went back into the office with the children and then we had further discussions with Dr Wyatt and the social workers.'

The nightmares of the Evans family were about to come true at twenty minutes past eleven that evening, for the social workers were back on the ward and they carried in their hands sheafs of paper.

They were not unlike those that had been served on the Charlton children and on Jane Foster's mother. They were place of safety orders. And they covered for the *second* time Jane Foster and Colin Charlton and also the children of Elaine and Dennis Evans. The children would be kept in hospital overnight but there would be no room for Elaine and Dennis Evans: 'It was like a cattle shed,' Elaine Evans recalled. 'There were three cots and a bed in a small room. You could not get into the room. We would have had to sleep in the corridor if we had stayed. It was impossible. My daughter looked as though she was in prison. You had a bed at the back of the room and three cots in front. You opened the door and looked through bars.'

The children were terribly upset. One minute Annette had been at home awaiting the return of her mother, the next she had been brought to Middlesbrough General Hospital, examined, and then confined to the ward. She was tearful. She was frightened. She did not want to be left on her own. Thomas was crying, the foster children were crying, 'possibly because we had gone into the room and unsettled them to say goodnight to them. My daughter said she did not want to stay, she said she did not like it there.'

Among these tragic events came a moment of black comedy. Despite the lateness of the hour neither Dennis nor Elaine Evans had any desire to return to an empty house. Elaine Evans wanted to tell Dr Higgs and Dr Wyatt that their eight year old had a voice and could speak for herself. She could tell them if someone had interfered with her. She would give honest answers. There might be some hope after all, if only they would talk to her.

She went looking for the consultant paediatricians. She found them sitting in the hospital kitchen. Their day was clearly over.

They were eating fish and chips.

21

As these human dramas were played out, was there no voice crying in the wilderness? Was there no common sense? Or had common sense slipped away like a thief in the night? Was the technique of reflex anal dilatation so foolproof, so invincible that paediatricians of eminence and respectability could not resist it? Or was there something wrong with the way the system was handling the diagnosis? Was it meant to be so decisive that it must be acted upon at all costs? Did Dr Jane Wynne understand the nature of the confirmations that were being sought by way of 'second' opinions? Did she know that place of safety orders would be issued immediately? Or did she feel her own medical examination would be part of a wider investigation? And did the paediatricians in Middlesbrough understand the legal problems, let alone the human ones, that would ensue from their own diagnoses?

Confidence in the diagnostic technique abounded in these early days of May. And this confidence was not limited to the paediatricians working out of Middlesbrough General Hospital and the North Tees outpatients' clinic. It was equally shared by the child abuse consultant Mrs Richardson. Her esteem and respect for Dr Jane Wynne was equal to that of Drs Higgs and Wyatt. She had first read the article by Drs Wynne and Hobbs in the *Lancet* in November 1986, a month after its publication. She had gone down to Leicester University on 26 March 1987 to hear and see a detailed presentation by Dr Hobbs, who was present with Dr Wynne, and she had ensured that her department would be in regular touch with Dr Wynne on a number of cases of alleged child sexual abuse. In all social services sent some nine children to Dr Wynne for her 'second' opinion. All confirmed the original diagnoses of Drs Higgs and Wyatt: the signs were consistent with sexual abuse. Mrs Richardson had even had the opportunity on 26 March to discuss with Dr Wynne the Ames case. According to Mrs Richardson she had been told by Dr Wynne that in her view the father was the perpetrator.

Not long after the detailed presentation on 26 March, Mrs Richardson made a further trip to hear Dr Wynne at a seminar at Leeds General Infirmary. She had contacted the senior clinical medical officer of the seminar to ensure that it would be open to professionals who, as she described it, were 'interested in the work of the Leeds paediatricians'. At this seminar Dr Wynne would mingle and mix with the professionals and talk to them 'on an equal basis'.

This particular visit to Leeds took place on 12 May, when the child sexual abuse figures for Cleveland were escalating fast. So fast that no one quite knew how many children had been diagnosed and where they actually were. Records showed that there had been *fourteen* children admitted over four days from 5–8 May; other records showed *eighteen* over the first seven days of the month. So great was the confusion that on 8 May Mrs Richardson held a meeting at the hospital with the fostering officer, Dr Higgs, a child psychiatrist and a social worker. They did a head count on the ward. When it was pointed out that it was rather unsatisfactory for the child abuse consultant of Cleveland Social Services to be reduced to 'a head count' to elicit the numbers of sexually abused children, Mrs Richardson replied: 'I would accept that as something with which I feel equally frustrated.'

The control of the numbers would not get any better as the crisis deepened and Mrs Richardson would be reduced to consulting the records of the night-duty team of social services at Middlesbrough General Hospital 'because a lot of these place of safety orders were taken out of hours, and that was normally brought to my attention the following morning from the night-duty-team log'. On 12 May, four days after the 'head count', she would be at Leeds speaking with other professionals at the Wynne seminar, speaking notably to representatives of the NSPCC and the National Children's Home, and police representatives from Leeds who were able to tell of their own experience of a similar increase in referrals. This reassured Mrs Richardson. As she was later to relate: 'I was particularly interested in the practice of the police in carrying out prompt interviews of adults, if necessary on the basis of medical evidence alone without disclosure, and that this sometimes resulted in admissions of guilt.'

Other points of interest, as she recalled, were that 'all the agencies had participated in a group on the subject of sexual abuse for some eight years, there was an established line of referral from long-serving paediatricians, and paediatricians were being used frequently for diagnoses which led to action by all appropriate agencies, including social services and police.' Nevertheless, there they were: eighteen children admitted to Middlesbrough General Hospital during the first seven days of May. And no doubts about the diagnosis. For once it had been made by Dr Higgs or Dr Wyatt it became 'unequivocal' in the mind of Mrs Richardson.

This left her, of course, with the problem of managing such a large number of children to be taken into care. And there would be more to come. On the day she had been to Leeds she wrote to her superior, Mike Bishop: 'The increase in detection of child sexual abuse has now become critical. As you will be aware, eighteen sexually abused children were admitted to Middlesbrough General Hospital during a seven-day period beginning 1 May 1987, highlighting major discrepancies in the department's ability to respond in concert with the police and health service. *Already there are more new cases pending and this increase in referrals is likely to continue.* Urgent plans, therefore, are needed to examine both short-term and long-term issues.'

Mrs Richardson suggested an urgent meeting with Mr Ian Donaldson, district general manager of the South Tees Health Authority, to discuss the setting up of a task force of nominated social workers to be able to deal with the referrals on a rota basis. Temporary facilities should be arranged for interviewing children pending longer-term plans: 'What is needed is a comfortable room equipped with play material, preferably with video equipment, available inside and outside office hours. There should also be long-term plans for specialist resources and shared training between social services, health and police.'

This innovative suggestion was taken up and converted into the Child Resource Centre at Middlesbrough General Hospital with Ms Deborah Glassbrook in charge. It was not, however, this suggestion that caused controversy. *Already there are more new cases pending and this increase in referrals is likely to continue.* How did Mrs Richardson know that? How could she know that if there had been *eighteen* children in seven days there would be equal numbers in the future? How did she know that there would be more cases of child sexual abuse before they had been diagnosed?

In her view, this avalanche of cases had been brought about by increased 'skills, detection and diagnosis'. It was a view she passed on to her boss, Mr Bishop. As Mrs Richardson later explained: 'My understanding was that more children were already on the wards at that time waiting to be allocated a social worker or otherwise dealt with by the department and that we were entering the point where we might not be able to manage that.' The 'head count', apparently, had encompassed not only children on the ward who had been allegedly abused, but those who were awaiting the allocation of a social worker prior to any diagnosis being made.

There were other reasons why the numbers were likely to increase and which arose out of Mrs Richardson's view of child sexual abuse. She accepted there had been challenges to the diagnosis of reflex anal dilatation, and although she had no doubts about the technique it had caused her some 'heart-searching'. But 'the end result has been to reaffirm my confidence in the diagnosis'. She also believed that child sexual abuse traversed all social strata and that it hardly mattered that the children came from perfectly respectable backgrounds with no previous histories of behavioural problems, with parents who seemed to be in every way ideal parents, who had brought their children to the doctors for routine check-ups and who had then had their children diagnosed as having been sexually abused.

'Certainly it is fairly novel,' she would say, 'but it doesn't come as a complete surprise to me in the field of sexual abuse as the more we understand about this problem the more we understand that perfectly respectable people do it.' When she was asked how she had come by that knowledge Mrs Richardson replied: 'It comes from cases now being detected and also adults speaking about what has happened to them in the past.'

Mrs Richardson and Dr Higgs and Dr Wynne and Dr Hobbs and Mrs Bray and Mrs Dunne were all in BASPCAN. But BASPCAN did not deal in the controversies of the medical diagnosis of reflex anal dilatation. Rather its members accepted it on merit: 'I have to say that at the seminars and conferences I have attended the topic had not been particularly controversial in that setting. [In] the setting I have heard this work described in, there seemed to be a lot of acceptance and a lot of support for this work.' Mrs Richardson nonetheless accepted that she was sailing into 'uncharted waters', to use the nautical metaphor, but she believed that sexual anal abuse was widespread and a hidden problem within the community.

Besides, the research of Drs Wynne and Hobbs was there, in the pages of the *Lancet*, although the disputes and contrary arguments put forward in other editions of the same medical journal by other paediatricians and police surgeons were not considered as other than spent bullets. Mrs Richardson had looked at child sexual abuse from 'the social point of view' and she had been 'particularly impressed by the subsequent number of disclosures that they have had from the children to substantiate the diagnosis and the number of successful cases in care proceedings; and also I believe in Leeds they have increased the prosecution rate, which tends to be extremely low for this type of offence.'

Mrs Richardson might diverge from Drs Higgs and Wyatt in that she did not believe in second opinions. She believed that social workers should take over to make their own assessments, particularly by interviewing the child. This meant that once a diagnosis of child sexual abuse had been made disclosures would follow. Therefore, again the problem in Cleveland was not one of diagnosis but one of management. How to cope? The rapid increase in numbers had begun on 1 May and had continued from that first bank holiday weekend. When Mrs Richardson returned to her office later that month after another bank holiday she found there had been *fourteen* children admitted over that weekend alone.

Mike Bishop, director of social services, addressed the South Tees Community Health Council on 12 May. This was the same day Mrs Richardson had gone to Leeds. This was the day she would write to Mike Bishop that there would be new cases pending. This was the day she would propose new management changes and techniques to cope with the influx.

For Mike Bishop it was a day of confidence, bouyancy and pride. For he was not at the South Tees Community Health Council to talk about child abuse. He was there to talk about Cleveland Council's work on behalf of the elderly, the physically handicapped, the mentally handicapped, the mentally ill, and children in need. Ironically, Mike Bishop would tell the council that the only group where need was decreasing was in the area of child care. This was a curious statement for Bishop to make at a time when the hospital was filling up with well children allegedly sexually abused, when already there were strains on the fostering system, but he made it in order to justify the county's policy of closing down children's homes and transferring children to foster care. As a result of this policy, Mike Bishop would proclaim, ten per cent more children a month were finding permanent substitute homes. And of course there was the incidence of known cases of physical and sexual abuse. They had doubled in three years.

It was not that the number of cases of sexual abuse in boys as well as girls under the age of five was increasing: it was that the detection rate was higher. There was never any doubt in his mind that the medical diagnoses were correct, since no one had told him otherwise and he did not read the *Lancet*; rather it was an opportunity for social services and the health authority to work more closely on such issues as to how long a child who had allegedly been abused should remain in hospital and where that child should be placed afterwards. Bishop's pride came from the fact that five years earlier social services had been regarded as the poor relation but now they were emerging as equal partners with their health authority colleagues.

While Mike Bishop would take responsibility for the events of his department, child sexual abuse was not a matter for his personal attention, although he would later recount how he had been aware of the increase in referrals beginning in late April. In fact they had begun on 1 May, when the news had been given to him that not only was there an increase in child sexual abuse but that in one case the alleged perpetrator was a foster parent on the books of Cleveland County Council's social services.

As Mike Bishop recalled: 'First of all the actual nature of this type of sexual abuse was fairly uncommon in my experience and frankly it was very difficult to comprehend how children could be abused in such a manner. To find that children who had been previously abused and placed in the care of the county council had similarly been re-abused in a caring situation, it was almost incredible to believe at that stage that such a coincidence would happen. That is why I said: "Something must be wrong. I want a second opinion." '

No one had told Mike Bishop of the earlier allegation that Alma Smith had been abused both at home and then in the hospital when the alleged perpetrator was already bailed to a hostel; or that of the two Dixon children only Vera aged four had been allegedly abused in the Steiner Unit, while the allegation now was that Vera and her sister Angela had been abused in the foster home.

In calling for a second opinion he was echoing the sentiment of Matthew Allan who had insisted that his own doctor be present when Dr Higgs examined his own children. But whose idea was it that this second opinion should be furnished by Dr Jane Wynne? Was he aware of the conversations Mrs Richardson had had with Dr Wynne on 26 March when cooperation between Leeds and Cleveland was to be enhanced? Did he know they were both partisans of BASPCAN? Did he know that Dr Jane Wynne had pioneered the technique of reflex anal dilatation which had been adopted by Dr Higgs and now Dr Wyatt on Teesside?

As it happened, Mike Bishop did not know who had thought to bring in Dr Wynne: 'I instructed my senior assistant director to obtain a second opinion. He in conjunction with Mrs Richardson would have told the area officer to obtain the second opinion. Who actually decided that it should be this particular doctor in Leeds, I am not sure.' This did not mean he would later disapprove of the choice: 'I said: "I want a second opinion from outside of Cleveland from a paediatrician who has got expertise in child sex abuse." In hindsight, it seems to me a perfectly sensible place to go to Leeds, where there already was a child sex abuse crisis.'

But if he did not know of Dr Wynne's 'exposed position' as the pioneer of reflex anal dilatation, perhaps with hindsight it might have been 'happier' had the reference for a second opinion been to somebody who was not in such an exposed position? 'I think it is impossible for a director of social services to pick and choose paediatricians. It seems to me to be eminently sensible to use a paediatrician in an authority which has had major problems with child sexual abuse. Whether these paediatricians have got particular skills or techniques of diagnosis I cannot comment on.'

Nevertheless, the case of Vera and Angela Dixon preoccupied him: a child or children allegedly anally abused in two different environments and on both occasions while in the care of Cleveland County Council; and in the case of one of them the alleged perpetrator being a foster father on the books of the council. As it happened, on 1 May the Dixons were trying to gain access to their children whom they had not seen since July 1986. Their case was to be heard that day by the adjudications subcommittee of the social services committee of Cleveland County Council. But the Dixons were not allowed access to their children either on this day or any other day.

However, because the subcommittee was meeting that day Mike Bishop instructed his deputy to inform the social services committee chairman of what he described as 'the circumstances of this latest abuse'. Perhaps neither bureaucrats nor councillors saw the significance of this for the Dixon family. Or if they did there is no evidence that an eyebrow, let alone a voice, was raised to ask how it had come about that a child who had allegedly been abused by its father in the Steiner Unit in Newcastle in July 1986 had now allegedly been abused in the foster home by a foster parent employed by Cleveland County Council – the medical diagnoses having been made by the same doctor. Nor did anyone wonder, if the allegation was true, who was going to hold accountable the social services department which allowed these things to happen. Nor did the Dixons discover this latest chapter in the lives of their young children until six weeks later.

Nevertheless, the Dixons again preoccupied Mike Bishop on 6 May: 'It was agreed that we should seek further advice from the county secretary and ask for a specific solicitor to help us handle these issues. Mrs Richardson should discuss the problem with both the solicitor and the police, particularly concerning other children who have been in this particular foster home.' What Mike Bishop was talking about was bringing in all of the children who had been in the Allan foster home over the past year, although unknown to him that decision had already been taken by others, and one of the children, Peter Chapman, had already been brought to the hospital and confirmed as sexually abused.

While Mike Bishop was preoccupied with the Dixon children, and the legal difficulties that were now looming for the county council, it was not till a few days later that he was made aware 'that a larger than usual number of children had been admitted into Middlesbrough General Hospital, on place of safety orders, as a result of suspected sexual abuse of a serious nature. These figures were confirmed in a memo from Mrs Richardson to myself, dated 12 May, confirming eighteen allegedly sexually abused children admitted to Middlesbrough General Hospital between 1 and 8 May.'

Mike Bishop later recalled: 'The position sprang into public prominence on 12 May when I addressed the South Tees Community Health Council meeting on general issues appertaining to the social services. At that meeting questions were asked about too many children being accommodated on wards in Middlesbrough General Hospital. I explained to the meeting that the admission and retention in hospital was a matter for the consultant paediatrician but that social services would make arrangements to accommodate the children appropriately when the paediatrician considered they were ready for discharge.'

The strict legalities of events surrounding Middlesbrough General Hospital were not uppermost in anyone's mind. The police were struggling in their endeavours to track down alleged perpetrators. The build-up of place of safety orders was heading towards the courts. Confusion and chaos resulted in 'head counts' to ascertain just how many children had been taken into care. It would take many months before anyone could come to terms with what was actually happening in Cleveland. This Tuesday 12 May, when Mike Bishop addressed the community health council, would be a busy day for him, as indeed it was a busy day for Mrs Richardson, who had gone to Leeds and back and written to Mike Bishop warning him of more cases of alleged child sexual abuse coming from the hospital.

It would also be a busy day for five-year-old Alma Mitchell, who had the misfortune of falling from a bench in the garden and injuring herself, requiring a visit to the casualty ward at Middlesbrough General Hospital, there to be treated by Dr Geoffrey Wyatt.

22

Alma Mitchell was the five-year-old daughter of Doreen and Albert Mitchell. They had married in 1980 and had three children: Alma aged five, Thomas aged six and Yvonne aged seven. All three children were on the small side, underweight but not undernourished, and there was no medical evidence that they had in any way been deprived in their short lives. They were hardy children and had no need of the assistance or intervention of Cleveland Social Services, or indeed of any of the welfare agencies that might have had a say in their upbringing.

The school doctor had noted their lack of height and weight and teachers had noted their somewhat unkempt appearance, but they were none the worse for that. In the tough life that existed on the Middlesbrough housing estates, they were neither better nor worse cared for than their young playmates going in and out of the school gates. There would be no complaints from neighbours, who brought their own children up in much the same fashion, and on one thing they were all agreed: the Mitchell children were surrounded by love and so therefore, whatever the financial circumstances of their lives, they were basically happy children.

Then there was the accident on Tuesday 12 May.

It is not entirely clear how it happened. One minute the five year old was playing. The next she was on the ground with blood staining her underclothing and the garden tiles. She was scooped up by Doreen Mitchell and rushed to a next-door neighbour. The neighbour had some expertise in first aid. It was the first thing that came to the mind of her mother. But they were unable to staunch the flow and therefore called an ambulance. Alma was conveyed to Middlesbrough General and admitted to ward nine. Her mother went with her. By the time they arrived at the hospital the blood flow had ceased but the child remained white and shaken, mystified by what had happened, how it had happened, and finding herself in her mother's arms but also in the strange environment of ward nine.

It was ten o'clock at night.

Dr Geoffrey Wyatt arrived to treat the injury to the child's vulva and did not dispute the accidental nature of the injury or how it had happened. He wished, however, to make an examination of the child's bottom. He therefore applied the reflex anal dilatation test. To the surprise of Doreen Mitchell he diagnosed findings 'consistent with sexual abuse'. It was a phrase that not only the Mitchells but the lawyers too would hear a great deal of. In fact, Dr Wyatt would be asked by His Honour Judge Hall what weight he attributed to this finding. As the judge declared, 'It then transpired that he considered that there could be no other explanation of these symptoms but buggery or digital penetration.'

Dr Wyatt regarded reflex anal dilatation as conclusive evidence of anal abuse. Therefore the Mitchells were called upon to bring their other two children to the hospital immediately: Thomas aged six and Yvonne aged seven. They were there before midnight. Thomas was the first to be examined. The doctor found relaxation of the sphincter muscles, no anal dilatation, but some bruising. He noted in the hospital record that 'dilatation might be detected the following day'. But in fact he found no further symptoms in Thomas either the following day or thereafter.

The sudden examination of Thomas Mitchell passed off without any great stress or emotion; but this was not the case with Yvonne. She was so upset that a High Court judge would prefer, when giving judgement, not to deal with what he described as 'the harrowing details of that distress', since they would form no part of the reasons for his judgement. Despite this distress and the undoubted difficulties of carrying out the examination, Dr Wyatt diagnosed reflex relaxation and anal dilatation, and concluded that these symptoms were consistent with sexual abuse.

All three children now found themselves bedded down in Middlesbrough General Hospital. Social services were informed, along with the police. All the panoply of investigation and place of safety orders was launched. Enquiries were made at the children's school. On this occasion there was certainly no lack of coordination between the services: the place of safety order was requested and obtained at one o'clock in the afternoon of 13 May and both Doreen and Albert Mitchell were arrested. But after they had been interviewed and when the enquiries were completed, there being no evidence against the Mitchells other than the diagnosis of Dr Wyatt, no action was taken and they heard no more from the police.

On 29 May Middlesbrough juvenile court granted an interim care order on all three of the Mitchell children. On 17 June there was a full hearing before the same court, when Dr Wyatt came forward to give evidence for some two and a half hours. On the day that he did so the magistrates' courts were engulfed in court orders and applications and more than forty cases were listed solely for the juvenile courts. One bench alone on that day granted interim care orders on more than a dozen children who had been diagnosed as allegedly sexually abused. Such indeed was the pressure on the court that the Mitchell case had to be adjourned

However, the Mitchells were able to make some points of their own before the adjournment. One was that they had not seen their children since they had been taken into care some thirty-five days earlier. The disruption to their family life was such that they did not know how they would pick up the pieces. And the court delays in getting back their children was playing on their nerves. Dr Wyatt, in his evidence, made much of the unkempt appearance of the Mitchell children: he told the court they were 'some of the most unkempt, dirty, miserable children I have seen in a long time'. He said that the girls had been sexually abused and had non-accidental bruises. The boy was 'dirty, underweight' and had eleven bruises, mainly to the spine.

The strain of thirty-five days without their three children, the disruption to their family home, the implication that Albert Mitchell was a child abuser, that he interfered with two of his girls if not the boy, that he had pushed something up their backsides, proved too much for this diminutive father who loved his children like any other father, and who felt desperately forlorn when they had been taken from him. He could not see how he could ever put his family life back together again. He did not see how he could endure more sleepless and stressful nights.

Albert Mitchell had a heart attack.

He insisted, however, on coming back into Teesside juvenile court for the continued hearing on 26 June. And so sure was he that his children would be returned, that there had been no abuse, that he asked his friends and family to decorate the house, to buy paper hats and bunting, to set up a nice meal of cakes and biscuits and orange juice and Coca-Cola for the children. So that night, some six weeks after his daughter had fallen from a bench and thus triggered these outlandish events, there would be a homecoming, a party, they could all rejoice, unite, bring back the spirit of the family that he had so much missed. Unlike other neighbours in other situations, there had been full support for the Mitchells in their fight to get their children home.

By now events in Cleveland had caught up with both the health authority and social services and, while the case was being heard, press and cameramen were outside awaiting the result. No expert evidence was given – that is, no paediatrician or doctor was called to challenge the evidence of Dr Wyatt. But having heard the submissions and spent some five hours on the case the juvenile court refused to grant a full care order to Cleveland County Council.

The council had lost its case.

When the magistrates announced their decision the Mitchells were overcome with joy and wept in court. In the impressive setting, with the dignity of the court all around them, with even the magistrates smiling, it seemed odd that there should be, in a court of law, tears of joy. But there they were. Their children back. Their family together again. And outside were the pressmen and the cameras, interviews conducted from behind, so that the children could not be identified. 'I'm just going to cuddle them, kiss them and play with them. I haven't been able to do that for thirty-five days,' Albert Mitchell said.

However, the orange juice and Coca-Cola would remain unsipped; the cakes would have to be thrown into the rubbish bin. Cleveland Social Services did not give up so quickly. Someone somewhere was not happy with the decision. Someone somewhere thought it wrong. Someone somewhere was convinced that Albert Mitchell had indeed interfered with two of his children. It had been open to Cleveland County Council, had they so wished, to appeal against the judgement of the juvenile court in releasing the three Mitchell children back to their parents and refusing the full care order; but they chose instead another route, one that would not have been open to the Mitchells had the case gone the other way. They made them wards of court.

A solicitor appeared at the house and, as compassionately as he could, explained to the family that their children would not be coming home that night; there would be other hearings at other courts, and therefore the due process of law would continue. Albert Mitchell was inconsolable. There were more tears, only this time tears of grief; there was more strain, so that neighbours, friends and family feared he would have another heart attack. Albert Mitchell had only one comment to make: 'I think what is going on at Middlesbrough General Hospital is wrong.'

The next hearing took place in the High Court before Judge Hall. It was the view of the judge, in the light of the evidence given by Dr Wyatt, that 'the bruising and undernourishment would not have justified removing the children from their parents' care without the evidence of sexual abuse'.

He therefore concentrated his attention on the evidence that two of the Mitchell children had, or had not, been sexually abused. Only this time, in contrast to the hearing at the juvenile court, there was expert evidence to contradict that of Dr Geoffrey Wyatt. One expert witness was Dr Raine Roberts. She had been a police surgeon for twenty years. She had made examinations in cases of suspected rape and child sexual abuse. She told the court that in 1986 she had examined no fewer than 160 cases. And she had been an early opponent of the diagnostic technique of reflex anal dilatation.

She had challenged Drs Wynne and Hobbs when their article had appeared in the *Lancet* in October 1986. There had been other challenges too, of course. Four consultant doctors at St James's University Hospital, Leeds, working in the department of gynaecology, paediatrics and surgery, took issue with Drs Wynne and Hobbs and cast doubt on reflex anal dilatation as a method of diagnosing child sex abuse. They pointed out that one of the consultant doctors had been dealing with a ten-year-old girl with a history of general swelling in the vulval region. Examination revealed a dilated anus and fissures, all consistent with the reflex relaxation referred to by Drs Wynne and Hobbs. A photograph which the doctors showed looked identical to those published in the earlier *Lancet* article by Drs Wynne and Hobbs to support their diagnoses.

But the child had not been sexually abused at all, a fact which the doctors had gone to great lengths to ascertain in their assessment: 'Further gentle questioning of the patient and her mother, both individually and together, failed to reveal any history of trauma, and the possibility of sexual interference was discussed and strongly denied.' The child was eventually admitted to hospital where Crohn's disease was diagnosed. This was a rare form of ano-rectal illness. The doctors therefore wrote their own 'government health warning' in the pages of the *Lancet*: 'While not wishing in any way to diminish the alertness of doctors in looking for evidence of sexual abuse in young girls, the case illustrates an alternative diagnosis which should be brought to the attention of all groups seeing children with ano-rectal and vulva-vaginal complaints.'

The doctors felt their case illustrated the importance of considering other diagnoses to prevent errors being made and 'the addition of severe stress to parents already deeply concerned by their child's illness'. Dr Graham Clayden, honorary consultant paediatrician at St Thomas's Hospital, London, also weighed in. He wrote that 'caution must be taken in interpreting findings on anal inspection'. Indeed,

Dr Clayden would go further: 'Apart from recent violent abuse where anal bruising, tearing and excoriation are evident, the appearance of the anus and findings on palpation per rectum are unlikely to prove reliable evidence to confirm or exclude penetration.'

Dr Clayden had for nine years been running a special clinic for children with severe constipation. He had seen about six new cases a week, all of them with a variety of bowel complaints: 'In children with significant constipation the anal canal frequently gapes when the buttocks are gently drawn apart, this being a normal ano-rectal reflex initiated by the distended rectum.' Dr Clayden wrote: 'When a child has recently passed a very large stool that has accumulated over two to three weeks fissures may be visible. Reddening of the anus and perianal region is very common in children.'

But the strongest criticism, and the one which foreshadowed the clash to come – the conflict between the paediatricians and the police surgeons – was to be found in a letter published in the *Lancet* on 8 November 1986. Dr Raine Roberts had read the views of Drs Wynne and Hobbs with increasing concern. They had made 'assumptions that are not justified' by the evidence presented: 'Their findings are based on inspection only, and this is inadequate to assess the tone of the anal sphincter and the extent of any damage to the anal canal.'

Dr Roberts also pointed out, as she perceived it, an inconsistency in the arguments of Drs Wynne and Hobbs: 'They do not do a more thorough examination because this might distress the child – yet they are prepared to come to conclusions which will have devastating effects on the future wellbeing of the child and its family.' Dr Roberts complained that many of the histories recounted on abused children by Drs Wynne and Hobbs were vague: 'Children of all ages may refer to their "bottom" or "bum" when they mean any part of their genitalia, and even older children's knowledge of their anatomy may be very inadequate. Without a more thorough investigation it is not possible even to be sure what is being alleged.'

Dr Roberts claimed that at least three of the photographs that had appeared with the *Lancet* article might well be within normal limits: 'It is very easy to pull on the buttocks and produce photographs which show apparent fissures and slackness of the sphincter.' Drs Wynne and Hobbs had shown five cases of reddening of the anus and perianal skin, but many children alleged to have been sexually abused were poorly looked after 'so any finding of redness is of little value'. Nor was reflex anal dilatation, or 'anal twitchiness', confined to sexually abused children.

It was to the experienced Dr Raine Roberts that the Mitchell family had turned in order to refute the evidence of Dr Geoffrey Wyatt. She had examined all three of their children on 7 August 1987, even though only two of them had allegedly been sexually abused. She then prepared an affidavit of her findings on 10 August. As Judge Hall remarked, Dr Raine Roberts had 'twenty years' experience as a police surgeon making examinations in cases of suspected rape and child sexual abuse'. In the case of Dr Wyatt, he had examined 'his first case of child sexual abuse on 8 May this year'.

This was four days before he had examined the Mitchell children, but since then he had 'examined some ten such cases'.

It was therefore left to Judge Hall to deal with what he described as 'a head-on conflict of evidence between Dr Wyatt and Dr Roberts'. 'During her examination on 7 August, Dr Roberts could detect no evidence of sexual abuse in any of these three children. She did not perform the reflex relaxation test because three months had elapsed since Dr Wyatt's findings and those are not symptoms which normally last for a very long time; she considered they could not be expected to survive that length of time. In addition to her physical examination, Dr Roberts examined the hospital notes in which Dr Wyatt had recorded his findings.'

Dr Wyatt, after examining the Mitchell children on the evening of 12 May, had repeated the examinations the following day in the presence of a photographer who recorded his findings. Dr Roberts had been able to examine these photographs in the preparation of her own evidence. There were two matters which the judge found striking. Dr Roberts was familiar with the reflex relaxation and anal dilatation test. She would say that it was essential, in carrying out that test, that the patients should be comfortable and relaxed before the test began, and that when applying the test the buttocks should be gently separated in order to allow observation of the anus when relaxation and dilatation can be observed.

The conclusion that Dr Roberts had drawn from an examination of the photographs was that the children's buttocks had been 'forcibly' drawn apart, which she described as 'quite the wrong way to carry out the test'. The effect of such 'force' had been to invalidate the test and therefore its result. Dr Roberts would find no signs of sexual abuse on any of the three children and looking at those photographs where some bruising had occurred she formed the view that such bruising 'was likely to have been caused by rough play and disclosed no evidence of ill treatment or of the use of force in the course of sexual abuse'.

Judge Hall would be most impressed by Dr Raine Roberts as a witness: 'She holds all the academic qualifications held by Dr Wyatt; she also has a diploma in medical jurisprudence. Over and above all this, a matter which I think is immensely important in cases of this nature, she has a long experience gained through being a police surgeon for twenty years, specializing in rape and sexual abuse. She is in fact a member of the Council of the Association of Police Surgeons. She is a consultant in child sex abuse to the NSPCC. She lectures on these topics. She is approached by social workers in the district where she practises and also by consultant paediatricians in that area to examine children where sexual abuse is suspected.'

But if Judge Hall was impressed by Dr Roberts' 'impartiality and objectiveness', which he felt to be 'the hallmarks of the expert witness seeking only to assist the court in matters requiring expert knowledge and experience', what of her medical opponent, Dr Geoffrey Wyatt? Was he not equally qualified by reason of his appointment and his experience as a consultant paediatrician? Unfortunately for Dr Wyatt, the judge carefully considered these submissions but found them difficult to accept: 'It seems to me to be indistinguishable from a suggestion that if a paediatrician were consulted in respect of a child patient with, say, a gynaecological complaint, he would be equally qualified to deal with the patient as an experienced gynaecologist.'

Even Euclid, the judge thought, would find that proposition 'absurd'. Judge Hall went on: 'Dr Wyatt would have done the prudent thing and either referred the patient to a gynaecologist of experience or at any rate would have sought a second opinion. So far as Dr Wyatt is concerned, in putting his experience of child abuse before me, the earliest date that he has put forward, as I say, is 8 May 1987 – four days' experience.' Yet the diagnosis of child sexual abuse was not one of 'academic study'. Detailed knowledge of the subject was available to those who had 'long experience of its practice; others can probably gain some knowledge by the learned articles which they write'.

But the judge would come to this consideration: 'A positive diagnosis of child sexual abuse is a very serious matter indeed because the child concerned is almost inevitably removed from its home and its family, and Dr Wyatt has agreed with me that taking a child away from its family and home can have, and indeed is likely to have, serious and harmful effects upon the child.' The judge felt in these circumstances it was 'surprising' that Dr Wyatt, 'with what I think I can fairly describe as virtually no experience of this diagnostic process, was prepared to accept the heavy responsibility of making this positive diagnosis of sexual abuse without taking the precaution of obtaining a second opinion from someone with a suitably lengthy experience of the process and the subject'.

And what of Dr Wyatt himself? 'I found him an unimpressive witness. In cross-examination he persistently refused to address his mind to the question he was being asked, instead he would look at his report and repeat what he had already told me which he thought came somewhere near the question.' Cross-examining counsel would have to ask Dr Wyatt the same question two, three or even four times 'before he could answer it'. It was the judge's duty to make a finding as to the facts of the matter. This he did. The Mitchell children had not been abused.

And what of those social workers who had so assiduously sought and obtained place of safety orders? Who had sought and obtained the involvement of the police which had led to the arrest of Doreen and Albert Mitchell? 'The social workers who have given evidence before me were obviously imbued with the concept of the infallibility of Dr Wyatt. Although they had ample authority under the interim care order to submit these children for a second opinion it did not seem to occur to them to do so. Dr Wyatt had held his consultant post in this area for some four years before he ventured into the field of diagnosing child sexual abuse; therefore social workers must at least have had suspicions of his lack of experience in this important field.'

However, 'when they came to face the grave responsibility of taking steps which might result in these children being permanently separated from their home and family, together with the harm that they might suffer therefrom, I am surprised that they did not see fit to seek a further opinion.' Nor had the social workers carried out any real enquiry into the Mitchell home situation: 'All the evidence before me points to this having been a normal happy family until 12 May this year. They had their problems as most families do. The children were small and thin, "X"[1] in particular, but steps had already been taken through the family doctor and the clinic to obtain advice on this.'

Judge Hall therefore dewarded all three children and returned

[1]Alma Mitchell

them immediately to their family. Cleveland Social Services, having lost before the juvenile court, had now lost before the High Court, though Judge Hall was anxious to point out that he was making 'no general findings nor any recommendations' as to the general issue of child sexual abuse in Cleveland. This time there were none of the scenes of joy that had accompanied the earlier decision of the juvenile court: no bunting, no cakes, no orange juice, no Coca-Cola. The entire Mitchell family had been subdued by their ordeal before the High Court. But they were now free of Cleveland Social Services. They were free of Middlesbrough General Hospital. They were free of the stigma of child sexual abuse.

And they had their children home again.

23

Judge Hall wondered aloud why social services had not sought a second opinion in the case of the Mitchell children. There had after all, though the judge did not know this, been second, third and fourth opinions on other children. At the juvenile court hearing on 26 June it was revealed that, while the children had been in the care of social services for some six weeks, there had been no attempt to obtain a second opinion until the day of the juvenile court case. A social worker blamed 'the heavy workload for the delay'.

This in fact was not the case. The truth was that, while second, third or fourth opinions from paediatric consultants would be satisfactory to social services when it came to the demand for a place of safety order, a second opinion from a police surgeon was not. Thus on 12 May, when five-year-old Alma Mitchell was taken to Middlesbrough General Hospital because of injuries to her genital area after she had fallen from a bench seat in a garden; when Dr Wyatt found evidence consistent with sexual abuse; when he found her to be 'dirty, thin and underweight'; when the two other Mitchell children were taken in to be examined; when place of safety orders were taken out on all three children, even though only two were allegedly sexually abused; when the police were called to arrest the Mitchells, there would be no corroboration of the sexual abuse by a police surgeon.

In the words of the chief constable of Cleveland Constabulary, Mr Christopher Payne: 'The three children were taken into care and a request for an examination by the police surgeon was refused.' There would in fact be *fourteen* such requests made by the police in their search for corroborative evidence that might lead to convictions. All were refused. The refusals had also worked the other way and led to a breakdown between the consultant paediatricians, social services and the police. Detective Inspector Walls had refused the request of Dr Higgs for photographs to be taken by members of his force of the intimate areas of children's bodies. Another detective constable received a similar request from Dr Higgs on 2 May. He too turned it down.

Then there had been the case of a two-year-old girl who had been admitted to Middlesbrough General Hospital on 15 April. She was suffering from what was described as non-accidental injury. Her brother and sister were examined and found to be in good health and not subject to abuse. All three children were taken into care. While the interim care order was still in force the children were returned to their parents, but on 17 June 1987 Dr Higgs re-examined the children and diagnosed anal dilatation. Again, in the words of the chief constable: 'The case was investigated by the police but a request for an examination by the police surgeon was refused.'

The chief constable added succinctly: 'No proceedings are pending.'

On 1 May ten-year-old Elizabeth Jones had voluntarily disclosed sexual abuse by her foster father. She alleged that he had touched her genital area and put her hand over his private parts. Social services placed the child in the care of other foster parents. The girl lived in that part of the county which was under the jurisdiction of North Yorkshire Police, and accordingly a woman police constable stationed in Richmond was asked to attend a case conference in Middlesbrough on 15 May to discuss the child. She was advised at the meeting that the alleged abuse had occurred 'frequently' between September 1984 and February 1987.

She advised the meeting that they were discussing serious allegations of crime and therefore a formal investigation would be required. This would entail Elizabeth Jones being medically examined; in addition, the child's name would be required to be added to the child abuse register. A social worker at the meeting requested that the medical examination take place as soon as possible because Elizabeth was now suffering from 'a nasty rash in the genital region' and this was worrying her. The woman police constable assured the social worker that she would be in touch with a consultant paediatrician at the Friarage Hospital, Northallerton, but the social worker replied that 'their department preferred their children to be seen by Dr Higgs, paediatrician at the Middlesbrough General Hospital'.

This, however, created a difficulty.

For the social worker told the woman police constable that Dr Higgs had 'a long waiting list and that it would probably not be possible for her to see Elizabeth in the very near future'. This being so, the policewoman suggested that she make immediate arrangements for Elizabeth to be examined by a Cleveland female police surgeon. The social worker at the case conference said she could not agree to this request either. 'I therefore stated that I would contact Cleveland police and request they arrange for Dr Higgs to examine Elizabeth as a matter of urgency so that she may be treated for her genital rash,' the policewoman recalled.

The social worker agreed and said that she wished to attend the interview. The policewoman thought this 'very helpful' since there had already been a voluntary disclosure from the child. On Monday 18 May she telephoned the Guisborough station of Cleveland Constabulary to ask them to arrange for the examination with Dr Higgs. The Guisborough station, however, had difficulty in making the arrangements with Dr Higgs and they were equally unable to arrange a police interview with Elizabeth. Cleveland Constabulary wanted a police surgeon involved but the policewoman pointed out this had already been refused.

The North Yorkshire policewoman wanted the matter to be 'treated with urgency' so that the alleged offender could be interviewed prior to the next case conference which had been arranged for 18 June. Dr Higgs did eventually examine Elizabeth Jones. The policewoman was told that 'the social worker who was present at the examination had asked Dr Higgs what her opinion was and that Dr Higgs had walked away stating that a report would be forwarded to the police in due course'.

Police were concerned when they learned that Dr Higgs might be diagnosing abuse of a more serious kind than that originally alleged by the child. Therefore it became even more important to have the results of Dr Higgs' examination rapidly. The policewoman, having failed to obtain information either through Cleveland Constabulary or Cleveland Social Services, telephoned Dr Higgs directly.

The policewoman recalled: 'Dr Higgs asked me who I was and what information I required. Dr Higgs was very cooperative and polite. She told me that she could remember examining Elizabeth but could not remember what her findings were without referring to her notes, and she was not at her usual place of work.' The policewoman told Dr Higgs that she had heard 'a suggestion' that the abuse might be of a more serious – even a different – nature from that first alleged.

Dr Higgs confirmed 'that was in fact the case but she couldn't remember what her findings were'.

Was she referring to anal abuse?

'She thought that possibly was the case. She also indicated that Elizabeth had made further verbal disclosures to her but again she couldn't remember the details. I asked Dr Higgs if she would forward a report as soon as possible or, failing that, that she inform me verbally of her findings prior to making a written report so that I was aware of the facts in order that the alleged abuser could be interviewed.' Dr Higgs agreed with this. Dr Higgs was also interested in the manner in which child sexual abuse was dealt with in North Yorkshire. She understood that liaison between the various services was 'harmonious'.

'She then asked if I could do anything to influence my fellow colleagues in Middlesbrough.' The policewoman, based as she was in Richmond, had not been aware of the friction between Dr Higgs and Cleveland Constabulary. 'She told me that the Cleveland police refused to recognize the extent of the problem of child sexual abuse. She asked my advice as to how she could change the situation and improve investigations.' The policewoman urged better liaison between the various agencies and the effective operation of a multi-disciplinary team.

By 22 July, however, when the policewoman contacted the social worker responsible for Elizabeth Jones, she was told no medical report had yet been received from Dr Higgs: 'She told me that their department had received nothing at all and she stated she would write a letter to Dr Higgs immediately asking for a report as a matter of urgency.' The policewoman was still awaiting the report on 1 August 1987. The upshot was that Elizabeth Jones was not examined by a police surgeon and the alleged abuser was not interviewed by police.

*

The case of Alma Mitchell, and the refusal of social services to allow a police surgeon to examine her, was but one of the fourteen. On 5 June one of these, five-year-old Joanna Forbes, was admitted to Middlesbrough General Hospital suffering from an injury to the vulva. Although the injury was consistent with the explanation given by the parents, Dr Wyatt found anal dilatation, from which he diagnosed sexual abuse. 'Even though the parents, who were annoyed by the implications of the diagnosis, requested a police surgeon, they were refused. Both parents have denied any offence and no disclosures have been made by the little girl. No prosecutions are pending.'

This polite language of the police belied the trauma the Forbes family would endure, but there was another case, of a three-year-old girl who was brought to Middlesbrough General Hospital on 5 June. Earlier she had been seen by Dr Wyatt because she was suffering from constipation. Dr Wyatt had prescribed medication. On 5 June, upon re-examination, he diagnosed anal dilatation. On this occasion there was a second opinion, only not by a police surgeon: by Dr Marietta Higgs. The girl was taken into care and both parents and the grandfather interviewed. A request for a second examination by the police surgeon was refused and no disclosure had been made by the girl. There were therefore no prosecutions pending.

The following day, on 6 June, a ten-year-old girl was referred to Dr Wyatt by her family doctor. The family doctor had diagnosed an infection of the urinary tract. Dr Wyatt diagnosed anal dilatation and in his opinion there had been penetration over a prolonged period. Two other male children in the family were examined by Dr Wyatt, who found anal dilatation in both boys and all three children were taken into care. The place of safety orders were continuing to flow. The parents were interviewed by the police, but denied all and any allegations of sexual abuse. Another request to have the children examined by the police surgeon was refused.

On 12 June, as a result of information she had received, a policewoman went to a Middlesbrough housing estate to investigate allegations that a sixty-two-year-old man had been exposing himself to young children. She took statements from the children and then cautioned and arrested the man, Albert Atkinson, on suspicion of indecency. He replied: 'I haven't been out all week.' He was taken to Middlesbrough police station and placed in a detention cell pending the arrival of his solicitor. The policewoman returned to the

Atkinson's home, where he lived with his daughter and grandchild. The grandchild was ten-year-old Sarah Atkinson.

The policewoman took from the home several pornographic-type magazines that belonged to the grandfather. His daughter did not know of their existence. The daughter, Anna Atkinson, was upset that her father had been arrested, but young Sarah confirmed the allegations of 'flashing'; she also shared in her mother's distress that her grandfather had been arrested. The policewoman suggested that, given the nature of the allegations, it might be in the child's interest to have a medical examination. This alarmed Anna Atkinson but she agreed to think about it. She said she would speak to the police officer again.

Other children in the street made statements corroborating the allegations of 'flashing' and Albert Atkinson was charged at Teesside Magistrates' Court, with a police request that he be remanded in custody because of the seriousness of the offences, for his own protection and since he shared a residence with Anna Atkinson, who might well be a prosecution witness, and also the ten-year-old Sarah. The court granted the request and the police continued with their enquiries.

On the morning of Monday 15 June, the policewoman spoke with a social worker who had been assigned to the case. The policewoman recounted police action to date and remarked that Sarah Atkinson's mother was still reflecting on whether her child should undergo a medical examination. A somewhat astonished policewoman, later that day, got a call from the social worker. Sarah Atkinson had been taken from her home, with her mother, to Middlesbrough General Hospital. The child had been examined by Dr Higgs. Dr Higgs had found anal dilatation consistent with sexual abuse. The child was on ward ten because ward nine was full.

Sarah's younger brother Malcolm had also been taken to the hospital; he had also been examined. And he too had been diagnosed as having been sexually abused. Or rather there had been reflex anal dilatation that was consistent with sexual abuse. 'I asked why such an examination had been carried out at all, considering the police intentions in the first place, and secondly, if such an examination had been carried out, why the police were not informed prior to such, considering the police involvement.' The policewoman was advised by the social worker that 'she was merely following her department's guidelines that, once she is aware of possible child sexual abuse, to involve a consultant paediatrician immediately'.

The social worker said she was not aware that the police needed to be 'involved'.

The policewoman contacted the social worker's supervisor, who agreed that 'a mistake' had been made but now that an examination had been performed and the children admitted to hospital, 'it would be up to the consultant paediatrician involved to consent to such a second examination'. Police request for such an examination was refused. The policewoman again rang the social services supervisor. 'I explained that the allegations made and admissions obtained were totally inconsistent with the medical findings and because of such I requested that, should no disclosure be forthcoming, then a second medical examination be performed in the future when the children came into his jurisdiction.'

Both Atkinson children denied their grandfather had ever sexually abused them and the original allegation made by Sarah Atkinson of her grandfather's 'flashing' was also withdrawn. Grandfather Albert Atkinson was still languishing on remand in prison. The Atkinson children were taken into care and Anna Atkinson had now to cope not only with the arrest of her father on allegations of indecency but also the fact that she had lost her two children to social services.

The difficulties of the police were compounded by this precipitate action, for when Albert Atkinson came again before the court on a second application to remand him in custody there were no longer children at his home address, and therefore now insufficient grounds for his being detained. Police were able to rely on the evidence of other children and Albert Atkinson was therefore not sent back to prison on remand but rather to a bail hostel, with a condition that he did not come near his own housing estate.

Cleveland Constabulary was concerned not only about refusals to let police surgeons examine allegedly abused children, and the photographing of the intimate parts of children who had no apparent injuries, but also about the interview techniques adopted by Cleveland Social Services after the diagnosis of anal abuse had been made. For the social workers, in the words of Judge Hall, the diagnostic techniques of Dr Wyatt were 'infallible'; so too, of course, were the techniques of Dr Higgs. Therefore, once they had made the diagnosis, it would be incumbent upon social services to extract a disclosure from the child.

However, a great deal would depend upon the skill of the social worker doing the interviews, and the techniques adopted during the question-and-answer sessions, if the video recordings of these interviews were to have any merit in a court of law. It had not occurred to social workers, however, that they would themselves be called to account for what went on in these sessions, that the law in its majesty would demand to know; they assumed that if they were able to obtain a disclosure from a child, this could be enwrapped in an affidavit and presented to a magistrates' court, or juvenile court, as *evidence*; at least, they could hand over the tapes to the police who would complete their work for them. It would be up to the police to enlighten and instruct the social workers on the 'foolishness' of these beliefs.

On 27 May Detective Superintendent John White gave social workers advice on their interview techniques. He had gone along to the social services department to see video recordings made with the Ames children in which, allegedly, one of the children had made a disclosure. He had been advised to go by Inspector Whitfield, who had so closely followed the case of Alma Smith. As Detective Superintendent White recalled: 'I was quite – upset is not the word because I do not get upset very much any more, but I was certainly surprised at what I saw.'

The video showed Carol and Nigel Ames, aged nine and eleven, being interviewed, or rather 'being asked questions which left no doubt in anyone's mind that the suspected abuser was the father'. In the words of the detective superintendent: 'There were leading questions; there were hypothetical questions. I think the partial disclosure finished up something like this, although this is purely my recollection from a long time ago: "Well, if it was anyone, it could be my dad, but I was asleep at the time."

"What did your dad do?"

"Well, he might have put something up my bum."'

As Detective Superintendent White recalled: 'That video lasted quite a while. It was perhaps fifty minutes – something like that. That was the extent of the partial disclosure. When it had finished I turned to the child psychiatrist and the other lady who was present and said:

"Did you see that as a partial disclosure? Because I did not. What about everything else that has gone on all the way through it? Are we going to take into account the fact that for the remaining however-many questions the children are saying that nothing has happened?"'

He added: '"What do you expect the police to do with that video?"

"You can re-arrest the father and question him again."
"We are living in different worlds, madam, if you think that is what can go on."'

The detective superintendent advised social workers that there was no evidential value in the video and stressed that all interviews leading up to a complaint of such a serious nature should be meticulously documented and seen to be fair.

There was, here and there, a bizarre twist to these various complaints and allegations and examinations. On 10 June a four-year-old girl purportedly disclosed to her mother that her father had subjected her to sexual abuse. The social services immediately arranged a case conference to deal with the welfare of the child. They were extremely keen to have the child examined by Dr Higgs at the earliest possible moment. Again, the suggestion that a police surgeon should be involved was quickly deflected. Instead, she was to be examined by Dr Higgs, and Dr Higgs alone. The child was duly taken to Middlesbrough General Hospital.

On this occasion, however, no evidence of sexual abuse was to be found.

24

At the height of the Cleveland crisis two men hanged themselves in Durham jail.

Francene Martha James was a housewife on a Middlesbrough housing estate. She was twenty-seven years old. She had been born Francene Thomas and had married Allan James just before Christmas 1983. Prior to that, Francene had been married to Walter Hanson, by whom she had two daughters: Elaine born in February 1978 and Caroline born almost a year later. As Francene recalled: 'Sometime in 1980 I split up with my husband and started going out with Allan James. We started living together as man and wife in 1981 and eventually we married on 20 December 1983. I gave birth to my daughter by Allan – Françoise – on 15 April 1982.'

Francene's first two children kept their father's name until January 1985, when they were changed from Hanson to James. As

Francene recalled: 'The reason for this was that Françoise was starting nursery school and we wanted the three girls to have the same surname. As from that time the girls have been known as James and all official records were altered accordingly, although they are not actually adopted by Allan.'

The three children were all attending school and it was at school that the eight-year-old Caroline James disclosed to her teacher that she was being sexually abused. The consequences were swift. At nine fifty-five in the morning on 17 June 1987, a woman detective constable at Cleveland Constabulary received a telephone call from a social worker to say that 'three' children were alleging sexual abuse against them by Allan Hanson. The fact that this was an amalgam of their stepfather's first name and the children's original surnames went unnoticed, for there was no such person as Allan Hanson.

The social worker listed the names of the James children and also gave their dates of birth. She said she intended obtaining a place of safety order on all three children and proposed to have them medically examined. The detective constable suggested that a police surgeon be used, but the social worker explained that she would have to follow 'guidelines' and have the children taken to hospital. The detective asked where the children were at that moment and she was informed they were being interviewed by another social worker in the presence of their head teacher. Thus at the crucial time when an eight-year-old had disclosed sexual abuse the police were not taking part in the vital interviews.

The policewoman was told that the head teacher could be contacted by telephone along with the social worker. She therefore telephoned the school and, as she put it, 'learned of the complaint in detail'. She discovered that the allegations against Allan Hanson had been converted into allegations against Allan Thomas, who was uncle to the children, being their mother's brother. The allegations appeared to be 'full sexual intercourse and anal intercourse upon the older two girls'.

The policewoman explained to the social worker that she had suggested using a police surgeon to examine the children but that the suggestion had been declined by the social worker's superior. The social worker explained that she was against a place of safety order because the alleged perpetrator had been named and he did not live in the family home. The social worker therefore saw no reason to take the children to the hospital, to hang around 'until eight o'clock tonight' and said that, so far as she was concerned, a police surgeon could be used.

The detective constable said that she would arrange for such an examination and contact her again with the details. Dr Alistair Irvine was called and arrangements were made for the two elder children to come to his surgery that evening. Shortly afterwards, however, the detective constable received another call from the junior social worker explaining that her superior had insisted the children attend 'a hospital and consult with a paediatrician, regardless that the normal guidelines in relation to a place of safety order were being ignored'.

The social worker 'apologized for the inconvenience caused' and the detective constable made arrangements to interview the children at a later date. The two elder children were still not interviewed by police. Dr Irvine was called and the arrangements for that evening's examination were cancelled. Three days later, on Saturday 20 June, the policewoman attended the Allan home and began a question and answer session with Caroline. During that time the child's mother, Francene James, was present. But as the session ended, and before the child had signed the statement, the alleged perpetrator came to the house.

Confronted by the police, Allan Thomas tried to get away. In the words of the detective constable: 'A violent arrest followed, with Thomas attempting to escape.' Allan Thomas continued to struggle and only became subdued when uniformed officers arrived at the house in response to an emergency call. Allan Thomas contended that he had been 'lured' to the house by his sister, and this was why he had run away when he had seen the police. He denied that he had resisted arrest but rather it had been the police who 'scuffled' with him and he was knocked on the head.

The elder children's stepfather, Allan James, helped hold Allan Thomas until police reinforcements arrived.

Thomas was taken to Middlesbrough police station where he was held in detention until his solicitor could arrive. When an interview was attempted Thomas refused to acknowledge that he had abused any of the children. He denied point blank all of the allegations. He was returned to the police cell. A police surgeon was called to declare him fit for interview at the police station and also fit to be detained there. The detective constable returned to the James' home to complete Caroline's statement and she also obtained a statement from her mother. On Sunday 21 June, Thomas was interviewed again, in the presence of another police officer. This time the interview was recorded.

When the interview was completed Thomas refused either to read the statement that had been made or to sign it. The record of the interview was read aloud to him, but still he refused to sign. He was returned to custody and the on-duty inspector at the police station endorsed the notes of the interview. At twelve noon Thomas was charged and cautioned with one offence in relation to the children. He was later charged with three additional offences.

There had still been no medical evidence to corroborate the allegations made. At four-forty on Monday 22 June the detective constable returned to the James household and collected Mrs James and her three daughters. She obtained from the mother written consent that all three of the children could be medically examined by a police surgeon. All were taken to the local health centre where they were examined by Dr Irvine. He informed the detective constable that the findings on the two older girls were consistent with their allegations but there was no evidence of penetration in the case of the youngest child.

Dr Higgs would also later provide a statement alleging sexual abuse against all three children. It later transpired that the two older girls had admitted to 'touching' the youngest child and that this had happened on two occasions. Since there was no corroboration of this no charges were preferred by the police in relation to the youngest child.

The mother of Allan Thomas, on being given the news that her son had been charged with sexual abuse, was so distraught that she tried to take her life. She was counselled by two local clergymen through a long night of anguish and despair. It was not that she believed her son to be guilty; she was convinced that he was not. She had long suspected the sexual abuse of her grandchildren and had been so concerned she had sought to have them examined by her own doctor. Of a nervous disposition herself, she knew that her son had inherited her fragile mental balance and dreaded what the impact on him would be when he was remanded to Durham jail at police request.

He was due to appear again before Teesside Magistrates on 29 June to enter a plea of not guilty. But in the very early minutes of that day he hanged himself in his cell. He was found by his cell mate just after midnight. An inquest on 9 September 1987 heard that the cell mate also found a suicide note in which Allan Thomas protested his innocence. In a statement issued later that day, Deputy Chief Constable Jack Ord pointed out that there had been 'no conflict between police surgeons and children's doctors regarding the Middlesbrough man found hanged in Durham jail'. It was also announced that there would be a major enquiry as to how Thomas had committed suicide while in prison.

Although there were troubling details in the allegations against Allan Thomas – the fact that eight-year-old Caroline had given a different name when first disclosing, the fact that Allan Thomas himself denied sexually abusing his nieces, the fact that Allan's mother refused to accept his guilt – the police file was closed. All that could now be hoped was that the two eldest children could settle down and forget the trauma.

The family went on holiday in Surrey in August. They were to stay with Tess and Jonathan Hall and their three children. They left Teesside on Saturday 8 August and the following day Francene James was asked if she fancied a night out with Tess on the following Monday, 8 August. The two mothers would go out on their own, for Jonathan would be working from nine o'clock and Allan would babysit. As Francene recalled: 'Caroline was in the room when this conversation was taking place but she did not actually say anything. I asked the three girls if it was OK that I went out. Elaine and Françoise said "Yes" but Caroline just shrugged her shoulders.'

For the remainder of that Sunday, Francene noticed that her eight-year-old daughter was 'particularly quiet' but she attributed this to the journey down from the north and the fact that she might be out of sorts. Her temperament did not improve the following day and while the children were having their tea Caroline 'just sat crying at the table looking at her dinner. She wasn't crying aloud, just sat looking at her dinner with tears running down her face. Allan was out of the house playing tenpin bowling with Jonathan at the time.'

Francene asked Caroline 'what was wrong' but the child said she had a pain in her tummy: 'For some reason I did not accept what she was saying and suspected that it was something more as her whole body was shaking as she sobbed. I thought that maybe she didn't want me to go out that night, so I asked her if that was the reason she was crying.' Caroline asked Tess if Jonathan would be at home after she and her mother went out. Tess replied that Jonathan would be going out to work.

'Upon hearing that, Caroline became visibly distressed and started shaking uncontrollably,' Francene recalled. 'I then took her upstairs into the bedroom in order that I could talk to her. Once upstairs I asked her what was wrong and Caroline begged me not to go out. I asked her why she didn't want me to go out and she said that she didn't want to be left with her dad. I could not understand why she should say this, so I cuddled her and stroked her hair and gently asked her why she didn't want to stay with her dad.'

Francene repeatedly asked this question but all Caroline would say was 'Cos' or 'I can't tell you': 'I realized that something was seriously wrong and in the finish I had to raise my voice to Caroline and say that if she didn't tell me, her dad would soon be home and he would come upstairs and she would have to tell him what was wrong.' Caroline then begged her mother not to tell her stepfather – whom she called 'dad' – what she was about to tell her. Francene agreed. The child then said:

'He's been doing the same as Uncle Allan.'

Francene asked her what she meant. She replied: 'You know. With his thing.'

Francene then asked Caroline some more questions.

'I realized my husband had been sexually interfering with her.'

The Jameses returned to Middlesbrough on Saturday 15 August. Francene told her husband that she was going shopping but instead took her three children to Middlesbrough police station. At half past five that evening the elder children were seen again by a police surgeon, and on 19 August another police surgeon, Dr Alistair Irvine, who had examined them earlier when their uncle had been charged, saw them again. He found evidence of past abuse in both girls, but no recent abuse.

Some facts are clear: Francene James did not know her husband had been interfering with her two older children when she made her statement to the police concerning her brother.

Allan James did not know of any allegation against his stepbrother-in-law before his arrest because the children never told him. James vehemently denied that he had touched Françoise, his own flesh and blood.

Caroline was asked why she had not told the teacher about her stepfather when she had told about Allan Hanson. The answer of the eight year old was: 'I thought about it but if my dad had come to school when I told about Allan he might have gone mad or silly or something.' The child also said: 'Cos on the telly the kids have gone in a home if their dad had done it to them.'

The nine-year-old child, Elaine, was asked the same question. She replied: 'Because I loved our dad and he said to me please don't tell on me because if you don't I won't do it again.'

Nor did he. When the children were examined by the police surgeon on 19 August, Dr Irvine found no signs of recent abuse. At the time of Allan Thomas's arrest, Allan James had gone round to the local newspaper, the *Evening Gazette*, and spent some time with one of their reporters. He denied that the sexual abuse of his children had anything to do with him. It was, with hindsight, a curious statement to make, since no one was accusing him of the offence.

At quarter past eight on Saturday 15 August, Allan James was arrested in the same house in which his stepbrother had been arrested. Unlike Allan Thomas, however, he admitted a series of offences against both his stepchildren, including buggery, intercourse and oral sex. He freely admitted having the children masturbate him, but it took a little while longer for him to admit to buggery and intercourse and oral sex with children who were only eight and and nine years old. That he was filled with remorse was understandable. He became very depressed and said he hoped that the judge would give him a maxiumum sentence.

While on remand he too tried to commit suicide, but recovered. The judge lived up to James's expectations with an eight-year sentence. On 9 November 1987 James admitted at Teesside Crown Court to raping his two young stepdaughters. The court was told that the girls had spent a 'year of horrifying sexual abuse'. James, aged thirty, admitted the two charges of rape, two of indecent assault and two of indecency with the girls. The judge, His Honour Sir Frederick Lawton, said: 'I cannot remember hearing a case of such depravity.'

The mother of Allan Thomas instructed solicitors to sue Cleveland Constabulary and the Home Office alleging wrongful arrest, false imprisonment and, in the case of the Home Office, negligence in that they failed to prevent her son Allan hanging himself in his cell. She had for a year been filled with anxiety that two of her grandchildren were being abused by their stepfather. She was 'suspicious' that he took baths with them. Her doctor had referred the children back to their own general practitioner and she urged the eight-year-old Caroline to disclose to her teacher.

And so the sexual abuse was revealed.

The second man to hang himself was Ronald Adams. He was thirty-six years old and a former soldier. He was unemployed. He had been separated from his wife for a year and lived in a bedsit in the residential part of Middlesbrough; he had a close girlfriend, Marilyn, who had her own flat, and by whom he had a baby boy, Steven. Steven was a year old in November 1987. Ronald Adams' wife had the custody of their three children, all of them daughters, aged seven, four and two. The youngest daughter had been taken to the family doctor because, according to Adams' sister, she had been bleeding from the back passage. Two days later she had a fit at playgroup and was taken to Middlesbrough General Hospital.

Dr Higgs diagnosed alleged sexual abuse. The other two children were brought to the hospital. Dr Higgs examined these two children, who were also diagnosed as having been allegedly sexually abused. The signs Dr Higgs had seen had been consistent with anal abuse. All three children were taken into care but on the arrest of Adams they were returned to the custody of their mother. Later, the mother of the three children would say that she was 'full of praise' for Dr Higgs, 'as she had no idea her children had been abused until the diagnosis was made'. She had 'no doubts about it'. She said the 'doctors and the social workers had explained each step' to her and she 'had agreed with all that had been done'. She made no complaints against the police or social workers, saying 'they acted with kindness throughout'.

She said she 'did not want her children to be interviewed' but she had been willing herself to talk and she wished the judicial enquiry in Middlesbrough to know of her 'experiences'. A police surgeon, not Dr Alistair Irvine but one who had recently taken up his duties, was in attendance when the other two Adams children were examined. Adams was arrested and charged with indecent assault. He was remanded in prison. He denied ever touching any of his children. Adams' sister claimed he had not been on his own with the children. She, together with her sister, and Adams' parents, claimed he had been separated for a year. 'He wanted them examined by another doctor,' one sister said. 'He was going to contest all of the charges. He couldn't have hurt his children. The bairns were his life.'

Ronald Adams was kept under observation while in Durham jail since, according to prison doctor Clare Foot, he was in 'a high state of anxiety' following withdrawal from alcohol and Valium abuse. He was deeply distressed at his incarceration on charges of alleged sexual abuse. He wrote to his mother on 5 July from Durham jail: 'I just cannot take it anymore mam. At the court my solicitor told me that I might going to St Luke's Hospital on Marton Road. I wish I was there right now mam. Mam I HAVE NOT DONE ANY-THINK TO THE CHILDREN. Its all right you telling me to pull myself together you are out there and so should I. I have not done anything it is just driveing mad in here(e) mum.'

In a second and final letter sent a week later on 12 July Ronald Adams expressed his deep concern that he might be sent down for crimes he had not committed: 'If I get sent down for this I may get anythink from three, eight to ten years for something I have not done.' Adams had also been charged with other offences arising out of his being in bed with his wife and another man, but it was the allegations that he had abused his children that preyed upon the mind of the former soldier.

Ronald Adams had with him in the cell in the prison wing of the hospital a photograph of his seven-month-old son Steven. He spent hours looking at it and he wrote to his mother: 'Now I have lost my son and the girl I wanted to marry. I could not care less any more if anyone comes to the courts or the jail. I will tell them the same if anyone comes to see me.' Ronald Adams went on hunger strike to protest at his arrest. He sorrowed for Marilyn and their son Steven. His mother, in order to cheer him up and get him back to eating, sent him the photograph of Steven. But Adams wanted a letter from Marilyn. He told his mother: 'If you want me to eat you will have to get Marilyn to write and tell me she loves me. I love Marilyn and Steven and want them back without them I am nothing to no one. If she writes and tells me she still loves me like she had told you [I] will eat something. If she does not write I will give up altogether. I just do not care anymore. I have no faith in myself anymore mam.'

His letter ended with a warning: 'Mam it's back to me again it's like I have wrote its Marilyn and Steven or no one else will get me I only want them two all I think about is them two I want them and if I can not have them all the kids will have no father at all and I mean that mam.'

Prison doctor Clare Foot would report that Adams had been examined 'at least twice by a psychiatrist'. He had suffered the 'severe anxiety' problem since 1974 and 'he was very upset about the charges he was facing. He had a wife and three girls and I understood they were separated. He had a girlfriend and a son by her. He was grossly anxious.' Pathologist Dr Harvey McTaggart said he believed Adams was 'upset and mentally hysterical.'

The assistant governor of Durham jail, Mr Stuart Mitson, later denied any claims that his staff had refused to treat Ronald Adams when on hunger strike. He confirmed that Adams had been under psychiatric observation and checked regularly 'because of the stress' he had shown. He said that the prison authorities took all reasonable precautions but nevertheless could not keep a twenty-four-hour watch on inmates. In fact, prison officer Victor Holloway told how he checked the cell 'every ten to twenty-five minutes'.

But fifteen minutes after his footsteps receded, on Wednesday 29 July, exactly a month to the day after Allan James, Ronald Adams barricaded himself in the cell with a bed and wardrobe, tore strips from the bed sheets and hanged himself from the window bars. It took three or four prison officers to break the door open.

25

One refusal to involve a police surgeon particularly irked the police. It concerned a handicapped child who had been treated in the past for constipation and who had been a regular patient of Dr Wyatt. On 12 July an examination revealed anal dilatation and fissures in the skin around the anus. These symptoms were diagnosed as consistent with 'recent anal penetration'. In the words of the chief constable: 'The child's sister was examined by Dr Wyatt without reason and anal relaxation and dilatation were diagnosed. He also found damage to the hymen. His opinion was recurrent anal and hymenal penetration.' But no statement was made available to the police for a fortnight after the examinations and 'a request for an examination by Dr Irvine was refused'.

It took some time for the chief constable to learn that these exclusions of a police surgeon were a deliberate act of policy, that the policy itself grew out of a determination to support Dr Higgs and Dr Wyatt in their diagnoses. Neither Mike Bishop nor Christopher Payne was aware of this determination when they bumped into each other at a cocktail party on 22 May. What Mike Bishop described as 'the growing crisis' in the child abuse sector was not far from either of their minds and they agreed to meet again on 5 June.

Mike Bishop held further formal meetings with his two senior assistant directors and the chairman and vice-chairman of social services. They were briefed on the situation, as Mike Bishop described it, and the fact that 'there did not appear to be an easy solution'. Mike Bishop recalled, 'the chairman and vice-chairman agreed to leave the handling of the crisis to ourselves as officers'. Thus Cleveland County Council's elected representatives would henceforth content themselves with briefings, but not positively involve themselves in action.

At the end of May the concerns of Cleveland Constabulary brought them into a direct clash with social services. There was an apparent antipathy between child abuse consultant Mrs Richardson and the police; and there was a concomitant antipathy between Dr Alistair Irvine and Dr Marietta Higgs. A meeting was therefore convened for 28 May by Mrs Richardson and Inspector Taylor to bring social services and the police together. Also invited were Dr Higgs and Dr Irvine.

The scene was set. The conflict would be monumental.

And it was a conflict for which both sides carefully prepared. On the one hand, Mrs Richardson wrote a memorandum for her boss, Mike Bishop. On the other, Detective Superintendent White wrote a memorandum for his superiors within the Cleveland force. Mrs Richardson set out her position on the day before the meeting. She was aware that Mike Bishop was to meet the chief constable on 5 June, and she pointed out to him the many difficulties that were arising but which she did not feel could be resolved other than at the highest level. The meeting between Mike Bishop and Christopher Payne had the aura of a summit, of being the only occasion where these matters of high policy could be resolved.

Mrs Richardson's specific criticisms of the police, as outlined in her memorandum, were that there was a 'shortage of police hours and/or overtime payments' and this was 'leading to delays in decision-making and appropriate placement of children'. There were also 'serious delays' in interviewing the suspected perpetrators of alleged child sex abuse 'due to the policy of Cleveland Constabulary of first establishing an unequivocal disclosure even where there is clear medical evidence'. This 'contrasted' with the policy of police forces 'in other areas of the country'.

There were also difficulties in establishing joint police and social work investigations and interviewing: 'At present the agreement is for "consultation" which is insufficient to prevent difficulties occurring, e.g. wish to exclude social workers from interview with the child. This includes one recent case where the child was in care on a

POS [place of safety order].' The 'current' increase in referrals was now outstripping resources, so that there was a need to 'consider specialist police abuse units which are becoming the norm elsewhere'.

But although Mike Bishop was meeting the chief constable on 5 June, it might be appropriate to have the chief constable along to a meeting which had already been arranged with the hospital authorities on 1 June, 'since the pace of police investigation is relevant to the length of time children are having to stay in hospital'. Mrs Richardson concluded her memorandum: '*I would value Dr Higgs' involvement in any meetings regarding child sexual abuse.*' Dr Higgs was consultant paediatrician working out of Middlesbrough General Hospital, with an outpatients' clinic at North Tees; insofar as child abuse was concerned there was also a role for her in management.

This was not a role she refused, for she had already accepted the invitation to meet with police officers on 28 May. But at that meeting did any of the participants from police, social services and health authority understand the nature of the crisis that was building all around them? Did they understand its impact on the lives of the people of Cleveland? Dr Higgs was there with her diagnostic technique, Mrs Richardson with her management skills. The police would bring their scepticism with them. All of the participants were representatives of their respective bureaucracies. Who would impose whose will upon whom?

They would find out on 28 May.

26

Detective Superintendent John White was one of those police officers who had been closely following events in Cleveland since 28 April, when he had attended a meeting of scenes-of-crimes officers held at the police headquarters in Middlesbrough. One of the items on the agenda that day had been Dr Higgs herself. The meeting was told that she had been recently appointed and was making requests for photographs to be taken of children's bottoms where the children were suspected of being sexually abused.

Officers attending the meeting were concerned that there was no sign of physical injury and therefore, in their eyes, such photographs had no evidential value; distress was being caused to the children, which apart from the ethics of causing distress was equally upsetting for police officers themselves. They were extremely embarrassed to be involved in a technique that turned children upside down so that photographs could be taken.

Detective Superintendent White, in the light of what he was being told, therefore instructed that no such photographs be taken until Detective Inspector Walls was consulted, and that the detective inspector should so advise Dr Higgs and explain policy on this matter. This Detective Inspector Walls did on 1 May. It was about this time that Detective Superintendent White became aware of the deep disquiet running throughout CID at the number of children now being diagnosed as having been sexually abused. Officers were particularly struck that there had been no complaints of sexual interference by the children themselves; the diagnoses were being made after the children had visited the hospital for non-sexually related matters; the children did not complain of abuse when interviewed by the police; the parents, who were the main suspects, completely denied that they had ever touched their children.

What also struck Detective Superintendent White was that the parents themselves, no experts in medicine or science or diagnostic techniques, simply did not believe in the diagnoses and kept calling for second independent opinions. But as he put it, there was also 'a gut feeling from experienced investigators that the suspect parents were genuine in their denials of abuse'. Following the conversation that Detective Inspector Walls had had with Dr Higgs on 1 May concerning the taking of photographs, Detective Superintendent White followed this up with a meeting at Middlesbrough General Hospital with the senior administrator.

Detective Superintendent White did not know at the time, but on the day he paid this visit to the hospital, a further *seven* diagnoses of alleged sexual abuse were being made in another part of the building. While these examinations were taking place the police officer was complaining to the hospital authority. Or rather he was complaining at what he described as 'the frequent diagnosis of "anal dilatation" where the surrounding evidence did not appear to support the finding' of sexual abuse. He was equally concerned at the abrupt response of Dr Higgs when she was informed that the police did not believe in the taking of intimate photographs where the diagnosis had been made.

The fact that the police were reluctant to follow Dr Higgs down an investigative line consequent upon her diagnosis had not, however, deterred her in any way. She had shown Detective Inspector Walls the door. She had not given up on the taking of photographs to provide her own back-up evidence of reflex anal dilatation. Detective Superintendent White learned that Dr Higgs had called a hospital photographer 'out of hours' to take the photographs. In the words of the detective superintendent, the hospital administrator 'informed me that he would approach Dr Higgs on this matter of the photographs and suggested that I spoke to Mr Drury, unit general manager'. The hospital manager was not available at the time.

In view of what the detective superintendent described as 'the escalating cases', a further meeting was held at Stockton on 8 May. Also there were representatives of the Crown Prosecution Service, who would have to deal with any criminal prosecutions, and Dr Alistair Irvine, the police surgeon. All were worried at the increasing number of child abuse cases where there was no corroborative evidence, and again it was decided that a new approach should be made to the administrators at Middlesbrough General Hospital and that Mr John Drury, the unit manager, should be seen on this occasion.

The appointment was arranged for Wednesday 13 May: 'I met with Mr Drury at Middlesbrough General Hospital,' Detective Superintendent White stated. 'I discussed with him the increase in cases of sexual abuse being diagnosed by Dr Higgs and the problems encountered by the police as regards the lack of supporting evidence. Mr Drury was well aware of escalating problems and informed me that on a particular ward (ward nine), twenty-four out of twenty-nine cases were of children diagnosed as having been sexually abused, in the main by Dr Higgs.'

The day before, 12 May, Mike Bishop had been present at the meeting of the Community Health Council. Questions had been asked and now the press were becoming aware of the somewhat startling position at Middlesbrough General Hospital. Fortunately for those involved in the management of the crisis, a general election had been called, and the media's attention was elsewhere. However, this was not known at the time of the meeting between the detective superintendent and the hospital manager. Mr Drury expected the figures to be published that day and anticipated a press response.

Detective Superintendent White himself began groping for a solution, one which had already occurred to the parents and which would occur to others.

Should there not be a second opinion on these diagnoses? 'Mr Drury stated that he would examine this possibility, but envisaged problems as regards paediatricians examining one another's patients unless invited to do so.' The ethics of medical consultancy were brought into play and therefore Detective Superintendent White steered back to his own remit, the operational problems that the police were experiencing in garnering evidence to back up the diagnosis and, if the evidence was there, to prosecute offenders. Later, his state of mind would not be assisted by seeing the Ames videos on 27 May, the day before the meeting had been arranged between Mrs Richardson and Dr Higgs on the one hand and police officers and a police surgeon on the other.

The meeting was held in Mrs Richardson's room at the headquarters of social services at Marton House, Middlesbrough. At the meeting were Inspector Taylor and Inspector Makepeace as well as Detective Superintendent White. There was Dr Alistair Irvine. And on the other side of the table, metaphorically at least, if not physically, were Dr Higgs and Mrs Richardson. The meeting focused on proposed amendments to circulated draft guidelines on how to handle sexual abuse, but it was really all about the medical diagnosis of reflex anal dilatation and the number of confirmations of child sexual abuse that had filled up Middlesborough General Hospital during the month of May.

The police representatives learned something new at this meeting. For Mrs Richardson told them that Dr Higgs had been appointed by South Tees Health Authority as a paediatrician with special responsibilities for child sexual abuse. And since this was the case the guildelines should be amended to take this into account. The amendment proposed was even more startling. Quite simply, there should be no further involvement of a police surgeon in the examination of child sexual abuse. This was to be the exclusive domain of Dr Higgs.

In the words of Detective Superintendent White: 'At this point the meeting degenerated into a heated argument between Dr Higgs and Dr Irvine, each doubting the other's competence and qualifications. Mrs Richardson frequently interrupted to condemn Dr Irvine's views. I was eventually able to bring order to the proceedings with the two doctors in total disagreement, in particular as regards the diagnosis of "anal dilatation" and their respective responsibilities in respect of child abuse cases.'

The detective superintendent then asked Mrs Richardson for her views on the differences of opinions between the two doctors: 'She told me that she was one hundred per cent with Dr Higgs and said her diagnosis could not be disputed. She was an expert in this field. She would endeavour to refer all sexual abuse cases to Dr Higgs. She did not support the views of Dr Irvine, in particular as regards "anal dilatation".' As to second opinions, Mrs Richardson was equally forthright: 'She said she was against it as they were not in the best interests of the child.'

Dr Higgs agreed fully with this view, put forward by the child abuse consultant: 'If a second opinion was absolutely necessary, then the child would be referred to Drs Wynne or Hobbs at Leeds who were the recognized child abuse experts in the United Kingdom. She would not be in favour of a joint examination between police surgeons and paediatricians.' Detective Superintendent White noticed the difference in the referrals from Hartlepool, where Dr Higgs did not practise, and that of Middlesbrough where she did. Mrs Richardson heartily agreed. It was her view 'something was wrong at Hartlepool, there was a failure to diagnose sexual abuse'.

Both Mrs Richardson and Dr Higgs referred to a survey conducted amongst adults which showed that one in ten had been sexually abused as children. The police officers and police surgeon were not told that this sample covered a wide range of so-called sexual abuse, including flashing, and that only seven in a thousand, in that poll, indicated they had been interfered with. This one-in-ten figure had been quoted in television programmes and news articles.

As Detective Superintendent White recalled: 'Mrs Richardson stated that they were now discussing the true problem in South Cleveland. I asked what percentage of that one in ten had been anally abused, as it was this diagnosis which was causing the problem. Neither Mrs Richardson nor Dr Higgs were able to answer this.' But if police surgeons were to be excluded, who would gather the forensic samples as evidence? 'Mrs Richardson stated that Dr Higgs could be given instructions on this. Dr Higgs expressed an interest in such training.'

And what about the late provision of statements?

To the astonishment of the police officers present, Dr Higgs replied that 'statements were not important. She gave them low priority. She said the police should accept and act upon her verbal account.' Dr Higgs would later state that this had been the practice during her days at Newcastle and she had expected it to be followed in Cleveland. She nevertheless did accept that the police would encounter problems if there continued to be a division of medical opinion. 'Dr Higgs had sympathy with the police in this respect and accepted that we would on occasion treat the diagnosis with caution.'

Throughout the 28 May meeting Dr Higgs stayed calm. She had put her views firmly but forcefully. She had held her corner before the police officers and in particular before Dr Alistair Irvine, who at one stage, and in a loud voice, called her 'incompetent'. Tempers had flared and later Detective Superintendent White expressed surprise that anyone could call the confrontation a meeting at all: 'I like to think of a meeting as people going somewhere. Meeting together, discussing things, maybe coming to agreement, maybe coming to partial agreement, maybe coming to disagreement, and hopefully agreeing to meet again to try to get things a little bit better.'

In accordance with this definition this was not a meeting at all: 'It was a forum for someone to say to me and the police surgeon, more or less: "Your role is finished." I was very very disturbed at what happened there. I think the next step along the line was perhaps for social services to say to us: "We will decide which cases the police will be involved with at all." That was the next step that I was very much afraid would come. They were very naive to think that that could happen, but it was, I think, the next step along the road as far as they saw it.'

Mrs Richardson, for her part, described the 28 May meeting as 'very difficult'. She had made a few notes at the meeting. She had indeed a high opinion of Dr Higgs and she had disliked the way she had come under professional attack: 'I think I certainly have some feelings in my own right on that account,' she recalled. This did not mean that she agreed with Detective Superintendent White's account of the same meeting. For example, he had been wrong in recording her forthright support for the views of Dr Higgs: 'He would not be wrong in recording that I will have made it clear that I had confidence in Dr Higgs and so did my department, but I think it is unfortunate the flavour that Superintendent White has given it by the way in which he has recorded it.'

Mrs Richardson denied that she had ever said she would endeavour to refer all cases of child sexual abuse to Dr Higgs: 'I think what I made clear at the meeting is that we would continue to work with Dr Higgs as normal; that we would not treat her work as suspect in the way the police felt obliged to do; that we would continue to refer cases to her and also continue to act on her diagnoses as we were obliged to do.' But was it not a fact that Mrs Richardson would actively prefer Dr Higgs to handle social services' cases because of her expertise and commitment to child protection? 'Certainly, throughout the department I think Dr Higgs was being selected by us to see children on our behalf.'

This did not mean that Detective Superintendent White had got it right. His note of the meeting, said Mrs Richardson, made 'the situation look very black and white and look as if we are working together in a professional way, which is not the case.' It is not entirely clear what Mrs Richardson meant by this remark, since she and Marietta Higgs had indeed been working as a professional team for some months, sharing an identity of views and approaches to the problems of child sexual abuse; but she had never said, nor would she have said, that she would refer all cases to Dr Higgs: 'That is far too black and white. The fact is that we might well be selecting Dr Higgs for certain cases but we would be working with other paediatricians as well.'

Mrs Richardson explained her own perspective on the diagnosis, 'in particular the fact that in the department, when we had investigated some of these cases, we had got some disclosures from children of these diagnoses'. She had apparently not been made aware of the deep concern the police had at the manner in which these disclosures had been made, or the views of Detective Superintendent White after he had seen the video recordings made with the Ames children. The diagnosis was 'unequivocal' and the disclosures would follow.

Mrs Richardson denied that she had said there would only be a second opinion if it was provided by Drs Wynne or Hobbs: 'I did say that I regarded Drs Wynne and Hobbs as leading authorities on child abuse in the United Kingdom. This is the only correct statement in that paragraph [of the note made by Detective Superintendent White]. I think the debate that took place on the use of Drs Wynne and Hobbs was that it was being put to me, particularly by Dr Irvine, that we were prejudicing our investigations in the eyes of the police by using someone whom he could not recommend. I think that the decision that was held, which I supported, was that when one seeks a second opinion one wants the best and most experienced you can find.'

Mrs Richardson said she was in favour of joint examinations, and yet she was to draw up a memorandum which would exclude police surgeons: 'I certainly recommended joint examinations *subsequently*,' she stated. 'I have recommended to staff in the department that they attempt to arrange a joint examination between the surgeon and the paediatrician.' She agreed, however, that she had said Dr Higgs might take over the collection of forensic samples: 'I think the issue was not whether or not a joint examination would be carried out. The concern was whether or not a repeat examination should be carried out.'

Therefore, if Dr Higgs were to collect the forensic samples, a second examination might be avoided.

But was it not a fact that the police saw themselves as being pushed out of what was described as 'an important area of responsibility'? 'Only if the police saw themselves aligned with the police surgeon. In fact, the police couldn't have failed but to be aware that as a department we were putting a great deal of pressure on them to become involved, that our request to the police was for more involvement, not less, and that was one of the difficulties of the issue which I decided, out of tact, not to pursue at the time.' But if tact came into it at all, had it been tactful of Mrs Richardson to make the bold statements that she did? Were not her own responses at the 28 May meeting a battle cry to the police?

'Not as far as the police were concerned. In that meeting I think I saw the social services department and the police in a very similar position, in which I could quite understand the police point of view, that they had difficulty if given contrary advice by the police surgeon. Equally, I explained the department's point of view that if we were given certain information by the consultant paediatrician, we couldn't ignore it. I saw it very much on a par.' Battle cry or not, the battle lines were set. But as Mrs Richardson later reflected: 'I had no idea at that meeting the police viewed it in the way that they subsequently reported it.'

The police may have been negative but there was high praise for Drs Higgs and Wyatt from Mrs Richardson: 'They were trying to be as open as possible to look at ways of handling this problem. The problem of sexual abuse was there, that we didn't at that stage in time know the best way of dealing with it, and that it was important to find a good way of dealing with it, and that they joined with us in seeking that way.' Mrs Richardson would add: 'I know that Dr Higgs discussed all the difficult cases with staff in the department, examining them from different angles and trying to consider what was the best outcome for the children. But that debate took place from a position of belief that the problem was there, that it was serious and that we had to look at what was best for the children.'

In short, there was 'an iceberg of undetected sex abuse below the surface of society's waters' and the doctors 'were beginning to get at it'. This deep belief in the perfidy of society towards its own children, and on such a widespread scale, might or might not be shared by police officers, whose main concern was to compile evidence that would convince a jury in a court of law beyond any reasonable doubt of the culpability of the accused. The 28 May meeting was not assisting this at all; rather, it seemed to the police their role would be further reduced, if that were possible.

The meeting ended abruptly.

One minute they were all seated in Mrs Richardson's room, and the next it was over. No conclusions were reached. No positions agreed. Aware of the forthcoming meeting between Mike Bishop and the chief constable, Christopher Payne, Mrs Richardson said that she would await the outcome of their discussions. The foreign secretaries and plenipotentiaries could not agree. It would now be left to the heads of government, or less grandiosely, in this case, the heads of the respective departments and bureaucracies. Detective Superintendent White took this to mean that the role of a police surgeon in the investigation of child sexual abuse would be discussed again.

However, while both sides indicated that they reserved their positions, neither in fact did. Detective Superintendent White immediately reported back to his assistant chief constable and made a note of the meeting. Police Inspector Colin Makepeace also made a note. He felt the meeting to be of such fundamental importance, the conflicts so deep, the consequences so grave, that he immediately wrote an account of his own. A solid police officer, he was trenchant in his remarks when it came to the altercation between Drs Higgs and Irvine: 'It soon became very clear that Dr Higgs is one of only three or so doctors in the country whose clinical practice and interpretation is at variance with the vast majority of medical opinion.' The other two were Drs Wynne and Hobbs.

Inspector Makepeace wrote that: 'Dr Irvine was of the view that Dr Higgs was frequently in error, which often resulted in care proceedings against innocent families which effectively tore them apart. What was worrying was the obvious lack of objectivity on the part of Mrs Richardson. She openly supported Dr Higgs one hundred per cent and even attempted to correct Dr Irvine, rather foolishly, on matters which really involved expert medical opinion. Dr Higgs gave me the distinct impression of being besotted with her own convictions, citing similar problems of recognition by an American doctor who tried to gain credence of his evidence of child physical abuse.'

This was Professor Kempe, who had pioneered investigation in child physical abuse in the United States in the early sixties.

Inspector Makepeace might not have been an objective observer of events at the meeting – it was alleged that there was a 'coloration' to his views – but nevertheless he made his notes contemporaneously and set on paper his own impressions: 'There was a definite sense of the evangelical present in Dr Higgs' attitude and without doubt Mrs Richardson is a convert and ardent follower.' There would also be a parting shot from Dr Alistair Irvine. His earnest hope, he said, was that both Mrs Richardson and Dr Marietta Higgs were 'both well insured'.

'You are going to need it,' he told them.

The fundamental dilemmas that preoccupied the police had not gone away. As Inspector Makepeace wrote: 'This leaves the police caught between two stools. On the one hand we have the weight of medical opinion in support of Dr Irvine, who in practice has proved to be one of the best police surgeons ever, and on the other a social services department which regards Mrs Richardson as the oracle and fountain of all knowledge on child abuse who is never wrong. It would seem that Dr Higgs, supported by Mrs Richardson, are out to serve their own interests and unfortunately are using Cleveland as the place to prove their theories.'

Inspector Makepeace never intended to doubt the sincerity of either Dr Higgs or Mrs Richardson in relation to these theories; they were clearly and obviously fully behind the diagnosis of reflex anal dilatation, and their desire was to protect children from the heinous crime of buggery. But their undoubted sincerity did not prevent the situation from getting worse, 'especially where irate families are objecting to Dr Higgs' diagnosis and social services' actions in taking care proceedings'. Inspector Makepeace described a case where one police sergeant had attended a case conference on child abuse where a solicitor representing a family requested that other children within the same family not be examined by either Dr Higgs or her associates. He wanted a paediatrician from outside Cleveland county. 'The sad result brought about by Dr Higgs and Mrs Richardson is that the good and effective relationships previously established are under great strain, with each agency under increasing pressure to cope with what the majority regard as unnecessary referrals.'

Inspector Makepeace might not doubt the sincerity of Mrs Richardson, but he did doubt her good faith: 'What is worse,' he wrote, 'is that I believe Mrs Richardson is mishandling the situation and perhaps deliberately so. She is making no attempt to bring about any appreciation or reconciliation of views and I have an uneasy feeling that if she got her way the police surgeon would not be used in the investigation of child sexual abuse.'

The following day a social services directive was signed that excluded the police surgeon altogether.

27

Following the 28 May meeting the police instituted new procedure for tracking Dr Higgs' cases: investigating officers would submit a report of all referrals on a weekly basis.

This information was then transferred to a work-board installed in the office of Inspector Makepeace, so there could be appropriate monitoring. A directive from Detective Superintendent White indicated that the police should seek 'substantial corroboration' of Dr Higgs' alleged findings before taking positive action, and that any diagnosis by her should be treated with 'caution'. The words of the Puritan elders seemed to be echoing down the ages, only they had urged 'exquisite caution' rather than simply 'caution'. Cleveland Constabulary were going to act with circumspection, meaning that, while police officers would seek a statement from the doctors, to have something in black and white, they would not interview possible or alleged perpetrators who might very well be parents. Not at an early stage. Investigations would mean talking to social services; talking to the children to seek a disclosure: everything that would be of any use to the police in carrying forward the investigation.

'Caution' would be specific to any diagnosis of reflex anal dilatation. As Detective Superintendent White explained: 'Dr Higgs is a well-qualified paediatrician who deals with many cases where her findings are not in dispute. Our actions in such cases are well established and will continue.' The detective superintendent meant by this that his concern was 'mainly over this particular diagnosis, which was referred from the initial diagnosis in hospital. Dr Higgs did deal with cases where there are court proceedings pending. There is no doubt that she does come across, and correctly diagnose – that might not be the right word to use – sexual abuse which is supported by corroborative evidence.'

The detective superintendent was referring to the case of the James children, where the uncle of the children had hanged himself in Durham jail, and four other cases that were pending and which were, according to the Crown Prosecution Service, of clear and explicit assault.

On 29 May White had a meeting with Dr Alistair Irvine. The assistant chief constable recalled: 'Dr Irvine told me that Dr Higgs was relying on a single clinical indication (anal dilatation) in her diagnosis of anal sexual abuse. He explained that this conflicted with well-established medical opinion which recognized the need for an internal rectal examination before concluding that abuse had occurred.' The assistant chief constable would tell his senior police surgeon that he had little knowledge of child sexual abuse 'but was surprised at the apparent incidence of anal abuse which was being diagnosed. Dr Irvine agreed that the number of cases was greater than he could have expected.'

Police concern ranged far and wide, so that on 29 May Detective Superintendent White had a further meeting with the deputy chief constable and Superintendent Saunders, who was stationed at police headquarters and was the officer in charge of the force community relations department. All were aware of the summit meeting pending between the chief constable and Mike Bishop on 5 June, and therefore the assistant chief constable decided that police officers should not attend the next meeting of the working party to establish child abuse guidelines which was scheduled for 3 June. Police officers later regretted that they had pulled out of this future meeting because it lost them the opportunity of putting their views to a wider forum. And if the consensus with social services had been ruptured it would hardly be restored by not attending meetings.

Assistant Chief Constable Fred Smith, however, at the time, in the heat of battle as it were, felt the amendments proposed on 28 May excluding a police surgeon were 'so extreme that it seemed unrealistic and pointless to allow them to be discussed by subordinate staff before the meeting of 5 June'. Detective Superintendent White therefore advised the social services department accordingly. Social services had themselves been busy following the breakdown of the meeting in Mrs Richardson's office. She and Dr Higgs had conferred with the assistant director, Bill Walton. Dr Higgs then left, and Mrs Richardson and Walton went to see Mike Bishop.

Bishop himself now wanted to move to centre stage: 'I was making it very plain to my senior staff that I wanted to know what was going on and I wanted to take a very personal responsibility for the crisis.' He referred to Dr Higgs as having 'exceptional expertise and talents'. But he did not know that the confrontation between Dr Higgs and Dr Irvine was a confrontation of medical schools and thoughts: the Dr Higgs school, straight out of Drs Wynne and Hobbs, that believed reflex anal dilatation was consistent with sexual abuse; and the Dr Irvine school which believed that it was not and could not be considered as anything other than prima facie evidence of sexual abuse which required a full rectal examination. Bishop perceived this simply as a clash between two doctors.

Mrs Richardson told Mike Bishop that the police were insisting on a police surgeon examining children, often some time after the original diagnosis had been made. He was further informed that 'this was contrary to *DHSS Guidelines in Child Abuse – Working Together*'. As Mike Bishop recalled it: 'This was the first time the police surgeons had taken this strong line, which conflicted with the practice concerning physically abused children where they accepted the diagnosis of the relevant consultant.' By then they had been joined by John Hughes, who was a child care adviser employed by social services. Dr Higgs had participated in the discussions with Bill Walton but not those with Mike Bishop.

As a result of this meeting Mike Bishop signed what turned out to be a fateful memorandum, although he himself did not consider it 'all important': it was one memorandum within the department 'among thousands issued in a year'. Nevertheless he admitted that it was a new directive to his staff and provided them with fresh mandatory instructions on how to handle child sexual abuse cases. And while Dr Higgs had not attended the meeting with Mike Bishop, upon her return to Middlesbrough General Hospital, Mrs Richardson called her there: 'I later had a telephone discussion with Dr Higgs regarding our mutual concern not to allow professional disputes to affect the interests of children, and the need to maintain high standards of professional practice.'

Shortly after this, having switched back from management to diagnosis, there was another telephone conversation between Mrs Richardson and Dr Higgs: 'Later that evening Dr Higgs telephoned me for advice on the immediate reporting of a new admission of a case of sexual abuse, since she was anxious not to alienate the police.' This would be the *forty-seventh* in a month for the paediatricians at Middlesbrough General Hospital. Mindful of the day's events, Dr Higgs clearly wanted to be on the right side of the law. She was advised by Mrs Richardson that the emergency duty team would alert the relevant persons and 'it would be normal practice to deal with the matter first thing the next morning'.

It had not been 'normal practice' at the hospital at any time during the last month, with the other forty-six cases, to deal with place of safety orders other than immediately; and while the anxiety not to 'alienate the police' was admirable on the part of Dr Higgs, this did not go so far as to invite a police surgeon to confirm her fresh diagnosis. In fact any fear of this was about to be made redundant since Mrs Richardson had already prepared a memorandum to exclude them. This she had done following her meeting with Mike Bishop, and although she had the assistance of John Hughes she ultimately took responsibility for its drafting.

Already she had spoken to Marietta Higgs on the evening of 28 May to let her know that an instruction would be issued and that this instruction would ensure that children would not go 'unprotected'. The memorandum was left with John Hughes so that it could be further discussed with Mike Bishop and then typed and distributed if approved by him. Bishop himself described the memorandum as a reaction to the fact that he knew 'the police were starting to be uneasy about enquiring into cases that had been diagnosed by Dr Higgs'. The memorandum would ensure that any 'unease' would be limited in future to joint investigation of child sexual abuse rather than medical diagnosis.

The memorandum was sent to divisional directors, senior area officers, area officers, court officers and the emergency duty team at Middlesbrough General Hospital. As Mike Bishop recalled: 'It was intended to reach all operational staff who would be in a field-work sense in contact with sexually abused children.' It was not circulated to residential and day care staff because it was not within their operational line of duty: 'It was aimed at all staff working in the field in the particular aspect of child care.'

The memorandum was headed 'The Management of Child Sexual Abuse' and its first paragraph read: 'In order to safeguard the welfare of children, pending guidelines from the Joint Child Abuse Committee, the following steps should be taken in cases of alleged or suspected sexual abuse.' The first step would be that there should be medical examinations carried out by a consultant paediatrician; the second was that 'initial protective action should be via admission to hospital'. That is, where the consultant paediatrician was of the opinion that there was medical evidence of sexual abuse, an *immediate* place of safety order should be taken to protect the child's interests during investigation. Of course, the police should be informed and every effort should be made to conduct a joint police/social worker investigation with the child.

What this meant was that the diagnosis having been made, police and social worker should investigate with the child in order to obtain, if possible, a disclosure: 'The obtaining of a disclosure from the child should be the key focus. The child should be interviewed as promptly as possible, preferably not in the presence of a parent, which may inhibit disclosure. Parental access may therefore need to be suspended or restricted during initial investigations.' And siblings should also be seen and medically examined.

But there should not be repeat examinations; they should be avoided. '*Where a statement is available from a clinician, it is not necessary for the police surgeon to re-examine the child. Forensic tests should be arranged in consultation with the consultant paediatrician, who will be able to assist the police surgeon as necessary.*'

This was a mighty victory for the young Australian doctor who had arrived as consultant paediatrician at Middlesbrough General Hospital less than six months earlier. Her diagnosis would be supreme; it need not be gainsaid nor verified by Cleveland Social Services. It was beyond dispute. This would equally apply to other paediatric diagnoses emanating from the hospital. Of course, the police would be needed in order to seek a disclosure; but the evidence of the paediatrician according to the edict of Mike Bishop would be sufficient, and where a police surgeon had any role at all it would be simply to obtain the forensic samples with the consultant paediatrician on hand 'as necessary'.

The police surgeon, reduced to laboratory technician in search of forensic samples, was now to be excluded from confirmatory examinations; child abuse guidelines were unilaterally rewritten; the work of civil servants in the Department of Health and Social Security, who laboriously turned out such guidelines for circulation up and down the country at the behest of their respective ministers, was redundant; and all this was done by the director of social services unbeknown to the police, to elected councillors, even to fellow officers within Cleveland County Council. Mike Bishop stated that the memorandum had been 'approved' by a DHSS officer from the Social Services Inspectorate 'prior to being sent out'. This was what Mrs Richardson had told him. Later he would amend that statement and say that only the last paragraph of the memorandum had been 'approved' by the Social Services Inspectorate.

This mandatory instruction was not only a landmark for the future in the treatment of child sexual abuse in Cleveland, albeit till proper guidelines could be agreed by the Joint Child Abuse Committee, it also served to consecrate the practices of the past month in Middlesbrough General Hospital. For during this month, in all the diagnoses made, there had been no corroborative evidence from a police surgeon; siblings had been brought to the hospital; place of safety orders, of which there appeared to be an abundance in photostat form, had been issued immediately (notwithstanding the 'normal practice' referred to by Mrs Richardson to Dr Higgs on the evening of 28 May); there had been attempts at disclosure work with police which the police did not believe had been successful; the parents had been denied access to their children.

And the medical diagnosis would be sufficient to have children immediately taken into care. These were the very amendments to child abuse guidelines that had been resisted by the police; indeed, resisted so fiercely that the meeting between police officers, Mrs Richardson and Dr Higgs had ended abruptly; so fiercely that a summit between the director of social services and the chief constable would be required to sort it out. This summit would indeed take place. But what was not known to police was that the guidelines had in effect already been rewritten, their views had not been taken into account. Social services had acted rapidly and effectively.

And unilaterally.

Rather, therefore, than social services and police moving closer to re-establish a consensus, that consensus was broken. On the one hand, the police were saying that they would attend no further meetings of the Joint Child Abuse Committee; on the other hand Cleveland Social Services had issued guidelines to their officers saying the police surgeon was to be excluded from future examinations until the Joint Child Abuse Committee was able to approve new guidelines. The stalemate was complete. Rather than establishing orderly managerial procedures to handle the influx of new cases of alleged child sexual abuse on the basis of reflex anal dilatation, there would only be the intervention of social workers, the participation of police in joint interview work, but no prospect of medical confirmation from a police surgeon that would bring alleged perpetrators into courts of law.

The children would indeed be protected. They would be saved from repeated medical examinations. (Mike Bishop did not know that when a child had been diagnosed as having been sexually abused this had often been the beginning of a series of examinations which, in the case of Alma Smith, numbered thirteen.)

Rather than draw the crisis to a close, the memorandum gave it a headlong push towards the brink. The paediatricians would continue their diagnosis of reflex anal dilatation and social services would continue protecting children, continue having them taken into care, all in the children's interests, without the checks and balances of thorough police investigation through their surgeon, against the will of their parents, without any dissenting voice emanating from social services, without any accountability to a wider county council audience, without any democratic intervention at all. Rights would be nullified.

It was as if those at the centre of the Cleveland crisis had spent all this time rehearsing their arguments, establishing their procedures, building up a partnership between health and social services, to build a road that was now open and could be signposted. It was not a yellow brick road that led to the Wizard of Oz and would enthral children through the decades. Rather, it was a grim road for those who would travel it, whereby in the course of another few weeks, some *forty-nine* more children would be taken into care, would be taken from their parents, would be taken into the maw of Cleveland Social Services, would fill up the hospital in a neverending turnover of well children looking for placement in foster homes, children's hostels and residences, new foster parents to be found, where social workers would turn video cameras on children who cried their innocence, while their parents languished and wondered where to turn next.

The road to Salem was now open.

28

'Hindsight is a blessed gift', Mike Bishop reflected.

The evidence that was available to him, as director of social services, was that children were at risk. He had acted promptly in appointing a child abuse consultant following the report of the Jasmine Beckford affair. The evidence he had – and from his point of view it was 'substantial evidence from a bona fide paediatrician' – was that 'these children had been quite seriously, in some cases quite horribly, abused'. He was not therefore prepared to 'balance the risk out' by sending children home to a situation where they might be abused again. 'I wanted to be satisfied that these children could be safely returned to the domiciliary environment.'

He added: 'I do not see any excuse for us trying to take risks that could result in children being further abused.' What, however, had been the impact of his 29 May memorandum? Could not its short effect be summarized thus: diagnosis equals immediate place of safety order equals disclosure equals limited access to enable disclosure to take place? Mike Bishop agreed that this indeed would be the flow 'once field workers received the memorandum and implemented it'. That was 'the appropriate technique that specialist members' of his team were advocating.

Had that management technique, however, been discussed with the Social Services Inspectorate of the Department of Health and Social Security? 'Not specifically on the memo,' Mike Bishop now recalled. But with hindsight or otherwise, as Mike Bishop pointed out, the memo was 'issued at the height of the crisis to protect children. If we had not issued that memo the children would not have been as well protected as they were.' However, whether the Social Services Inspectorate were fully aware of the content of the memo, nevertheless the management technique adopted by Mike Bishop had approval from other sources.

Some time between 1 and 12 June there was a knock upon his office door. There to see him, without appointment, were Dr Marietta Higgs and Dr Geoffrey Wyatt. Mike Bishop had had lunch with Marietta Higgs on 1 June and therefore he was 'mildly surprised' to see her turn up at his office. The lunchtime appointment on 1 June had been arranged by Mr Ian Donaldson of the South Tees Health Authority. Also at the lunch were Dr John Drury, manager of the Middlesbrough General Hospital, Mr Bill Walton, deputy director of social services, Mrs Richardson and Dr Higgs, and the new district medical officer, who had taken up his appointment only a day or so earlier.

Of this lunchtime meeting, Mike Bishop stated: 'Discussion took place at this meeting about the increase in child sexual abuse in Cleveland and the fact that Drs Higgs and Wyatt were responsible for the diagnoses.' The debate should have been about the increased incidence of anal abuse rather than child sexual abuse in general, since this was where the diagnosis lay, but as Mike Bishop recalled: 'A frank discussion took place on the validity of these diagnoses, also pointing out that once a diagnosis had been made, the department had little option other than to consider our statutory duties to take appropriate legal action.'

Mike Bishop later recalled that there had been some 'fairly critical questioning of Dr Higgs'. The critical questioning, as he recalled, came from himself, Ian Donaldson and John Drury, but their questioning was not to 'resolve the issues between conflicting medical opinion'. Rather, Mike Bishop felt, 'it was for Dr Higgs to convince us that her techniques were accurate and that these children had, in fact, been sexually abused in the way that she had diagnosed they had'. Mike Bishop would accept this might sound 'terribly naive', but he had even asked whether the diagnosis could not be attributed to 'massive constipation'.

Dr Higgs was able to convince him on this and other points: 'She was very cool and very convincing and very professional in her handling of our questioning and I am not saying that we were bowled over by her but her arguments were very very professionally strong and there was nobody in the room who could show that Dr Higgs was, in fact, wrong in what she was diagnosing.' Dr Higgs must have felt grateful that, unlike her meeting of 28 May with police officers and Dr Irvine, there had been no heated discussion: 'It was a cool, professional assessment of questions that we wanted to ask of her and we received cool, balanced, very carefully thought-out replies.'

Both Dr Higgs and Mrs Richardson expressed the view that child sexual abuse was much more widespread than had been realized and it therefore required a coordinated action and response. Was Mrs Richardson supportive of the views that Dr Higgs was expressing? 'She did not play a very active part in the meeting because we were – I do not like to use the word cross-examining in this context – giving Dr Higgs a fairly intensive grilling, those of us who were not *au fait* with her thinking. I would not say that Mrs Richardson was supportive of Dr Higgs. In fact, she kept out of it and let Dr Higgs answer for herself.'

In short, Mrs Richardson 'enjoyed her lunch and did not say an awful lot'.

Whether or not Dr Higgs raised the issue of the 29 May memorandum with Mike Bishop after that lunchtime meeting, the fact is that she and Dr Wyatt came unannounced to his office to praise the director for the strong support Cleveland Social Services was giving them in their work and to encourage him and his staff to continue on that course. As Mike Bishop would point out: 'Irrespective of whether that memo had been isssued or not, I would have expected my social workers to take control of the situation and, if they were not able to be satisfied a child could go home safely, to take a place of safety order. I would have expected strong action from the department throughout the crisis. The memo was simply clarifying how that action was to be conducted and taken.'

There was another question which the doctors wished to discuss.

The pressure on wards nine and ten of Middlesbrough General Hospital was now so great that it had been proposed *another* hospital should be opened to accommodate those patients who were the subject of the diagnosis of reflex anal dilatation. The Hemlington Hospital in South Middlesbrough appeared to be ideal, since a children's ward there had in the recent past been closed down. The scenario now envisaged was that it could be reopened to take the strain from Middlesbrough General Hospital where, as the hospital administration had turned the corner from one month to another, some twenty-four of the twenty-nine beds were taken up by children allegedly sexually abused. While superficially this course of action might seem attractive, the doctors did not agree.

They had in fact 'strong objections'. These objections were based on the fact that Hemlington was some distance away from Middlesbrough General, and the doctors therefore felt it would create difficulties with the services that the children needed from the hospital or indeed from Cleveland Social Services. It was, as Mike Bishop explained, 'more than that. They were very afraid that we were going to create a ghetto of abused children on the southern extremity of the county removed from mainstream services.' Hemlington was some five miles from the town centre.

While Mike Bishop could not recall precisely when these discussions on the opening or otherwise of a ward at Hemlington Hospital took place, the idea was finally rejected at a meeting which took place at Middlesbrough General Hospital, on Saturday 20 June, between Mr Ian Donaldson, Mr Mike Bishop and Dr Higgs.

There were other matters which Mike Bishop raised at this impromptu meeting between himself and Drs Higgs and Wyatt. As Mike Bishop recalled, they believed, 'particularly Dr Wyatt, that the detection of child sex abuse was a major breakthrough in the care of children and could explain many problems of child health which had previously not responded to treatment. I took this opportunity to raise the question concerning examination of children for sex abuse who had been referred for other symptoms, such as asthma, as I had heard that such examinations had taken place.'

Both doctors were able to assure Mike Bishop 'they would not examine for sexual abuse as a matter of routine, but if a child had been referred with some form of chronic or long-standing complaint, and if other causes for the symptom could not be established, then sexual abuse would be considered as a possible cause of the symptom and investigated further by medical examination.' Mike Bishop would have to admit that he was not qualified to question their diagnoses, 'but that the effect of uncovering so much sex abuse of children was placing serious strain on other services.'

As Mike Bishop pointed out: 'The existing resources could not cope with their numbers of referrals and I wondered whether there was any way in which they could reduce diagnoses to allow us to obtain the resources which would enable us to provide proper services for children and families.' Both Drs Higgs and Wyatt said that this was not 'professionally acceptable to them' and that other services needed 'to realize that this was a major development in child health which required an appropriate new initiative, in terms of resources and effort, to ensure that the opportunity was not missed to create a whole new integrated service to identify and combat the effects of child sex abuse.'

As Mike Bishop recalled: 'The meeting concluded with an acknowledgement that problems lay ahead that would need to be faced by us all.'

The summit meeting between Mike Bishop and the chief constable was held at police headquarters in Middlesbrough on 5 June. The senior advisers were also present: the assistant chief constable in support of the chief constable and Bill Walton in support of his director, Mike Bishop.

Mike Bishop led off by expressing concern as to 'the increased incidence of alleged child sexual abuse in the county of Cleveland'.

He expressed concern that Cleveland Constabulary appeared reluctant to play their part in the multi-agency approach. In turn, both the chief constable and his assistant spoke of the difficulties which the police were facing in trying to pursue enquiries into allegations that children had been sexually abused when those allegations were frequently based solely on the controversial medical diagnosis of Dr Higgs and were not accompanied by a written statement.

In the words of the assistant chief constable: 'We told Mr Bishop and Mr Walton that the standard of evidence was unsatisfactory and that the method of diagnosis used by Dr Higgs was controversial. We referred to Detective Superintendent White's written report of the meeting of the 28 May and expressed our concern that neither Dr Higgs nor Mrs Richardson saw any future role for the police surgeon in matters of this nature. We also referred to the fact that Dr Irvine had already been refused access to an alleged victim of abuse.'

Both the chief constable and his assistant emphasized that it was necessary for the police to obtain the best evidence available when investigating a crime. 'We could see no reason why an expert witness who had been used by the police for many years, the senior police surgeon Dr Irvine, should be unable to gain access to an alleged victim of sexual abuse. At the same time we assured Mr Bishop and Mr Walton that, like them, our main priority was the welfare of the child.'

The police were aware and agreed that the 'child's welfare was of paramount importance' and therefore they sympathized and understood that Mike Bishop and social services had 'to act positively when they received information that a child was in danger'. They also accepted that social services might have to accept a standard of evidence less than would be expected in a criminal enquiry. 'However, the chief constable and I suggested to Mr Bishop and Mr Walton that there must be some way of obtaining the best medical evidence while allowing the social services department to discharge their responsibilities while also ensuring that no unnecessary discomfort in the form of repeated medical examinations was imposed on an alleged victim.'

Somewhat delicately, both Mike Bishop and Bill Walton assured the police that they too were anxious to continue the cooperation which had traditionally existed between Cleveland Constabulary and Cleveland Social Services, 'but Mr Bishop indicated that Dr Higgs had been appointed to the post of community paediatrician and that he was obliged to accept her advice. He suggested that her evidence should also be sufficient for police purposes.' Christopher Payne, the chief constable, was firm in his assurances that this was not the case. Christopher Payne said that the examining doctor did not have to be a police surgeon, but did need to know what evidence to look for, how to collect that evidence and how to present it.

There was no communiqué following this summit, no statement to the outside world, for the outside world did not know of the upheaval that was taking place in Cleveland; the outside world was steering itself into the final week of a general election. If there was ever a time to reach any agreed solutions on how to handle this crisis, now was the time to do it. This fact was not realized by any of the participants. Their positions were set and demarcation lines had been drawn. While the constabulary agreed to keep a low profile, issuing no press statements, no one sitting around the table this day in police headquarters knew that it would not be long before the crisis took itself on to the streets.

Cleveland Constabulary were not insensitive to the need for efficient handling of child abuse. They had been discussing for some time the establishment of 'a dedicated unit' to deal with child abuse. Now they planned not only to establish this unit but to have it functioning by 1 July. Mike Bishop and Bill Walton were asked to participate in that they might attach social workers to the unit 'so that a genuine corporate approach could be established'. The two sides were able to agree in principle to this suggestion and agreed to discuss it further.

The police, however, were still going to treat with 'caution' any diagnosis of Dr Higgs, who the police complained had been 'reluctant and slow' to provide evidentiary statements. If place of safety orders were to be issued *immediately*, in accordance with the 29 May memorandum, each place of safety order had to be converted into an interim care order by the juvenile or magistrates' court. The place of safety order might be for seven, fourteen, twenty-one or twenty-eight days, but at the expiry of whatever time limit there had to be a presentation in court. On 8 June, when there was a first hearing on youngsters Lorna and Katherine Halliday, both diagnosed by Dr Higgs as having been allegedly sexually abused, there were a further *forty-five* other cases standing in line. Thirty-two further interim orders were asked for and obtained; thirteen new interim orders were obtained, taking the total to forty-five. There were, in addition, for the sake of the record, a further four applications withdrawn, with another seven adjourned, and three full care orders taken out.

In all *fifty-nine* care cases in a single day. All of the magistrates and juvenile courts in the Teesside Crown Court complex were embroiled in the making of these care orders.

Though the crisis was acute, Alan Cooke, the clerk to the Teesside justices, did not feel that his services were 'overwhelmed'. Certainly they were 'hard pressed'. Alan Cooke revealed that there were *two hundred and seventy-six* applications for place of safety orders between 1 January and the end of July 1987: a truly 'astonishing' number by his reckoning. But would he not agree that a danger existed that the application for a place of safety order, in the eyes of a justice of the peace, was nothing more than responding to a complaint or a summons?

Response of Alan Cooke: 'If there is one thing that I have insisted on telling magistrates, it is that what they are being asked for is a deprivation of a child's custody. And a very serious matter. I have compared it to remanding on a criminal charge in the adult court. Magistrates in the adult court are not allowed to deprive an alleged criminal of his liberty for longer than eight clear days, and here magistrates in the juvenile court have the power to deprive the parent of a child for up to twenty-eight days.' He would therefore stress, and stress repeatedly, that this was a very serious step, one which he would not equate 'with the judicial exercise of granting a summons'.

Of these two hundred and seventy-six applications, most had been made at the home of a justice of the peace rather than before a court of law. The previous understanding with social services had been that an application would always be made to a court in the courthouse unless it was a dire emergency; and then only a senior magistrate would be used for that purpose. This would be a senior member of the juvenile court panel or, if not available, a senior member of the bench. The ultimate decision would, however, be left to social services, who would be provided with a magistrates' yearbook containing the names and addresses of all of the magistrates.

In all some forty magistrates were called upon to sign the dreaded place of safety orders between 1 January and the end of July. Such were the numbers that it was impossible to establish how many were issued by the court in full sitting and how many were issued in the home of a justice of the peace: 'I suspect some of the orders that were obtained were obtained in court,' Alan Cooke recalled. 'But because the times at which they were obtained are not recorded I cannot confirm this.'

On 10 June the part-heard hearing on Lorna and Katherine Halliday came back before the juvenile court. There had been a hearing all morning and the case had been resumed at five-thirty in the evening. A doctor had been called independently by the parents and he supported Dr Alistair Irvine in stating that neither child had been anally abused; whereas the court officer of social services, Mr Jim Marsh, was seeking to put a contrary view on the basis of 'hastily scribbled notes' supplied to him by a consultant paediatrician who was seated at the back of the court.

This was Dr Marietta Higgs, who found herself in her third role: not that of an examining doctor, not as one participating in the management of the crisis her diagnosis was causing, but now sitting in a courtroom advising the court officer of social services. In the words of Alan Cooke: 'The answers being elicited were highly technical and capable probably of being properly understood only by experts equal to those by whom they were being asked and given.' How on earth were magistrates on Teesside to cope with such conflicting evidence? It seemed to Alan Cooke an unfortunate development, 'for not only was it taking a great deal of time but it appeared to be shifting the focus from the children to the doctors'.

What should have been at issue before the court was what was best for the children; instead there was 'a trial of strength between medical experts in which the interests of the children were in danger of being obscured and even lost sight of amid the claims and counter-claims of two doctors who each thought they were right'. The battle-ground between Dr Irvine and Dr Higgs had moved from the offices of social services, where the last struggle had been fought on 28 May, to the juvenile court in Middlesbrough on 10 June. Soon it would be joined by other eminent specialists, including paediatricians.

Alan Cooke arranged an urgent meeting with Mike Bishop, so urgent that it took place at quarter past eight in the morning on 11 June. In the prosaic words of Mike Bishop: 'A meeting took place between myself and Mr Cooke, the clerk to the Teesside justices, who was so concerned about the growing situation that we met at 8:15 in the morning in my office.' By now, following the traumas of 28 May, the tone of the meeting was as important as the content for those whose duty it was to record what had transpired: 'Again this meeting was cordial and Mr Cooke was fully understanding of the social services' position and did not question our entitlement to apply for place of safety orders.'

In the words of Alan Cooke: 'I wanted to discover how it had come about that two doctors, or four doctors, were opposed – two either side – that was the first thing I wanted to discover. I also wanted to get a move on with the case so that the guardian could be assigned and we could deal with the case completely. What was exercising me was that we had already spent two days on a case merely to decide whether an interim care order should be made. We were probably faced with a further two days before we finally disposed of the matter.'

Clearly the to-and-froing of medical argument had left an indelible impression in the mind of Alan Cooke. Like others in the Cleveland drama, he was experiencing something new, something different, something so out of the ordinary that it required action on his part. 'The situation in that court that night was like a medical seminar,' he would recall, 'where a diagnosis having been put forward was being countered by argument and suggestion that was really only capable of being understood by people who were trained to be medical people.' He had noted, however, that the application had been 'bitterly opposed by parents' who had been denied access to their children.

Alan Cooke did not know about the memorandum of 29 May. He did not know of the following lines: *The obtaining of a disclosure from the child should be the key focus. The child should be interviewed as promptly as possible, preferably not in the presence of a parent, which may inhibit disclosure. Parental access may therefore need to be suspended or restricted during initial investigations.* However, at his meeting with Bishop on 11 June, he learned that his procedural legal problems were being caused because 'access was being denied across the board and that began to show me why I was getting this avalanche of extensions of place of safety orders'.

Without mentioning his memorandum, Mike Bishop explained the difficulties by saying that 'disclosure work was essential and that he was being advised that the access by parents to the children was inimical to the disclosure work'. Alan Cooke was so alarmed at this news he immediately reported back to the chairman of the Teesside juvenile court panel, Mr Leonard Davies. They met at the law courts on that same morning, Thursday 11 June. Alan Cooke was due to accompany Leonard Davies to a seminar on juvenile justice that was being conducted at the nearby Teesside Polytechnic. 'It had been Mr Cooke's intention to be present at the seminar to which I had been invited as a speaker,' Leonard Davies recalled. 'Mr Cooke told me that a new situation had arisen in the juvenile court on the previous day – 10 June – which could have very significant ramifications if repeated before other benches.'

The alarm had now spread to the chairman of the juvenile panel. He was alarmed not only by the conflict of medical evidence, but also by the fact that parents were being denied access to their children, which was pushing them before the courts in order to contest interim care orders. The parents were fighting back. Through their solicitors they were now agitating for the return of their children, not on ward nine of Middlesbrough General Hospital, but before magistrates in a court of law. And there had been some fifty-nine suits in a single day. Notwithstanding that Alan Cooke had left Mike Bishop only an hour or two ago, he was instructed to arrange another meeting with him, which the chairman of the juvenile panel would himself attend.

As Leonard Davies recalled: 'I could appreciate that Mr Cooke would have particular difficulties coping with the sheer logistics of the additional work coming before the juvenile court, but in my view there were three matters of special concern to magistrates receiving the applications: the number of applications, the denial of parental access, and the conflicting medical diagnosis of alleged abuse.' There was an additional logistical reason: 'The large number of applications meant that other matters of longer standing were being delayed to the annoyance of the parties concerned. When people have waited in vain to have their cases heard, it is the custom in Teesside courts for the chairman to express regret for the unavoidable delay.'

Such now was the case load of child abuse cases that other aspects of litigation were being delayed, and complaints began to mount both from solicitors who were appearing in the courts and the clients themselves. Even when the care orders came before the courts, the case of the parents was receiving some sympathy. As Leonard Davies would say: 'The denial of access is recognized by the magistrates as a most serious deprivation for parents and children and knowledge that it was now a common practice was a matter of deep concern. The reasons for denying access in particular circumstances were known to magistrates but there was unease that access might be denied too readily.' The meeting was therefore arranged with Mike Bishop for 15 June.

What concerned Bishop at the moment was how best to manage what was now privately recognized as a crisis by social services, the health authority, the police and now the courts. There was also a fine legal point: this was whether social services had any right in law to deny parents access to their children when under a place of safety order. Mike Bishop had said so in his 29 May memorandum. But was it lawful? 'I am aware that the law allows access to be denied under an interim care order,' Alan Cooke would say. 'I am doubtful in my mind whether access can be denied under a place of safety order. I am aware that some people take the view that under a place of safety order access can be denied.'

The legality or otherwise of denying access to parents whose children were subject to place of safety orders was not raised by Alan Cooke with Mike Bishop because it was already happening, 'in the sense that he had obtained place of safety orders for which now he was seeking extensions. I could not deny him the right to come to court and ask for extensions. If he were to get an extension, he then had an interim order and under the Child Care Act of 1980 he then could deny access.'

Alan Cooke had hoped, on 15 June, to share problems with Mike Bishop, but he was equally hopeful that they might find solutions. However, Mike Bishop had none to offer. 'And what was worse he had no predictions as to when this work was going to drop away.' The plain fact was, however, that Alan Cooke had no solutions either. They were all faced with a crisis. None knew how to break it. Men do strange things in a crisis. They reach strange conclusions. The reason for the visit by the clerk to the Teesside justices and the chairman of the juvenile panel was their concern, among other things, that parents were being denied access to their children and were bringing their grievances to the courts.

In this context the solution put forward by Alan Cooke was startling.

'We were back in a situation of a manager being presented with problems and no one offering any solutions,' Alan Cooke recalled. 'At that stage, quite spontaneously, I said: "Well, why don't you apply for twenty-eight-day orders. If it is so important that you should have this period for disclosure work, would that not give you a longer period?"' The suggestion was quickly taken up by Mike Bishop: 'Mr Cooke thought that some respite might be obtained in this unprecedented situation if place of safety orders were sought for twenty-eight days in the first instance.'

From 10 June there had already been a sharp increase in twenty-eight-day place of safety orders, although Alan Cooke denied this had anything to do with him. The clerk to the justices now found himself entangled in the crisis when all he had been trying to do was be helpful. By now the place of safety orders were 'coming thick and fast and with little notice and taking precedence as emergency applications over other cases that had been in the lists weeks and even months earlier'. On the twenty-eight-day place of safety order, Alan Cooke would say: 'It was a spontaneous suggestion on my part, made by me after hearing his difficulties as a means of helping both of us to deal with a situation in which, so far as we knew, there were no precedents to guide us.'

In fact this suggestion was never acted upon by Bishop for in what seemed no time at all, the crisis was out in the open and running. By 15 June, it hardly mattered what had been discussed between Mike Bishop and Alan Cooke and Leonard Davies. It hardly mattered if the clerk had suggested a twenty-eight-day place of safety order. None of the participants had been able to get a grip on the crisis and each step they took not only did not resolve the crisis but made it worse.

Someone else came knocking at Mike Bishop's door on 15 June. It was his second-in-command, Bill Walton. The news from the Western Front was bad; or rather the news from Middlesbrough General Hospital, on the west of the town, was hardly encouraging. Over the weekend of 12–14 June a further *eighteen* children had been admitted and diagnosed as having been sexually abused.

And the strain was beginning to tell even within the walls of Middlesbrough General Hospital.

29

Dr Marietta Higgs and Dr Geoffrey Wyatt were still up at five o'clock in the morning of Sunday 14 June.

When Dr Higgs came to Middlesbrough General Hospital on 1 January, she had not been slow in letting the nursing staff know that she had an especial interest in child sexual abuse. This information was imparted to Sister Morrison who passed it on directly to Mrs Iris Chambers, who was employed by the South Tees Health Authority as a nursing officer for the medical and paediatric unit. It was not, however, as Iris Chambers would accept, unusual for 'a consultant paediatrician to have an interest in many areas of paediatric medicine'.

The hospital staff at Middlesbrough General Hospital had not noticed any particular increase in admission to wards nine and ten of children with a diagnosis of sexual abuse in the early part of 1987. A number of children of all age groups had been housed on wards nine and ten, but there had been scant, if any, admissions of children who had allegedly been sexually abused. In fact, there had been only three cases in the month of April. There were, however, twenty-five admissions in the first twelve days of May, and while there was some abatement in the numbers towards the middle and end of the month, the figures climbed dramatically again in early June, culminating in the eighteen fresh admissions on the weekend of 12–14 June.

Crisis point had been reached.

Mrs Marjorie Dunne was employed by the South Tees Health Authority as senior nurse and designated officer for child abuse in the Langbaurgh district of Cleveland. She had held the job for five years. Prior to this, she had worked as a health visitor in Scotland, where she had become a member of BASPCAN. Later she became the chairman of BASPCAN's north-east branch, following in the footsteps of Dr Christine Cooper, who had done so much to encourage Dr Marietta Higgs.

Mrs Dunne initiated training programmes for nurses in child sexual abuse which often took the form of informal lunchtime sessions and 'annual study days'. She also talked to emergency staff at Middlesbrough General Hospital: midwives, general practitioners' groups and nurses training in mental health care. Mrs Dunne had not been aware of any difficulties among nursing staff at Middlesbrough General in March or April but she was not surprised that problems developed as the crisis broke. She felt sexual abuse was such a difficult topic that 'some people find it extremely difficult even to listen to us talking about it'.

From May relationships between herself and the nursing staff deteriorated. As she admitted: 'It was a complete breakdown, really.' Mrs Dunne learned that the nurses were finding it increasingly difficult to cope with children who were entering the wards diagnosed as sexually abused. One day she telephoned the ward at Middlesbrough General Hospital to speak to one of the sisters. The sister did not come to the telephone. Mrs Dunne thought this unusual. She realized 'something was afoot'. She recalled: 'It was a sign of the great stress that they were under, that she would not talk to me.'

On 22 May Mrs Dunne visited the hospital to see the staff and to talk to them about 'sexual abuse and the feelings associated with it'. In response the nurses voiced their frustration. They asked: Why didn't someone tell them what was going on? Mrs Dunne tried to involve the nurses at a later meeting arranged by social services so that Dr Higgs and others might talk to them about sexual abuse. She became concerned, however, when she was not informed of the names of those children in her district who had been either admitted, discharged or referred to the newly created Child Resource Centre with a diagnosis of alleged sexual abuse.

She found the delays mounting in getting relevant information. On one day, she recalled, 'a hospital social worker telephoned me with *twelve* referrals'. Parents requested information from health visitors who had no information to give; case conferences were delayed because there were no witness statements from consultants; police investigations were delayed because of conflicts in the diagnosis. Dr Higgs herself was on several occasions unable to attend case conferences or to provide notes. One day Mrs Dunne left a case conference and called the ward to ask the sister to give some information from hospital notes so that the conference could proceed.

Mrs Dunne discussed these problems with Mrs Richardson and learned that the resources of social services were also being stretched: 'I think this was one of the most difficult things to deal with, that as professionals who had been feeling they were fairly competent, suddenly we just felt helpless in the face of this crisis which rolled on and rolled over us all.' Mrs Dunne went to see Ian Donaldson. She agreed to make written recommendations. She also decided to canvass paediatricians and other child abuse experts to try to get some consensus on the diagnosis of reflex anal dilatation Among those canvassed were fellow member of BASPCAN. As she recalled: 'I was very concerned about the possibility of a neverending chain of "Yes it is", "No it isn't", with all the awful effects on the child.'

Mrs Dunne also questioned the increase in referrals in a direct conversation with Dr Higgs. Dr Higgs replied that the signs were all there. Mrs Dunne accepted this response from her BASPCAN colleague: 'It was not a surprise, particularly once I had adjusted to the idea of what it meant in numbers.' Mrs Dunne regarded Dr Higgs with great respect. She had been impressed with her at their first meeting at a case conference in Newcastle prior to Dr Higgs' coming to Teesside, and she had also heard of Dr Higgs from earlier

BASPCAN meetings: 'I realized that we had at last got a paediatrician that seemed to be prepared to acknowledge child abuse and actually act on concerns from nursing staff.'

The nurses needed all the help they could get. They had difficulty coping with each sudden influx of alleged child sexual abuse cases. It was not the numbers that gave rise to concern, for often in the northern winter the numbers of children admitted with coughs and flus and other ailments would rise dramatically. It was the nature of the allegations that caused the problems. Normally when new patients were admitted information about them was forthcoming, either from doctors directly, or from notes. But in the case of this sudden influx of alleged child sexual abuse, when the doctors were not on the wards and the nurses looked to the notes, they found them blank.

Did this mean there were no notes at all?

There were indeed notes, but they were kept by Dr Higgs, not at Middlesbrough General Hospital but in her office in the town's maternity hospital. There was a file on each child who had been diagnosed as sexually abused. Dr Higgs felt it important that 'certain documents should not be included in the child's medical notes. For example,' as she later explained, 'case conference minutes and reports, photographic slides, and details of information about parents obtained from them or their children.' These 'subfiles', as she described them, also included 'information on cases other than sexual abuse, such as physical or emotional abuse'.

This stockpile would not be revealed until some months later, but for the nurses, dealing with the immediacy of everyday life on the ward, the fact that there were no notes, or that the notes stayed blank for several days, was particularly distressing. For while they knew that alleged sexual abuse had been diagnosed, the children were often suffering from common ailments, such as constipation or asthma. Parents complained that these specific ailments were not being treated. The nurses had the additional difficulty of knowing the legal status of each child: they had become surrogate social workers who needed to know which parents had access to which children, what those access arrangements were, if they existed at all, and who had authority to take a child from the ward and who had not.

Social workers bustled in to take children for photographic sessions at North Tees General Hospital – now that it was clear the police were no longer to lend a hand taking photographs of the children's intimate parts – parents wandered in to see their offspring, although the records sometimes indicated they were not allowed access. Sometimes the records gave no indication at all. Some children were under place of safety orders, some under interim care, one was even under a place of safety order before a medical diagnosis had been made. This was in the case of a new admission where records other than the name of the child did not exist at all.

Apart from confusion over the status of children's records there was confusion over procedures for their admission. Often a health visitor or social worker arrived unexpectedly. The normal procedure when a child entered hospital was that a general practitioner would make a referral and send case notes. But in the case of a referral by a health visitor or social worker there was neither.

In normal cases, a child would be brought to children's outpatients'. A report would be made to reception and the parents would give the child's name and time of appointment, together with the name of the consultant designated to see the child. The receptionist would then hand over the case notes to the nurse on duty. The nurse on duty would weigh the child, measure him and, according to what was provisionally wrong with the child, would test urine, put parents and child alike at ease, explain procedure and tell them what was likely to happen.

These procedures could not be followed, however, when all that the nurses knew from the health visitor or social worker was that there was a query regarding alleged sexual abuse. They had to tread warily with the child. They had to tread warily with the family. They could not explain what was going to happen. They could not explain the likely outcome.

All they could do was weigh and measure the child and say that he or she would shortly see a doctor.

Even with these limited procedures the nurses coped, but they began not coping at all as May turned into June and the numbers of admissions increased so considerably that children began to be left sitting in corridors and in spare rooms, often for hours at a time. Indeed, the inflow became so great that often the nurses were reduced to knowing the child's name but nothing else. They did not know what was medically wrong with the child or even what was supposed to be wrong. They saw health visitors and social workers coming and going, they saw police on the wards, there were case conference huddles, and one evening three boys on ward nine, two aged eleven and one aged twelve, became aggressive and began fighting.

All three had been admitted as victims of alleged sexual abuse. One boy stabbed another with a sharp toy. Two policemen who were on the ward investigating other suspected cases of child sex abuse were called in to calm the children down. The children came from one of the rough council estates on Teesside, and when the nurses sought to intervene prior to the police, the nurses were assaulted too, only with verbal abuse. This caused great agitation among the nurses. In all their years of experience they had never witnessed scenes such as these in a hospital.

One such nurse, Mrs Susan Bareham, who had entered nursing in April 1973 and had nursed in a variety of hospital units, said that the scenes she had witnessed and the treatment meted out to both patient and parent alike during this month of June, were 'disgraceful'. She recalled the different attitudes of the parents: 'Many were distressed that they had to bring the children to Middlesbrough General Hospital at all. They were very wary, fearful of saying too much in case it was picked up the wrong way. And in some cases people just cancelled their appointments.' This hardly pleased the nurses, who had always maintained a good rapport with both parents and children, seeking to be, as Nurse Bareham said, both 'very honest and very open'.

The nurses had sought to be friends, so that the children would not treat the uniform with suspicion. But because of the diagnosis of alleged sexual abuse, with the examinations which this entailed, the parents were becoming distressed, and this was being communicated to the children. The atmosphere of gentle reassurance was being replaced by fear, anger, frustration: 'frustration from the nurses' point of view because all they could do was make them a cup of tea'. Nurse Bareham said the nurses were left to cope by themselves because there were no guidelines on how to deal with such an unexpected situation and no guidelines were given.

An added complication which caused anxiety was that once a child had been admitted for alleged sexual abuse, social workers would bring in brothers and sisters. The cloud of suspicion extended to them too. As emotions built up, children who were about to be taken from their parents began to shout, thus charging the atmosphere still further. Confidentiality was lost, and staff and patients in the clinic next door to the mayhem of ward nine could hear everything that was going on.

What happened if a child was brought to the hospital needing emergency treatment, when all the beds were occupied with well children who had nevertheless been diagnosed as allegedly sexually abused? Into this atmosphere was admitted one little boy who had been in a road accident. The beds were full. There was not even a cubicle in which the child could be nursed. 'He needed peace and quiet,' Nurse Wendy Hornby recalled, 'and in the middle of the ward, with children running around, throwing paper airplanes and Dinky toys, he did not really get the rest he needed.'

In the end parents became aggressive and abusive, and nurses – considered with respect by all users of the health service – found that the abuse was beginning to be directed at them. A great deal of time was being consumed by the nursing staff on these extraneous events: 'Quite a lot of my working shift was spent trying to smooth things over,' Nurse Hornby recalled, 'trying to explain to parents what was happening and that we would help in every way we could.' But because of this Nurse Hornby had not the time to do the job for which she was trained: that is, look after children.

Confusion was added to this already confused scene because some parents were allowed to stay on the ward with their children, and in fact became residents of the hospital, while other parents had no access at all. On one occasion the brother of a suspected abused child was allowed to come on to the ward to stay. This meant there was a brother, sister and mother all sleeping in the same ward, the mother on a campbed on the floor, the brother taking up a bed on the ward that an ill child might have taken. And if parents had no authorized access, according to social services, but nevertheless appeared, it was left to nurses to tell them they could not see their children. 'Sometimes the parents were not even aware they had no access.'

The sudden arrival of the consultant paediatricians did not help matters. Dr Higgs and Dr Wyatt would arrive on the ward without any warning at all and nurses would be expected to accompany them. Sometimes children were examined in the presence of their parents; sometimes not. This was because some parents had access to their children but access to others had been forbidden by social services. Those children who were examined without their parents present were quite distressed at the fact; this was especially true of the smaller children. These smaller children were aged between two and three. After examination, these children were admitted to the ward. For this there was a special admission ward separate from the main ward, but when admissions were made at night nurses did not wish to disturb children who had settled down to sleep.

The side effect of this was that while some examinations were made by Dr Higgs and Dr Wyatt in a day unit at the far end of the ward, some were equally made by the consultants in the admissions ward, thus preventing this ward from being used by acutely ill children, who had to be admitted immediately on to the open ward. The main lights were therefore required to be on and children already settled for the night were disturbed after all. Sick children were also being moved in the middle of the night. One angry anaesthetist phoned Nurse Hornby to complain that children who were listed for the theatre the following day had been moved from ward nine to an adult ward.

One night, when Nurse Eileen Middleton, a sick children's nurse, came on to the ward for night duty, she found that ward nine was already full. Nurse Middleton had been a staff nurse on night duty at Middlesbrough General Hospital for six years and worked on both wards nine and ten. A girl had been admitted with a minor head injury. She was examined by a junior doctor and then discharged. But in addition to the full ward seven children were in the playroom awaiting examination for alleged sexual abuse. Nurse Middleton came on duty at quarter to nine. She was told that the children in the playroom were to be examined in the day unit, these examinations were now proceeding, and the children would not be allowed home that night.

Discussions then ensued with doctors, nurses and a consultant as to where to place the children, since there were no beds for them. The consultant who took part in the discussions was Dr Geoffreey Wyatt. The suggestion he made was that two older boys in the second half of the divided ward, that is beyond the nurses' cubicle and entrance, should be transferred to an adult ward. The boys were aged eleven and twelve. One boy, who was a diabetic, was wakened and refused to go. The other boy, who had befriended the first while in hospital, said that if his friend was not going he would not go either.

'Eventually,' Nurse Middleton recalled, 'five children were transferred over to an adult ward, an adult orthopaedic ward. Two of the children who were originally on the ward were transferred to ward ten, so we kept seven.' That is, two children aged approximately two and four were sent to sleep upstairs, and when the child with the minor head injury had been discharged at two o'clock in the morning, the numbers on the ward righted themselves. As it happened, the mother of the injured boy did not mind taking him home at two o'clock in the morning, because he was due to leave the hospital at six anyway, and this meant his place would be taken by an acute admission. But as Nurse Hornby said: 'It seemed odd that if the child was ill enough to warrant admission at seven-thirty at night, then the child should have stayed'.

Nevertheless, on this particular night the children on ward nine were unsettled and it was not until eleven o'clock that some calm was re-established. Another nurse who had difficulty in coping was Nurse Deborah Cunliffe, who was so upset by one specific incident that she called in the nursing officer. This concerned the moving of a diabetic child: 'He was actually moved in the evening and was brought back the following morning by the house officer,' she recalled. 'The child was uncooperative and [the move] had an adverse effect on him. With being a diabetic, he would not take his diet, so we had to get him back on the ward where we controlled him again.'

This took place on 19 June.

Another case involved a child with a fractured femur. The child, actually on traction, was moved across the grounds to another ward. This upset both the child and the parents. By now the ordinary routine of the ward was so severely disrupted that it was affecting the recovery of the sick children; their parents were complaining; but the children who were fit and healthy, 'running about the place', as Nurse Cunliffe recalled, were having a damaging impact on those poorly children struggling to get well.

The nurses had lost control of their own wards.

These criticisms would mystify Dr Higgs, who on Tyneside had always been used to involving nursing staff in discussions about day-to-day management of cases. She had done this both informally and on ward rounds. When she arrived in Middlesbrough she found there was no current programme of weekly clinical meetings attended by junior medical and nursing staff, and she therefore arranged a series of lunchtime meetings on alternate Tuesdays at Middlesbrough General and Middlesbrough Maternity hospitals for nursing and junior medical staff, 'though attendance by nursing staff was not high'.

These meetings had started in February, and in April Dr Higgs began to show some videos on the subject of child sexual abuse which she had obtained from Leeds, together with a short booklet which had been introduced following the admission of the Ames family, 'since it was clear that both junior medical staff and nursing staff would find them helpful'. These meetings were held in the children's outpatients' clinic and nursing staff were 'strongly encouraged' to attend. There would be a discussion following the showing of the videos and copies of the booklet were left on the ward for nursing staff to read.

As Dr Higgs said: 'I also tried to make myself available to the nursing staff who wanted to discuss points arising from the cases on the ward. This was usually in the evening, either before I went home when I was not on call, or after the night round when I was. These discussions covered many different topics and increasingly involved sexual abuse in May and June when admission of children so diagnosed increased.' BASPCAN would also be helpful. There was a BASPCAN meeting on 4 and 5 June, to be addressed by a child psychiatrist, and Dr Higgs made sure this was publicized in the nursing sister's office on wards nine and ten. She arranged a further discussion on 23 June at a meeting of her Cleveland sexual abuse group, but by then events had overtaken her.

Mrs Chambers, as nursing officer for the medical and paediatric unit, wrote: 'In May there were no problems of well children running around the wards or of parents being 'disruptive'; these developments occurred in June when numbers rose again, communication deteriorated and the critical events of 12–13 [June] and the days following took place.' Deterioration? Critical events? The ever-calm, ever-cool, ever-logical Dr Higgs would express it somewhat differently: 'A particular concern of the nurses was that they did not have experience in dealing with parents in such circumstances. My advice was that they should act towards them just as they would to any other parents.'

She would add: 'I think there was some frustration on the part of some nurses that they were not able to take an active part in treatment of such children as they would normally do, a feeling which I could understand.' She certainly did not think that 'the care of ill children on the wards was being compromised, nor was any such concern expressed to me by the nursing staff that this had happened, although they were worried that it might do so and they were also concerned about the lack of supervision of the more active children'.

Just as Mike Bishop did not see the ground falling away from him in his discussions with the chief constable and the clerk of the Teesside justices, together with the chairman of the juvenile panel, nor did Dr Higgs see the dangers in the frustration, deteriorating relations and downright worry of nurses who dedicated their lives to patient care. Dr Higgs was not an insensitive woman; her care for children – and especially those who had allegedly been abused – was all-consuming. She worked every possible minute of the day and night and was expected to cope, and although she could understand the 'frustration' of the nurses, she did not understand, until the nights of 12–13 June, that there was more to it than that.

It was open rebellion.

30

Mrs June Drummond was a staff nurse at Middlesbrough General Hospital two nights a week. She had worked on the paediatric wards since October 1970. Her work was exclusively on wards nine and ten, the children's wards. She had been particularly preoccupied by the influx of sexual abuse cases and had taken up the matter directly with Dr Higgs and Dr Wyatt. Both assured her that their diagnoses were based on sound clinical techniques. Nurse Drummond's concern reflected the rumblings of other nurses and junior doctors. Nurse Drummond knew that as a nurse it would be the worst case of *lèse majesté* to question the medical diagnoses of two eminent paediatricians. However, on one occasion she could not help but blurt out:

'Well, surely it isn't possible for anyone to be a hundred per cent certain of anything. There must be areas of grey.'

Nurse Drummond was on duty at midnight 12–13 June.

Dr Higgs and Dr Wyatt came on to the ward to do what is described as 'a ward round'. There was nothing unusual in this. Nurse Drummond had now known Dr Wyatt for some years. Often he looked in at children at night. After all, as Nurse Drummond later explained, children are often sick at night as well as during the day, and there had been times when Dr Wyatt had been extremely helpful to Nurse Drummond. There had been times in the past when she had become concerned for the wellbeing of a child, and no matter how late or early, he would come and see the child immediately.

Dr Higgs was less well known to the nurse.

As it happened, Dr Higgs had been on the ward earlier to examine a child, and now she and Dr Wyatt examined the same child again. In the words of Nurse Drummond: 'They in fact looked at one child who Dr Higgs had seen briefly at nine o'clock. They re-examined the child and then they stated that they thought they should look for a child with a normal anus on the ward.' As Nurse Drummond followed them around, they went into another cubicle to examine a child who had been vomiting. Nurse Drummond pointed out the child had been on intravenous feeding. The child was not well at all. Notwithstanding this advice of the duty nurse, the doctors proceeded to examine the child.

This was not, however, the full paediatric examination, only examination of the chest and abdomen, genitalia and anus. Other children were also examined that night. It was the recollection of Drs Higgs and Wyatt that one of these was looked at because a nurse had told Dr Higgs that when the child's nappy had been changed the nurse had seen a bottom that seemed to be 'rather gaping'; in another child Dr Higgs found skin tags around the anus; and it was Dr Wyatt who had asked Dr Higgs to examine another child because of his 'failure to thrive'. Another child was examined, but there were no signs of sexual abuse and he was put back to bed. This child had been admitted with what the medical fraternity call *otitis media* (inflammation of the ear).

It was also the recollection of the doctors that on this occasion they examined four children on the ward, although Nurse Drummond would say there was a fifth: 'They wanted to examine yet another child who had been in the hospital for a number of weeks, who was a child with quite serious chest problems, and I pointed out that in fact the child's mother was present on the ward and that, in fact, she appeared to be "educationally subnormal", and I did not think she would be able to understand the reasons for the investigation and so Dr Higgs and Dr Wyatt did not examine that child.'

When examined by the two doctors, a child would be put in a prone position on the nurse's knee, the nappies having been removed; there was no internal examination in the case of reflex anal dilatation, but glass rods were used to the front of a female child. As Dr Higgs herself would explain: 'Before using the rods, and depending on the child's age, I show the rod to the child, saying that I need to touch her with it where I had been looking. I then touch the end of the rod on the child's hand and say it should not hurt but if it does then tell me and I will stop.' Describing the test of reflex anal dilatation, Dr Higgs would say: 'I employ the same technique as I have always used when examining a child's bottom for any other reason, namely inspection with the buttocks parted adequately to visualize the anus.'

There would therefore be an anal examination on all of these children that night. Parents were already sleeping on the ward with their children, but none of the children who were examined that night had their parents with them.

And what was the reaction of the doctors when they were on the ward? In the words of Nurse Drummond: 'I think that they felt, and of course this is really a personal opinion, that they were glad, not presumably that they had found a case of sexual abuse, but that in fact it had been diagnosed, so that the child and the family could be treated accordingly.' In her written statement, Nurse Drummond used the word 'elated'. 'Yes – because I feel that was sort of quite important, in that that is the only word I can find to describe it.' A state of high excitement? 'I think that they, in all sincerity, believed that this problem of sexual abuse was reaching such proportions and was in fact going to become even worse.'

When the night sister, Sister Chaytor, heard what had happened on the ward this night she asked Nurse Drummond to make out a written report. But there was another nurse who had been on duty on 12–13 June, working downstairs on ward nine while Nurse Drummond worked upstairs on ward ten, and she too would make a statement in her own handwriting and submit this to the hospital authority. This was Nurse Middleton.

She described the atmosphere on ward nine: 'Several families were on the ward being investigated for possible sexual abuse.' She recalled: 'This involved having police officers, social workers and medical photographers present. Several children were being examined anally and vaginally, using special glass rods to measure dilatation of these areas. Photographs were taken. When this was completed the consultant asked if there was a child that was not suspected of abuse that would be photographed as a comparison to the abused children. They selected a child with a minor head injury and suggested we photograph him. I said that I didn't wish to waken him and be part of his examination as abuse was not indicated. These incidents occurred from around eleven o'clock at night to one o'clock in the morning.'

Sister Chaytor herself formally complained to Mrs Chambers as soon as she arrived for duty on the morning of 13 June. It was Iris Chambers who instructed Sister Chaytor to get the formal statements. These statements were handed to management on 15 June. They rapidly found their way into the hands of the district general manager of the South Tees Health Authority.

Ian Donaldson had had his first brush with Dr Higgs when she had signed a letter prepared by Dr Geoffrey Wyatt accusing the South Tees Health Authority of 'asset stripping'. The letter had been sent on 18 September 1986, before Dr Higgs had taken up her appointment. Ian Donaldson had responded sharply, calling the letter 'a mixture of fact and serious misunderstanding', or 'fantasy in other parts'. And while Dr Higgs had taken up her post on 1 January, in February the chairman of the local medical advisory committee had drawn Ian Donaldson's attention to the fact that 'he had heard that Dr Higgs, who had been appointed with special interest in neonatology, was widening her activities considerably into child abuse and social medicine'.

As Ian Donaldson recalled: 'If true, this gave us some concern, not as such, but in that there had been strong paediatric professional pressure in the autumn of 1986 very substantially to increase the number of consultants working in neonatology.' His concern was such that he wrote to the regional medical officer, Dr Liam Donaldson, informing him of this development in Dr Higgs' practice and 'suggesting that a timetable of her activities be obtained'. Then there had been the lunchtime meeting with Mike Bishop on 1 June, when among other things they had sought to quantify the likely levels of child sexual abuse in Cleveland. Mrs Richardson and Dr Higgs offered to produce a report, since information at the meeting had been 'vague and anecdotal'.

When Ian Donaldson received the three formal complaints from the nurses he sought legal advice. As he later recalled: 'It was and is no part of my role to comment upon the clinical judgement of a consultant.' However, he also talked to the regional medical officer and sought his backing in telling Dr Higgs and Dr Wyatt what the law was and how and why it was they needed to conform with it: 'I saw both the clinicians in the early evening [of 16 June] in the children's unit and spelt the situation out in an amicable meeting in which I sought to convince them to stay within the ethical and legal limits.'

The doctors, in turn, sought to convince Ian Donaldson 'how imperative it was to unearth abuse and of the consequent long-term damage to the child'. Dr Wyatt gave Ian Donaldson some startling news. 'In the course of the conversation, Dr Wyatt told me he had radically changed his clinical practice about a month previously, having seen what Dr Higgs was doing, as he now thought that this was the most important aspect of child health.'

Mike Bishop was also taking action. Information on the eighteen admissions over two days had been so 'alarming' that he was now seeking a second opinion. His own 29 May memorandum excluded a police surgeon; his discussions with the chief constable at the summit of 5 June had not persuaded him that this second opinion should come from the senior police surgeon in Cleveland county; and one of the reasons why he had issued his memorandum in the first place was to prevent too many examinations of children. Mike Bishop knew too that he could not 'interfere with clinical judgements of paediatricians', but he nevertheless now turned to the Social Services Inspectorate for advice and help.

The strategy of the second opinion was therefore devised. But it was all coming too late. For between 12 and 16 June inclusive, there were *thirty-seven* admissions for alleged sexual abuse, thus completely blowing all systems. The hospital could no longer cope, the police were excluded, and social services simply ran out of foster homes and residential homes and could not place the children. As Mike Bishop later stated: 'It is likely that this rapid increase in diagnoses and place of safety orders over a five-day period, and the consequent delay in explaining the situation to parents and children, provided the seeds of massive discontent, parental concern and the enormous outcry which ensued.'

On 18 June events got so completely out of hand on ward nine that the police were called.

Tim and Mary Hall had two children: Naomi and Nelson, both of whom suffered from constipation. A local doctor prescribed suppositories and Mary Hall was given plastic gloves in order to insert the suppositories. The suppositories, however, turned out to be 'uncomfortable' and she stopped giving them to her children. Nelson was eventually taken to see Dr Grant at Middlesbrough General Hospital, who advised that the child be put on a high fibre diet. Since Naomi also was still suffering, Mary Hall put her on the same diet.

Nevertheless, because both children complained of 'itching in their bottoms', Mary Hall took them both back to the doctor. He diagnosed threadworms. But since the constipation persisted in

Nelson an appointment was made with Dr Geoffrey Wyatt for 16 June. The appointment was for twenty past four in the afternoon. Dr Wyatt arrived at twenty past five. 'I explained about Nelson's constipation. Dr Wyatt examined his back passage. I never saw what the doctor done. I was sat next to Nelson's head while the doctor examined his bottom.'

Dr Wyatt left the room and returned with Dr Higgs: 'She looked at my son's bottom, nodded her head, and then asked if I had any more children.' When Mary Hall referred to her daughter Naomi, Dr Wyatt asked if she too could be examined. 'I agreed immediately. My daughter, who was at the hospital with me, became very upset when she found out she was to be examined and to what extent the examination was.' Dr Wyatt allowed Mary Hall to look at the children's bottoms and indicated that there were signs 'consistent with sexual abuse'. Mary Hall did not believe a word. She immediately asked that the police be brought in, but she was told that she must take her daughter to ward nine.

'When I arrived I had to tell the nurse on the ward what had happened, because they weren't expecting us and didn't know anything about it. We were then left for five and a half hours wondering what was happening when Dr Wyatt came along wanting to examine my daughter's vagina. I immediately refused because I thought my children had gone through enough.'

By now the place of safety orders were flowing instantaneously: 'I was then given an emergency twenty-eight-days protection order by a social worker which had a photostat signature of a justice of the peace,' Mary Hall recalled. 'At eleven o'clock that same evening I was asked if my husband and I would leave the ward and return the next day. The following morning, 17 June, I went back to the hospital to be greeted by my children who were both very upset and wanting to come home to me and my husband.'

Mary Hall called the police herself and asked if they would come to the hospital and make enquiries as to 'what extent my children had been abused'. She was informed that it was not within the power of the police to do this until the social services had reported the abuse. 'I left my name and address and those of the others in the same shocked state and position and was told to ring back.' Mary Hall rang the next day, 18 June, and was told that none of the cases had been reported to the police.

It was at this time, with angry and frustrated parents milling around, that Dr Higgs and Dr Wyatt appeared on the ward. They were harangued by the mothers and retreated into their office where Mary Hall and others collared them and asked what was going on. The invective stung Dr Higgs. Dr Wyatt was jostled, pushed and shoved, and felt so threatened he felt it prudent to call the police. The ward was now in uproar. There was mayhem in the playroom, and the teacher who came to assist children in care to keep up with their education refused to teach. Cigarette ends littered the ward. Taps had been left running and water spilled on to the floor; there were wet paper towels all over.

The toilets used by the children were in a miserable state: their floors were damp with urine, paper towels had been thrust down the bowls, and cleaning ladies refused to accept that cleaning up this mess was any part of their job. Neither Dr Higgs nor Dr Wyatt, nor any of the nurses, were hurt in the disturbances. The parents were calmed down sufficiently for a delegation to visit the hospital manager. They were told by the acting unit general manager how they could and should complain. A police inspector and a police sergeant now arrived. As Mary Hall recalled: 'They came to talk to the parents concerned and the inspector told them to see a solicitor.'

A call was put through to Mike Bishop. Would he attend the hospital? Mike Bishop refused. The police inspector therefore advised parents as a group to go to social services and put in a petition. Rather than investigating a disturbance at the hospital and arresting the alleged culprits, the police fully understood and sympathized with the plight of the parents: they had been living with the crisis throughout its build-up. And while Mike Bishop would not come this Thursday 18 June to see for himself the turmoil on the ward and confront the anger of the parents, he did accept an invitation on to ward nine two days later, Saturday 20 June.

He had felt it 'inappropriate to confront an angry emotional group and therefore reiterated the offer that I would see anyone who wished to come into the social services headquarters'. Two parents took up the offer and came to see him. Mike Bishop promised that their children would not be moved from the hospital to a foster home without further consultation. This promise was easy to give, as it happened: the foster homes were all full. As Ian Donaldson recalled his conversations with Mike Bishop on 17 June: 'His immediate concern was that he had run out of children's homes and foster families and couldn't move the children then in Middlesbrough General Hospital.'

The suggestion of a spare ward at Hemlington by way of

additional accommodation for the children was still being discussed. Meanwhile Bishop and Donaldson had agreed to set up a panel to give clinical second opinions, and a greater part of Thursday 18 and Friday 19 June was taken up with setting this in motion. On the Saturday, when Mike Bishop was taken on to ward nine, he was shown round by Dr Higgs: 'The atmosphere was peaceful with no sign of tension between staff and children on the ward. Some parents were present who spoke to us informally. The only forceful representation was made by a child's uncle who was very critical of the consultants.'

But after the disturbances on Thursday 18 June the parents remained restless. Mary Hall took the police inspector's advice and went to see a solicitor. She saw Graham Brown at his office in the centre of the town. To her surprise, Graham showed her a stack of files on his desk. He told her they were all allegations of child sexual abuse. He told her: 'You are now one of seventy.' He explained that he had called for a second opinion from an independent qualified paediatrician. The same day, wandering the streets in her desperation, Mary Hall called in at the studios of Tyne Tees Television and explained what had happened at Middlesbrough General Hospital. The general election was now over, the dust of the electoral battle had settled, and Tyne Tees immediately despatched a television crew and an experienced reporter, Miss Kim Barnes, to the hospital. It was her first of many door-stepping visits.

Mary Hall also went to the offices of the South Tees Community Health Council, where she met the secretary, Mr John Urch. John Urch had been seeking to bring an end to events at Middlesbrough General Hospital since the Community Health Council meeting of 12 May which Mike Bishop had attended. He had himself visited ward nine and described the scenes he had seen as 'hellzapoppin''. He was filled with sympathy for Mary Hall and her fellow mothers. He was also categoric. He did not agree with the diagnosis of reflex anal dilatation or the diagnoses of the two doctors.

Ian Donaldson had returned to the hospital and was told how Dr Wyatt had been 'harangued'. He sought to calm the hospital staff. 'It was very tense,' he recalled. 'Totally different to when I had been there two days previously.' No violence had been done but he found that 'the children were overactive, resistant to being in, and the parents were meeting, sharing experiences, which was creating real tension, and they were blaming the doctors for taking the children even when they had done nothing wrong'. Ian Donaldson had 'a long talk' with Dr Wyatt and they were joined by Dr Higgs. 'I said I could not accept the present position and would have to do something radical to reduce tension.'

Ian Donaldson proposed closing down the children's ward of the hospital.

'I said I did not wish to do anything as crude as that and would they ease back on admissions for four or five days to reduce the tension.' There was some digression in the discussions but neither doctor was prepared to budge: 'Essentially, they maintained that if they came across sexual abuse they had to do something about it and they could not shirk their duty.' Unsure that he had made any impact at all on the doctors, Ian Donaldson rang the chairman of the local medical advisory committee and they agreed that a panel of senior doctors should see the two paediatricians the following morning, 19 June.

Ian Donaldson met the panel at quarter past eleven and they saw Dr Higgs and Dr Wyatt at lunchtime. What was the panel of distinguished medical experts on Teesside to tell the doctors? What was the purpose of the meeting? Who could gainsay consultants making diagnoses in the exercise of their duties? Or was the meeting to instil into the minds of the two doctors that there was a serious problem in the hospital, that they were a part of that problem, and that while no one would wish to interfere with them in the course of their duties, there were wider considerations? Whatever those wider considerations were, Drs Higgs and Wyatt were adamant: their behaviour was ethical and they had a duty to diagnose child sexual abuse where they believed they discovered it.

Having lived through a sequence of extraordinary events, whereby there had been disturbances at Middlesbrough General Hospital, with the police called in; having threatened to close down the children's ward; having brought in the wise men of the local health service; having sought to second-guess the consultant paediatricians with a new panel of medical experts; having seen calm restored to the ward, Ian Donaldson said that he 'kept in close touch with the situation on an hour-to-hour basis'. And rather like the communiqué that was issued on 11 November 1918, that it was 'all quiet on the Western Front', he wrote: 'There were no other significant developments during Friday 19 June.'

He was wrong. For there was one further call that Mary Hall made on behalf of the parents congested at Middlesbrough General Hospital.

That was to her Member of Parliament.

Book Three

BRANDLINGS PLUCKED FROM THE BURNING

31

On the same day as the summit between Mike Bishop and Chief Constable Christopher Payne – 5 June 1987 – five-year-old Joanna Forbes was playing with a toy truck in the front room of her home on a Middlesbrough housing estate while her mother fastened the buttons on the coat of her young brother Carl, aged fifteen months. As the mother fumbled with the buttons she heard a shriek from her daughter. Joanna had tried to sit on the truck, holding the wheel, with her legs on either side, and push it along the carpet. In doing so, she had fallen badly. She had fallen forward, but the truck had tipped up, rearing its rubber front wheels, causing her an injury.

June Forbes was a single parent. She and her husband had separated some eighteen months before this incident, but although they no longer lived together they had remained good friends and were in regular contact. Since birth their daughter had been in and out of hospital, not because she was accident-prone, but because she had a palsy that affected her arm movements. Her consultant paediatrician at Middlesbrough General Hospital was Dr Geoffrey Wyatt.

In fact, while Dr Wyatt regularly saw the child, she was also seen by other specialists, and had regular physiotherapy to assist her with her arm movements. She had been attending hospital on a weekly basis until she was three years old, when she started nursery school, and then when attending primary school she had special treatment from a physiotherapist who would visit the school regularly. In addition, there were exercises to be supervised at home and June Forbes had seen to these without difficulty. She had also taken her daughter to Dr Wyatt because she suffered from constipation.

Dr Wyatt had suggested a 'colour-free' diet that might assist the child combat the difficulties of constipation. There was, however, another reason for the colour-free diet. It was to improve Joanna's temperament and moods. She was regularly afflicted by temper tantrums. Whether or not this had any effect, the fact is that Joanna Forbes was known to Dr Geoffrey Wyatt, who had been treating her almost since birth, and there was no difficulty in the relationship between June Forbes and the doctor. She found him 'a good doctor' and she was happy with his treatment of Joanna: 'I felt I was able to talk to him. He had always reassured myself and Joanna in the past about about any problems.'

The incident with the truck had occurred prior to Joanna going off to school. The result of the fall was that Joanna had injured her bottom and vaginal area. She was very upset. She was screaming and crying and her mother tried to settle her down: 'I comforted her the best I could,' June Forbes recalled. The child went upstairs to the toilet and her mother heard her crying. The child had blood on her knickers and so her mother carried her into the bedroom and laid her on the bed. She was red and a little swollen. June Forbes took Joanna to school and asked the school nurse if she would take a look. She wanted the nurse to keep a check on Joanna throughout the day. When she returned that afternoon to pick Joanna up from school the nurse suggested that she be taken to the doctor and June therefore called at the doctor's surgery on the way home. It was closed but she was told it would be open the following morning. Joanna suffered no distress that evening, she settled down happily at bedtime and went to school the following morning. During the middle of that morning the school nurse came to the house to see June Forbes.

'The nurse arrived at my home the following morning about eleven-thirty. She said she had made an appointment for me to take Joanna to Middlesbrough General Hospital to see Dr Wyatt,' June Forbes recalled. June therefore put on her coat and went to the school with the nurse, where Joanna was picked up and taken to the hospital. June Forbes, however, had not been best pleased at the interference of the school nurse. Her husband had come by the evening before and together they had looked at Joanna's injury: 'When Joanna's dad came for his tea, both me and Joanna's dad had a look and Joanna's bottom was a little bruised. She said it still stung her when she went on the toilet.'

Notwithstanding her crossness with the nurse, June Forbes went off to the hospital with Joanna. She waited two hours before seeing Dr Wyatt. This did not improve June Forbes' temper, but she had calmed down by the time she arrived at the hospital and kept her daughter quiet by reading some stories to Joanna on the ward while they waited: 'I kept asking the sister in charge when Dr Wyatt would be coming and we were offered a cup of tea and were told Dr Wyatt would be with us shortly.' Joanna, however, wanted to know what she was doing in the hospital, why she was there and 'she was a little bit distressed as well because she had been taken from school and she had not even had any dinner'.

By this time both June Forbes and her daughter were very anxious, and when Dr Wyatt eventually arrived June Forbes found him 'very flustery and sort of busy. I thought he must have had a very off-day. Then I tried to explain to Dr Wyatt all about Joanna's accident and I could not because Joanna was made to undress and get on the couch straight away.' By this time the delicate Joanna was more than fidgety and cross: she was 'crying, screaming and very distressed'.

This made it difficult for Dr Wyatt to deal with both Joanna and her mother, but it was June Forbes' view that Dr Wyatt should have spent more time talking with Joanna and herself, reassuring Joanna and 'getting to know the actual facts of what happened' before any examination took place. The examination was not to be easy, with the crying child, the cross mother, and now two nurses on the scene to assist Dr Wyatt to quieten things down.

The nurses talked to Joanna and held her hand but she was kicking and trying to get off the examination couch, so the nurses had to hold her down so that she could not move. Or were the nurses simply holding the child's hands and trying to reassure her? Response of June Forbes: 'One of the nurses did try to reassure her but they had to hold her down so she could not get off the couch.' There was, however, one thing on which June Forbes was absolutely clear: she gave no consent for any doctor to examine her child for alleged sexual abuse. 'Joanna was made to undress. She had to lay on the couch, crouched down with her knees tucked under her. She was crying and very distressed. Dr Wyatt then pulled her buttocks apart and observed her bottom for three to four minutes.'

It was the view of June Forbes that Dr Wyatt could have been 'more gentler and reassuring than he was'. Joanna was still crying and screaming. In fact she was hysterical. According to June Forbes, Dr Wyatt then said to the child: 'Come on, Joanna. Be bloody reasonable, old girl.' It was the recollection of Dr Wyatt that while he did all that he could to encourage Joanna and to quieten her down, and also quietly encourage June Forbes to quieten down too, he at no time swore at Joanna. In the words of June Forbes, however: 'The doctor was trying to examine her but she was all tensed up. The doctor forced the examination upon her and it was a terrible experience.'

The upshot of the examination, which concentrated on the child's anal rather than vaginal area, was that a diagnosis of alleged sexual abuse was made. There was a firm statement from Dr Wyatt to June Forbes that 'something had been repeatedly pushed inside Joanna's bottom'. This statement was made in the presence of the five-year-old child. As June Forbes recalled: 'I was very shocked and deeply upset. I knew it was all very wrong. I understood what he meant by what he was saying – there had been something repeatedly pushed inside Joanna's bottom – but at the same time I was very very confused and very upset.'

All June Forbes wanted now was to get out of the hospital and take her child home, but she was to find that she had lost her legal rights to her own child. Dr Wyatt told her that the child could not be taken home: 'His exact words were: "If you dare to take your child out of the hospital she will be placed straight into care."' Now suitably cowed, June Forbes watched her child admitted to hospital and she was allowed to stay with her. Throughout all this time she had with her the fifteen-month-old Carl, for the school nurse had offered to run them both home after the hospital examination. The hospital nurse in charge told June that Joanna would be kept in over the weekend 'just for observation' and therefore, when June Forbes retreated from the hospital, she did so with only one of the two children she had brought with her several hours earlier.

In the despair that overwhelmed her, June Forbes went to the home of her mother-in-law where her husband lived. They were as startled by this turn of events as June had been and the two of them rushed off to Middlesbrough General Hospital. June Forbes returned later with Carl, but she missed the further examination of Joanna by Dr Higgs. However, her husband was there and it was his recollection that Dr Higgs was 'undecided' as to whether Joanna had been sexually abused or not. Now back in the hospital with Carl, June Forbes was asked to allow this child also to be examined. He too was examined by both Dr Wyatt and Dr Higgs but there was no allegation that he had been sexually abused.

Dr Wyatt's view of these events was that he was firm with June Forbes and her daughter Joanna, but never rude, never abrupt; he had been trying to encourage the mother to participate so that there could be a proper examination; that he simply wanted Joanna to stay on the ward so that he could examine her again; and that in fact this second examination took place that evening – 5 June – with Dr Higgs. It might have been the recollection of June Forbes that Dr Higgs had been 'undecided' about the alleged sexual abuse and the diagnosis; but it was put to her that in fact Dr Higgs had been 'undecided' about how the injury to the vagina and vulval area had occurred.

There was never any doubt in the mind of Dr Higgs about the medical diagnosis. And in the discussion which had ensued it was not that Dr Wyatt had been brutal, rather he had been firm and kind and had told the Forbes that there were signs consistent with sexual abuse. Response of June Forbes: 'He was never kind, no. My husband asked Dr Wyatt "What do you mean, sexually abused?" and Dr Wyatt was still shouting and very angry and he said, "I am on about this, Mr and Mrs Forbes," with explicit hand gestures of penetration.'

On Saturday 6 June, June Forbes returned to the hospital with Carl and spent the whole day on ward nine with her daughter Joanna. She saw neither doctor nor social worker this day, but spent the time as pleasantly as she could settling her daughter and trying to explain why it was she was being kept in hospital, although withholding from the five year old the *real* reason: that there was an allegation of child sexual abuse. On Saturday evening she again went to stay with her mother-in-law and husband.

In fact, June Forbes could not stand the idea of returning to her own home without Joanna. It was as if she had been involved in a car accident, as if some sudden event had taken her from her, which it had, but an event so unforeseen, so unforeseeable, that she could not cope. Who would have imagined her daughter would allegedly have been sexually abused? All the worries she had had about her health, the palsy in her arms, the constipation, paled into insignificance. And she could not understand what had happened to the caring Dr Wyatt. Where had he gone to? Who was this sudden apparition who had changed so totally from the caring, loving doctor who had been so conscientious in his treatment of Joanna?

It was all a profound and worrying mystery to June Forbes. She knew nothing about the law. She knew nothing about the next steps. She did not know what the next day would bring, let alone the next weeks and months. She was preoccupied by the diagnosis, casting around in her mind to see if it could have any basis in fact, but finding none. She might be separated from her husband but it never crossed her mind that he would sexually interfere with their daughter. Who else could it be? There was no one. Therefore, for June Forbes, the diagnosis had to be wrong, though what she could do about it, what she was supposed to do about it, was beyond her.

It was in this state of bewilderment that she returned to her own home this Saturday evening to collect some clothes for herself and Carl prior to returning to her mother-in-law's house. Concentrating as she had done on the diagnosis itself, she had not looked ahead to what might happen in the long term to Joanna. She was now about to find out. She found an envelope on her doormat. It had not been sent through the post for it bore no stamp. Therefore, it must have been hand delivered.

June Forbes opened the envelope. As she explained later: 'I was in a complete state of shock. I was trying to read it, but I was too upset. I thought at the time it meant that there was somebody going up to the hospital to take Joanna there and then, and that she would be placed straight into care. So I did not bother to get any clothing, I just flew straight back out and straight back up to the hospital.' There would be no explanations, no social worker to explain what the document meant, simply a terrified – and horrified – mother tearing back to the hospital.

The document in the envelope was the dreaded place of safety order.

32

Not everyone in social services, this first weekend in June, approved the rush to issue place of safety orders on children where there had been a diagnosis of alleged sexual abuse. One concerned social worker was Mrs Olga Caswell, a senior caseworker based at Middlesbrough General Hospital. She had been employed there since March 1985 and prior to that had been doing similar work at Hartlepool General Hospital. Her work generally dealt with cases more difficult and complex than those related to the medical diagnosis of reflex anal dilatation: she dealt with mental health and child care, but she was the senior social worker at Middlesbrough General Hospital.

On 5 June Olga Caswell received a referral at about half past twelve from Dr Wyatt. The doctor had diagnosed sexual abuse of a ten-year-old girl whom he had seen on a number of previous occasions for a urinary infection. This was Audrey Rose, who had two brothers – William born in 1973 and Rodney born in 1974. Her father, Albert Rose, had been one of a tribe of Teesside skilled workers who had found employment elsewhere in the country. He was thus away from his home for most of the year and had been away on 5 June, when his wife Mary had taken Audrey to Middlesbrough General Hospital for a check-up.

Dr Wyatt had, in the past, prescribed a course of antibiotics for Audrey Rose, but still the infection had persisted. While examining Audrey on 5 June, he had parted the child's buttocks and watched the anal orifice. Over the next twenty seconds the anus dilated to approximately two centimetres. There was also a deep fissure to the right of the anal canal. There was no abnormality of the genitalia and no bruising. Nevertheless, the anal signs were consistent with alleged sexual abuse and he sought and obtained confirmation from Dr Higgs.

Dr Wyatt asked Mary Rose if she could bring her other two children to the hospital. Rodney was the first to be examined. The child had no history of bad health. Nevertheless, applying the buttocks test, Dr Wyatt noted reflex anal dilatation, to the level of two centimetres, that he felt was 'consistent with sexual abuse'. In the case of William, Dr Wyatt noted that he had undergone a kidney operation in 1985. Since then his health had been generally good. He parted the child's buttocks and watched the orifice. After a period of time he saw a large orifice. This too he felt was 'consistent with sexual abuse'.

All three children were taken into care and Mary Rose telephoned her husband requiring him to return home immediately. Albert Rose returned to find that his entire family of growing and essentially healthy children had been taken from him. He would not return to work for many months. His firm would give him unpaid leave, but prior to that he had been home for only two weeks in the last year. He would also throw his entire life savings into a legal battle to get back his family.

The referral on Audrey Rose came to Olga Caswell at half past twelve in the afternoon of 5 June: 'I received a referral from Dr Wyatt that he had examined Audrey Rose and he had concluded that she had been sexually abused. I went to see the mother in ward nine of Middlesbrough General Hospital. She was in a very distressed state, apparently due to shock at the revelation that her daughter had been sexually abused. Dr Wyatt requested that the two brothers be brought to the hospital for examination. They were brought by their aunt at about four o'clock.'

All three children were jointly examined by Drs Higgs and Wyatt. After the examination the doctors told Olga Caswell that they agreed that all three children had been sexually abused anally. Mary Rose had been present when this was said. 'The doctors left me with the mother, at which time, at the request of the doctors, I made arrangements with the mother that the children would remain on ward nine over the weekend. The mother agreed to her children remaining on the ward. I confirmed that I would discuss the case in more detail on Monday morning, 8 June.'

Mary Rose had telephoned her husband at half past five that evening. Olga Caswell passed on the information to the nursing staff in the ward office that Mary Rose had agreed to the three children remaining on the ward. She also left instructions that if there were any problems, that is threats of the children being removed from the ward, the emergency duty team should be contacted and place of safety orders requested. A note of these instructions was lodged in the case file of the Rose family. Her work done, Olga Caswell left the office this Friday evening and did not return until the following Monday, 8 June.

By this time Albert Rose had returned home and was at the hospital with his wife: 'Both parents said they had talked at length with the children over the weekend and that they [the parents] were convinced that they had not been abused. They told me that place of safety orders had been taken out. Neither parent gave any indication of an intention to remove the children from the ward or of reneging on the agreement I had made with the mother.' Olga Caswell later learnt that the place of safety orders had been requested by the headquarters emergency duty team at five to ten on Friday evening, 5 June 1987.

A justice of the peace had been contacted in his own home after ten o'clock on this summer's evening and required to sign place of safety orders on three children, without the knowledge of their parents, and without even the knowledge of the social worker handling the case, and despite a promise from the mother that of course her children could stay on ward nine for the weekend if it was thought this was in the best interests of the children. The justice of the peace had not been told of the view of Olga Caswell that no place of safety order was necessary because the children were in the hospital and not under threat. There was no doubt in the mind of Olga Caswell as to who had contacted the emergency duty office. Following his diagnosis of alleged sexual abuse on Joanna Forbes, confirmed by Dr Higgs, following the discussions he had had with June Forbes and her husband, notwithstanding the lateness of the hour, it was Dr Geoffrey Wyatt who had personally called the emergency duty office and requested the place of safety orders on the Rose children.

As Olga Caswell would state: 'I was not aware of any reason why Dr Wyatt should have needed to contact the emergency duty team and request a place of safety order. It was later confirmed to me by the receipt of a copy referral prepared by [another member of the staff] that place of safety orders for seven days had been taken at the specific request of Dr Wyatt at 9:55 p.m. on the Friday night, 5 June. I did not have the opportunity to discuss this with the doctor, as I would normally have done, because of the sudden excessive pressure caused by the number of referrals and the number of children in the hospital wards.'

Olga Caswell was sufficiently upset to alert her team leader to the concern she felt about the precipitate taking of place of safety orders: 'I felt that the taking of the orders in this case was a premature decision because it denied me the opportunity to discuss the circumstances more fully with the parents. It may have been necessary to take place of safety orders later, but at that time I did not think it was appropriate and it undermined the trust between the parents and me, which at that time was important to begin the process of planning and assessment for the family.' Olga Caswell would later acknowledge that she had no knowledge of the Bishop memorandum of 29 May which required an *immediate* place of safety order where there was a diagnosis of sexual abuse, no matter what the circumstances.

Dr Wyatt later expressed the view that it was for social services to apply for place of safety orders and that whether they did so was a matter for them: 'As I have indicated, my concern was to get the child admitted to hospital, and unless the parents resisted this idea, I would not necessarily raise the question of a place of safety order when notifying social services.' Dr Wyatt accepted, however, that 'in appropriate circumstances' he would warn parents that 'if they did not cooperate', action would be taken to ensure that they did not prevent either a further examination of the child, the examination of siblings, or admission to hospital.

The place of safety order on the doormat of June Forbes clearly had nothing to do with Dr Wyatt, but this Saturday evening 6 June there she was back on ward nine seeking to assure herself that her daughter was indeed still there. Her fear was she would already have been whisked away. The sister in charge of the ward found her upset and crying. The sister herself was sympathetic. 'She said that the place of safety order should not have been delivered in that way. She seemed surprised that we had not talked to any social workers.' The sister went off to arrange for the emergency duty social worker to come to talk to June Forbes.

This social worker was also sympathetic: 'She told me that Joanna would not be able to come home to me, but would be able to go out of the hospital and possibly stay with one of the family. She also advised us to go to the police station voluntarily and to go and get a solicitor.' This both Forbes did, but when they arrived at the police station at ten o'clock on the Monday morning they were told that no interviews had been arranged and there would be no police enquiries made into this alleged incident of child abuse. They contacted a solicitor and June Forbes found herself beginning to claw back her legal rights.

What she needed, however, was what all the other parents in this situation began to need: that is, a second medical opinion. For the parents never regarded a second opinion of Dr Higgs confirming that of Dr Wyatt, or Dr Wyatt confirming that of Dr Higgs, as being a second opinion. They wanted an independent opinion. In the case of June Forbes, she asked for a police surgeon to look at Joanna. But she of course was not aware of the 29 May memorandum signed by the director of social services, Mr Mike Bishop, which excluded a police surgeon.

All she knew was that when she broached the subject with the sister in charge of the ward, the sister looked 'concerned' and said that she doubted whether a police surgeon could get involved because there had been no 'official complaint'. At the police station June Forbes had asked if they could send their own doctor along, but there were now other parents on the ward, all in the same position, the same situation, sharing the same doubts, the same bewilderment. Most of the children on the ward suffered from the same complaints, as June Forbes recalled: 'Bowel disorders and constipation, bladder complaints. They never received any medical treatment for those complaints.'

This was hearsay, of course – the word of one parent to another parent, statements that would consistently be denied by the doctors, but statements equally consistently made, independently made, and which would later preoccupy those who were designated to sort out the tangle of child sex abuse in Cleveland. A case conference was to be held on the future of Joanna Forbes, and though her mother was assured she would be able to attend it, instructions came down the line that this would not be possible. The fate of her child would, apparently, be decided without her.

Police officers did eventually see Joanna Forbes at the hospital and she was also introduced to anatomically correct dolls. The five year old did not particularly take to these, however, describing them as 'rude'. Social services applied for an interim care order on 12 June and the Forbes appeared in court for five minutes. 'We were not even allowed to say anything at all. There was only the social worker asking for an interim care order and it was granted with no further evidence than Dr Wyatt's.' It was agreed that there would be a full hearing on 24 June, but June Forbes' solicitor achieved what was for her an important breakthrough: the magistrates agreed that there should be an independent medical report to challenge the report of Dr Wyatt. Battle was now to be joined among the medical men and women.

The following Saturday, 13 June, Joanna was moved from Middlesbrough General to North Tees Hospital, a move that hardly pleased June Forbes, who would now have to make her way using two buses to cross the river to the second hospital. The news was conveyed to her by Dr Wyatt and the hospital social worker. The anger that June Forbes felt towards Dr Wyatt spilled over at this meeting.

For in all this, what had happened to the child's original complaint? Had the damage to her bottom and vaginal area healed? The original injury seemed to be subsumed in the drama around child sexual abuse. Nor, of course, had June Forbes seen any more of the school nurse. She had not been round to ask after either Joanna or her mother, on whose behalf she had kindly arranged the appointment at the hospital. The parental control of a mother over her own daughter had been grossly interfered with by outside agencies, the consequence being that she had lost her daughter to the social services and, apparently, the health authority, for she was now to be moved from one hospital to another.

As June Forbes sought to articulate it later: 'I was still very, very confused and very upset. So I was asking them, you know, why she had to be transferred, and I had a little bit of an argument, as I was very angry and upset.' This was something that failed to impress those to whom she was talking: 'When we were told that Joanna would have to be transferred to North Tees

Hospital, Dr Wyatt said to me that I was just an hysterical mother and that I could not accept what had been happening to Joanna.

Joanna Forbes was eventually fostered out, but even that was mishandled in the eyes of June Forbes. As she explained it: 'A social worker arrived at North Tees Hospital early one morning about ten-thirty and told me that she would be coming back the same day at three o'clock to take Joanna to be placed with foster parents.' She thought the five year old should be told that she was going away 'on a little holiday'. When she came back at three June Forbes walked with Joanna to the social worker's car: 'She was strapped in the back of the car with the safety belt and she was very, very upset. She was shouting and screaming, "Please don't leave me, Mummy, please come with me, Mummy."'

Alas, this was not to be, and as the car drove out of the hospital grounds this 17 June the young child shouted: 'I love you, Mummy.' Joanna Forbes was then physically sick in the car and it drove on out of sight. The major preoccupation for June Forbes was: would social services tell the foster parents that her daughter had palsied arms that required physiotherapy? 'I strongly said to the social worker to tell the foster parents all about Joanna's needs, especially concerning her arms, as there were some things she cannot quite manage to do for herself and she needs help. She told me she would tell the foster parents.'

But when June Forbes finally ascertained where her daughter had been taken and visited her in the foster home, she was astonished that the first question of the foster mother was: 'Has Joanna got something wrong with her arms?' It transpired no one had passed on the message that Joanna needed physiotherapy and exercises.

For June Forbes, her separated husband, the child's grandmother and the child herself, the nightmare mercifully soon came to an end. On 16 July, June Forbes was taken by a social worker, together with her daughter Joanna, to Newcastle, where Joanna was examined by a panel of independent specialists appointed to confirm or reject the findings of Drs Higgs and Wyatt. The panel found no evidence of sexual abuse. On the way back the social worker told June Forbes that it was probable social services would drop all care proceedings. The report of the independent specialists was sent on 17 August to Mr Mike Bishop, on 18 August there was yet another case conference on Joanna Forbes, and on 19 August all care proceedings were withdrawn in the juvenile court.

There had been no sexual abuse of Joanna Forbes after all. But

June Forbes would remain perplexed that social services had not taken a background history either of herself or her husband; the only visits they made to the house were after 25 June. And when the social worker did appear June Forbes showed her some of Joanna's work in the home, 'drawings and pictures and so on'. The social worker stated that Joanna was 'an articulate, intelligent girl'. It has to be presumed in all this that the original injury to the child, caused by falling on a toy truck, had cleared up, that she was now fit and well, that she would be able to resume school, and that ultimately, as she was so young, she would forget the experience of repeated examinations, two hospitals and a car ride to an unknown destination with her mother disappearing beyond the car window.

But what had been the impact of these events on the Forbes family? On this June Forbes has the last word: 'All the family have been heartbroken, devastated, we have suffered so much mentally and emotionally. I myself could not hardly sleep, I have lost nearly one stone in weight. All the family's nerves have just been completely shattered, even my nineteen-month-old son lost his appetite, he could not understand the changes from his daily routine and his home environment.' There was one consolation for June Forbes and it was a slim one at that. Throughout her desolation, her bewilderment, her sadness, her anxiety, she knew one thing that helped keep her going through these early weeks of June.

She was not alone.

33

Her Honour Judge Cohen QC gave judgement in open court.

This was the case of *Cleveland County Council* v. *Jane and Robert Harris*. They were the parents of two small girls, Alyson and Bernadette. Both children had been diagnosed by Dr Higgs and Dr Wyatt as having been sexually abused. Bernadette was two years old, 'a normal healthy child'; Alyson, aged four, 'has always been a very sick child with behaviour and development problems. She suffers from a brain deformity which causes her to have regular fits.'

During the course of April and May 1987, Alyson had a brain

scan, together with other tests, and she was finally diagnosed as having 'a small brain' which was the cause of her poor health. She had fits 'at least once a week. Nearly every week. At times every day.' Sometimes, as Judge Cohen stated, these were mild, *petit mal* kind of fits; sometimes they were more serious *grand mal* fits. So poor was her health that from July 1986 through June 1987 she was admitted to Middlesbrough General Hospital on no fewer than seven occasions. She suffered as well from inflamed eardrums, which caused deafness; there were also urinary infections and 'problems with her feet'.

A series of drugs was administered to Alyson, but they had serious side effects: crying, scowling, moaning. 'The moaning got much worse in the earlier part of this year and there can be no doubt whatsoever that the mother in this case has endured an enormous amount of strain and stress, which may account for her present state of mind.' Judge Cohen pointed out that anyone who had any knowledge of dealing with a mentally handicapped child would 'understand this and sympathize with her'. The mother, Jane Harris, released her own anxious sentiments by keeping a school book, in which she made notes for the child's school teacher, and in which she referred to herself as 'deserving a medal' in what she had to put up with.

Notwithstanding the serious problems which afflicted Alyson Harris, and the fact she was a regular patient of Dr Geoffrey Wyatt at Middlesbrough General Hospital, no hospital records were produced for Judge Cohen: 'I have been told that they have gone missing. I have been given no other explanation for their absence. This I do not understand. For a child with her problems I would have thought that it was essential to have her records showing her symptoms and her treatment, in order to treat her in the future.'

Judge Cohen thought such records would be vital, following the diagnosis of alleged sexual abuse by Dr Geoffrey Wyatt on 5 June: 'It is essential to have these records in order to compare her pre-5-June condition with the condition that Dr Wyatt found on that day to see if there was any connection. Because, in order to justify a finding of sexual abuse, it is in my view necessary to look at the whole of the child's physical make-up and physical condition in order to exclude any other possibility.' Dr Geoffrey Wyatt admitted that the loss of the records was 'unfortunate'.

But as Judge Cohen would declare: 'I believe that to be a great understatement. I regard it as gross negligence on the part of whoever was responsible for keeping and filing them. I do not know who that might be, but it is certainly more than "unfortunate" to have lost records belonging to a child with a brain disorder, when that condition may (or may not) be relevant in the present case, and may be needed to be considered.'

Alyson had been taken by her mother to the Friday outpatients' clinic on 5 June. This was a routine visit to discuss with Dr Wyatt the results of a brain X-ray and scan that had been carried out on Alyson in the preceding month. Dr Wyatt examined Alyson Harris. He looked at her anus. But as Judge Cohen asked in open court: 'Why, when a child is taken for a brain examination, is it necessary to carry out this type of examination?'

The reason given by Dr Wyatt was – and it may well be 'a valid reason' – that 'because the mother at this stage was complaining of abnormal moaning' by Alyson, he felt that such 'moaning and distress' could be associated with sexual abuse. The consultant paediatrician was doing his duty, 'although the mother had previously always associated this "moaning" with a variation in the dosage of her tranquillizers'. Alyson was examined by way of reflex anal dilatation.

Alyson Harris was found to have been sexually abused and she was kept in hospital. Dr Higgs was subsequently invited by Dr Wyatt to see the child. She came on to the ward at ten o'clock on the evening of 5 June and confirmed Dr Wyatt's diagnosis. Dr Wyatt had already told Jane Harris to bring her other child, Bernadette, to the hospital. This she did at around seven o'clock. It was not until between midnight and one-thirty in the morning that Drs Wyatt and Higgs examined Bernadette: 'They found a similar dilatation in her anus and drew the same conclusions, that she had been abused. The doctors say she was awake before that examination.'

If sexual abuse was suspected, why did Dr Wyatt not look at the girls' vaginas? 'One would have expected him to do [this] if he was suspecting sexual abuse in the case of little girls. He said in his evidence, "the only thing I was concerned with was anal dilatation. I rely one hundred per cent on this test. I have my opinion. I am obliged to give it."' Judge Cohen pointed out that Dr Wyatt would modify that view somewhat during the course of cross-examination. As for Dr Higgs, she agreed that the technique of reflex anal dilatation was 'controversial'. It had been on the scene for only about a year and was a 'fairly new theory'.

Both Dr Higgs and Dr Wyatt fully accepted the theory and as

Judge Cohen said: 'They may well be proved to be right, and there is nothing that I wish to say in this judgement or that I wish to be interpreted in this judgement as meaning they are wrong in that. Time alone will tell whether or not they are right or wrong. At some stage all medical certainties were only theories and were at the theoretical stage.'

But what of the evidence in the case of Bernadette and Alyson Harris?

'On 5 June the diagnosis was made in respect of both these children by both doctors. Dr Higgs made no record or notes whatsoever of her findings. Indeed, she did not even read and/or initial, and/or verify in any other way, the subsequent notes made by Dr Wyatt.' It was not until 14 October, a week before the Harris hearing, that Dr Higgs first committed to writing in her affidavit what 'she now purports to have seen some four months ago on 5 June'. And this was after the two expert witnesses called on behalf of the Harris family, Dr Clark, an experienced police surgeon for Liverpool, and Dr Raine Roberts, had examined the children. At that time Dr Higgs had read their reports and noted that they disagreed with her diagnosis.

Of Alyson Harris, Dr Higgs would say: 'There was reflex relaxation, dilatation of the anal sphincter and fissuring of the anal verges.' So far as Bernadette was concerned, she had 'relied on reflex dilatation only'. In evidence, Dr Higgs produced photographs and stated they had been taken at the time, together with her interpretation of these photographs. But she was asked by Judge Cohen: 'How can anybody possibly remember details of a case some four months ago when no notes were made by you at the time?'

She assured the judge that she had 'a good memory and she can remember and that the photographs help her to do so'. As Judge Cohen declared: 'I accept that if a doctor has one isolated rare condition to diagnose, he or she may possibly be able to remember details of that case months, years, decades later; but on 5 June, round about that time, Dr Higgs was seeing and diagnosing so many cases of child sex abuse that I believe it is impossible to remember any one specific case without notes, and merely to rely on a slide, which has now been blown up to photograph size by a hospital photographer, who may or may not have the expertise or accuracy or experience of a police photographer, and who has never been called to give evidence or file an affidavit to prove the photograph being referred to, in my view would be extremely dangerous.' This was especially so in the case of Bernadette, where the photograph seemed 'to show the buttocks have had some pressure exerted, because the skin around the anus appears to be "puckered" and pulled, which might pull apart the anal orifice.'

As Dr Higgs told the court, on 5 June she had examined eight other children, *seven* of whom she diagnosed as having been sexually abused; and within a space of two weeks before and two weeks after that date, in all she had examined seventy-one children, *fifty-two* of whom she had diagnosed by this same test as having been sexually abused. 'I do not criticize her for that. It may well be her diagnoses in some, if not all, of these cases are correct,' Judge Cohen recorded, 'but what I do say is that her evidence in this court is absolutely unreliable and useless when there is no documentation made at the time to confirm what she now says.'

It would be 'beyond the realms of human recollection or credibility', having examined seventy-one children over a period of a couple of weeks – and eight on 5 June – 'to be able to remember all the details four months later, with that degree of accuracy necessary to satisfy any court on a balance of probabilities in a case like this'. Judge Cohen also noted that during one part of her cross-examination Dr Higgs was saying her findings were 'consistent with sexual abuse; in another she was saying there is no other explanation'. To the judge's mind, this was not the same thing.

Dr Wyatt, the senior of the two consultants and doctor to Alyson and Bernadette Harris, disclosed in his evidence 'an extraordinary state of affairs in his department of Middlesbrough General Hospital'. As the judge said: 'I would be failing in my duty to the public at large who are concerned by the large number of children diagnosed as having been sexually abused in this area, and more particularly (and this is now my only concern) to the particular family in this case, if I do not express the very strong views and worry that I have felt as this case has developed.'

Judge Cohen repeated the view of Dr Wyatt, that he relied one hundred per cent on the anal dilatation test as being evidence of sexual abuse: 'That is his opinion. Others may disagree, but he is entitled to his views and any criticism of him that I express is not directed to his opinion. I have been spared the difficulties, being experienced by some of my learned brother judges in these cases, of having to decide which set of medical opinions I prefer. My criticism of Dr Wyatt is not directed to his opinions but to his procedures, or rather the lack of them.'

Dr Wyatt had examined both children twice on the evening of 5 June and, after all, when a patient was admitted to hospital, old or young, he was entitled to expect that proper records would be kept of his case, 'whether he goes there for a sprained ankle, an appendicitis or a suspected case of sexual abuse'. Perhaps Judge Cohen, as she herself remarked, was being 'facetious' in comparing a sprained ankle to child abuse, but in her view 'the effect and the result is for the patient alone. When the ankle is cured it is over and done with. In a case of sexual abuse there can be dreadful consequences.'

One witness had said there could be 'monumental consequences for the child who may be taken away from his family; for the parents who may be deprived of their children . . . In a case like this, for a father who can lose his reputation among his family, his friends and workmates, possibly even his liberty if the police pursue the matters.' There could therefore be no case more important for the keeping of 'carefully and accurately detailed' records. Yet when Dr Wyatt saw these children on 5 June 'he made no note or record whatsoever on that date'.

The first note that he made was on 8 June and when asked to explain this he said: 'I omitted to make a note. I continued to work until dawn on the sixth. I went home. I was not on duty until the eighth and so I did not make my note until then.' But if he had seen ten children on 5 June, five of whom were admitted to the Middlesbrough General Hospital as having been sexually abused, 'how can one be sure now that if he was making his notes three days later relating to any one of these five children he can distinguish one case from the other?'

Even the notes he did make were so 'scrappy as to have little value'. In regard to Alyson Harris the note indicated that both he and Dr Higgs 'had difficulty with the child not being relaxed, but after an hour or so on the ward there was no doubt she had reflex anal dilatation. Diagnosis: sexual abuse.' In the case of Bernadette, Dr Wyatt noted he examined her on the night her sister came in: 'She was difficult to handle initially, but after she relaxed there was no doubt she had reflex anal dilatation. Diagnosis: Sexual abuse.'

It would have taken no more than a couple of minutes to write that down at the time, Judge Cohen recorded. 'It would have taken even less time to use the recording machine which he says he used, whether it be midnight or dawn, or however tired Dr Wyatt may have been. He says it was unfortunate that he did not make a note. I asked him, if he was so tired he could not make the note when he examined the children, why he didn't get the nurse on duty to write it down for him. That would have been so easy because I have always understood hospital practice and etiquette to be that a nurse always attends a consultant on a visit to a patient.'

After all, his status as a consultant demanded that courtesy. But Dr Wyatt would respond that he saw the children on his own, 'only with the mother, without a doctor, without a houseman, without a nurse. That is his practice, which means that no one else can confirm his findings on admission.' And when eventually he did make a note he agreed that it should be a 'full and an accurate account of his clinical examination'. That had not been the case either for Alyson or Bernadette Harris.

The reason why Alyson Harris was in hospital at all was because of the delay in her development which eventually, in May 1986, had been discovered to be due to a brain deformity. 'That was the root of her problem. That was the reason why the mother took her there on 5 June in the first place. The abnormalities in her muscle power and the neurological functions thereafter could well have been a result of the brain condition, and yet in the whole of Dr Wyatt's affidavit of 13 October 1987 he makes absolutely no reference whatsoever to the brain condition.'

He dealt with some of her medications and some of her other conditions, but 'totally ignores the brain handicap. In his view any distress that she was feeling at that time was consistent with sexual abuse and so no mention is made of her brain deformity.' Judge Cohen would therefore be drawn to 'the irresistible conclusion in this unhappy case that on the 5 June Dr Wyatt's only concern was to look for sexual abuse and he was not interested in investigating any other cause for his findings or any other condition from which the child was suffering.'

Even Drs Wynne and Hobbs, in their *Lancet* article, described by Judge Cohen as a 'controversial paper', emphasized how important it was 'to eliminate other causes for the symptoms that they find'. The judge was obliged to find that Dr Wyatt's 'only concern' on 5 June had been to look for sexual abuse in children. Therefore his evidence could not be considered 'objective'. This applied equally to Dr Higgs. She would find that Dr Wyatt kept no proper records, that Dr Higgs kept no records at all, that Alyson's vital previous records were lost by the hospital and ignored; that the doctors were 'unimpressive and not objective'.

Cleveland County Council, the plaintiffs in the case, readily admitted through counsel that there was 'no evidence whatsoever to support a finding that the father has sexually abused either child and he does not invite me to find that he has'. Therefore, as a finding of fact, Judge Cohen would declare that neither child had been sexually abused, either by their parents or anyone else. The judge would go further. Not only were the procedures at Middlesbrough General Hospital unacceptable: 'They fell far below the standards of efficiency that one expects and demands from departments in our hospitals, and, indeed, so far below the standards that, as I have said, it amounts to inadequacy and/or incompetence and/or negligence in his department for which Dr Wyatt must be held responsible.'

Judge Cohen had decided to give her judgement in open court. She had done so for a particular reason. Her judgements on the procedures and the routines at the hospital were directly specific to the Harris family and their children, but the 'devastating result (and I make no secret of the fact that I cannot think of a worse result) is that great human tragedy has followed this unhappy sequence of events'.

The tragedy in this case was that Jane Harris genuinely believed that her husband Robert had abused both children. She could not get this out of her mind. She and her family looked back in their minds. Could it have occurred on 3 May? Could it have occurred on 21 May? So convinced was Jane Harris that Judge Cohen stated that 'any decision I may make is immaterial to her. She believes the father to be guilty. She has convinced her family so and I suspect her neighbours as well, and so as far as she and they are concerned her husband is now labelled by them as some sort of monster who would abuse a mentally handicapped child.'

Robert Harris did not give evidence before Judge Cohen. Nevertheless, she observed him in court, she had heard evidence from others, she had read affidavits on his behalf. She found him to be a sensible decent man. It was very much to his credit that on 11 June, after the diagnosis of Dr Higgs and Dr Wyatt, when offered the option by social services of leaving home, or having his children taken into care, he had opted to leave home 'despite his own discomfort and unhappiness'. Robert Harris remained separated from Jane Harris and the question now before the court was the terms of access he should have to his children.

Judge Cohen said that there was no reason why he should not have access. But so thoughtful, so caring, so considerate was Robert

Harris that he himself proposed that access should be supervised 'to break the ice and help mother get over what clearly is a traumatic experience'. Judge Cohen explained that the reason for her giving judgement in public was because 'I am trying by so doing to convince mother of what I say'.

She decided to continue the wardship of the children, not because they were in any danger, but 'solely in order to help mother to get over what clearly I have already described as being a difficult and traumatic time.' Social workers too, though they might be 'imbued with the infallibility of the doctors' were urged to do all that they could 'to bring mother to her senses'. It was no part of the court's duty to say that parents must be reconciled. 'If mother has decided that her future lies separate and apart from father, of course that is her decision, but as a result of my judgement what she must not do, nor must any member of her family continue to do, is to say that the marriage is over because father has abused his children. He has not and that must not be said by her or by anyone on her behalf.'

This was plain forthright speaking from one of the north's distinguished judges, who not only set down in simple judicial language the heartache and tragedy of a family with a handicapped child, a family destroyed by the trauma of misdiagnosis, but also had the courage to go into open court so that the family would know, the neighbours would know, friends would know, and in years to come two children would know, that their father was not a child molester. He was a simple, kindly human being who loved his children but who had the misfortune of seeing them enter Middlesbrough General Hospital on 5 June and the course of their lives and his own changed irrevocably, irretrievably, leaving emotional and psychological damage.

We have seen that Dr Wyatt had been busy on 5 June, so busy that he had been unable to keep notes and maintain hospital records. So busy that he had seen ten children, five of whom he had diagnosed as having been alledgedly sexually abused. But such was his dedication to rooting out child sexual abuse in Cleveland county, such was his conversion to the technique of reflex anal dilatation, such was the course on which he was now embarked, that he did something that was extraordinary even by his own standards of energy.

At quarter to nine in the morning of Friday 5 June he telephoned Ms Daphne George, a social worker with Cleveland County Council who had worked at Middlesbrough General Hospital since 1 March

1985. She was responsible for referrals from wards nine and ten at Middlesbrough General which did not involve non-accidental injury. The call she received was one she was never likely to forget. On the line was Dr Geoffrey Wyatt, asking to see all of the children at a certain school in the area. He wished all of the pupils to be at the hospital before five o'clock that day. He wanted to know if this could be organized.

There were *one hundred and twenty children* at the school. One hundred and twenty children to be brought to Dr Wyatt and his fellow paediatric consultants at Middlesbrough General Hospital. Dr Wyatt told Daphne George he would be 'willing to cancel his clinic for that day, and that the other paediatricians would also cancel their clinics in order to cover this situation'. A call was therefore put through to the education department at Cleveland County Council. An immediate note would be made for the records.

The crisis in child abuse in Cleveland was now about to become a crusade.

34

'You do whatever you like.'

These were the soothing words that greeted the seven-year-old Elaine Yardley as she entered the special playroom devised by Cleveland Social Services. The carpet was plush, coloured in a brown and yellow swirl, but sturdily woven to withstand even the most energetic childish play. And then there were toys. A large dolls' house stood near the centre, alongside it a big box of puppets, funny rubber faces, large dolls, and other special items. Elaine's pleasant appearance completed the happy picture: she wore a trim yellow dress with a white collar, white tights, sandals, and a big yellow bow in her hair.

It was as if Elaine Yardley had followed the yellow brick road to a Technicolor dreamland of Oz. Or been transported to the delights of Disneyworld. Wherever her imagination took her, there was a smile of pleasure and curiosity on her face as she searched around, wondering where to start, fixing her attention first upon the dolls' house, removing the miniature furniture and rearranging the pieces. So interested was she in interior redecoration, shunting around the model furniture, that she failed to notice, or did not respond to, a troubling instruction that came to her from a social worker.

'If you want to do something you think is naughty, it's not naughty in this room.'

The social worker had been assigned to the Yardley children on 15 June 1987. She checked with Cleveland police and was told they had been 'informed' of the situation. The children had been fostered into separate homes. Social services' attention was concentrated upon the seven year old, the talkative child, the extrovert: Elaine Yardley. The police never did interview the Yardleys, there was no taking of family background, no allegations made, no arrests, no charges: but that did not mean police would not be involved in disclosure work with their daughter.

The Yardleys had been devastated at the taking away of their children. As the social worker pointed out, however, the children had taken to it none too badly. It was true that Elaine had 'shed a few tears, but entered the car calmly and settled during the journey to the foster home'. Susan had shown no distress on parting with her mother and father. She was two years old. And as the social worker later described it: 'I understand from foster mother that Elaine cried for her mother on the first night but since then has not shed tears and has not asked for either parent.'

The social worker felt it significant that 'in the foster home she never talks about her parents'. On Sunday 28 June, Elaine told her foster parents she did not want to go home but would prefer to go to the swimming baths with the foster family. The social worker also said that the foster parents had observed a variety of behaviour patterns in both Elaine and Susan that were 'indicative of possible sexual abuse'. It was Elaine Yardley to whom social services looked for their disclosures.

Now removed from the care of her parents, safely ensconced within the confines of a place of safety order, stamped as a child sexually abused because of a diagnosis of reflex anal dilatation, it was now left to Cleveland Social Services to extract from Elaine Yardley the corroboration of the medical diagnosis. Elaine was now in her first play session. And the girl of 'sunny disposition' who, it seemed a long time ago, was happily at home with her mother and father and two sisters, was now in the comfortable but artificial environment created by social services, not to make the child happy, but to extract from her the disclosure that she had been heinously interfered with.

The social worker succeeded in at least one thing. Elaine was neither anxious nor frightened in her presence. Indeed, Elaine seemed so comfortable that she busily set about arranging the toy furniture, turning her back on the worker, though not on the video camera that duly taped the entire scene. The social worker saw Elaine seven times – four times in joint interviews with a policewoman, once in a joint interview with Dr Marietta Higgs, and twice for non-directive play therapy which was nevertheless recorded on video. Three video recordings were made. Only two survived.

In this first video Elaine moved from the dolls' house to other toys. Each new activity was a new mini-world which sent her enthusiasm sparkling. She laughed at first at a toy spider which for others might seem scary. Then she wasn't so sure. She displayed that uncanny, stubborn logic peculiar to young children. This, as it turned out, would serve her well in the days to come. For upon discovering a toy phone, she said matter-of-factly:

'It doesn't really work.'

Elaine already knew the difference between the real and the pretend world.

The social worker nevertheless saw possibilities here.

'Is there anything you ought to tell me?' she asked.

'No.'

Elaine then moved on to the larger anatomically correct female doll. She undressed the doll but paid little attention to its prominently displayed body parts. Elaine quickly adopted a mother role, treating the doll with great care by stroking its hair and making everything neat and tidy and nice. Perhaps the most revealing part of the play session, if there were revelations at all, came near the end of the video when eventually the seven year old got round to the problem that had truly been troubling her. It had worried her ever since she was taken from her parents and placed in a foster home.

She had missed a school trip.

Social worker: 'I'm sorry you missed your trip.'

Elaine: 'I paid for it as well.'

Social worker: 'Not to worry. Not to worry.'

This first play session took place on 17 June. It took place without a policewoman present because on 15 June the social worker had sought and obtained permission to commence disclosure work before a policewoman could be assigned. The policewoman put in her first appearance at the second session on 22 June, when Elaine returned to the special room. This time there were no dolls' houses or toys on the floor. Elaine wore the same pretty yellow dress, the big bow in her hair. She was introduced to the policewoman, whom we shall call Valerie. Elaine sat down on a big red sofa, politely tucking her hands under her knees while her legs dangled above the floor. To her left sat Valerie, on her right, sitting on the floor, sat the friendly social worker.

Valerie talked about how brave a little girl Elaine had been.

She then tried the first investigative shot.

Valerie: 'You've got secrets don't you?'

Elaine: 'No secrets.'

Valerie: 'We've all got secrets.'

Elaine: 'I know, but I haven't got one.'

Valerie and the social worker then moved on to a more specific topic. It must have struck Elaine as odd that both these friendly grown-ups were so interested in her bottom.

Valerie: 'Why would your bottom get sore again in a few weeks if you went home?'

Elaine: 'Because it gets sore again.'

Valerie: 'Can you tell me why it gets sore?'

Elaine: 'I don't know.'

Valerie: 'Can you tell me, is it somebody that makes it sore?'

Elaine: 'No.' (Shakes her head.)

Valerie: 'It isn't . . . I think, Elaine, I really think that maybe it is.'

The line of questioning continued for some time, gentle but firm and persuasive; only it did not persuade the seven year old of anything in particular. With both adults doing the talking, Elaine, responding as best she could, would turn her head back and forth to follow the conversation, her attention wandering. She was getting tired and not a little confused. She began turning her gaze towards a different corner of the room. Finally, there would be a break-through. At least a breakthrough of sorts. Elaine at last pleased her interrogators with a bold statement, and it was about her bottom.

'It's because nobody's touched it.'

This was not satisfactory.

Valerie asked Elaine what made the bottom sore?

Elaine gave the adults the only answer she could think of.

'Hot water.'

This failed to satisfy those grown-up people who continued to ask more questions. By now Elaine was thoroughly bored. She began to fidget. First putting her right foot in her hand and then lying back with her hands over her head.

Valerie: 'So we're still very concerned about your bottom because it's all right now, isn't it?'

Elaine: (emphatically) 'Nothing has happened.'

Valerie: 'I think Elaine still has a secret that she can't get out.'

Elaine: 'Truth.'

Valerie: 'What's true?'

Elaine: 'That nothing has happened.'

But of course something had happened. There was the medical diagnosis. And so the questioning continued, but both the social worker and the policewoman were hard pressed to persuade Elaine to tell them anything more. At last the social worker had a brain-wave. Perhaps Elaine was not saying what had happened to her because whatever had happened had happened while she was asleep. However, Elaine Yardley's childish logic saw through the transparency of the question.

'If someone touches me, I can feel it and I wake up.'

The social worker and policewoman at least managed to convince Elaine to think about the problem of her sore bottom when she went to sleep that night. 'You're going to be with foster parents for quite a while, OK – you know that don't you? Whatever happens you've got to be with foster parents. Even if you don't tell us, we're not going to let you go back. I'm going to fight really hard for you not to go home, OK?'

The interrogation continued on 23 June, the following morning. This time Elaine wore a white blouse beneath a red play dress, and again she sported a bow in her hair. The pattern had now established itself. No dolls. No toys. No tinsel. No make-believe. This was the cruel world of adults. As Mrs Richardson would say, if child abuse was about anything it was about the power adults wield over children; but it was equally about who wielded power over children in society. Whether this should be parents, or social workers and policewomen and consultant paediatricians. And health visitors. And whoever else happened to come along and interpose themselves between a family and its children.

Elaine Yardley was at the sharp end.

But the policewoman and the social worker were acting with the best intentions. They were seeking to protect the child. They were acting their parts for Elaine's own good. The child would be better after she had disclosed. She would be freed from the horrible family who had abused her. So there they were, in the playroom, in the same positions: Elaine in the middle of the sofa, Valerie to her left, the social worker sitting on the floor at eye-level to her right. Valerie and the social worker returned to the interview tactics of the previous day. They talked about how brave Elaine was, how she should think of her little sister Anne, not yet one year old, and how many other girls had problems too with their bottoms. Valerie tried again the direct approach.

Valerie: 'Do you want me to ask and you to tell or do you want to just tell us?'

Elaine: 'I can't tell because there's nothing to tell.'

Elaine was now a sad little girl. Gone was the 'bright, sunny disposition' that had so appealed to the next-door neighbour. The deputy head teacher had said that she knew all about 'unvoiced emotions' and had seen no sign of them in Elaine. The deputy head had written that Elaine was 'a happy, lively and friendly girl, gently confident and secure, with a close, loving family'. The deputy would not have recognized this sullen little girl who now looked towards the corner of the room and repeatedly clenched her fingers. But if Valerie and the social worker had asked her to be brave, she *was* brave: she was putting up with their questions and fending for herself as best she could, as each adult spoke in turn, whispering in soft, encouraging tones.

Social worker: 'Try to think of all the things that worried you about telling me your bottom's sore. Can you think of one of them?'

Elaine shakes her head up and down.

Social worker: 'Tell me.'

Elaine: 'Because you keep thinking it's a grown-up when it isn't.'

The child was more visibly confused throughout this morning interview, but nevertheless remained spontaneous and alert. The social worker, by way of analogy, said that one must be brave when going to the dentist. Elaine quickly volunteered: 'I don't like fillings.' She smiled. 'I don't like the noise.' Thus Elaine had not withdrawn from the battlefield. She was still defiant. She was not defeated. She was not cajoled. She just had nothing to say about her 'poorly bottom'. Near the conclusion of the interview, the adults asked Elaine to draw a picture. Perhaps she might find some release in this. Elaine smiled, eager to please, eager to do something else for a change.

She started colouring in the sky at the top of the paper.

Three days later, Elaine returned for her next play-therapy

session. The dolls' house and other toys were placed back in the centre of the room. Elaine appeared more relaxed, especially after the social worker informed her it was a play day and 'it's your day off talking if you want it to be'. Elaine laughed in approval and started by drawing. She was very much at ease and spent most of the session playing a guessing game with the social worker. She also investigated the other toys, including a big pink sword and an elephant. While Elaine no doubt enjoyed herself, the session was a wash-out for the adults: they were still a long way from corroborating the diagnosis of sexual abuse made by Dr Higgs.

As it happened, the social worker sustained an injury to her foot which put her leg in plaster, and because of this she was not able to meet again with Elaine Yardley until the following week. This was 2 July. Elaine began this play-therapy session by heading straight for the dolls' house and dismantling it. She was now in the demolition game. She asked after 'the other little girl' who she was told also played in the room. But the social worker, having lost a bit of time, steered their conversation back to her problem.

Social worker: 'I think that you're a little bit worried about your secret at the moment.'

Elaine: 'I haven't got a secret.'

Social worker: 'Well, that's it you see.'

The social worker suggested that they play a new game: the wishing game. She asked Elaine what three wishes she would make if they could come true. Elaine thought it over. She said she wanted a Barbie doll. She wanted to be able to swim without arm bands. And she wanted to go home.

'Do you know what the judge said? What would you have liked him to say?'

Elaine: 'That I can go home.'

Social worker: 'Well, he didn't say that, Elaine.'

The social worker then told Elaine that the judge had allowed her parents to visit her and Susan and Anne, although the social worker would have to remain present the entire time. Elaine did not know anything about legal niceties. She did not know that her own case had been due to be heard before a registrar at Middlesbrough High Court on 29 June, but such now was the public outcry at events in Cleveland that, on the instructions of the Vice-Chancellor, directions had been given for it to be heard in the High Court at Leeds. A date would be set for the hearing. It would be late July and early August when the presiding judge, Mr Justice

Hollis, would give his judgement in open court.

Elaine, in the play-therapy room, was remote from these outside events. She did not understand court hearings. Why should she, when her major preoccupations had been missing a school trip, a Barbie doll and swimming without arm bands? But she liked the answer about seeing her parents again. Indeed, so satisfied was she that she did not mind further questioning about her sore bottom. But it was hardly helpful to the social worker.

The fact is that after so much time in the foster home the bottom was no better than it had been at home.

'It hurt,' the young child said. 'It stung.'

There was no letting up. And on 5 July there they were again, Elaine Yardley and the social worker, returning for yet another session of play therapy. The social worker decided to play their phone game again. The social worker now opted for a different approach. She pretended to be Elaine's foster father. She talked to a female doll which she pretended was Elaine's foster mother. The social worker turned to the doll. 'What is it that is bothering Elaine? Do you suppose it's the willy-snake?' At this point she raised the toy snake for Elaine to see. If the young girl understood this suggestion she ignored it. She merely imitated the social worker. She mimicked her words.

But soon she became bored. She no longer liked the toys in the special playroom. She wanted to look at an empty bookcase in the corner of the room. The social worker wanted her back in the centre of the room to play with the toys, but the young girl's response showed her irritation, her boredom, her frustration, her anger, her weariness. Or her plain dissatisfaction with all of these proceedings. She stuck the toy snake into the social worker's mouth. Was this a sign of overt sexual behaviour?

Social worker: 'What sort of taste do you think it would have been if you had a snake in your mouth?'

The thought astonished Elaine.

'Ugg. Horrible.'

Social worker: 'Do you think it would have a special taste?'

Elaine: 'No.'

Social worker: 'Wettish or dryish?'

Elaine: 'Wettish.'

Social worker: 'Wettish all the time. Or not after a while?'

Elaine: 'All the time.'

Time was clearly running out for Cleveland Social Services'

representative to extract their disclosure from Elaine Yardley. But if there were to be disclosures at all, they came from the social worker. What was her view of the case now that there had been so many video sessions, when there had been interviews by an experienced policewoman, when there had been play sessions, and when none of these revealed anything of significance? Elaine, despite her ups and downs, the vicissitudes of play therapy, had nevertheless remained a bright, curious child whose deepest anxiety had been that she wanted to return home.

Had the social worker by this time begun to doubt the diagnosis? Had she begun to doubt Dr Higgs? Certainly she now had the opportunity of evaluating the child on her own ground, in an environment created for her, with the time and leisure to put to her all manner of questions. Surely this left her with some doubt about whether Elaine Yardley had been abused? Not at all. The social worker revealed her own state of mind when she explained to Elaine that, due to a new ruling by the judge, the Yardley parents could now come and see their daughter three times a week, that is Monday, Wednesday and Friday.

Social worker: 'I'm a little bit cross with the special judge. Yes, a little bit. I'm very pleased they didn't send you home.'

Elaine: 'Don't tell him.'

Social worker: 'I can tell the special judge, why of course I can. Why can't I tell him?'

Elaine: 'Because in case he says: "Oh well, you can't see your mom and dad." So don't tell him.'

Social worker: 'Well, I'm going to because I don't think you should see your mommy and daddy.'

Later, Elaine asked, 'Are you going to tell him you're cross with him?'

The child added by way of an afterthought:

'Maybe he might send you to prison.'

Of course the social worker did not go to prison. She did not go to see the 'special judge' either. The penny began to drop that if the tapes she had made with Elaine Yardley ever got into the wrong hands, that is to say, if they were shown to a judge in a court of law, they might be open to misinterpretation. She therefore destroyed a tape containing two interviews, the contents of which would never see the light of day. Two were handed over for the court, but in the event no judge ever saw them. Cleveland County Council thought it prudent to withdraw them as evidence.

On the tape that was destroyed, what kind of pressure had been applied if she felt it more prudent that no trace of the interviews should survive? All this began to prey on the mind of the social worker, who after all had been only doing her job as she had perceived it; only doing her job as she had been told. Only doing her job because others elsewhere had diagnosed sexual abuse and she had been assigned to the case to obtain corroboration. She was a woman of thirty-seven, married with a teenage daughter.

The destruction of the tape, however, solved nothing. She began to worry even more. Did she begin to think that somehow, rightly or wrongly, she had let the side down? Did she begin to realize that there might after all be consequences in seeking a disclosure from a young child of seven years old, of putting ideas into her mind, of leading her on? And what about those remarks she had made about the judge, who had allowed access by parents to their children? Did she blame the judge for the fact there had been no disclosure, because the will of the child had been strengthened in close proximity to her mother and father?

All this so played upon the mind of the young social worker that her world came apart. The world of Elaine Yardley had come apart when she had been taken to Middlesbrough General Hospital on 13 June so that a doctor could look at her bottom. The world of her parents had come apart when they had taken all three of their other children to the same hospital and had seen them taken from them. Now the world of the social worker was about to come apart. On the night of 20 July, the social worker, Mrs Kathleen Angouin, wrote out a suicide note and recorded final messages for her family and friends. She then drove off in a blue Mini Metro.

She disappeared on to the Yorkshire moors.

35

On 17 June the local evening newspaper, the *Evening Gazette*, published an inside-page story on the 'Crisis Over Tide of Child Abuse': 'A surge in child abuse cases, particularly sexual abuse,' wrote the paper's municipal correspondent, Malcolm Race, 'is putting so much strain on social workers in Cleveland that some are near to breaking point. And because the authority is running out of foster homes for abused children there is a possibility that a former children's home, now closed, may be reopened.' On 18 June Tyne Tees Television carried its first reports of the crisis when Miss Kim Barnes, their Middlesbrough presenter, held interviews with parents who denied that they had interfered with their children.

The *Evening Gazette* moved the child abuse story to its front page on 18 June. The hard news continued to be provided by Cleveland County Council: 'All residential homes are full, every foster place is taken, and a child care emergency would leave social services unable to cope,' Malcolm Race reported. The crisis had also engulfed the courts: 'Teesside magistrates face heavy workloads as they battle with surging numbers of child abuse cases.'

Tyne Tees Television returned again to the story on 19 June, and on Saturday 20 June, in an important news breakthrough, the *Evening Gazette* published the name of Dr Higgs. In this they had a bit of a scoop, for they were able to refer to an earlier interview with Dr Higgs: 'We should regard child sexual abuse in a similar manner to TB,' the *Gazette* reported Dr Higgs. 'Once TB was a disabling and fatal disease. Now with improved and earlier detection it is a preventable disease.'

Dr Higgs added: 'Our aim should be prevention. But at present we are concentrating on earlier detection to redress the amount of long-term damage to the child. There is now an increased awareness and increased medical knowledge in order to detect sexual abuse of children at an earlier stage than previously.' Dr Higgs issued a press statement on 25 June and allowed an interview with a reporter from the *Observer*; she also gave one interview for television news. But for the rest the press had to rely on pictures of her arriving for work at Middlesbrough General Hospital or attending court hearings. The significance of the *Evening Gazette* publishing her name on 20 June was that this was the first time Dr Higgs had been linked to the child sex abuse crisis, and such was the respect for paediatricians that BBC Radio Cleveland was advised not to use the name of either doctor or even Middlesbrough General Hospital in any of its news bulletins.

On 30 June the High Court in Leeds freed from the care of Cleveland Social Services some twenty children and returned them to their parents.

The parents had hired a coach to take them to Leeds for the hearing. Their cases had been removed from Middlesbrough because of the publicity now surrounding what the press were calling the 'children of Cleveland'. The decision to move the cases had come from Lord Justice Watkins, Vice-Chancellor, and they were now to be heard before Mr Justice Hollis. The twenty children were released immediately and there were scenes of jubilant parents running to the coach that would take them back to Teesside. There were also test cases and on these the judge ruled that the parents should be allowed access to their children.

One of the test cases was that of Bill and Norma Yardley. The access they had been granted by a High Court judge had led to the exchange between Elaine Yardley and the social worker on 2 July. The Yardleys had collected their wits as best they could following events at Middlesbrough General Hospital over the weekend of 12–13 June. How to get their children back? They had not known that within the space of those few days thirty-seven children had been taken from other parents, who had the same worry, the same anxiety. They perceived more quickly than others that if they were to get their children back, if arrangements were to be made to see them, they would have to take a legal route.

But they were not entitled to legal aid. All their savings would now have to come on the line. Nevertheless, they consulted David Scourfield of a Middlesbrough law firm. He promptly arranged second independent opinions with independent specialist doctors in Newcastle upon Tyne. The children were made wards of court. They appeared before the High Court, and on 29 June limited access was granted. This did not entirely suit Cleveland Social Services, who arranged that these access sessions betwen the Yardleys should be recorded on video. A social services spokesperson later stated: 'We do this with all our families.' A copy of the video would be given to the families' solicitors so that 'if anything happened it would be used as evidence in court or used to stop further access'.

The attitude of social services alienated still further the much-alienated Yardley family, but with two independent opinions now arranged on their behalf they felt they were on their way. The first independent opinion came from Dr Edmund John Eastham, consultant paediatrician at the Royal Victoria Infirmary, Newcastle upon Tyne. Dr Eastham was a fellow of the Royal College of Physicians and a member of the British Paediatric, Gastroenterology and Nutrition Association. One has to recall that the Yardleys were slight of build; so too were their children. But as Dr Eastham remarked: 'A child may be unusually small because he takes after his mother or father in that respect.'

With this in mind, Dr Eastham began his examination of the parents. Bill Yardley he found to be in good health, though on the small side; his wife Norma he found to be tall and thin and in good health. He found the seven-year-old Elaine to be in good health and showing no nutritional deficiencies and, in his opinion, the discrepancy between her height and weight almost certainly reflected her genetic make-up. She had her mother's *habitus*. He added: 'Had I been seeing her in my own outpatients' clinic for the first time, I would not have labelled her as "failing to thrive".' The doctor found Susan not to be cooperative when it came to gauging her height, but she was the sturdiest of all the children and was not failing to thrive: 'She is in good health, although she does have a dry skin.'

The smallest child, Anne, he found to be a very sleepy baby who would not feed. 'Following a chest infection at ten weeks, for which she was admitted to hospital, it was felt necessary to feed her at home for two or three weeks via a tube passed down the nose into the stomach.' In addition, she had been noticed to be rather floppy, with increased reflexes in her lower limbs and 'slow to develop'. The doctor believed she showed all the evidence of development delay, 'not being able to sit or roll over'. He felt the combination of 'a poor feeder and sleepy baby', together with her development delay and floppiness with increased reflexes, strongly suggested an 'organic rather than an emotional' basis for her weight.

Dr Eastham felt that a further on-going evaluation of Anne was necessary, which he understood was being undertaken by a local paediatrician.

The second independent medical opinion on the three Yardley children came from Dr David M. Paul, a registered medical practitioner and member of the Royal College of Surgeons of England and Licentiate of the Royal College of Physicians in London. Dr Paul had been engaged in the practice of clinical forensic medicine for the past thirty-one years. He had been examining cases of suspected sexual abuse of children since 1958, and since 1967 he had medically examined most of such cases throughout the Surrey Constabulary area.

He examined the Yardley children at the Cleveland Nuffield Hospital on 24 June. The day before, incidentally, Elaine Yardley was examined by Dr Higgs at Middlesbrough General Hospital. She found all the signs consistent with sexual abuse that she had seen present on 13 June. Dr Paul, however, was concerned with all three children, for whom the medical records were passed over to him.

There was, he found, little information on Anne, who was now nearly nine months old.

She presented as a happy baby, smaller than normal for her age. Dr Paul found her alert and happy, able to follow a light source with ease. She attempted to grasp his torch. However, the doctor was there to examine for anal abuse. He used a magnifying glass that magnified eight times. The magnifying glass did not disclose any scarring or other injury. Dr Paul was categorical: *There were no abnormal findings and no evidence of any kind to indicate that Anne Yardley had been sexually abused.*

It was now the turn of Susan Yardley to be examined. No medical history was available from the social worker present. This child Dr Paul found to be 'happy and relaxed; chatty but not articulate'. She too was examined with the magnifying glass. And again the doctor's opinion was categorical: *There were no abnormal findings and there were no clinical signs of sexual abuse.*

Elaine Yardley was also now examined. Because she was older she was given a more thorough examination by Dr Paul. However, he reached the same conclusion as he had with the other two children: *there were no abnormal findings on his clinical examination and it was therefore his opinion that there was no evidence whatever of any sexual abuse involving penetration of the anus or of the genitals in the past. There was therefore no clinical evidence of sexual abuse in this case.*

To the quiet relief of the Yardleys, the doctors had confirmed to them what they had known all along: none of their children had been sexually abused either by them or by any other person. Dr Paul, with his vast experience, thought it appropriate to add some general comments to his medical opinions. He had not found, in the first instance, social workers who had been present at the examinations to have been 'entirely helpful and cooperative' in every respect; in the second instance, he found 'no abnormal signs present on anal or genital examination of any of these children'.

Dr Paul recalled that Anne had been taken to Middlesbrough General Hospital for a 'check-up' as a routine following her chest and feeding problems, and had then been admitted as she was found to be suffering from a chest infection when seen in outpatients'. Dr Paul wrote: 'I am not aware of any reason for the examination of her anal area, nor indeed am I aware of the clinical findings that caused the diagnosis of sexual abuse to be made in her case.' He added: 'The other two children were seen at the hospital for no specific reason as far as I can understand, other than the fact that sexual abuse had been "diagnosed" in the case of Anne. The examination of these two children would seem to have taken place on Saturday 13 June – eleven days prior to my medical examination of them.'

Of Elaine Yardley, Dr Paul had this to say: 'She is very definite in her denial of anyone touching either her anal area or her genital area. I see no reason to doubt her word any more than I would see reason to doubt it if she had made such an allegation. She would seem not to have made any allegation to her social worker either, for the social worker (complete with a plaster cast on her leg) was not slow in reminding Elaine about the feeling of "stretching" of her bum that it would appear she had mentioned to the social worker but did not initially mention to me.'

Dr Paul also went on to say: 'The sign of so-called reflex dilatation is not, and has never been recognized as being, *indicative* of repeated anal penetration.' He introduced the notion of *false positives*, which he declared could so easily be produced by more than mere very gentle separation of the buttocks: 'If there is more than very gentle separation the anus will always "open up" in response to the lateral traction on the anal verge skin and a false positive will result.' Dr Paul also pointed out that 'by the deliberate relaxation of a patient who has undergone previous anal examination or instrumentation some patients will exhibit this sign in any case'.

Dr Paul said that it was for these reasons that 'this so-called test is never relied upon by itself as an indication of anal sexual abuse'. It was 'no more than a very minor guide in the course of a full examination', and he expressed surprise to be told that 'the consultant paediatrician in this case had declined my invitation to be present and to undertake a joint examination with me'. The second opinions, however, were now in the pocket of solicitor David Scourfield. The parents were satisfied. But the examinations of Drs Eastham and Paul, conclusive though they might seem to Bill and Jane Yardley, would not have the same aura once they found their way down to Marton House, headquarters of Cleveland Social Services.

Kathleen Angouin, in her affidavit prepared prior to her disappearance on the moors, admitted that disclosure work with Elaine had not been productive; but the fact that Elaine had refused to admit she had been abused was not conclusive. Kathleen Angouin wrote: 'From the sessions so far the following has been revealed indicative of possible sexual abuse – Elaine accepts my role as keeping her and her sisters safe; Elaine acknowledges that her bum and bottom might get sore again if she returned home; however, she says that her bum and bottom have not been sore since placement in the foster home.'

This latter statement was contradicted on a tape that was not destroyed; but there was other circumstantial evidence on which Kathleen Angouin chose to rely. A great deal was made of the sleeping arrangements in the parental home. Elaine, apparently, slept in her mother's big bed. She would go to bed first, and she slept either with her father or with her mother: 'When she was in bed with one parent the other parent sleeps in Elaine's own bed in Elaine's own room which is shared with Susan. On occasions, Elaine sleeps with both parents in the same bed, says that this only happens when nan comes.'

Kathleen Angouin also found significance in the fact that, during an early interview, 'Elaine told me that her mother had told her to say this: that is, that she and parents together in one bed only occurred when grandparents were staying. Elaine was asked if her parents ever slept in the big bed together. She replied that they did sometimes and when this happened Elaine drew pictures illustrating the above sleeping arrangements.' Elaine, notwithstanding her tender years, was endowed with remarkable insight on more worldly matters: 'Elaine sometimes said she pretended to be asleep when she was really awake. She said her mother did this also when she wanted dad to leave her alone.'

Kathleen Angouin made the following recommendations: 'In view of the observations by foster parents of the children's behaviour while at the foster home, and the information revealed by Elaine so far, I feel that there is reason to suspect that the children have been sexually abused and that a further period of time is required in order to carry out the necessary investigations.' Only one of the three Yardley children had been involved in disclosure work, the other two being too young. Kathleen Angouin gave another reason why time was required: 'A number of studies have shown that children are unlikely to disclose sexual abuse while continuing to have access with their parents. I feel strongly therefore that access should be suspended for the period of investigation.'

The High Court in Leeds gave access to the Yardleys three days a week. And with the date coming up for a full hearing in Leeds, now set for 29 July, Kathleen Angouin destroyed one of her tapes and disappeared. On Sunday 26 July, her husband picked her up from Marton House, where she had been preparing the Yardly case, and brought her home. That evening she got into her car and drove off.

There was understandable panic within social services and Cleveland County Council. On finding her suicide note and tapes for families and friends, senior representatives and officials feared the worst. A press conference was held in the Municipal Buildings, Middlesbrough, and messages were sent to the unfortunate social worker via the air waves.

Mike Bishop said the note she had left gave cause for 'serious concern'. He acknowledged: 'We don't know where she is or what she has been doing. She has been working on a very complicated child sexual abuse case and is very anxious about one detail of her work on that case. I know what she is worried about and I can give a categorical assurance that if she gets in touch with me we can make sure she has no cause for anxiety.' Messages were also sent from her husband and teenage daughter: 'We love you and miss you and want you to come home.'

Cleveland County Council's chief executive, Mr Bruce Stevenson, said: 'This shows the enormous pressure that some of the people in this case are facing.' All these statements were made in the hope that Kathleen Angouin would not fulfil her stated intention. The statement was broadcast nationally. The police began to search the moors. Fifty police officers with horses and dogs searched around the village where her car had been found. An underwater team searched rivers and ponds.

Cleveland County Council meanwhile announced that Kathleen Angouin had destroyed a tape that was to be used in legal proceedings. Had this amounted to the destruction of evidence to be used in a court of law? The council themselves were nonplussed. The council's deputy secretary stepped briefly on to the scene of the Cleveland child abuse saga, but refused to give details of the tape's contents; the fact is that he did not know them. Mike Bishop announced 'a sensitive enquiry' into how the tape had been destroyed, but the deputy secretary was unable to say whether Kathleen Angouin had accidentally or deliberately wiped the recording 'which is believed to be with a seven-year-old alleged victim of sexual abuse'. The bubbly Elaine Yardley was continuing to make headline news even though she did not know it.

Mike Bishop would confirm that 'it is the practice with some children to video disclosures to protect them from having to repeat what they say on many occasions and to ensure there is a correct record available to both sides'. The inherent contradiction in this statement seemed to evade Mike Bishop. If a tape had been destroyed how could it be 'available to both sides'? Mike Bishop denied that pressure was placed on children by social workers to reveal details of abuse and their abusers.

Kathleen Angouin had disappeared on 20 July. The search for her proved fruitless, but in the early hours of Wednesday 22 July, a young dishevelled woman, wet, cold and exhausted after wandering for two days on the moors, fell into the arms of a local policeman in the small North Yorkshire village of Gribdale. She was immediately driven to the Friarage hospital at Northallerton suffering from exposure and exhaustion.

Kathleen Angouin had been found and at least one tragedy had been averted.

36

Mr Justice Hollis gave his judgement in the Yardley case in open court in Leeds on 3 August.

Dr Marietta Higgs and Dr Geoffrey Wyatt had given evidence and sat through the days of the hearing, as had the expert witnesses called by the Yardleys, so that battle had been joined on both the legal and medical fronts. Mr Justice Hollis explained that in view of the exceptional number of children that had been taken into care, in view of the public outcry, in view of the fact that the government had stepped in and announced a judicial enquiry, he had decided to give his judgement in open court.

Mr Justice Hollis would also decide upon the case of the Rose children: Audrey, William and Rodney, who had been taken into care on 5 June, when Albert Rose had been called from his work in another part of the country, and when the social worker, Mrs Olga Caswell, had complained that a place of safety order had been taken out after Mary Rose had agreed that the children should stay on ward nine. Just as for Bill Yardley, there would be no legal aid for the Roses, but they had committed every penny of their savings to getting their children back.

And just as the Yardleys had been helped by solicitor David Scourfield, another local solicitor had promptly acted to have the

Roses' case heard. This was Graham Brown, who had told one parent that he had on his desk some seventy cases dealing with children taken into care over the past weeks on a diagnosis of reflex anal dilatation. He too had arranged two independent medical opinions on the Rose children. They had been seen on 24 June by Dr David Paul and Dr Raine Roberts. As Mr Justice Hollis would say in open court, 'so far as the girl was concerned both found no reflex relaxation'. Again the examination had been carried out with a magnifying glass. The independent experts had found 'no evidence of any kind to suggest anal sexual abuse'.

One worry for Mr Justice Hollis was the time lag between 5 June and 25 June, but nevertheless Dr Raine Roberts had found Audrey Rose to be 'a perfectly healthy girl'. In the case of her brother Rodney, Mr Justice Hollis noted that Dr Paul found no reflex relaxation. There were no fissures or scarring and no medical evidence to suggest anal penetration. Dr Roberts said that Rodney had denied there had been any sexual abuse: 'She found however a slight reflex relaxation on examination. She thinks that may be because his anus, like that of his brother, was very deep set. The anus was completely normal.'

In the case of William Rose, Dr Paul had found one healed scar on the anal verge; on digital examination, he found the anus to be lax: the initial opinion of the doctor was that this was consistent with the boy having suffered anal penetration on a number of occasions. However, it then emerged that William had been constipated prior to his examination, and that on 19 June he had been given glycerine suppositories at North Tees General Hospital, and that on the following day he had been given a microlet enema, and when this had not worked it had been followed the next day by a phosphate enema. He was still being prescribed laxatives until 28 June.

In the words of Mr Justice Hollis: 'There is no doubt at all he was suffering constipation at that time.' But was he suffering constipation prior to his examination on 5 June? On 30 June, following the transfer of cases from Middlesbrough to Leeds, Mr Justice Hollis, on 'the spurious evidence' put before him, had released all three Rose children back into the care of their parents pending a full hearing beginning late July or early August. He saw no reason, when he delivered his final judgement on 3 August, to contradict his earlier decision.

Mr Justice Hollis added: 'I come to the conclusion that the evidence of Dr Paul and Dr Roberts, and indeed the other medical evidence that I have mentioned, taken together with the other facts that I have mentioned, cast such a doubt upon the opinions of Drs Higgs and Wyatt that I would not be justified in holding that there was a real possibility that any of these children, except one case, had suffered penetration per anum. The one exception is William and I confess that I am very concerned about him in view of the findings of Dr Paul.'

It was the opinion of the independent expert rather than that of Dr Higgs or Dr Wyatt that so concerned the judge. But since the family had been reunited he proposed to keep them united, 'wholly in the expectation that now everyone was alerted to the serious allegations, a fourteen-year-old boy, hopefully, could fend for himself'. Mr Justice Hollis decided to continue the wardship in the case of the Rose family, with care and control to the parents, plus a supervision order. The judge expressed the desire that William be periodically examined for a time.

In his judgement, Mr Justice Hollis stated that there were 'a number of unusual factors' present in both the Rose and Yardley cases. He felt these 'unusual factors' needed comment by him.

The first was that in the case of each child the diagnosis of sexual abuse had been derived from clinical examination alone (Cleveland County Council had withdrawn as evidence the tapes of Kathleen Angouin).

Second, in the case of each child the evidence had consisted of a diagnosis of external penetration of the anus.

Thirdly, none of the children had had a deprived upbringing.

Fourthly, none of the children showed any of the signs of a disturbed childhood, such as bedwetting, withdrawal symptoms, overt sexuality or other behavioural problems.

Fifthly, none of the children of school age had been noted at school as behaving other than 'normally and averagely'.

Sixthly, none of the children had complained of having been sexually abused in any way; those who could speak and understand had denied it.

Seventh, no parent or anyone else had complained of the children being sexually abused.

Eighth, the respective parents seemed 'on the face of it' to be 'caring parents of happy families'. There was abundant evidence to support this by respective parents and Mr Justice Hollis would agree with their findings, 'having heard them in the witness box'.

Ninth, the local authority, through its Queen's Counsel, did not point the accusing finger at any particular individual as suspected of interfering with any of these children.

Tenthly, all the children appeared to have led entirely normal and protected lives, and all those children who were old enough to express any feelings at all wished to go home.

Mr Justice Hollis pointed out that no criminal prosecutions could possibly succeed against anybody: 'I doubt whether it is really helpful to talk about the standard of proof and the balance of probability. No person has been charged, not the parents nor anyone connected with the family or children; nor in a different sense the social workers, the local authorities or the doctors.'

Mr Justice Hollis could not avoid the fact that he had been placed in an invidious position, that he had to decide between two differing sets of medical opinions. For if the Roses and the Yardleys had their own independent medical experts, Dr Higgs had prayed in aid Dr Jane Wynne. Who was right and who was wrong? Mr Justice Hollis was particularly intrigued by the fact that the independent medical experts had seen Elaine Yardley on 24 June, the day after she had been seen by Dr Higgs. This was important 'because all the opinions agree that signs of anal penetration can disappear within a matter of weeks or even a few days unless penetration has been persistent over a period of time, or fissures remain visible and scars'.

Dr Wynne said that 'you must take account of the specific clinical findings, together with all the other signs'. She said one cannot be too dogmatic and 'I think this is a very wise remark concerning this field. She points out that in all the thirty-five cases covered by the [*Lancet*] article there was a history of signs corroborating the clinical findings.' Dr Wyatt linked Audrey Rose's urinary tract problems with the interference to her anus. This appeared in his written evidence to the court. But as Mr Justice Hollis said, 'I can see no possible connection between urinary tract troubles and discoloration of the anus.'

Elaine Yardley had indeed put on weight while in care, but it was pointed out to Mr Justice Hollis that this might equally be as a result of 'anxiety at being parted from her parents; it may not be; one simply does not know'. But he felt there really was nothing in the question of weight because Elaine 'is the same build as her mother, tall, very light and thin, and her daughter has simply taken after her. Elaine wants to go home and repeatedly says so.' Mr Justice Hollis also noted that all the children had 'good, loving relationships with their parents'.

The judge summed up the dilemma which faced many of the Cleveland families: 'Once such allegations, whatever the source, have been made it is generally impossible to refute them absolutely.' But the question for Mr Justice Hollis would be: Of all the children, is there a real possibility that these children, or any of them, have been sexually abused? 'I think that Dr Higgs was clearly wrong about her findings as to Elaine's *fourchette*[1] and I refer to Dr Paul's experience as to his findings on 24 June concerning that.'

Mr Justice Hollis was far from saying that Dr Higgs or Dr Wyatt were 'necessarily wrong', but he had 'considerable doubt about their findings concerning reflex relaxation and dilatation'. It would be impossible to say they must be wrong, but what was unusual was that all of the cases 'start and finish' with a clinical finding: there was no back-up whatsoever to the diagnosis. In the case of the Yardley family they had a good case for dewarding their children, but nevertheless the judge remained 'a little concerned' about Anne, who had still to attain her first birthday, and thought it wise to be 'cautious'. He therefore proposed to continue the wardship but with care and control to the parents so long as the children were taken for three-monthly check-ups to their local doctor.

Mr Justice Hollis was rightly being cautious at a time when few of the facts were known about what really had been happening in Cleveland; but they would become clearer as time passed. So clear that when the Yardleys took the decision of Mr Justice Hollis to the appeal court on 18 December 1987, the court set aside the wardship and freed the Yardley children from any legal constraints. The battle which had begun at Middlesbrough General Hospital on 13 June was over for Bill and Norma Yardley.

It had taken them all of six months fully to regain control of their family and restore them to the situation they had been in prior to that fateful confrontation with Dr Higgs. It was over for Bill and Norma Yardley, over for little Susan and the baby Anne, and over too for Elaine Yardley, the delightful seven year old who had been thrust into a world of dolls' houses and toys and anatomatically correct dolls and willy-snakes and social workers and police officers and examinations and missed school trips and missing parents: in short, all the paraphernalia of the state exercised through Cleveland Social Services.

All of the Yardley family were free: free of the courts, free of

[1]Part of the external female genitals

doctors and free of social workers telling them when they could or could not see their children. Free to rebuild their family and their relationships. Free to take their children next door again to the neighbours. Free to have them returned to their own school with their own friends. Free to consult the family doctor who had stood by them throughout and given evidence for them before courts of law.

And free to forget.

37

Each statement put out during the Cleveland crisis by social services would end with the following words: '*The children's interests are paramount.*' How then did Cleveland Social Services go about protecting these interests? And how did the children themselves perceive their intervention? The fourteen-year-old William Rose recalled how he had been collected from his school with his brother Rodney, a year younger, and taken to Middlesbrough General Hospital by an aunt. The aunt had been unable to tell them the purpose of the visit.

William Rose had waited an hour and a half before being examined by Dr Wyatt. He had not been told the nature of the examination and felt it 'daft' when Dr Wyatt had examined his 'bum'. What was equally mortifying for a fourteen-year-old boy was that his mother had been present when this examination had taken place. Following the examination, William recalled Dr Wyatt's comment:

'That's all right.'

There were no further questions.

William Rose saw Dr Wyatt on three or four other occasions. Dr Wyatt always asked if William had been interfered with. William always denied this. He found Dr Wyatt friendly, but one night in the hospital, around midnight, when he was sleeping, he was wakened by his mother. Dr Higgs had arrived and wanted to examine and photograph his bottom. After his initial examination with Dr Wyatt, William was told that he was to be admitted to hospital. His mother stood on the ward crying. It was his mother who told him that he was being admitted because Dr Wyatt thought someone had been 'interfering with his bottom'.

William Rose denied this.

His mother asked: 'Are you sure?'

Social workers then arrived on the scene and William Rose was questioned on no fewer than four separate occasions. He was questioned about his home life. And again the same question – had he been abused? William began to get annoyed and then upset because no one believed him. He spent a week in Middlesbrough General Hospital before being transferred to North Tees General. He was later examined by two independent doctors, Dr David Paul and Dr Raine Roberts, and he found their chat 'interesting'.

Hospital, however, he found boring. He mostly sat around and waited for his parents to show up. They came to see him daily. He found his brother, Rodney Rose, 'moody'. And when he returned home and the inevitable questions came from classmates and friends as to where he had been he replied that he had been to visit his father who worked elsewhere in the country. He was too 'embarrassed' to tell his friends the real truth. He had badly missed his schooling and now he had to work hard to catch up.

As for his brother Rodney, he recalled that it was at about two o'clock one afternoon when he had arrived at Middlesbrough General Hospital. He had been told that he was visiting the hospital to be checked for 'an infection'. He too had been examined by Dr Wyatt. He was not upset by the examinations nor was he told anything. He was moved to a bed and when his father arrived he explained what was happening. His mother had been too upset to communicate. Later he was interviewed by police and asked if anyone had stuck 'anything up his bottom'. He was told the doctors thought someone had. He denied that anything had been put up his bottom.

He had 'vague recollections' of being woken and photographed at night when he was very sleepy. He could not remember whether it had been Dr Higgs who had examined his bottom. There had been two discussions with Dr Wyatt but neither of these had touched upon abuse. A social worker described abuse to him as 'someone sticking something up your bottom'. He too found hospital 'boring'. He too missed school. He mentioned that because the hospital was full 'some children slept on campbeds'.

He had been particularly worried when in hospital a social worker had said he might have to go to foster parents, and that he and his brother and sister might be placed separately. He was then concerned that he might not be able to go home. This he found 'very upsetting'. Ten-year-old Audrey Rose had been the most confused of all. She had suffered from the urinary infection which had ended in three children being admitted on suspicion of child abuse and her father being brought back to Teesside.

She recalled the night she had been woken by Dr Higgs and Dr Wyatt who both examined her and had taken photographs. A social worker told her she might be going into care. The social worker also asked if anyone had put anything up her bottom. She replied: 'No.' The question was repeated. Her parents asked the same question. She felt 'bored and sad' in the hospital and was happy to see her parents. She whispered that she found the examination 'a bit embarrassing'.

Audrey was happy to go home and happier still when life got back to normal. She too was worried about seeing another doctor because she feared that doctor might put her back on to the hospital ward and into care. Mary and Albert Rose expressed their concern as to the long-term effects on their children's health and wellbeing. They worried too lest they end up in the records 'as potential abusers'. And they were particularly exercised that Audrey Rose had never been treated for the urinary infection.

The Burtons had two children: Emily aged nine and Maurice aged seven. Maurice had been examined by Dr Wyatt when on all fours. According to the children's mother, Marjorie Burton, Dr Wyatt had 'fed the boy biscuits to make his bottom open'. Dr Wyatt had then seen Emily. After the examination he had invited in Dr Higgs, who had repeated the examination on Maurice. Marjorie Burton was 'amazed' at the change in attitude of Dr Wyatt.

When Dr Wyatt examined Emily, according to her mother, he wanted 'to go into her front'. Emily later said that Dr Wyatt was 'talking not very nice'. He was shouting at her and she was afraid. Dr Wyatt later apologized. The Burton children stayed in hospital for two weeks. They liked Dr Paul and Dr Raine Roberts who 'never shouted or forced them'. It was their recollection that 'these doctors did not hurt them or pull their bottoms, they only looked at them'. Dr Wyatt, however, had 'hurt'. Emily said that Dr Wyatt made her 'grandfather have a heart attack'. They found Dr Wyatt 'kinder' when he came round their beds at ten o'clock at night.

The children, however, felt that he was just being 'kind so that they would go with him'. No one told either child what was going to happen to them and Dr Wyatt changed the subject if they asked. Maurice thought Dr Wyatt was 'coming to get us', as he never came when it was light. He said Dr Wyatt was 'horrible', although he was 'all right' until Dr Higgs came in. Emily Burton did not like her social worker. She did not let her go to the swimming baths because she was too busy. The social worker did not tell her what was going to happen to her.

A policewoman who interviewed Emily was 'nice'.

The allegations of child sexual abuse against the Burton children were dropped. No counselling was offered to either Maurice or Emily. Even their local doctor was not told that the allegations had been withdrawn. But Emily, when she returned to school, was called 'a child abuse kid'. Marjorie Burton would never forget the examinations of Emily. Even when she had given her agreement to a photograph being taken of her daughter's bottom, Emily 'panicked' while dressing herself afterwards since the room was full of people. 'She became upset and was sick, soiling and wetting herself.'

When the children had been examined by the independent doctors they had emerged 'laughing'.

The Davison girls were aged ten and eight and their brother nine. Ten-year-old Maureen Davison acted like 'a mother figure'. All three were in the care of Cleveland Social Services on allegations of sexual abuse, but Maureen was anxious to get home. She got 'upset' at night because she wanted to return to her mother and father. She was also 'bullied' in the children's home where she had been placed.

She believed that she was in the children's home because her father had 'done dirty things to their babysitter'. He had done these 'dirty things' on her bed. She said that if she went home there would be no more 'dirty things' but she could not 'take much more'. Everything was going round in her head. She wanted to go home and did not care about all the hearings and 'whatever else has gone on'. All three of the Davison children missed their mother and father and wanted to be home with them.

The parents had access to their children twice a week with a social worker present. The social worker did not leave them alone 'a moment' and the social worker continually took notes. She did not think much of the venue for the access but the social worker had told all three of them they were not going home and that anyway it was up to the court. Maureen Davison described her social worker as 'really fussy'. She had been examined by four consultant paediatricians and was now seeing a doctor. None of the children had been troubled or distressed by the examinations which were not 'painful or embarrassing'.

According to Maureen, Dr Higgs had told her 'somebody had touched' her.

'This was just not true.'

The doctor whom Maureen was seeing in Darlington was 'nice' but not 'nicer than mum'. Maureen would 'pull a face' when Dr Higgs' name was first mentioned to her. Eight-year-old Angela Davison knew nothing of the babysitter or her father's dirty things; all she knew had come from Maureen. Both children were looking forward to the birth of their mother's new baby and whatever had been wrong with their day-to-day lives in the past it was the 'only life they had known' and they wanted to return to it. At the children's home the housemother would confirm that all three children desperately missed their parents.

She felt that the 'constant questioning' and examination of Maureen Davison had been 'mental torture' for her.

38

What was it that had pushed Dr Geoffrey Wyatt into asking that an entire school of some *one hundred and twenty* children should be brought to Middlesbrough General Hospital to see him and his paediatric colleagues; or if necessary that he and his colleagues should visit the school to see the children?

Andrew and Margaret Temple had two children: Allan aged eleven and Cheryl aged four. Allan had had the misfortune of being involved in an accident at an early stage which had left him with brain damage. This had created difficulties with his schooling and over a four-year period he had attended several special schools, finally being placed in a residential school on Teesside. This was one of several schools in the area for children with educational problems.

The school had an open day in March 1987 and Andrew Temple

and his wife attended. Andrew Temple was called into the head teacher's office. The deputy head was also called in. As Andrew described it, 'I'm afraid I have to tell you your boy has been sexually abused,' the head teacher said. He explained that Allan Temple had been abused by another boy, who had since been expelled as a resident because of his conduct, but had been taken back as a day pupil. In all, five children had been involved in allegations of sexual abuse and a decision was taken by Cleveland Social Services to examine at Middlesbrough General Hospital not only these children but also their siblings.

On Friday afternoon, 29 May, the head teacher and his deputy appeared at the front door of the Temple home and suggested that Allan be medically examined by Dr Geoffrey Wyatt. Allan was therefore taken to Middlesbrough General by his father where he was diagnosed as having been 'regularly sexually abused'. This diagnosis was made by both Dr Wyatt and Dr Higgs. Allan was admitted to ward nine and Dr Wyatt asked Andrew Temple if he had any other children at home.

'I have our little girl, Cheryl.'

A social worker brought Margaret Temple and her daughter Cheryl to the hospital, where Dr Wyatt diagnosed sexual abuse of the girl both front and back. Dr Wyatt had diagnosed in Allan reflex relaxation and anal dilatation 'indicative of repeated anal penetration', whereas Cheryl was diagnosed as having 'a perforated hymen which had a ragged outline'. Both children were admitted to ward nine and place of safety orders were taken out.

That evening – still 29 May – when the Temples returned home, Andrew called his brother who had been working as a trained professional in the hospital service for twenty-three years. 'He was distressed by the terrible turn of events,' Andrew Temple recalled. 'He said the best thing I could do was to go back to the hospital next morning and have a word with Allan before he vanished into care.' The trained professional accompanied his brother to the hospital. They were able to take Allan into a side room. Allan revealed he had been pushing felt pens into his sister's private parts on his weekends home from the residential school.

The information was passed on to Dr Wyatt and found its way into the reports of social services. At a case conference called on the Temple children on 9 June the minutes showed that 'it was also agreed that the children should be separated as there was clear evidence that Allan had abused his sister and had attempted further abuse within the hospital. Later, social services would make an important discovery – that Andrew Temple was what is known as a Schedule One offender. The case notes record: 'It was purely by chance that this was brought to the attention of the department and referral was made to the police on 24 June 1987. The police then made checks and ascertained that in June 1981 Andrew Temple was charged with two offences of indecent assault on an eight-year-old girl, with a further offence taken into consideration. Social services had great difficulty in persuading the police to investigate Andrew Temple, given their caution in relation to any diagnosis of Dr Higgs and Dr Wyatt, but on the evidence that Andrew Temple had a record he was arrested and imprisoned.

When the twenty-eight-day place of safety order expired application was made for an interim care order. Andrew Temple made an eight-page statement to the police, in the presence of his solicitor, and he was discharged. There would be no criminal proceedings against Andrew. But this did not mean he would be getting his children back. In fact, by a decision of the High Court he and his wife would lose their children.

It was against this sombre background of five children involved in alleged sexual abuse that Dr Wyatt had requested that every child in the residential and day school should be examined. He would not later recall referring to *every* child, but nevertheless he did view the school as 'a large family, especially the residential part of it'. The question would then be raised that if he *had* investigated the whole school, and diagnosed abuse in half or three quarters of the children, what then? What would he have done next? Where would it have taken him?

Response of Dr Wyatt: 'No further than in any of the other children in whom I have given an opinion.'

But why had he demanded instantaneous action – the whole school being brought in a single day? 'I had nothing else to offer. I could have done the same the next week. If I offered to do it the next day it was because I could have arranged my calendar in order to do that.' Did he look upon it as an emergency? 'No. I was seeing it as something that I could offer. I can do it today.'

But Dr Wyatt did not examine the children of the school on that or any other day. For when Ms Daphne George contacted her team leader and indicated that Dr Wyatt wished to see all of the pupils from the school he replied:

'Is this a joke?'

She insisted that it was not.

She suggested that the chief education social worker of Cleveland County Council be informed. He in turn offered to tell his divisional director. The divisional director passed it up the line. The telephones were busy in the headquarters of Cleveland County Council's education department. So busy that full notes were studiously taken of the telephone calls and who said what to whom. Astonishment had passed from social services to the education department. It was the director of education who made the decision. There would be no wholesale examination of pupils for alleged anal abuse within his authority.

A call was put through directly by a senior person in education and Dr Wyatt was told that no such examination would be necessary.

There was concern that more children might be brought into Middlesbrough General Hospital than the staff could handle. In the early afternoon of Saturday 18 July three children aged eight, five and three were seen in the day unit on ward nine. They were examined by Dr Higgs in the presence of a staff nurse. In the words of Nursing Officer Mrs Carol Dargue: 'These children were already in care in a children's home and had been brought by the social services to the day unit for this examination.'

The ward sister, Nurse Hornby, telephoned the nursing officer to say that the examination had taken place, the administrative forms had been completed and were ready for collection. Nurse Hornby also told the nursing officer the children had left. By now, however, a panel had been set up to review any diagnoses of child sexual abuse at Middlesbrough General Hospital. The request for second medical opinions had come from Mike Bishop on 17 June, when he had run out of foster homes and children's residences. Dr Liam Donaldson, of the regional health authority, had expressed the view that 'in the circumstances a single second opinion might be difficult because of the importance of the decision and that in the present controversy it might be wrong to concentrate the decision in a single person.'

The concept of a panel rather than a single examining doctor was born.

Under the new procedure, two opinions had to be sought, that of the police surgeon and that of another consultant paediatrician from out of the Teesside area. Nursing Officer Dargue ascertained that the children had not gone far: they had crossed the river to North Tees General Hospital so that they might be photographed. In the words of Carol Dargue: 'I felt that neither social services nor the doctors were as forthcoming with information about these children during this afternoon as I would have wished.' On Sunday 19 July the night sister informed the nursing officer that there was 'a possibility' that the remaining children from this children's home might be coming to the hospital to be examined.

That might mean some *fifteen* further admissions when there were only twelve beds available.

On hearing this at eight-thirty on Sunday morning, Carol Dargue telephoned the hospital manager and he contacted the South Tees Health Authority's manager. The telephones were now busy on a Sunday morning. Both the hospital and district managers came to the hospital to speak to Dr Higgs and find out what was going on. Dr Liam Donaldson of the regional health authority was increasingly being drawn in. He received a call from Dr Higgs who told him there was 'trouble' in a care home and that she needed a second opinion on three children.

The two doctors ran through the names of those who were on the panel but Dr Higgs said they were all unavailable for 'one reason or another'. Dr Higgs felt that the 'needs' of the children were being lost sight of in what she described as the 'present controversy'. Both Dr Higgs and Dr Wyatt would later say that they had never made a decision to bring in the rest of the children from the home; Dr Higgs felt she had been misconstrued and said 'she would be careful of what she said to the nurses in future'.

Neither Dr John Drury, hospital manager, nor Dr Ian Donaldson, district general manager, returned to their homes this Sunday 19 July that the Cleveland child abuse crisis was coming to its end. The regional health authority was becoming increasingly alarmed. Mr Ian Donaldson had called on 15 July to say that the region's administrators should be prepared for further admissions over that weekend; Dr Liam Donaldson had then telephoned both his chairman and regional manager saying how 'increasingly difficult' it was becoming to run the health service because of the 'perceived public confidence issue'.

On Friday 17 July Mr Ian Donaldson had again called Dr Liam Donaldson and said that a second opinion by an independent paediatrician and a police surgeon had not confirmed Dr Higgs' original diagnosis of the children of one of the principal families caught up in the sex abuse crisis. Dr Donaldson could not recall whether this was a child from the Dixon or the Allan family. But Mr Donaldson warned that if this story reached the public there would be further controversy.

Individual cases were also intruding upon Dr Donaldson's time. 'On one particular day I had been involved in discussion with a duty police office, a social worker and a second opinion paediatrician about a family.' Dr Donaldson accepted the obligation to help the families concerned, but pointed out to his superiors that he was now doing nothing else. The crisis that had overwhelmed the staff at Middlesbrough General Hospital, that had broken relations between police and social services, that had submerged the legal system, that had taken children from their parents, that had frayed public confidence, was now lapping as far as Newcastle upon Tyne and impeding the administration of the Northern Regional Health Authority.

Clearly, something had to be done.

39

Mandy Taylor was six years old.

She was at school painting flowers when the school secretary arrived to tell her that her mother and a social worker were waiting to take her to the hospital. Mandy was a talkative and confident child with a noticeably outgoing manner. She was 'possessed of a positive self-image' and could 'confidently recognize her own strengths and good points'. She set down the brushes and obediently left the classroom. She did not know why she had to go to the hospital, but on arrival she saw Dr Higgs, who looked at her bottom and allegedly told Marlene Taylor that 'her uncle' – that is Matthew Allan – had 'done things to her bottom'.

Mandy discovered that her playmates from the Allan family were also in the hospital. She was happy to see them because she was 'lonely', but eventually they were moved. It was the view of the six year old that they had been moved so that she could not see them any more which 'upset her'. Her brother Luke, aged thirteen months, was also brought to the hospital but he screamed whenever Mandy went out of the room. Her only complaints about hospital life, however, were that her mother was not with her and that she had fewer meals than she did at home. She impressed the staff as an 'intelligent and chatty' child.

Mandy Taylor had been taken to Middlesbrough General Hospital when Cleveland Social Services had decided to trawl every foster child of the Allan family. This had been at the beginning of the Cleveland crisis in May. Both she and her brother Luke were detained in Middlesbrough General Hospital from 6 until 12 May.

Mandy was visited on at least two occasions by police officers while on the ward. She always denied that anyone had abused her. She was upset with her mother whom she blamed for having put her in hospital. Marlene Taylor said that Mandy had 'lost trust in her' and that she herself had been distressed because she had not believed her child could be taken away from her. She had been told not to allow either of her children anywhere near the Allans, whom she had known for some time, who had fostered one of her children, and whom she trusted. Nor was Mandy allowed contact with the Allan children when in hospital, a fact which she found difficult to understand.

The independent panel created to review the diagnoses of Dr Higgs were unable to make their own 'confident diagnosis' of sexual abuse of either child in the absence of any other criteria and declared: 'The period of hospitalization for six days appears to us to have been an unnecessary disruption and separation of both children from their natural mother, despite the allowance for regular visitations.' Mandy had been given the anatomically correct doll to play with. She had been straightforward in responding to any direct questions. Had anyone 'inappropriately touched' her? The response had been a firm 'no'. She had been questioned in several different ways 'using degrees of facilitation' but there was no indication in her response that she had experienced any form of sexual abuse: 'Additionally, she did not give the types of responses associated with children who are fearful and withholding information for fear of repercussion.'

Mandy had been taken to Newcastle for the examination by members of the independent panel. She was petrified of the hospital staff. The child had been examined in an annexe to the hospital 'on two chairs' because she was so afraid. Marlene Taylor later complained that Mandy, having played with the anatomically correct dolls, now knew too much about the facts of life: 'She had never previously seen a naked man and was now showing an unhealthy interest in her brother.' Nevertheless, it was ultimately decided by the panel that 'while there is no evidence currently that the children have suffered harm from this [stay in hospital] Mrs Taylor has been disturbed and upset by the process'.

The trauma would live with this single-parent mother for many a long month; her child would have to live with sex abuse taunts at school, despite efforts to protect Mandy's identity; and Marlene herself soon fell ill, requiring major surgery. Throughout, however, she had the comfort of her friendship with Matthew and Ruth Allan. And she was luckier than others. She had been separated from her children for only a few days and had regular daily access at Middlesbrough General Hospital.

Marlene was advised by her solicitor that since there was no place of safety order there was no legal impediment to her simply taking the children home. But this sounded easier than it was. She recalled: 'There was still a fight to get them out of the hospital the day I was told to take them home. I went on to the ward, got them dressed, got the cases packed, approached the sister and said:

'"I'm taking the children home now. Is it all right?"'

The sister said that so far as she was aware there were place of safety orders on the children. '"There's no way the children go out of this hospital. I've never been told anything about it and as far as I'm concerned, there are safety orders on the children."'

Marlene had to wait another hour before she could take the children by the hand and, with their luggage, leave the hospital.

The fact that there was no place of safety order on them meant there was no trace of Mandy and Luke Taylor in the statistics. So that when the tale of the Cleveland children came to be told, when the county officials and computer operators began compiling the figures of how many children had been taken into care in those fateful weeks in May and June, when they sought to discover how many had been diagnosed as sexually abused, how many had been returned to their parents by court order, how many had been fostered out, there was no record of those mothers like Marlene Taylor who were allowed to take their children home.

Matthew Allan and his wife had been fostering children on behalf of Cleveland County Council since 1982. Their registration was now cancelled. There was no follow-up from social services. No family histories were taken, no family background ascertained, no one enquired how or why it came about that foster parents of Cleveland County Council could find themselves in this predicament. There was no courtesy, no consideration, for in the minds of social services he had been perpetrating sexual abuse on no fewer than *six* children. Matthew Allan learned what it was like to be treated as a child abuser and molester.

On 21 May Mr Allan went to the local police station where he was arrested on suspicion of indecently assaulting his daughter Rebecca, aged eight. He was held for questioning from eleven o'clock in the morning till five o'clock at night. The only allegation that was held against him was that he had put cream on his daughter's bottom. There were no other specific allegations as to what he might have done.

There was also, of course, the question of Selina and the sponge.

Matthew Allan explained: 'The police referred to the question of a sponge. The child had used a sponge that had hair on it and unfortunately the hair had entered part of her body. They said that Selina had said that she had inserted fingers into her body to remove that hair. I said as far as I knew that was correct. But I had only seen the sponge in the bathroom once and when I had seen it I threw it away.'

Even the act of throwing away the sponge was seen to be suspicious.

Matthew Allan was bailed to return to the police station on 8 June, but two days earlier, on 6 June, a policeman came to the door. Matthew Allan was told that there were 'insufficient' grounds to pursue the matter further. That was the last he would hear or see of the police. There remained the question of getting his children back. The children of Joseph and Mary Dixon, Vera aged four and Angela aged eighteen months, had disappeared into the clutches of social services. Now Matthew and Ruth Allan made their own children wards of court. But what about access? Where were the children? There were further discussions with social workers, but the Allans made no progress in explaining to the social workers their children had not been abused.

The Allans were told that these were not 'allegations'. They were 'fact'.

As Matthew Allan recalled: 'We attempted to point out that this, with all due respect, was the opinion of a doctor. We were told, and the conversation was repeated like this a few times, "No, this is a fact. You must accept it."'

Matthew Allan would feel it was like being in 'a parrot shop'.

'"You must accept your children have been abused."'

Matthew Allan was 'the principal suspect', even though the police said there was insufficient evidence. One social worker expressed a wish to strike up a relationship with Matthew, which he was happy to do. The social worker said: 'Perhaps we can then get to the bottom of this and find out what has happened.' In vain did Matthew Allan explain that nothing had happened. And since the conversation fell into dull repetition it was left like that.

Matthew Allan was particularly upset that all of his children's recreational activities came to an abrupt end. He wanted them to continue with their music lessons. This was not allowed. He wanted them to continue attending the Girls' Brigade. This was out of the question. He wanted them to attend the St John Ambulance Brigade, even if he had to pay for this himself. He was told that there had to be 'a period of separation and when they were taken into care all their friends, school friends, all their outside activities stopped'.

It was not till much later that Matthew and Ruth Allan had the mortification of learning that social services had trawled, for medical examination, other children who had passed through their foster home. They knew, of course, about Marlene Taylor's children, but not about their other foster favourites. Nor was it until 13 July that the Allans were able to get an independent second opinion from police surgeon Alistair Irvine. In his view none of the children had been abused.

And what of the children?

Eleanor was too young to express any opinion. Selina, Matthew Allan described as 'a very truthful girl', but Rebecca would 'tend to sometimes exaggerate and sometimes tell untruths'. Rebecca was a girl who tended to make rather a fuss out of nothing: she made 'mountains out of a molehill'. Both children, however, were 'devastated' to be separated from their youngest sister. Theirs was a close-bonded family, the Allans were religious people, they had an integrated home life, and the separation devastated the parents as well as the children.

Selina and Rebecca Allan did not see their father for four months, although they began to be visited by their mother at weekly intervals. They remembered arriving home from school and being told they would have to see Dr Higgs. A 'lady and a gentleman' told the girls they would have to stay in hospital. No explanation was given to them as to why they had to stay in hospital. They had not been allowed to see their parents. Two days later they were made to take part in a 'play session' which was videotaped. They had been videotaped on a number of occasions but had 'lost count'.

When the crisis developed on local and national television both

Selina and Rebecca followed it with interest. And when police surgeon Alistair Irvine went on television on 26 June to castigate the medical diagnosis of reflex anal dilatation, and added a rider that many children who had not been abused had been caught up in the crisis, both Selina and Rebecca thought he was referring to them. They had been upset, while in hospital, that their mother had not been allowed to see them; another mother had been able to visit her child. So why not their mother? Rebecca would later remark that she never liked doctors and 'did not want to see one again'.

Nor were they particularly enamoured of their foster home. As for school, there were bullies in the yard. Later they moved to a new foster home, which they liked better, but for them there was no place like their own home. At the hospital they had tried through six-year-old Mandy Taylor to smuggle out a letter to their parents, but this had been intercepted. They had better luck next time.

On 6 August, in an effort to get his children home, Matthew Allan offered to move out of the house, but this was refused by social services. It was equally resisted by the guardian *ad litem* appointed to look after the children's interests. It emerged that the guardian, who was a member of social services staff, had attended the 'play sessions' with the Allan children. It was her view that if there were no disclosures coming from the two older Allan children, it was 'because they had something to hide'. She accused Ruth Allan of encouraging this passive approach because on access visits she was involved in 'non-verbal communication' with her children. This was social services parlance for 'kissing and cuddling'.

The guardian said there was 'a wealth of evidence' indicating that the Allan and Dixon children had been abused in the Allan household, but this statement was not supported by evidence. It was further thrown in that Vera Dixon, aged four, was making 'unprompted and unsolicited allegations' against Matthew Allan. However, the children said that they refused to talk to the guardian *ad litem*, who had told them that unless 'they told who had done it, or persuaded either mummy or daddy to move out, they would not get home'.

The registrar at Middlesbrough High Court had granted Ruth Allan access to her children at a hearing on 22 May.

Selina and Rebecca had been placed in the same foster home while Eleanor was placed elsewhere. When Ruth Allan saw her children on access visits she found them very 'upset and whispering' quite a lot because they felt that whatever they said 'the social workers and everybody would not believe them because they're saying nobody had hurt them'. They were glad, on these visits, of the comfort of their mother. But Ruth Allan was 'rebuked' for whispering during 'supervised access' and she was told she should not allow her own children to whisper in her ear. On returning home from one visit, Ruth Allan found a letter had been pushed into her bag by her eldest child, Selina. There was a second letter on another occasion. Both letters reflected what the children were thinking and feeling during their enforced separation from their parents.

The letter smuggled out by Selina early after the events which had deprived her of her home and family, read:

> Dear Mum and Dad:
>
> I miss you very much. In the hospital very early Saturday morning Dr Higgs woke me up to take photographs of our bottoms, and about Saturday in the afternoon she took Eleanor, Vera and Angela[1] for photographs with June the nurse. The man who took the photograph, his name was Ken he was horrid.
>
> Did, you know that they were telling Marlene[2] that dad made bottom sore? which is not true. Do you that the Wednesday you came, Eleanor went into care on the Friday, Kathleen[3] came on the friday because I was upset so took me to staff canteen to get a sandwich and some orangeade, got a egg and tomato and she got a egg sandwich that was my pudding and that was Kathleen's dinner. The Friday Kathleen came it was her day off so she came all the way to Guisborough* with us. The place where Leanor is stay it is big. I love Kathleen not as much as you two.
>
> The place where we are stay is in Middlesbrough 45 Cheviot Avenue* we went on the Staurday on the Friday I went for a walk with kathleen as we to the canteen we met Nana and Marlene.
>
> The people we are stay with are clathics.
>
> Love you
> very very
> very very
> much with
> lots of hugs and
> kisses love
> Selina and Eleanor
> xxxxxxxxxxxxxxxxxxxxxxxxxxxx
> xxxxxxxxxxxxxxxxxxxxxxxxxxxx

[1]Vera and Angela Dixon
[2]Marlene is Marlene Taylor
[3]A nurse from Middlesbrough General Hospital who befriended the children when on ward nine
*Locations and identities changed

PS ~~Wher~~(There was 6 children in for the same reason as under Dr Higgs.)
PS Open at home
don't let social
worker look at
this letter

And by the way our foster parent are called Margaret Tom Bennington and Eleanor are Sarah and Allan somebody Allan is a foreman*

xxxx
X X

Elean at Fell View*, Middlesbrough

Both envelopes were marked: To Mam and Dad, open at home.

The second letter from the eight-year-old Rebecca was addressed to Matthew Allan:

dear daddy I love you very much.
I will soon be
very ill because
i think ive
got ~~ger~~ german
measles. I will
soon be home
because i am
fighting to
get home.
plese will you
send me 5 pence
because i need
it to buy a
present for
Eleanor, Selina
But I am afraid
that we will
never get home
in our life

turn over

please will
you send us
lots of letters

*Locations and identities changed

tell us whats
happening down
in middlesbrough
Tell mammy
that she
can read this
letters

and aske
nana if
she had a
nice party
and asked
Marlene if
she will tell
Karen like
that we are
in middlesbrough*
lots and lots of love
Rebecca

xxxxxxxxxxxxxxxxxxxxxxxxxxxxxxxxxxxxxxxxxxxxxxxx

I love
daddey

Eight-year-old Rebecca Allan was fighting to get home; her mother and father were fighting to get her home; her solicitors and counsel were fighting in the High Court; and there were other battles on other fronts in order not only to get Rebecca Allan home but all those other children, in the foster and residents' homes, who found themselves in the same predicament. The Cleveland children were discussed on the floor of the House of Commons on 29 June and on 9 July the government announced a judicial enquiry. The enquiry would sit in Middlesbrough. Its doors would open on 11 August.

For Rebecca Allan, however, the dream would have to wait a little longer.

*Location changed

40

On 17 November 1987 Cleveland Social Services brought to an end the long-drawn-out court battle over the future of the Dixon children.

By this time Joseph and Mary Dixon had gone seventeen months without seeing their offspring. Following their arrest on 25 July 1986, police had taken swabs from the four-year-old Vera Dixon, and Joseph Dixon claimed that these had been taken in the presence of her eighteen-month-old sister: 'My younger daughter watched her older sister get swabs stuck up her backside, screaming,' he recalled. Once a diagnosis of sexual abuse had been made by Dr Higgs on Vera, the Dixons found themselves on their own.

Released from the prison cells in Newcastle, where their children had been taken from them, they were given £8 in an envelope and told to make their own way home to Middlesbrough. They had no further consultations with social services until September 1986, but so upset had been Mary Dixon at the allegation she was a poor mother because of her own unhappy and troubled background that she had seen a psychiatrist. The consultant psychiatrist found the 'consequences of your early upbringing have been grossly exaggerated and that neither you nor your husband have any evidence of sexual deviance'.

The Dixons campaigned vigorously to get their children back, or even to see them, but without success. 'When the case began,' Joseph Dixon recalled, 'we just could not believe it. We were in a shocked state. We could not take it in. Nobody we turned to would listen to us. Social services closed all doors. We saw Mr Bishop on numerous occasions and Mr Walton and we could get no answers, no explanations.' The Dixons obtained character references from their neighbours, from Mary Dixon's father and stepmother, but these were of no avail.

It was in June 1987, some six weeks after the event, that the Dixons learned of the alleged abuse of *both* their children in the Allan foster home. The allegation against the Dixons had been that one of them, or both together, or someone else, had interfered with Vera; but this was the first time they had heard that allegedly Angela too had been interfered with. Their children had been subjected to a *second* place of safety order. Having been fostered once into care they were now about to be fostered a *second* time. Although the Dixons did not know it, discussions took place in the hospital concerning whether their children should stay in the ward or whether they should be fostered out again.

When the Dixon and Allan children had been admitted Dr Higgs wished to keep them at Middlesbrough General Hospital under her own personal observation. She felt they were 'disturbed' children. She wanted to keep them for a period of assessment. Mrs Iris Chambers, nursing officer for the medical and paediatric unit, felt it wrong that the children should be on an acute ward taking up beds. Mrs Chambers remembered the conversation well because, in the course of it, a little girl came in, one of the Cleveland children caught up in alleged sexual abuse, and said: '*Come and play with me, Marietta.*'

However, on learning the news about their children, the Dixons being told by a senior officer of social services that it was 'only anal abuse', they made their way to the local police station. They were told by the acting officer that he would be in touch with them around eleven o'clock that evening. 'We waited till half past eleven and the police constable did not turn up. We walked to the police station in the rain to find out what had happened to our children in foster parents' care. When we went to the police station we could get told very little because the police station were not aware of the new situation.'

Following a case conference on 1 May, the Dixon children had been sent down to Leeds to see Dr Jane Wynne for a 'second' opinion. What had actually been sought was not a second but a third opinion, since Dr Peter Morrell had already confirmed the alleged abuse the evening before. A decision was taken to postpone wardship proceedings until at least the elder of the Dixon children could enjoy the benefit of disclosure work. And this could not begin if the children were wards of court because High Court consent would be necessary.

Those who attended the 1 May case conference were aware of the difficulties that faced them. The Dixon children – or at least one of them – had allegedly been abused in the Steiner Unit in Newcastle. Both had now been allegedly abused in the foster care of Cleveland Social Services. There was some talk that the condition of Vera might be caused by a 'neurological condition', but Dr Higgs was concerned to monitor the recovery rate of an abused child. As the head social worker at the meeting pointed out: 'It was also felt that in that particular case the contentious issue was the question of alleged re-abuse of these children in two totally separate living situations and that that would be a source of some contention in court proceedings.'

Dr Wynne confirmed that there were signs consistent with sexual abuse, but the independent medical opinions called from Dr Clark and Dr Paul found no abuse. The polarization of opinion between those who believed that reflex anal dilatation was consistent with sexual abuse, and others who felt that it might be a factor, but no more, remained as acute as ever when it came to Vera and Angela Dixon. And if there was conflicting medical evidence what else did social services have to rely upon before a court of law?

Attempts were made to show that Vera and Angela Dixon had put on weight since they had been taken into care, the inference being that they were thriving in the foster home whereas they had not been thriving at home. Mrs Madge Bray, interviewing the children in the Allan foster home, wrote: 'With regard to Angela, it is very clear that she showed many of the signs of a grossly emotionally deprived little girl upon her entry into the foster home, and I was able to observe, even now after nine months have elapsed, that many of these difficulties have as yet not been resolved and that she remains, to a worrying degree, a detached, developmentally delayed, emotionally flat little girl'.

Mrs Bray made this report before the allegation was made that the Dixons' children had been interfered with in the foster home. It therefore became an embarrassing line of questioning to suggest that the children were prospering in a home where *two* of the children had allegedly been abused. And while the children had certainly put on weight following their dramatic visit to Newcastle, where both had fallen ill with diarrhoea and vomiting, no one knew what their weight had been when in their own home and before their voyage of medical diagnoses had begun.

Attempts were made to show that Vera's speech was also improving. But as Joseph Dixon put it: 'Vera could speak but she was not putting sentences fully together. She would say a sentence and half way through the sentence she would make — maybe two or three words out of a sentence of maybe seven words she would not get out. She would not say them right.' The allegation was equally made that Vera had been 'cowed and frightened' on arrival at the home of the foster parents. A four-year-old child examined in Middlesbrough by Dr Wyatt, examined again in Newcastle by Dr Higgs, examined by Dr Ellis Fraser, examined by a police surgeon who took swabs from her body, having suffered illness while in hospital, having been taken from her parents and placed in an alien environment, might well appear 'cowed and frightened', though for reasons different from those suggested by social services.

Dr Higgs was asked at the judicial enquiry whether she would agree that 'the practical application' of the teaching she had received in Leeds in June 1986 at the Wynne seminar had been enormous? That it had led to enormous consequential problems and difficulties, not only of 'a medical nature but also of a social and legal nature'? Yet reflex anal dilatation had not been 'definitively established in science and medicine'? Dr Higgs: 'I think the sign itself is a very important sign. I believe that it is a good indicator of sexual abuse and that it is the diagnosis that we need to look into very carefully. I think it does highlight the importance of making sure that assessments of these children and their families become broadened outside the medical sphere.'

Cleveland Social Services sought to have the cases of the Allans and the Dixons treated separately by the court rather than taken together. However, the High Court judge chose to hear both cases together. And after several days of hearings, Cleveland Social Services were minded on 17 November to make a settlement, behind the judge's chair as it were, in both the Allan and Dixon cases.

The Allan children would be allowed home provided they remained wards of court and were subject to regular medical examinations. There would be supervision by a probation officer. Allegations of sexual abuse were dropped. All this meant that the Allans would have no further involvement with social services and they could have their children back. They accepted. The first medical examinations showed that the children were in good health. The family were united and for Matthew Allan his long leave of absence – his 'long day's journey into night', as he would describe it – was over.

He was able to return to work.

The Allans were both regular church-goers. They had taught their children never to tell a lie. Therefore, what were the eldest children to say when they returned to school? How would they parry the questions? Where had they been all these months? This was a worry for Selina, aged ten, for she was reluctant to go to school at all; Rebecca was, as her mother described, 'a little bit funny'; but when they did return they weathered the curiosity of the other children and simply told the truth. They had been in another school in another place. Soon the two children were playing in the schoolyard with the rest of the children.

However, although the apprehension of returning to school was out of the way, there was still the apprehension of the knock on the door. When Matthew Allan's mother decided that it was time for her to retire into an old people's home, and a requisite application was made to Cleveland Social Services, the senior citizens' department sent a social worker round to interview the children's grandmother. This was a different activity of social services, but the children heard the knock on the door, saw the strange woman standing there, and fled to their bedroom, locking their door behind them.

The Dixon children too were allowed to return to their parents. But Cleveland Social Services first asked for a period of rehabilitation because the Dixons had not seen their children for fifteen months. They also asked that the children should remain wards of court. In order to bring the proceedings to an end, and to get their children back, the Dixons agreed. There was some difficulty in finding a rehabilitation unit for them where they could stay as a family for the agreed period prior to reunion; but in the end, with an irony to end all ironies, the Dixons would find a place in the Steiner Unit commencing 29 December 1987.

They were to stay there six weeks.

So the Dixons were reunited in the very hospital ward where they had been separated. But for Joseph and Mary Dixon there was one joy that was overwhelming. It was that after fifteen months of separation, with two children bigger and sturdier than when they had last seen them, with one daughter now five and another two and a half, after the stays in hospital, in one foster home and then another, after many examinations by consultant paediatricians in both Leeds and Middlesbrough, having had a guardian *ad litem* into the bargain, the overwhelming joy for Joseph and Mary Dixon was that the children had not forgotten who they were.

The children remembered their parents.

41

The Ames became what was described as 'a high profile family'.

Notwithstanding four paediatric reports that their children had allegedly been abused, notwithstanding that Bryan Ames had been treated as a child abuser, the resolve of both husband and wife to get their children back and clear their name remained unflinching. Theirs was a deep sense of grievance. And that sense manifested itself through organizations such as Parents Against Injustice, through their Member of Parliament, through the media and 'wherever they had an opportunity to mobilize their feelings'. Jennifer Ames appeared on television, suitably blacked out to avoid identification, and her cool, articulate manner upset some and irritated others.

Together they were tireless in their quest for justice, and equally tireless in seeking to put back together what they conceived to have been destroyed – a happy home life with their children. The frustration and distress of their children was clear to Jennifer Ames on her access visits and if it added to her distress it added too to her determination. Their eldest son Nigel had been upset on several occasions. He had been taken into care on his birthday. He had been deprived of his family on this of all days, but worse: he had been deprived of his birthday present. He had been promised a bicycle and this had not materialized.

Nigel had been to an international scout camp where as leader he had been able to organize a patrol, but he was taken from the camp and subjected to further examinations, those of the independent medical experts Dr Roberts and Dr Paul. His mother had not been able to attend. He had seen his mother and younger brother, aged two, just once a week; and when Carol, aged nine, heard that her small brother was going home – when Bryan Ames vacated the family home – this deeply upset her. She had thought she too would now be allowed home.

The Ames, with the assistance of two local clergymen, organized a branch of Parents Against Injustice, an organization founded by parents who were innocent of child abuse or neglect, but who had nevertheless found themselves involved in child abuse and care procedures. The organization had been founded by Mrs Sue Amphlet and her husband, Steve, who wrote: 'It is impossible to describe adequately the anguish, anxiety, shame, helplessness and fear that is expressed by parents in this situation.'

The Reverend Michael Wright had been an ordained priest for some twenty-five years. He specialized in pastoral counselling throughout his ministry. He worked as a part-time priest in charge of St Cuthbert's Anglican Church in Middlesbrough, but was fully employed by the social services department in Cleveland. It says much for the courage of Michael Wright that he involved himself with families at all; he knew his actions would displease many in social services and might well cost him his job, but so upset was he at the injustice he perceived all around him that he coordinated a Cleveland Parents Support Group to help those famiies who had been deprived of their children.

He was supported in this by a Church of England minister, the Reverend Peter Langford, working out of the Teesside Industrial Mission, and together they provided succour for those families who, in the early days of the crisis, did not know where to turn. Some thirty-three families attended regular meetings of the group. Michael Wright had first become involved on 17 June when parishioners of his who were not church members had called him: 'What happened was that the couple had had their three children taken into care the previous weekend, and although they are very friendly with their next-door neighbour, who is a member of the church, they had not felt able to talk about the fact that the children had been taken into care following a diagnosis of possible sexual abuse.'

The parents, Bill and Norma Yardley, had been 'upset and distressed'. They had wanted to go to church to pray. They had wanted to talk to a priest. A meeting was arranged for the lunch hour on 18 June.

When he met the Yardleys, Michael Wright was struck by what they were telling him. It seemed to be true. 'I thought it very odd indeed that a child who was then seven months, who had been under the care of the same paediatrician for six months and had been regularly examined by this paediatrician . . . and for now a diagnosis to be made that this child, the youngest of three daughters, was the worst abused of the three, seemed to me very difficult to accept.'

One of the things the mother told Michael Wright was that she had had great confidence in Dr Marietta Higgs because she was known to have a special expertise in neonatal care. It had seemed odd to Michael Wright that 'no rational person, if they were going to abuse a child, was going to choose the youngest who was under the regular care of Dr Higgs rather than either of the other two'. The third point that concerned him was that the parents had told him they had found that their three children were among *nineteen* taken into care on the very same day.

On Wednesday 24 June Michael Wright held a candlelight vigil for those parents and children in Cleveland involved in the crisis. He also held a meeting in his home, with families present, at which two Members of Parliament were briefed. The Ames attended this meeting and the vigil. In an attempt to get his children back, Bryan Ames moved out of the family home into a bed-sit. However, social services looked upon this as a temporary rather than a permanent move, and so Bryan Ames went to live with his brother. Bryan Ames was suspended from his job and there were moves to have him dismissed. When the crisis broke on 19 June, these moves were deferred and never, in the end, took place; but the suspension continued. Once again, as with the Dixon and Allan families, the High Court overtook Cleveland Social Services and the Northern Regional Health Authority, employers of Dr Higgs and Dr Wyatt, and Judge Eastham gave his decision on the Ames case in open court on 7 December. He gave it in open court, as he explained, for two reasons:

'Firstly, [although] this case has undoubtedly aroused a great deal of local interest, that is not the main reason why I give judgement in open court. The main reason why I give judgement in open court is to try to assist the three wards and their parents to resume a normal family life after the trauma which has overtaken them since March of this year.' Bryan Ames was now forty-two years of age, his wife Jennifer was thirty-six. 'They both have professional qualifications, although the mother was looking after the children full-time. Before 19 March they were a well-integrated, happy family, of no concern to any authority, local or otherwise, but in March 1987 the parents took the youngest child to hospital because he had a long-standing bowel complaint.'

The child had been examined by Dr Higgs, 'who thereafter examined the other two children and reached the diagnosis that all three children had been sexually abused and the chief suspect was undoubtedly from that moment onwards the father.' The police had become involved on 21 and 22 March and on 23 March there had been the diagnosis of 'a female colleague', Dr Jane Wynne, who also diagnosed sexual abuse. In those circumstances, 'not surprisingly', Cleveland Social Services had obtained a place of safety order and the Ames children were separated and fostered to three separate foster homes.

There had been a series of interviews by representatives of the local authority who, 'on the information before them, treated this as an unanswerable case of sexual abuse'. The interviews were not 'on the basis of trying to discover where the truth lay but in trying to obtain disclosure from these children'. As Judge Eastham went on: 'On 15 April 1987 another doctor, Dr Steiner, who had previously made a report in which he doubted the diagnosis of sexual abuse, following a conversation with Dr Higgs, changed his view, with the inevitable result that an interim care order was made by the juvenile court in that month.' In May family life was disrupted: 'The father moved out in the hope that the mother would be allowed to have the children, and on 27 May he was suspended from his professional job and he remains suspended, although in the view of the findings of this court, it is the earnest hope of this court that he will be reinstated without further delay.'

By 26 June the decision had been taken by Cleveland County Council not to proceed in the juvenile court but to proceed in wardship, and on 26 June the children were made wards of court: 'The parents, from the inception of the wardship, fought back for their family.' On 22 June a guardian *ad litem* was appointed. In July the children were examined by Dr Raine Roberts and by Dr Paul: 'They discovered in respect of the girl that the diagnosis of Dr Higgs and her colleagues in relation to the girl in one respect was palpably wrong and they also formed the view that the evidence of sexual abuse against the boys was not as seen by Dr Higgs and her colleagues.'

That view was made known, certainly with respect to the girl, as Judge Eastham would point out, 'pretty firmly in July', and on 31 July the two-year-old Malcolm had been returned to Jennifer Ames, under supervision, with Bryan Ames 'an exile from his own home'. On 3 September Bryan Ames had been allowed some access to his children as a result of an order by Judge Hall. At that time Nigel and Carol were also returned to the mother and from this time the father's access was increased.

A third independent medical opinion had now been obtained on behalf of the children. This was provided by 'an extremely well-known consultant who has given evidence in many of this type of case'. The consultant had made 'a full and comprehensive report'. The consequence of this was that 'very late in the day' Cleveland Social Services on legal advice had decided 'not to pursue the allegations which had been persisted in since March'.

Judge Eastham added: 'I am satisfied that these children were not sexually abused by their father: I am satisfied that they were not sexually abused at all. The result of all this has been that children who required no psychiatric attention whatsoever as at 19 March, because of the relentless questioning, albeit put in good faith by social workers during the period April to July, have left psychiatric scars on these children and they will need some help.' The children would be dewarded and returned fully to their parents: 'I am satisfied that they have caring and loving parents who have not harmed them in any way whatsoever.' Judge Eastham hoped that 'whatever tongues may have been wagging in the locality may now be stilled and that this family will be left to pick up the pieces after their awful experiences since March of this year'.

There were no conditions on the release of the Ames children to their parents; no supervision orders, no wardship, no medical examinations. The Ames were completely exonerated and their integrity and honour maintained. Judge Eastham said that the children had gone through 'a very worrying period, their father not in work and out of the house, and everything must be done in my view to enable this family to get back on an even keel as quickly as possible'.

And what of Cleveland County Council?

The Ames had not had legal aid until late in the day. Jennifer Ames had obtained it on her own behalf on 21 July and Bryan Ames was able to obtain it on 25 September. An application was therefore made for Cleveland County Council to pick up the legal bill. As Judge Eastham said: 'Now the local authority is under a statutory duty to take action in the event of any child living within its jurisdiction being in need of care, and I have taken the view that although, as I now find, the allegations of sexual abuse were groundless, in my judgement the local authority had no alternative when faced with the views of no less than three doctors, that is Dr Higgs, Dr Jane Wynne and another doctor who was called Morell, who was rather inexperienced in comparison – and also faced with the change of mind of the doctor instructed originally by the parents, Dr Steiner – but to pursue the course they did, at least until July.'

However, 'if any criticism is to be made of the local authority it is for their persistence in branding this father with the smear of sexual abuse after they became aware of the conflict in medical opinion which originated with the examination of Dr Roberts and Dr Paul and was subsequently enforced by the cogent and trenchant views' of the consultant brought in by the Official Solicitor. Cleveland County

Council volunteered to pay £4000 towards the Ames' costs. Judge Eastham had the last word: 'At least, at the end of these proceedings, they leave here with their reputation untarnished, they are parents who love their children, who have children who love them, and they should now feel free of the dreadful suspicion and trauma which has been hanging over their heads since March of this year.'

There had never been the slightest doubt in the minds of either Jennifer or Bryan Ames that they would win their action; it had only been a question of when. Not for them any compromise. Not for them any conditions. And now they were vindicated in open court.

Both Jennifer and Bryan Ames would give evidence to the judicial enquiry in Middlesbrough Town Hall. A High Court judge would preside over the enquiry and she would be promoted to the court of appeal before the proceedings were over. Queen's Counsel and junior barristers would represent the various parties. Her ladyship the judge would have three assessors, one with police experience, another as a medical practitioner, and a third with experience in social work.

The enquiry would last seventy-four days. Jennifer Ames would sit through most of the proceedings, as would her husband. However, when his suspension was lifted he went back to work and therefore, on the final days, his wife, tall, slim, brunette, her face drawn and pale, her head bowed forward, listened to the proceedings alone. Throughout the same proceedings, sitting just in front of her, was the slim Dr Marietta Higgs, always impeccably dressed, always impeccably calm, spending the first weeks of the enquiry, as she had done throughout the court proceedings in which she had been involved, making copious notes.

Both women sat and listened to the final submissions. On behalf of Dr Higgs, her counsel asked the rhetorical question: *Where could it be said that the doctors in principle have erred?* At that point Jennifer Ames left the proceedings and entered the foyer where coffee was served, where councillors could mingle, where the press held court, where visitors who could not get into the council chamber listened to the proceedings through amplifiers. She had lived with the crisis from the time she had taken her child to see Dr Higgs on 19 March. It had occupied her thoughts, waking and sleeping, all that time. Her children had been told she had been 'a poor mother'; she had been described as 'a poor mother' too by social workers because she would not agree with them that her husband was a child molester.

And with that curious inversion that is part of the British psyche she would feel guilty: guilty that perhaps some of the criticisms were true. That she had not been a good mother. Her children had told social workers how often she felt tired; therefore now when she felt tired she would seek to hide it from her children, lest they spot it and lest they feel she was not after all 'a good mother'. She had kept a diary of events. The diary had helped her express her feelings on paper, to assuage her deep sorrow that these things could happen to her; that she, who had cared so much for her children, should be accused of putting them into a situation of purgatory: the purgatory of child abuse.

Jennifer Ames had lived through it all. Now she could stand no more. She sat down next to her Member of Parliament. Her shoulders shook. Tears came to her eyes and rolled down her cheeks. Her dark hair trembled around her face. She wept as silently as she could, embarrassed to be crying in public. She was passed a handkerchief. And then a cup of coffee. A nurse who had been attending the enquiry took her hand and massaged it gently. Finally Jennifer looked up. She tried to put on a brave face. She tried to smile. She tried to hide that sense of guilt, that sense of embarrassment. All these months she had held it back.

'It's the first time I've cried,' she explained.

EPILOGUE

42

The party was held at Pyrgi's restaurant in Linthorpe village, Middlesbrough.

It had been organized by the restaurateurs, Mimo and Anna Peretti, for those Cleveland children caught up in the child abuse crisis who had been reunited with their parents. It was held for those parents who had lived through a traumatic experience, the most traumatic in their lives; for their children had been taken from them, not by death or destruction, but by the power of the state through its agents, the health and social services department.

They had found themselves, in the summer of 1987, in a situation that mirrored similar situations in the United States, proving that the spirit of Salem is still not absent from the North American continent. The governor of Massachusetts, Sir William Phips, in those far off days, wrote to the home government on 12 October 1692 that he had found his province 'miserably harassed with a most horrible witchcraft or possession of evils'. In the United States of 1986 a million families were *falsely* accused of child abuse both physical and sexual; they had endured their own particular witch-hunt, the humiliation of investigation before being 'cleared'; but their names remained in government files as suspected child abusers, sometimes for five years and sometimes for life.

In the words of Mary Pride in her book *The Child Abuse Industry*[1]: 'Others, not so fortunate, found themselves in compulsory counselling programmes. Still others lost their jobs and emptied their bank accounts fighting these unjust charges. Many lost their jobs. Others, the saddest of all, lost their children.' The governor of Massachusetts wrote in 1692 that similar happenings to the events in Salem had occurred some thirty years earlier in Sweden; the contagion of Salem would spread to Andover; and while Cleveland saw the first child abuse crisis of its kind in this country, it would not be entirely alone.

On 24 February 1988 another enquiry would be announced, not as extensive as the judicial enquiry into affairs in Cleveland, but sufficiently detailed to embrace both Hereford and Worcester social services and representatives of the Department of Health and Social Services. This review had been inspired by the fact that large

[1]Crossway Books, Westchester, Illinois

numbers of children had been diagnosed as having allegedly been anally abused; the basis of the diagnosis had been reflex anal dilatation; and the first court battle of a family to get its children back would be heard in the High Court in Birmingham before Mr Justice Bush.

Some eighty children were taken into care by Hereford and Worcester Council during a two-month period in 1987 on allegations that they had been sexually abused, and the county had been warned by consultant paediatrician, Dr John Nicholson, after fifty-four diagnoses had been made, that a further one hundred were likely. Dr Nicholson worked out of the Worcester Royal Infirmary and was one of four consultant paediatricians there. Hereford and Worcester had 333 referrals of child abuse in 1987 compared with 150 in 1985. The figure leapt in July and August when there were fifty-four reported cases dealing with some eighty children. The council had set up a Sexual Abuse Child Consultant Service, but had not adopted the Cleveland approach of automatically separating children from parents, thus scaling down the crisis.

On 22 February 1988, when giving judgement in the first case to come before the High Court from Hereford and Worcester, Mr Justice Bush declared that the parents were entitled to be completely exonerated and the county council accepted that it was likely to lose cases where it acted on medical diagnosis alone. They declared that they had since introduced procedures which required suspected child abuse cases to be corroborated by additional evidence. Mr Alan Ferguson, the council's principal officer for children and family services, declared: 'We were caught on the hop. A number of families slipped through the net.'

Mrs Jean Hadley, chairman of the council's Social Services Committee, regretted what she described as an 'overzealous attitude'. She added: 'I have tremendous sympathy with the families. Parents were afraid to take their children to the doctors in case they were examined.' The Malvern father who had taken his case to court, and who had been separated from his four daughters for six months, echoed the plight of other parents both in Hereford and Worcester, in Leeds and in Cleveland: 'When I heard the verdict it was quite a hollow victory. The desperate thing is that you can only say you have done nothing, but you have no proof.'

What he had discovered, as had others in Cleveland, was that the Anglo-Saxon concept of justice had been reversed. A man was no longer innocent until proven guilty. In the case of alleged child sexual abuse, or where a child had been injured, it became necessary for the alleged perpetrator to *prove* his innocence in a civil court. And if he could not, social services through their case conferences could decide that children should be removed from their parental home, for a period of assessment, till they decided what to do. Parents would have no access to these case conferences and could not take part in the decision-making.

And where place of safety orders were converted into interim care orders parents again found themselves with no rights of appeal except with regard to access. The child might appeal through the guardian *ad litem*, if one were appointed, but while parents were entitled under the Children and Young Persons' (Amendment) Act 1986 to appeal against any such order, the enabling legislation had never passed Parliament, thus leaving parents deprived of legal rights in relation to their own children. Parliament, without realizing it, had allowed a further seepage of power away from the family to the state in the guise of social services departments. Power had been seeping away like a tide going out in the night. It had channelled itself into social services and regional health authorities and had become so overpowering that not only could these bureaucracies combine to take children from their parents, decisions would be made that also excluded the police.

For each tragic death fastened upon by the media, such as Jasmine Beckford or Kimberly Carlisle, power would rush away still further; for if social workers were to be chastised and criticized for failing in their duty, how much more eager did they become to ensure that children were taken from their homes to 'safe' surroundings, another euphemism that rapidly came into vogue. The 'safeness' was to be found in hostels and foster homes, and therefore not only the resources of social services but the lost powers of Parliament were converted to lethal instruments in their hands. Thus a place of safety order became repressive and allowed children to be literally spirited away in the night; the clinical judgement and freedom of doctors became similar instruments of coercion.

Why should a consultant paediatrician, or any other doctor, not be held accountable for the judgements that he makes, especially where these judgements lead to children being taken unjustly from their homes? Even the South Tees Health Authority would admit it could not interfere with paediatricians in the exercise of their clinical judgement. The National Health Service remains the jewel in the British social crown, a health service free for all, regardless of their ability to pay, yet in May and June 1987 it became an oppressive 'state within a state'.

Parents suffered because the stigma of child sexual abuse – the allegation – was enough to drive them into silence. This had been happening up and down the country for years. Parents had cried in the wilderness. But the crimes which they had allegedly perpetrated upon their own children were so offensive, so obnoxious, that any public doubts were drowned by the professionals. Events in Cleveland only came to public knowledge when Middlesbrough General Hospital was filled to overflowing with well children allegedly sexually abused who began to interfere with the progress back to health of poorly children. And when the parents were lodged together, their children in the same hospital, it became impossible to conceal one from the other that all were there for the same reason and on the same allegation.

When these parents took their story on to the streets, they began their own social revolution; a revolution that would swing power back to parents and their families, that would check social services, that would make consultant paediatricians and their employers more accountable to the public, and would restore to government and Parliament a proper interest in family life. Indeed, the government promised new child care legislation in 1988–9. Paradoxically, a proper balance between the family and the state would enhance rather than detract from the rooting out of child sexual abuse; for with the help of nationwide guidelines, applicable from John O'Groat's to Land's End, with the help of multi-disciplinary proceedings, whereby police, social services and health authorities worked together by consensus rather than confrontation, children in need could reach out for protection; and families concerned with their children's health need not worry that a random check at the hospital would see their children taken from them.

Those parents who rejoiced at Pyrgi's restaurant this 21 December 1987 did not take the high philosophical road but, rather, like the father who greeted the return of his prodigal son, they celebrated their own family reunion, and because it was Christmas, felt a special sense of gratitude that their children were home. This would be their first Christmas party of the season, with a local businessman providing the balloons and funny hats and Mimo and Anna Peretti the food, the drink and the festive bunting.

The party was also therapeutic. Some hundred children and parents had turned up. Many of the children had not seen each other since those confused and chaotic days on ward nine of Middlesbrough General Hospital. The children listened to the carol singing led by the Reverend Michael Wright and gazed at the Christmas tree and decorations. Many asked what other children were doing there? They seemed to feel a sense of reassurance, a sense of belonging, when it was explained to them that these children too had been taken from their parents. These children too had lived through the same experience. They too had been told they had been abused when they had not.

It had not, after all, been a lone experience.

There was Martha Johnson. She had three children, Paula aged twelve, Edward aged nine and Liz aged three. She had taken baby Liz to the doctor and asked if she could see a specialist because she worried about the child's asthma. Liz had suffered from croup since she was seven months old.

Then there was Heather Walker who had been given an appointment at Middlesbrough General Hospital on 18 June. She had sat 'over the other side in the outpatients''. She had gone into the hospital at ten-thirty in the morning but not until the afternoon had her child seen Dr Higgs.

'Dr Higgs asked if I had other children at home.'

Heather Walker's two other children were picked up from school and brought to the hospital. All three were made subject to place of safety orders and Heather Walker found herself on ward nine when Dr Wyatt was physically threatened as the parents decided to take their case to the public. No reasons were given for the place of safety orders on the Walker children: there was simply a tick against that clause in the place of safety order which declared that a court would be satisfied that the terms of the 'preceding paragraph' had been fulfilled.

The 'preceding paragraph' referred to the proper development of a child, that this proper development might be being avoidably prevented or neglected. But there was no tick against this paragraph. The justices of the peace nevertheless had signed not one, but *three* such orders, which placed the Walker children on ward nine for a period of not less than twenty-eight days. All three Walker children would be returned to the family home, but had there been a look of doubt or suspicion from Heather Walker towards her husband? When informed that all three had signs 'consistent with sexual abuse' had she doubted her husband? Did she mistakenly believe he was the perpetrator? The children might return home, but her husband Frank would leave. So that while the Walker children enjoyed themselves in the restaurant this 21 December, while the carols were sung, Heather Walker sat disconsolate, thinking of other happier Christmases.

Then there were the Turners. Tony and Beryl Turner had two children, Philomena aged two and a half and Roberta aged nine months. Philomena had weighed three pounds at birth. She had a chronic weight problem and weighed just over eight kilos when she went to Middlesbrough General Hospital on 22 June. Both children were diagnosed as having allegedly been sexually abused. The examinations had taken place in the morning of 21 June and the irony for the Turners was that as their children were taken into care and settled on ward nine, they were able to see that evening's local television news.

The story of the Cleveland children was given top billing.

Both Turners would reflect how their lives might have been different had their appointment been for the following day rather than 21 June. But they too would get their children back. On 8 February 1988 a judge sitting in the High Court at Middlesbrough not only returned the children to the Turners but ordered the county council to pay costs. Their ordeal had lasted a period a little short of eight months. Curiously, just as this was the length of time it took to unravel the Cleveland crisis, so it was the length of time it took for the governor of Massachusetts to get a grip on Salem.

Tony Smith also visited the Christmas party on 21 December. He had slipped away from work to be with those friends he had made in the parents' support group. But like Heather Walker he was disconsolate, unable to join in the spirit of the occasion. He had lost his wife and two children; his daughter Alma had been the *cause célèbre*, having been diagnosed four times as allegedly abused in three environments. He had been divorced from his wife. All he could hope for through the courts was that they would grant him access to his children, and in the granting of that access clear him of any taint that he had abused Alma.

As in other cases, Cleveland County Council would deem it prudent not to test their case in open court and on 18 February 1988 a settlement would be made. Tony Smith would have access to his children; the child psychiatrist who had been holding the therapy sessions with Alma, and whom Tony and his family had felt to be an 'invidious' influence, was to be removed from the child's supervision. Tony would be free to begin his life again, with the knowledge that all was not entirely lost; access to his children would claw him back from the insanity of events in 1987. Yet this Christmas would be the first without his family. On the morning of Christmas Eve, he spent the first hours crying with his sister. By lunchtime the tears were dried, and they had gone to a local club.

Tony's sister had a friend – Angela – who had lived locally but then found work in Manchester. She was back home to see her family. In the chemistry of Christmas and clubland Tony struck up a conversation with Angela, so that with the holidays over, and when she had returned to her work, if they were not writing to each other they were telephoning regularly. In March 1988, with the court case out of the way, Tony putting on a new suit to see his children for the first time in nearly a year, Angela returned to Teesside to see him. As his sister said: 'It's early days. But with a little time – who can tell?'

For Tony Smith the long road back had begun.

43

On 25 June 1987 Dr Marietta Higgs and Dr Geoffrey Wyatt had received the following identical letter from Dr Liam Donaldson, regional medical officer:

This letter confirms our telephone conversation today. I informed you that you are required not to undertake any examinations to look for signs of child sexual abuse in children without parental knowledge and permission except in circumstances where a court order removes the necessity of such permission.

The Northern Regional Health Authority had attempted to come to terms with the Cleveland crisis from 16 June when Mr Ian Donaldson, district general manager of the South Tees Health Authority, had alerted them to the complaints he had received concerning both Dr Higgs and Dr Wyatt. These complaints alleged that they had been examining children on the wards late at night 'without parental permission' and that they had examined children for sexual abuse who had been admitted for other conditions.

The district general manager had called Leeds to ascertain how the Yorkshire Regional Health Authority handled allegations of child sexual abuse. Some doubts had been expressed as to whether it was appropriate to investigate for sexual abuse 'unless there was an indication at the time of presentation and whether they should be examined, in any case, without explicit parental consent'. Dr Liam Donaldson immediately indicated that the complaints should be 'taken seriously'. Copies of these complaints should be sent to him forthwith.

Dr Donaldson took up with a senior consultant paediatrician the question of whether it was within the remit of a consultant paediatrician to examine all aspects of a child's body: 'Neither of us could see how looking for sexual abuse or any other kind of abuse in children could be restricted to those in whom the person referring raised the possibility that it was present.' The question of consent would again be raised the following day, 17 June, when Dr Donaldson visited Newcastle.

Dr Donaldson expressed the view that 'while consent was implied in every paediatric examination of a child, since parents would accompany a child and would be in a position to object, it would probably seldom be asked for. Given the normal trusting relationship between doctor and parent, we doubted whether any examination in the absence of the parent would constitute assault.' Did this equally cover the examination of private parts? 'I expressed the view that many doctors would regard such examination as part of a normal, thorough paediatric examination, although there might be a greater need to explain to parents when this part of the examination is carried out and seek their cooperation and indeed that of the child.'

On 23 June Dr Higgs and Dr Wyatt met with Professor Sir Bernard Tomlinson, chairman of the Northern Regional Health Authority, and Dr Donaldson at the Newcastle offices of the authority. They pointed out to the consultant paediatricians that 'as a result of the apparently large increase in the incidence of child sexual abuse in Cleveland pressure had been put on resources, and public concern had been raised on how children could have been taken from their parents.' There had also been specific complaints made against both of the consultants.

Dr Higgs and Dr Wyatt were offered copies of the complaints so that they could look through them and get a view of their general 'nature and tenor'. Both refused. They indicated that they were not willing to do this since the meeting was 'informal' and they wished to have the opportunity of consulting first with their Defence Union. Thus on 23 June both Dr Higgs and Dr Wyatt knew of the serious predicament they were in. Dr Wyatt did say that he thought such complaints could be part of the 'phenomenon of child sexual abuse'. He said it had a lot to do with who 'controlled' children.

Those at the meeting felt he had meant by that that if the children were returned home, parents would regain control and would silence the children from making disclosures. Dr Higgs said that child sexual abuse was now a serious problem countrywide and that the 'size of the problem' in Cleveland was a reflection of this. She pointed out that not all the cases referred to social services had originated within the South Tees district. She agreed, however, that a majority of the cases had indeed been diagnosed either by herself or Dr Wyatt.

Dr Higgs said that the start of the sudden increase had been the diagnosis of sexual abuse in a child who had been fostered and that the foster home had a large throughput of children. The record of the meeting did not indicate that Dr Higgs told her employers that Vera Dixon had first been diagnosed by Dr Higgs in Newcastle before she had embarked upon her Middlesbrough consultancy, and that she had diagnosed the child a second time as having been allegedly abused in the foster home; and that on this occasion she had also diagnosed the child's sister. It was the activities within the Allan foster home, as Dr Higgs perceived it, that had led to 'a large number of children being admitted for investigation over a short space of time'.

She accepted there had been few cases diagnosed prior to 1 May. But she thought that the 'current difficulties' had been caused by the absence of adequate back-up both by the police and social services. Had they undertaken the required investigative work with the children – that is, obtaining disclosures to go with the diagnosis – neither the complaints nor the anxieties of the parents would have been as 'manifest' as they had become. There had not been the counselling or support that was normally required when parents found themselves confronted with allegations of sexual abuse of their children.

Dr Higgs denied she had been 'seeking out' sexual abuse.

The majority of cases, she claimed, came from referrals, that is to say social workers, doctors, health visitors and other professions. What about the complaint that they had been examining 'normal' bottoms to contrast these with those they suspected as not being normal? Both doctors denied this and said that it was not their 'normal practice to examine children without parental permission', nor did they seek normal 'controls' for research purposes. Beyond this, however, neither doctor would enter into detailed discussion of the complaints.

They first wanted to take legal advice.

Dr Wyatt said that when he gave his opinion on child sexual abuse it was his clinical judgement as a doctor that counted. This clinical judgement, as he described it, was 'carefully considered'. But both doctors were in agreement that in order for further work to be carried out the child had to be removed from the family environment 'in order to give it the security to disclose the abuse to trusted professionals'.

For both Dr Higgs and Dr Wyatt the disclosure was the 'gold standard' in diagnostic terms. The young consultant Dr Higgs, in her post for barely six months, expressed the view that many paediatricians did not look for the evidence of child sexual abuse, and when they did, they were not 'experienced' in diagnosing it. This assertion was challenged by her seniors: 'Dr Higgs readily agreed that it appeared to be arrogant but said that she had made considerable efforts to feel competent to diagnose this condition and felt that few others in this region were yet at that stage.'

On the basis of information before them both Professor Tomlinson and Dr Liam Donaldson concluded that, nothwithstanding the complaints of parents, who after all were the consumers within the health service, there was no 'prima facie case for suspending the consultants pending serious disciplinary action on grounds of professional incompetence or professional misconduct'. Notwithstanding the best intentions of the regional health authority the difficulties of running a normal paediatric service in Middlesbrough were overwhelming. There was now intense media speculation on each child going into Middlesbrough General Hospital. The parents had solicitors. The solicitors were getting legal aid and making the children wards of court. With an independent panel in place to review any diagnosis of child abuse, neither doctor now had unfettered control over his or her practice. Both were called again to Newcastle. 'I mentioned some of the key points that needed to be observed,' Dr Liam Donaldson recalled. 'Prompt calling of the second opinion; allowing the second paediatrician to see the child suspected of having been abused with only a nurse and without one of them in attendance.' Dr Higgs pointed out that this presented difficulties from her 'perspective' because it seemed that her opinion was 'discredited' when the second opinion became publicly known and disagreed with her own.

She again emphasized the importance of photography for accurate recording of findings but said that it was now 'very difficult' to get parental agreement to the photography. Also a lot of time was being spent trying to arrange for the second opinions of busy consultants. Both Dr Higgs and Dr Wyatt, although they did not choose to accept this, were being submerged in legal work as they had to prepare each case meticulously for the courts, and were unable to run 'a normal service'. They were asked whether they might not like to 'withdraw' from paediatric practice until the court cases were resolved.

Both said: 'No'.

Although no one knew this at the time, Dr Higgs' discussions concerning the admission of fifteen children into Middlesbrough General Hospital from a children's home on 17 July would be her last major involvement in the diagnosis of child sexual abuse on Teesside. While into her eighth month at Middlesbrough, the criticisms of Mr Justice Hollis in open court on 3 August led to the Northern Regional Health Authority discussing the 'voluntary withdrawal' both of herself and Dr Wyatt: 'Failing agreement on voluntary withdrawal, the clinicians would be told that they must withdraw from clinical activity for a time, this to be accompanied by a public statement on their need to spend all their available time over the preparation of the evidence required by court proceedings and for the [judicial] enquiry.'

But when the enquiry drew to a close on 27 January 1988, it was announced that Dr Marietta Higgs was returning to Newcastle to continue her work in neonatology, the speciality which had sent her to Middlesbrough in the first place, while Dr Wyatt would stay in Middlesbrough. The regional health authority felt he had built up a clientèle over four years and he should continue with his 'well-established paediatric practice' from 1 March. There would, however, be an important proviso. Dr Wyatt would no longer be involved in examination for sexual abuse. And if there were cases of such abuse, or where abuse was suspected, he would refer them to another paediatrician.

Dr Higgs too would no longer be involved in the diagnosis of child abuse. In neonatology she would deal only with newborn babies. Dr Higgs declared herself 'pleased' with the move. She was happy that she had been asked to return to Newcastle but her move was 'tinged with regret' because she was leaving Middlesbrough which had presented a 'special challenge' in child health. Dr Wyatt was also 'happy' with the arrangements. Both consultants now had limitations upon their practice but both believed that paediatrics is 'primarily concerned with promoting the overall health of children and their role, wherever possible, should be that of preventing illness and disease.'

And what of Mrs Richardson, member of BASPCAN and child abuse consultant to Cleveland county?

She was criticized by counsel to the judicial enquiry for not fully informing her director, Mr Mike Bishop, that the diagnosis of reflex anal dilatation was controversial rather than sure. She was criticized for not telling Mr Bishop that following the meeting of 28 May, between herself, Dr Higgs and officers from Cleveland Constabulary, including Dr Alistair Irvine, the police had issued their own memorandum instructing their force to treat with 'caution' any diagnosis from Dr Higgs.

Nor had Mrs Richardson wavered from her view that no case had been mishandled by social services throughout the crisis; there had been no misdiagnosis; and so far as she was concerned, according to counsel to the enquiry, 'there were no errors that had been made either of omission or of commission'. Mrs Richardson had embarked upon a crusade. That crusade had been to 'eradicate from the Cleveland area the evil of undetected abuse'. She believed that sexual abuse was rarely a dysfunction but rather an abuse of power by an adult over a child.

In April 1988 Cleveland County Council agreed to release Mrs Richardson to embark upon a child abuse course at Newcastle upon Tyne Polytechnic. The course would last for at least one year. And by one of those curious ironies that were the hallmark of the Cleveland crisis, she would find herself studying not more than a few hundred yards from the Princess Mary Hospital where Dr Higgs would be developing her skills in neonatology.

In France, children pinch themselves each time they see a green Citröen two-horse-powered car. They call it a *deux d'oche verte*. At the height of the Cleveland child abuse crisis a red Citröen two horse power – a *deux d'oche rouge* – would leave the North Yorkshire village of Great Ayton and make the seven-mile journey to Middlesbrough. The car would stop at Roman Road, a long winding street on the main highway, and pick up a passenger before driving the few hundred yards to Middlesbrough General Hospital. Dr Wyatt's consideration for Dr Higgs was such, in these weeks of crisis, that he would regularly pick her up and accompany her to the hospital, sometimes passing the television cameras and reporters, to park his car before the outpatients' clinic.

On 1 March 1988 he made the trip alone. All weekend the weather forecasters had been threatening snow from the North Pole, hurried down by stiff winds, but it was not until Tuesday that the snow arrived. It was lying deep at Great Ayton when Dr Wyatt left. It was less deep in Middlesbrough, the town protected as it was by the Cleveland Hills and the heat generated by the ICI and British Steel plants. Outside the hospital he posed for photographs. He did not smile. He was pleased, he said, to return to his post and his patients. He paid tribute to his colleagues who had carried a 'substantial extra burden due to the unavoidable absence of myself and others at the public enquiry'. He did not mention the restrictions on his practice nor that his position would be reviewed when the judicial enquiry published its findings.

Some forty miles up the A19 at Newcastle upon Tyne, Dr Marietta Higgs was more forthcoming. She smiled for the photographers. She even had her picture taken at the Princess Mary Hospital with a newborn baby who appeared to be struggling for life in intensive care. As the regional health authority explained: 'All we were doing was showing what Dr Higgs' work will be.' Dr Higgs was accompanied by Dr Edmund Hey, who had suggested she apply for the Middlesbrough post in the first place. He said: 'We have been short staffed for a while and are grateful to have her help for some months to come.'

Dr Higgs herself would not speak to journalists but a statement was made on her behalf. In it, she said: 'I am very pleased to be working in Newcastle again with newborn babies, which is one of my special interests.' Her position too would be 'reviewed' in the light of the findings of the judicial enquiry. Dr Hey admitted that some parents in Newcastle were 'worried' about Dr Higgs' examining their children. 'I know of their anxieties,' he said. 'I can reassure people that every clinician who has worked with Dr Higgs says she is a skilled and experienced neonatal and general paediatrician.'

Dr Higgs continued to smile as she posed with her hands upon a newborn baby.

'I look forward to returning to Cleveland,' she said. 'Some time in the future.'

AUTHOR'S NOTE

I returned to my constituency on Friday 19 June 1987.

A week earlier I had stood in the town hall of Middlesbrough and heard the returning officer declare the result of the general election in the constituency. I had been returned to Westminster with a majority of 14958, an increase of some fifty-five per cent from the majority I had gained in 1983. On Monday, true to the traditions of the Commons, I had high-tailed it to London in order to get an office for the new Parliament.

After the swearing-in on Wednesday 17 June, I returned to Middlesbrough to receive a series of messages from my constituents. They all had the same anguished tone. *Their children had been taken away*. I at first thought these were hoax calls, some kind of fall-out from the general election. It had not been uncommon for jokers to call on election day with a series of spurious messages to distract or delay the candidate.

These calls were assuredly of that ilk.

The information which accompanied the calls was even more dubious. The children had all been diagnosed as allegedly sexually abused. The implication was that their fathers were the perpetrators. My first reaction was equivalent to that of others when they either heard or saw the news or read their newspapers; there was some kind of paedophilic ring at work in Middlesbrough which had been busted by the police, the fathers arrested and the children detained in hospital. This was clearly a time for caution.

But the calls persisted.

My constituency secretary rang to say that she was also getting calls and that she had been told Tyne Tees Television were running a news programme that evening on 'events' at Middlesbrough General Hospital. It seemed wise to speak to the news editor and urge caution upon him too. 'I hope you know what you're doing,' I said. The response was frank. The news editor did not know what was happening at the hospital, but they too had had parents coming in all day vehemently denying they had abused their children; some wanted to know who had; others said the children had not been abused at all.

Shortly before six o'clock I received another call. This man had a gift for the graphic. He painted for me a picture of the children's casualty ward at Middlesbrough General Hospital. There were children on the ward with 'nothing wrong with them'. Parents were sleeping on the floor alongside their children. The day before there had been a 'near riot'. I asked: 'Are you telling me this is happening in Middlesbrough?'

Could I come and see for myself?

I agreed to meet the constituent at Middlesbrough General Hospital at half past six that evening. I watched the Tyne Tees Television programme *Northern Life* at six o'clock. This told a similar story of children having been diagnosed for sexual abuse by a 'new consultant at the hospital'. There were pictures of parents telling their own story, their backs to the camera, and there was an explanation of how the children had been taken into care. The pictures were dramatic.

I went down to the hospital and was led into an anteroom between the two parts of ward nine where the parents had congregated. They were all excited, all shouting, all waving pieces of paper which they described as place of safety orders. The fathers were saying they wanted to know who had abused their children, the mothers were worried about getting their children back. There was a general feeling of anxiety. I asked them to write their names and addresses down in my notebook and to hold on to their place of safety orders.

A nurse appeared and asked me to see the sister in charge of the hospital. I was introduced to Sister Ball. There was also the district general manager of the South Tees Health Authority, and another nurse whom I did not know and to whom I was not introduced. I could see through the cubicle windows of the nursing office that the ward was full and very active, with children running around.

My own son, Malcolm, aged five, had been confined to ward nine for a few days before Christmas 1986, following a bad fall at home when he had fractured his skull, and it surprised me to see so much additional activity on the ward. My first thought was for casualties who might not find beds available, but Sister Ball assured me that they were able to cope with emergencies.

Since no one volunteered any explanation for the extraordinary scenes I was witnessing with my own eyes, I asked what was going on. I said that I had seen nothing like it in my parliamentary career, in my days in politics, nor in my life-long experiences. Mr Donaldson said something about 'the high level of detection in child abuse'. He also said that it was a legal matter which did not concern the hospital 'except insofar as social services have run out of accommodation'. I said I could not understand how these children had been taken from their parents with such rapidity and Mr Donaldson said that the place of safety orders had been before a magistrates' court and that it had all been legally sanctioned.

As he spoke, I scanned the place of safety order which had been given to me by one of the parents. I tried to make it out. It began with the name of a social worker. It went on to name the child. It went on to refer to a justice of the peace. It seemed to me that what had happened was that a medical diagnosis had been made, a social worker had filled out the order, and a justice of the peace had authorized it. I said to Mr Donaldson that I doubted whether any of these place of safety orders had been before a full magistrates' court; rather that they had been presented to a justice of the peace in his own home.

I went back to the parents who were still milling around in the anteroom. I already had some names and addresses written down, but since I could make little progress in understanding their individual grievances, I offered to return the following morning when things would be quieter and I could make a full note.

Thus began for me an involvement with the families caught up in the Cleveland child abuse crisis. As the Member of Parliament for Middlesbrough, I would have to see them through a great deal of anguish and heartache in the weeks and months ahead, when the future was not at all certain, when they were reacting to a totally unexpected event, some with fortitude, others with panic, some to recover, others never again to find their equilibrium, and at all times seeking not to lose sight of the fact that we were dealing also with the future of very young children, plucked from their homes, and where access by their parents was being denied. The situation was emotional and traumatic, affecting nervous systems and feelings alike, but there was nothing any of the families could do but live with it, seek to extricate themselves, and do this as patiently as they could in all the circumstances. Some succeeded, others did not, and some of their stories are told in this book.

That there would be one or several books about the Cleveland child abuse crisis was inevitable. That it should be about the families was less so. Those families who felt a great wrong had been done to them found, to their surprise, that while they might give evidence to the judicial enquiry which the government had announced, this evidence would be held in private and the public would never know what they and their children had endured. The decision that the families' stories should be told in private was made in the best interests of the children, but it meant that the public would never understand the full extent of the crisis, how it had affected relationships, how it had affected marriages, how it had affected both children and adults; and it was from the willingness of all those families – those who had given evidence to the enquiry and those who had not – that this book was conceived. Without their full cooperation and their desire to ensure that these events should be recounted in order that they not be repeated, this book could never have been written.

The comparison between the Cleveland crisis and the Salem witch-hunts stood out a mile: it was the first thought that went through my mind when I was confronted with the families at Middlesbrough General Hospital on Friday 19 June; and yet it somehow baffled those in charge of social services. So much so that their counsel would question me about it at the Cleveland enquiry.

I am grateful to my research assistant, Richard Saver, who declared his willingness to be acknowledged only on the understanding I would not change his name; to my wife Margaret, acting as my secretary, who had to cope with the hundreds of letters that came from all parts of the country when the crisis was revealed, who had to classify these letters and assist me in my efforts to deal with their many genuine grievances at the hands of authorities elsewhere. I am grateful to the press for giving the Cleveland crisis the widest coverage, and in particular Kim Barnes, Neil Bennett, Luke Casey, Simon Cole, Mike Gillings, Alan Powell, Roger Scott and Brian Unwin; especially Brian Unwin who, reporting for the Press Association, ensured that events were given international as well as national coverage. I am grateful to the *Evening Gazette*, my own local newspaper, which stayed with the story throughout, and to Ailsa Mackenzie and Mike Clark; and to the *Northern Echo*, which through Steve Hilton and Ted Young gave extensive and even verbatim coverage of the judicial enquiry. I am grateful to Richard Shears and the *Daily Mail* for allowing me to use material gathered in Australia and West Germany in relation to Dr Higgs' background.

I am grateful to the Department of Health and Social Services, to the transcript firms Laidler Haswell Ltd, 4 The Paddock, Rothwell, Leeds, to Humphreys Barnett and Co, official shorthand writers, and now suitably merged with Laidler Haswell Ltd; to Palantype Reporting Service, 2 Frith Road, Croydon, Surrey; and I would like to acknowledge and pay a special tribute to the late Mr Ivor Eastwood, leading transcriber and supervisor of the majority of the judgements referred to in this book who died on 15 January 1988.

His work will live on and might well have a place as important, in years to come, as those written observations of contemporary events in Salem in 1692. They too did not write for posterity, but rather the living moment; but they too found their work increasing in significance as the years passed.

I am grateful to Mimo and Anna Peretti for opening their restaurant to the parents and children in their busiest season, just before Christmas. I am grateful to local businessman and friend, Cyril Thompson, who provided the balloons and bunting and presents for the parents and children; to my friend and solicitor Donald O'Rourke who guided me through some of the anxious moments that occur when even Members of Parliament take on powerful bureaucracies. I am grateful to my wife Margaret, who saw me disappear over the Christmas holidays only to surface with a manuscript that was well on its way to completion, and to my six-year-old son Malcolm. He cannot understand why his father votes when a bell rings, nor how books are written; but he had patience and forebearance when his regular football in the park was curtailed so that the manuscript might advance further.

I am grateful to the Earl of Stockton, who anxiously followed events in Cleveland; to William Armstrong of Sidgwick & Jackson, who encouraged me to write the book. And finally I must record my thanks and appreciation to the staff at Pan Books, and Hilary Davies, who not only suggested to me the form the book should take, but who also guided me through the manuscript, who gently made sure I kept deadlines, and who corrected a grammar that owes more to the French than the English language. The cheerfulness of all those at Cavaye Place was a wonder to behold after the rigours of life within the precincts of the House of Commons.

Pauline Cutting
Children of the Siege £3.50

Children of the Siege is Pauline Cutting's moving account of life and death in the Palestinian camp of Bourj al Barajneh, Beirut.

It is an impassioned record of a heroic struggle to save lives in near impossible conditions of bombardment, starvation, malnutrition and dwindling medical resources – a struggle which is still going on.

Above all, it is the story of courage and comradeship shown by the doctors and nurses who have come to the camps from all over the world, and the people they are trying to save.

Dr Cutting spent eighteen months in Beirut, working day and night in makeshift operating theatres and helping the wounded – many of them children – while bombs exploded around her and snipers lay in wait outside.

Children of the Siege is her true story, an unforgettable testament of the fight to save lives in the face of death.

Mark Mathabane
Kaffir Boy £3.50

Growing out of apartheid

'I have sought to paint a portrait of my childhood and youth in Alexandra, a black ghetto of Johannesburg, where I was born and lived for eighteen years, with the hope that rest of the world will finally understand why apartheid cannot be reformed: it has to be abolished'
MARK MATHABANE

Angry, authentic, intensely personal, this autobiography graphically reveals the truth about being black in South Africa.

Mark's first memory is of being woken at dawn by a police raid. Too terrified to speak and reveal where his parents were hiding, he was beaten up. He was five. As he grew older, it got worse: life was a constant battle against starvation, cold ignorance and the ensuing violence.

Drawing readers into the turmoil, terror, and sad stratagems for survival, Mark Mathabane makes us see what it means for his people to live under the prevailing conditions. It may make your blood boil, shock you, or leave you emotionally drained, but it is too important *not* to read. Mark escaped. The rest remain.

'A rare look at life inside the festering adobe shanties of Alexandra. Rare because it comes not from the pen of a liberal white novelist, but from the heart of a passionate young African who grew up there'
CHICAGO TRIBUNE

Gordon Burn
'Somebody's Husband, Somebody's Son' £3.99

It seemed the case of the notorious Yorkshire Ripper was finally closed when Peter Sutcliffe was sentenced to life imprisonment in May 1981. *Sunday Times* journalist Gordon Burn spent two years researching Sutcliffe's life, living in his home town of Bingley, talking at length to everyone who knew him. His definitive account of the man and his crimes is a penetrating examination of the mind of a murderer.

'A book that will undoubtedly become a classic in the field of investigative criminology' COLIN WILSON

Emlyn Williams
Beyond Belief £3.99

The story of the Moors Murderers, Ian Brady and Myra Hindley.

'I keep remindin' myself' Superintendent Talbot said to me, 'that this isn't a tale – that it's been happening . . .'

'Perhaps the greatest value of this book is that it shows us that the human monsters Brady and Hindley were not one and the same, but two different kinds of monster' TIMES LITERARY SUPPLEMENT

'An appalling subject, and overpowering book' SUNDAY EXPRESS

Robert Hughes
The Fatal Shore £4.99

'Robert Hughes' magnificent epic book traces the fate of the 160,000 men, women and children transported between the despatch of the first fleet in May 1787 to Botany Bay, and the arrival of the last convict ship in January 1868 in Western Australia. This gory, grim but always compelling panorama evokes the almost unimaginable horrors and atrocities, both of the passage itself and the disciplinary apparatus of what amounted to a police state . . . a hell-hole of chain gangs ruled by the cat o'nine tails' LISTENER

'With its mood and stature . . . becoming the standing opus on the convict years' AUSTRALIAN SUNDAY TELEGRAPH

'A unique phantasmagoria of crime and punishment, which combines the shadowy terrors of Goya with the tumescent life of Dickens. THE TIMES

'Popular history in the best sense . . . its attention to human detail and its commanding prose call to mind the best work of Barbara Tuchman' WASHINGTON POST

'An impressive book, written with power and passion, lit by flashes of wit and imagination' SUNDAY TIMES

'One of the most carefully and brilliantly researched books I have ever read . . . compelling, hard-driving narrative' JOHN HOOKER, THE AGE

Charles Humana
World Human Rights Guide £4.95

This unique survey – the very first of its kind – of 120 major countries throughout the world records human rights performance and responses to the Universal Declaration of Human Rights and United Nations treaties. The information on which it is based has been drawn from world human rights organisations, official and unofficial sources, international institutions, as well as individuals.

The survey is in the form of forty questions and answers, covering both traditional human rights, such as freedom of expression, association and movement, and the wider area of state power-censorship of the media, telephone tapping, extrajudicial killings, independence of courts, the right to practise any religion, to use contraceptive devices, to practise homosexuality between consenting adults. The results are calculated and summarized by an overall rating.

Basic data about each country is also provided, together with a short commentary on factors affecting human rights and a list of compulsory documents required by citizens.